THE QUEST FOR UNDERSTANDING

A Historical Introduction to Philosophy

Douglas Giles
Elmhurst University

Kendall Hunt
publishing company

Cover image source: Douglas Giles

Kendall Hunt
publishing company

www.kendallhunt.com
Send all inquiries to:
4050 Westmark Drive
Dubuque, IA 52004-1840

Text ISBN: 978-1-7924-5760-9
PAK ISBN: 978-1-7924-6041-8

Published in the United States of America

CONTENTS

CHAPTER 11. BERKELEY: MATTER DOESN'T MATTER 151

CHAPTER 12. HUME: THE END OF PHILOSOPHY? 161

CHAPTER 13. KANT 177

CHAPTER 14. GERMAN IDEALISM AND HEGEL 193

CHAPTER 19. PROCESS VERSUS POSITIVISM: PHILOSOPHY'S GREAT DIVIDE 271

CHAPTER 20. LUDWIG WITTGENSTEIN 289

CHAPTER 21. PHENOMENOLOGY AND EXISTENTIALISM 299

CHAPTER 22. ANALYTIC PHILOSOPHY 321

CHAPTER 23. TEARING DOWN PHILOSOPHY: POSTMODERNISM 335

CHAPTER 24. CONTINENTAL SOCIAL PHILOSOPHY 349

CHAPTER 25. RETHINKING PHILOSOPHY: FEMINIST PHILOSOPHY 365

CHAPTER 1

WHAT IS PHILOSOPHY?

You have probably cracked open this book because your college or university has required you to take an Introduction to Philosophy course. Welcome. It's a wild ride, and you are about to have a lot of fun, if you allow yourself. You quite possibly will learn more in this course than any other undergraduate course you will take.

Philosophy is unusual among college or university courses in that most students have never encountered it before. For some reason, most high schools in the United States do not teach philosophy. Oftentimes, students in their first philosophy class feel the material is strange, even bizarre. They are being asked to think in a way they never have before and may feel out of their element. That's okay. We'll deal with that.

On the one hand, you may feel overwhelmed by what seems a sea of contradictory ideas. On the other hand, you will discover like-minded thinkers in the great minds of history. Philosophy is a voyage of discovery, and I'm not kidding when I say it will be a lot of fun. Like with all good things in life, the more you put into reading and thinking about the material in this book, the more you'll get out of it.

WHAT IS PHILOSOPHY? PHILOSOPHY IS A QUEST

Many people, because they've been allowed so little experience with philosophy, have a negative view of it. They see philosophy as the obscure arcane thoughts of odd reclusive men from bygone times. They see the study of philosophy as dusting off moldy ideas that have little relevance to their daily lives. ***Not*** true!

Literally, the word "philosophy" comes from the Greek words *philo* ("love") and *sophia* ("wisdom"). Thus, the label "philosophy" means "the love of wisdom." Clearly though, the act of philosophy is much more than simply loving wisdom. It is something deeper, broader, and more involved. Many people have attempted to explain what philosophy is. Some have said philosophy is thinking about thinking, reflecting on experience, a pursuit of truth. Philosophy is all of those things, but it is also something much more.

Here is my definition:

Philosophy is the active intellectual search for fundamental principles on which we can build a better life.

What does that mean? Let's break it down, concept by concept.

Philosophy is *active*. It's not passive. If you simply believe what you are told, you're not being a philosopher. An active mind is important for philosophy, and philosophy is not satisfied with comfortable feel-good answers. Philosophers question assumptions, and philosophy is a live pursuit for better explanations and better ideas. The most important ingredient in being a good philosopher is to be an active and open-minded listener.

Philosophy is *intellectual*. Yes, it's about thinking. It's not accepting ideas because they feel nice but because they make rational sense. Most philosophers prize reason above all else, and many of them dismiss emotions. You do need to use your rational powers a lot when doing philosophy. That's intimidating, especially because what philosophy explores are some of the most difficult concepts possible. We need to think diligently and critically to explore these concepts, discuss them, and arrive at solutions.

Philosophy is an active intellectual *search*. We are looking for something. Philosophy is not an aimless pursuit. It's not just navel gazing, and we aren't thinking for its own sake. Philosophy is a quest. We are searching for answers to life's most vexing questions by actively using our minds.

Philosophy is searching for *fundamental principles*. That means that the answers that we are searching for aren't superficial but are fundamental to the concepts we consider and our view of the world. One of the main differences between philosophy and other intellectual pursuits is that philosophy searches for the meaning behind concepts and phenomena. Science is fabulous at measuring phenomena and gathering data. Philosophy is fabulous at forming a worldview that strengthens our ability to perceive phenomena and make decisions about it. All of the data in the world don't give us wisdom. Philosophy searches for the foundations of our perceptions and understandings and what we do in the world. Identifying the fundamental principles that underlie our world and how we think about it is necessary to understand our world.

Philosophy has a purpose for its search for fundamental principles. With a few exceptions, philosophers are engaging in philosophy with the purpose of improving our lives. This is one of philosophy's greatest strengths. Philosophers engage in philosophical inquiry with the hope of more fully understanding the world they live in. Whether that understanding leads to directly practical benefits or just the satisfaction that having an answer brings, the goal of philosophy is to improve life. Philosophy has a concern for the quality of human life. Different philosophers have had different views on how life could or should be improved, but one way or another, they all share the same desire to better the human condition through better understanding. By understanding the fundamental principles of what reality is and how we perceive it, we can build a better life for ourselves and future generations. Philosophy is a quest for understanding.

We need to think actively, diligently, and critically about the problems we face to arrive at solutions and improve our lives. That is the answer to what philosophy is and why people do philosophy.

PHILOSOPHY IN CONTEXT—PHILOSOPHY IS A CONVERSATION

Perhaps the most important thing to keep in mind throughout this book is that philosophers do not create their ideas in a vacuum. Sadly, philosophy is often, though quite wrongly, portrayed as the product of esoteric thinking detached from the "real" world. The reality is that philosophy is not something that occurs out in "left field" but is a reaction by real people to the society in which they reside. All philosophers are (as are we all) embedded in a culture. All philosophers are a product of their society and culture and are affected by their environment and the events of their time. Thus, the philosophies they create are likewise products of their time and place.

It also works the other way. Philosophers help create culture and change society. The ideas of the philosophers have shaped human history, a fact that is sorely underappreciated. Philosophers identify fundamental principles on which we can build a better life, and subsequent generations have taken on the task of using those principles in changing their society. The wisdom of philosophers has shaped many governments, businesses, and individuals. So much of who we are today and how we think is a direct product of the work of major philosophers. That reality is one of the things you will learn in this book.

You cannot understand history without understanding philosophy, and you cannot understand philosophy without understanding history. That's why this book discusses philosophy chronologically. It begins at the beginning of philosophy's history and shows how many major philosophers all built on the ideas of their predecessors. Philosophy is fun and exciting because it is a quest for understanding who we are, where we have been, and where we are going.

NECESSARY CAVEATS

This book is a culmination of my twenty years of teaching, which means twenty years of learning what works for students who are learning philosophy for the first time. My goal is to present to students and instructors a textbook of manageable size and scope that can cover an introductory history of Western philosophy in a single university term. In any textbook on philosophy, people will naturally ask why certain philosophers or certain ideas of philosophers aren't mentioned. No textbook could possibly cover all of Western philosophy or cover every idea of who it includes. (One of the best histories of philosophy, Frederick Copleston' *History of Philosophy*, spans over 5,300 pages.) My intention with this book is to discuss the main threads of the Western philosophical tradition that have had the most influence on who we are today. That, of course, necessitates many, many judgments about who and what is more important than others, and those judgments are open to debate. People will naturally ask why I didn't discuss this philosopher or that idea more, or why I didn't mention such and such about a philosopher. My basic guiding principle has been to provide a book that helps higher education instructors teach and students learn philosophy. That necessitated making literally hundreds of decisions about what to cover and how to simplify difficult concepts for introductory students, all in keeping the book at a manageable length. To keep attention focused on the ideas, I have kept biographical details about the philosophers to a minimum. Certainly, I include historical and personal influences on the philosophers that are relevant to their thinking.

I have chosen to not have this book reliant on primary source material. Some instructors think that philosophy is best taught through source material. I respect that, but I have had too many students in my courses who dropped out of an earlier Introduction to Philosophy section in which the instructor threw complex source texts at them and expected them to sink or swim. They sank and learned little to nothing. These students aren't stupid, and they aren't lazy; they weren't helped. I designed this book to help students understand philosophy. Primary source texts are widely available in the public domain, and I encourage instructors to share them with students as I do in my courses. I feel that the role of a textbook is to be a secondary resource that helps instructors explain the philosophers' ideas, so this book references the primary texts without reproducing them. This saves page space for explanation and discussion, while keeping costs down for the students paying for the book. It also gives instructors more freedom to add what primary texts they deem fitting.

My chief regret is that this book covers only Western philosophy. This is in keeping with the widespread ethnocentrism of the cultural canon adhered to by U.S. institutions of higher learning. Philosophy departments need to satisfy the requirements handed down to them by their states and institutions, and non-Western philosophy is never part of those distribution requirements. It is a recent trend in some textbooks to include a few paragraphs of the *Dao De Ching* and the Buddha, but these inclusions serve more as sidebar curiosities. They give the false impression that philosophy in China and India ceased about 2,000 years ago, so I think they do more harm than good. Those two cultures, and many other cultures, deserve adequate attention and background—in other words, a book much larger than this one.

Distribution requirements also guided two other pedagogical choices. I didn't include logic because most schools cover that material in their critical thinking courses. This book doesn't ignore moral philosophy, but it concentrates less on the subject than on other areas of philosophy because most schools teach stand-alone courses on morality or ethics. Leaving out logic and spending less time on moral theory allows the book, and courses that adopt the book, to spend the limited class time on other topics.

There are not enough women represented in this book. History has excluded women's voices in all areas, and that means we do not have their voices. This prejudice cannot be ignored, especially because women are still underrepresented in philosophy. I have included notable women philosophers, not as sidebar curiosities, but because of the integral roles those women have in the history of Western philosophy. The same can be said about people of color who were also excluded by history.

ALL THE GOD TALK...

Finally, I have learned in my decades of teaching philosophy that it's helpful to make a general statement about the interaction between philosophy and religion. There's a lot of "God talk" that some students find odd in a philosophy course. It is not odd, though it may cause some difficulties for some. Almost everyone comes into a philosophy course with an opinion about religion. That's fine. What is important, regardless of your feelings about religion, is that we are all open-minded about the ideas we encounter in this course. The "God talk" by the philosophers we discuss in this course is not old-fashioned or irrational. It is highly rational and deeply influential to who we are as a society today.

Whenever a philosopher uses the word "God," you need to ask, "What does this particular philosopher mean by that word?" Chances are that this particular philosopher means by "God" something quite different from what you mean by the word or what you think others mean by the word. There is no universal definition for "God," despite what some people might want to think. You need to dig beneath surface appearances and discover what each particular philosopher means by each term he or she uses.

So, we begin. Enjoy!

CHAPTER 2

PLATO

To study philosophy and to have any hope for understanding it, we must begin at the beginning. That beginning is Greek philosophy because it was out of the Greek civilization that Western philosophy developed. Many present-day students initially find Greek thought difficult to grasp. That is because Greek culture is alien to our present-day world; there are many centuries of history between them and us. Present-day Western civilization is the product of a long history, the foundations of which are in the Greek world. We sit at the end of a long story, and like any story, it is most easily understood by starting at the beginning. So while the Greeks may seem strange and at times silly in their thinking, grasping the essence of Greek philosophy is the beginning of understanding all of philosophy.

The giant of ancient Greek philosophy is Plato. There is no overestimating the influence of Plato on philosophy and Western civilization. There were philosophers before him, but Plato was the first philosopher to develop a complete system of philosophy. Plato's system didn't have much influence during or shortly after his lifetime, but in later centuries, his approach to philosophy became one of the two main pillars of Western philosophy, the other pillar being Aristotle, who we will meet in Chapter 3.

THE GREEK CULTURAL CONTEXT

The ancient Greek world was an amalgam of cultural influences of various regions and city-states. Geographically, it encompassed not just the territory of modern Greece but also the shores of Asia Minor (modern Turkey), Crete, Cyprus, Sicily, and colonies in Italy and North Africa. All of the many Greek city-states shared a common language and culture and at least loosely a common pantheon of deities and mythology. These myths were recorded by the great Greek poets, most notably Homer and Hesiod, and the stories became the basic cultural backdrop for Greek culture and society. The tales of the poets informed the Greeks about who they were—their history and their current reality. Most importantly, they taught the Greeks about the natural and moral order for the society. Education for a Greek meant knowing the poets. The works of Hesiod and Homer were not just entertaining stories, they were considered authoritative about not only the gods but also the nature of human society and the world around them.

The Greek philosophers emerged within this worldview but not as rote followers of the cultural tradition. Philosophical discourse in ancient Greece was born from the willingness to question established answers and search for new and better ones. The point of these philosophers was to live as good a life as possible. A principle means to that end for the philosopher was to find some fundamental principles that provide stability amid the chaos of capricious leaders and deities. For this, many Greek philosophers looked to geometry and mathematics. In geometry and mathematics, the Greeks saw order and certainty and the promise of a language to explain the world.

Most prominent among the philosophers in this movement was Plato, who was active as a writer and teacher from approximately 399 to 347 BCE. He lived in Athens, Greece, during a time when the power and prestige of that city-state was in decline. Like so many other philosophers we will meet, the social and political situation of his homeland affected his thinking. Athens had suffered an embarrassing defeat to Sparta in the Peloponnesian War, and this created political and social uncertainty among the proud Athenian aristocracy. The defeat called into question the idea that Athens had a successful social system, and Plato's work can be seen as an attempt to find a way to build a better society.

PLATO'S WRITINGS

Plato wrote all of his works in the form of dialogues that almost always featured his teacher Socrates as the lead character. Why Plato wrote the dialogues is a mystery, especially given that Socrates apparently taught that writing philosophy was antithetical to philosophizing. The heart of philosophy for Socrates was the dialogue between two people working to reach the truth through reasoned dialectic (back-and-forth conversation). What Plato does in his dialogues is to put the dialectic in writing, granting the thoughts within them a form of permanency. This is consistent with Plato's beliefs about the nature of Truth and probably also reflects his desire to have a lasting effect on his society. Perhaps Plato's intent in writing the dialogues was to pass on to future generations the vision he had for society and the agenda that he couldn't complete in his lifetime.

A common plot runs throughout the dialogues indicating that Plato has a deliberate intent. That basic plot is that a concept such as Justice or Piety is brought up. Socrates says he does not know the exact meaning of the concept, could someone please explain. An answer is provided by someone, often a well-known someone who claims to be an authority. Plato often used the rhetorical device of placing actual Athenian public figures in the dialogue expressing their views to Socrates. Socrates points out that the answer given by the alleged authority is merely an example of the concept and he presses for a *definition* of the essence of the concept. Numerous commonsense definitions are examined and discarded as being insufficient to describe the essence of the thing being defined until eventually we are left with no answer.

The lack of satisfactory conclusions frustrates many readers, but it is part of Plato's intent and is the theme and purpose of the Platonic dialogues. Plato's purpose is not to inform the reader of the answer but to ignite in the reader a desire to find the answer. The answer cannot be said in mere words. The truth cannot be captured in the written word of preformed static sentences, nor can the truth be captured in rhetorical oratory. The truth takes time and nurturing to develop, and many conversations are necessary, for the truth is a life's work. Knowledge and Virtue must be cultivated in a student over many years.

DEFINING JUSTICE

Plato's longest and most detailed dialogue was *The Republic*. One of Plato's central topics in the book is the question of what Justice is. For him, justice is both an ethical issue and a political issue. Justice concerns how individuals should interact with each other and how society should be structured and ruled. In exploring the question about defining justice, Plato uses his usual literary device of Socrates discussing the question with alleged authorities. They give Socrates examples and definitions of justice; each one, in turn, Socrates shows to be inadequate.

The complex arguments of the back-and-forth between Socrates and his interlocutors are interesting, but let's step back for a moment to appreciate the complexity of the question of what justice is. How do you approach defining a virtue like justice? You cannot see justice. You cannot handle it. You cannot measure it or weigh it. It has no color or texture or any material quality we can discern with our senses. We can see actions that we call "just," but do we ever see justice itself?

Frustrating our attempts to define justice is that we have never seen an example of perfect Justice that we can use as a standard to judge particular circumstances. Our concept of perfect Justice does not come from any experience we have had. However, we feel that we can see how one situation is more just than another. Although we cannot measure justice, we still feel that we can discern differences in levels of justice and injustice. So how is it that we can make such judgments? What is the standard of justice to which we compare acts, societies, and times, and say how just they are? Plato argued that there must be a singular, unchanging standard of justice. If the standard of justice was changeable, then we would have no real standard by which we could measure acts. It would be as if the standard of measure that is a meter changed and was a different length each place we looked. How could we know how long anything was? Only by having a universal objective standard that says *this* is a perfect meter can we say with any confidence that a particular object is a meter long. Plato says that justice must be something universal and real; otherwise, justice is a mere word and has no real value.

So if Justice is universal and real, what sort of thing is it? Justice is not a physical thing like a tree or a person. So, justice must be a nonphysical, yet still real, thing. What kind of thing is that? How would we know anything about that kind of thing? First, we need to ask, what is knowledge?

WHAT IS KNOWLEDGE?

Plato fervently believed that genuine knowledge is universal, unchanging, and nonphysical and thus is not perceivable by the physical senses. True knowledge must be objective and grounded in reason. To be objective means to be independent of individual perception. In other words, to be objectively true, it must be true for everyone. Opinions are not worth much until one gives an account of the reason why they are believed. It is only when our opinions are attached to knowledge that our opinions are of any value.

Plato agrees with the earlier Greek philosopher, Heraclitus, that our physical senses are poor witnesses unless they are informed by the understanding that is brought about by reason. However, Plato will not go so far as Heraclitus in saying that the physical world was in continual flux, ever changing and unknowable. Plato pointed out that the particular objects in the world do fit into discernable patterns. We can identify a large number of qualities that particular objects share that allow us to identify them. For example, Plato and Socrates are particular individuals, but we call them both "human." The term "human" is a universal concept that refers to each particular entity that shares the similar characteristics that compose the definition of a human being. We can look at particular trees that differ in their particularness, but we can recognize that they are trees. "Tree" is a universal concept.

The question that Plato asks is how is it that we recognize objects or concepts? Let's look at an example.

What is it? If you said, "a circle," your answer is understandable but not exactly accurate. What is the definition of a circle? A circle is a shape whose curved boundary consists of points equidistant from a fixed center point. Is the circle on this sheet of paper an object that fits the definition? Not exactly. If we measured it precisely, we would find that the "circle" on this page is not a perfect circle. What is on the page is not a circle but an attempt to *portray* a circle. Almost all things are like this, Plato is saying: They are copies of something perfect. We have never experienced a perfect Circle, just as we have never experienced perfect Justice. The "circle" on the page is not really a circle; it is an object that is "circular." It has qualities that cause it to resemble a circle.

PLATO'S FORMS

So how do we come to the conclusion that something is a circle if we have never seen a perfect circle? In the simplest terms, we recognize a particular object as a circle because the object partakes of the Form of circularity and we have knowledge of the Form of circularity. When our senses experience a particular object, we can compare it to our understanding of the Form of circularity and understand that it is circular.

For example, we perceive an object and say, "That is a tree." How did we come to the conclusion that the object we perceive is a tree? Certainly part of the answer is because of the information provided by our senses. We would answer that we think it is a tree because it looks like a tree, and it feels and perhaps smells and sounds like a tree. But to say we think it is a tree because it looks like a tree doesn't answer the question of why we think it looks like a tree. What *is* a tree anyway, and how do we know something is a tree?

Let's say we are looking at some oak trees. We see one oak tree, a second oak tree, and a third oak tree. Despite their differences, they share something in common, and this common set of characteristics we call an "oak tree." This "oak tree" concept is a universal: It applies not just to one or even several objects but to a class of objects of a certain type. In Plato's philosophy, all oak trees are oak trees because they take on the universal Form of the oak tree.

Plato says that the objects of our sense experience and universal objective truths are intertwined. Any particular tree is a tree in that it participates in the Form Treeness—in other words, a copy of a perfect Tree. In the world of visible objects, we find that particular objects have a number of constant, universal qualities. This is why we can identify and talk about things. For example, Tom, Diego, Svetlana, and Neha are all distinct individuals, yet we refer to each of them with the universal term "human." Despite their differences, they share certain qualities. Corresponding to the names we use, like "human," "tree," and "justice," are Universals that consist of the essential qualities common to all objects within that kind of object. When a botanist seeks to understand trees in general, he or she is seeking not knowledge about a particular tree but what is universally true about all trees. Plato would say that the botanist is seeking to understand the Form of Treeness.

This is also how we recognize qualities within objects. For Plato, every quality we can think of—circularity, tallness, blueness, humanness—we know because there is a perfect, objective, universal Form of that quality. We recognize an object as a "circle" because it participates in the Universal of circularity. Circular objects, whatever they are, all have the Form of Circularity in common. Any occurrence of Justice is the result of the Form of Justice. Likewise, in the realm of human thinking, the Form of Justice is the cause of our idea of Justice.

Here's an example of our knowledge of the Form of Justice. Let's say you study very diligently for your next philosophy paper. You hand it in, and the professor immediately gives you an F. Meanwhile, one of your fellow students walks into class, takes out a blank sheet of paper, writes their name and hands it in to the professor who immediately awards that student an A. Chances are good that you would say the grading was unjust. Why? How did you come to that judgment? Plato would say that you were able to make judgments about the professor's grading because you have some knowledge of the Form of Justice.

So, in Plato's philosophy, there are particulars and universal Forms. All objects that are beautiful have the universal Form of Beauty in common. Particular objects come into being and go out of being. A rose grows from a bud and flowers into beauty but then gradually withers and dies. The rose has lost its beauty, but does beauty itself go away? Of course not. The Universal of Beauty does not change and is unaffected by the world of particular objects. Forms exist in and of themselves, separate from any objects that partake of it.

Plato refers to "justice itself" and "beauty itself." We have an idea of justice, and by this he does not mean a subjective idea, a product of a person's thought. The Forms are not dependent on particular minds. They are realities that are independent of all minds. Circularity exists even if no human mind is thinking of Circularity; it exists even if there are no objects that are circular, and the same is true with Justice, Beauty, and all the other Forms.

What, then, are these universal Forms according to Plato? They are the true objects of knowledge. Like Truth, they are universal, unchanging, and nonphysical and thus are not perceivable by the senses, are objective, and are grounded in reason. The universal Forms are unchanging, perfect—a perfect Circle—but particular objects are imperfect because they are only copies that partake of the universal essence of the Form. The Forms must be real, not imaginary, so then where do they exist? The Forms do not exist in physical space; they are perfect entities beyond this realm.

Confusing? Here is an example that should clarify. Consider the multiplication table. Does it exist? Obviously it must, for it would be silly to say that $5 \times 5 = 25$ is not true, or is not real. Where does the multiplication table exist? You can write the table down, yes, but those are just characters that represent the reality of the multiplication table. You have not created $5 \times 5 = 25$ by writing it down. Erasing or destroying what you wrote won't destroy the reality of the multiplication table. The reality of the mathematics is not changed by what you or anyone else says or does in regard to them. Wouldn't it also be the case that if all human beings somehow forgot the multiplication table the reality of it would still exist? Finally, isn't it also true that no human being ever thought up the table but rather we each at some point discover its existence?

LEARNING THE FORMS

Perfect justice, justice itself, differs from any and all of the limited and deficient particular examples of justice that we experience in the world. Plato said that rather than try to learn about justice from the imperfect happenings in the visible world, we learn about justice by contemplating the perfect Form of Justice.

To begin with, Plato has a different meaning of "learning" than we usually think of today. For Plato, learning is really a process of recollection, and the Greek word is *anamnesis*. We learn by remembering. We know the Forms because they are already within our souls. What a teacher does is awaken the dormant knowledge within the student. Although Plato never explains how, the knowledge of the forms is in our minds prior to our birth in this world. Since he believed that human souls were uncreated and immortal, having always existed, the knowledge of the forms must have somehow come to us in a previous existence. Thus, we have innate knowledge of what is true. Unfortunately for us, though, this knowledge from our previous existence is forgotten. We are unaware of the knowledge that we have buried within or soul.

The Forms cause both the particular objects in the world and our ideas about them. How Plato thought we perceive objects is like this. We perceive a particular object, and our reason discovers in our perception the universal Form. Through the insight of reason, we recollect (*anamnesis*) our knowledge of the Forms, and we are able to identify what the particular object is.

For Plato, though, knowledge of the particulars was a secondary pursuit if not a waste of effort altogether. Knowledge of the Forms is our one and only true goal. We do not study examples of justice; we study Justice itself. We do not bother much at all with the study of trees and animals; they are not what is ultimately important. They merely point us to the Universals.

True knowledge of the Forms is available to us through reason independent of sense experience. This must be the case because, as we have discussed, we recognize a circle but have never experienced through our senses a perfect circle. We know about perfect circles and perfect justice not from experience but through the innate knowledge of the Forms. Experience of particulars in the world reminds us of what we dimly remember, and in remembering we recognize that the object partakes of the Forms, which should point us to studying the Forms.

Problematic for Plato's theory of Forms is how it all works in the world. How does an object actually partake of a Form? Plus, if all particular oak trees partake of Oak Treeness, aren't an oak, a maple, and an elm all particular trees because they partake of the universal From of Treeness? Then don't all plants partake of Plantness? Going in the other direction, the leaves of an oak tree appear green, so it must partake of Greenness, but the trunk is brown and so must partake of Brownness; and what about the tree's size, shape, texture, and other characteristics? It would seem that every single quality of an object—color, size, shape, and so on—would have to have a corresponding Form. How many Forms are there, and how many are reflected in any particular object? And what about relative qualities like tall and short, thin and wide? When a tree grows and its trunk widens, is it partaking of less Thinness and more Thickness? It gets complicated real fast.

THE ALLEGORY OF THE CAVE

Plato does provide some lucid examples of his theory, especially his famous Allegory of the Cave, which explains the nature of reality. Plato has Socrates tell a long, poetic story. Here's a paraphrase.

A group of prisoners have been trapped in a cave since birth. All their lives they have been seated on the ground, their backs against a low wall that runs across the cave. They are chained such that they cannot turn their heads and can only look straight ahead at the wall opposite them. (Yes, this is a strange story.) The cave is lit only by a fire behind the prisoners, and it shines over the low wall and onto the wall opposite the prisoners. Between the low wall behind the prisoners and the fire, various people regularly pass by holding up puppets of people, animals, and other objects. (Yes, very strange story.) The prisoners are unable to see the people, the objects they carry, or the fire itself; they can see only the shadows cast on the wall in front of them. Consequently, they come to believe that these shadows are all that exist. The prisoners can talk with one another, and the words they use refer to the shadows that pass before them.

Plato, through Socrates, now asks us to imagine if one of the prisoners is unchained and allowed to roam free. First, the prisoner turns around and can now see the puppets over the wall. The sight of these puppets thoroughly confuses the prisoner, who naturally had thought that the shadows were the true reality. Having seen nothing but the shadows, the prisoner assumes the puppets are illusions. Worse for the prisoner, the light of the fire is blinding, and it is so foreign to prior experience that the prisoner turns away and flees back to the familiar shadows. But then, the prisoner is forcibly dragged up the cave entrance's rough and steep ascent and out into the light of the sun outside the cave. The prisoner feels pain and anger at this rough treatment but is immediately overwhelmed by the dazzling brightness of the sun. It takes some time for the prisoner's eyes to adjust to the glare of the sun. At first, the prisoner is able to make out only vague shapes and the reflections of objects in a pool of water. Eventually, adjusting to the new level of light, the prisoner can see the objects of the world—the real objects of which the puppets in the cave are mere copies. Thus enlightened, the liberated prisoner now sees how pathetic the lives are of those still in the cave. Returning to the cave to share these new revelations and set the other prisoners free, the prisoner's eyes are filled with darkness, now unable to see the shadows clearly. Those still imprisoned against the low wall refuse to believe the story about the outside world and the real objects in it. They ridicule the now liberated former prisoner for no longer being able to function in their world of shadows. Ominously, Socrates then says, "If they could lay hands on this person who was trying to set them free and lead them up, they would kill him."

Everything in the story is symbolic. The cave represents the physical world in which we live. The chains represent our ignorance within the darkness of the cave. The world outside the cave is the realm of Forms. In the cave are the particular objects that are copies of the Forms, though it is unclear whether the puppets carried behind the low wall or the shadows on the cave wall are meant to represent the particular objects in the world. My personal interpretation is that the puppets represent worldly objects and the people carrying them to cast shadows on the wall represent human artistic activity, the shadows being artistic creations like sculptures. This interpretation matches Plato's general antipathy for representational art, which he rejected as empty foolishness. Whatever the specifics, the Allegory is telling us that the objects in the physical world are like shadows of a higher reality. What causes the reality is a light above and beyond the objects of the world. Even the fire in the world is inferior to a greater light that is beyond the world. The sun represents the highest reality, a light that gives life and intelligibility to everything. The liberated prisoner is the philosopher, who now witnesses the Forms and understands that they are what is truly real, not the objects in the cave. Finally, the former prisoner's return to the cave to witness to the other prisoners represents Socrates. Plato's teacher had discovered wisdom, but when he tried to share that wisdom with others, he was ridiculed. Eventually, Socrates was killed by his fellow citizens of Athens. In the Allegory of the Cave, Plato teaches lessons in knowledge, reality, and politics.

PLATO'S DIVIDED LINE

The Allegory of the Cave represents Plato's view of the cosmos as being divided into two realms. This dualistic cosmology is the most influential and enduring aspect of Plato's thought. For Plato, knowledge and reality are inextricably connected. The levels of knowledge correspond to levels of reality, and he drew a firm line separating the two realms of existence—the visible realm and the intelligible realm—on the basis of how we can perceive each realm. Everything in the cosmos is either above the line or below the line. We can picture the divided line and the two realms in this way.

THE GOOD

Intelligible Realm:	Forms	Mind	Knowledge	Virtues	Unchanging
Visible Realm:	World	Bodies	Opinion	Shadows	Change and decay

Plato's Divided Line

Plato's intent is to categorize the different ways that we perceive and think. We live in the visible realm, which is the world of physical objects that we perceive through our physical senses. Plato further divides the visible realm between our perceptions of physical objects and mental images. We have a kind of knowledge from sensory perception of objects in the physical world, but this knowledge is only about the appearance of particulars. Our awareness of mental images is at the lowest level: These are optical illusions, dreams, fantasies, and imagination. They can't be considered knowledge.

Above the line is the intelligible realm. Even though this nonphysical reality is not accessible to the senses, Plato refers to it as the "intelligible world" because this realm is intelligible to reason. This highest level of knowledge is the realm of pure knowledge and rational intuition of the pure Forms and Virtues, like Justice. The Forms and the Virtues are perfect and unchanging, unlike the bodies in the visible realm, which suffer change and decay.

The first principle of the whole cosmos is what Plato calls "The Good." It is the highest realm of existence; it is perfect in every way. Plato gives us little explanation about what The Good is, though from the Allegory of the Cave, we get the idea that it is the light of reason that gives the Forms existence and makes them intelligible to us. Plato writes, "The good may be said to be not only the author of knowledge to all things known, but of their being and essence, and yet the good is not essence, but far exceeds essence in dignity and power." (*Republic* 509) The Good is the author of all things and yet surpasses them in beauty.

Below the line are the changing particulars of the world. The physical world is a world of flux, somewhat like Heraclitus' view that the physical world is one of constant change: We can never step into the same river twice because the river is different every second. Plato admits that this world of change is real, the objects in it are real and can be encountered by the senses, and we can even take in information about them. However, these objects cannot be understood rationally because they are constantly changing. This visible realm is less real than the realm of Forms, which are unchanging and therefore perfect. Our physical senses can be so easily deceived that we cannot hope to learn much from observing the visible world. We can, at best, get only partial, temporary ideas about particular objects.

Clearly, there is a relationship between a particular object and the universal Form, but what that exact relationship is, Plato never quite answers. An incomplete answer may be found in the Allegory of the Cave. The particulars in the world are the "shadows" of the universal Forms. That means that each particular object somehow "participates" in the Form. How can we think about this? A photograph "participates" in the reality of the object of which it is an image. Even an artwork participates in the same way. The more realistic the image in a photograph, painting, or drawing is, the more fully it participates in the object. However, this is still comparing one physical object with another. Perhaps a more accurate analogy would be in the Allegory of the Cave itself, a shadow cast by an object. A shadow "participates" in the reality of the object that casts it. The particulars are still real, just as a shadow is real. They are not phantasms or illusions. They are real projections of a higher reality. They are projections of the Forms, but unlike the unchangeable and eternal Forms, the particulars do change, and they degenerate into nonexistence.

Somehow the Forms cause the existence of particular physical objects. Physical objects resemble their Forms. Particular objects participate in their Forms. Forms represent the standards by which we judge whether particulars are excellent or deficient. We can understand anything in the world in terms of the Form that gives it its existence and "what it is." The "what it is" is not just its physical characteristics but its function. To understand any object, we must understand the Form, and that understanding gives us the standard of excellence the object is "trying" to fulfill.

In the dialogue *Timaeus*, a direct follow-up to *The Republic* and its story of the Allegory of the Cave, Plato tells a story that's a kind of creation myth for the two realms. The story is of a divine Craftsman who created the world and gave it order and goodness. The Craftsman admired the Forms and created the visible realm to resemble it. This explains how everything in our world is a copy of the Forms. The problem is that a copy is never as perfect as the original; therefore, our world is composed of imperfect copies of the perfect Forms.

MORALITY AND THE PERSON

For Plato, morality was as objective as geometry. Morality was not relative to the individual or even relative to social convention, time, or place. Moral truth was absolute. However, morality for Plato is not a series of dos and don'ts; instead, it is a question of what sort of person one is. Crucial to being a good human is rationally understanding what is good and what is evil. That means understanding what the Form of Humanness is and how we are supposed to be. Humans, like all other things in the world, are things that partake of the Forms. The Form Humanness causes particular humans to exist and gives them their qualities. Therefore, all humans are essentially the same; individual people are particulars of the Form of Humanness.

Plato considers what it means to be human not in terms of physical characteristics but nonphysical characteristics. The core of a human is the psyche. The psyche is not the same as what came to be understood as the soul in the religious traditions of the West. Psyche is the ancient Greek concept of a human self with all of its emotions and thinking. "Psyche" is the root for the word "psychology." Plato considers the psyche to be divided and in conflict, and he says that the psyche needs to be brought under control and be well ordered.

In the dialogue *Phaedrus*, Plato portrays the psyche in a dramatic analogy. The picture he paints is of a chariot driver holding the reigns of two horses pulling a chariot. The charioteer and the two horses symbolize the three elements of the human psyche. One of the horses is the appetites that are found in human bodily instincts, such as hunger and thirst. The appetites do not employ much reason but respond to stimuli of pain and pleasure. The appetites are related to the body and keep it alive but can get out of control when the body's demands for physical gratification are too strong. The other horse is the spirit. It is a higher function of the psyche, not tied to the body and its purely physical desires. By "spirit," Plato means the sense of a spirited horse, not a ghostlike being. It is a willful, dynamic part of the psyche full of energy that desires to do what is good, like a loyal horse. The spirit possesses strength of courage. Like a brave and loyal horse, it obeys whoever commands it. If the appetites are in control, the spirit will expend its energy to appease the appetites.

The charioteer is reason that controls the reigns of the two horses, the appetites and the spirit. Reason is the source of our love for truth and doing what is just. When reason reigns in the two horses of the appetites and the spirit, the chariot of the psyche travels in a controlled and productive manner. Reason needs to keep a firm reign on the appetites to guide those instincts to keep the body healthy while controlling the appetites' desires. The spirit will eagerly obey the commands of reason, but reason needs to keep the spirit's energy in balance, not letting it go too far too fast.

All of this pertains to morality because Plato thought that a well-ordered psyche is what makes a moral person. Plato states that there are four cardinal moral virtues: Wisdom, Courage, Temperance, and Justice. Foremost among these is justice. Justice is the well-ordered person in whom the parts of the psyche each possess the appropriate virtue. Reason must practice the virtue of wisdom and use it to control and guide the other parts of the psyche. The spirit properly manifesting the virtue of courage will subordinate itself to reason and apply its energy to the tasks at hand, ignoring the coercions of pain and pleasure. The spirit manifesting courage does what is noble. The appetites must always possess the virtue of temperance. Like the spirit, the appetites must subordinate themselves to reason, tempering their desires and compulsions. The well-ordered person displays self-control. Note that this is not asceticism—a denial of all bodily needs—but temperance—a moderation that avoids excess. When the parts of the psyche are each manifesting the virtue, it is designed to fulfill, the person as a whole manifests the virtue of justice. The just person is one who has each element of the psyche playing its proper role and maintaining its proper place.

MORALITY AND THE CITY-STATE

Plato talks about the morality of a person, but consistent with his central concept that the Forms are the source of all that is good, he takes a top-down approach to morality. Justice is not arbitrary or subjective; it is objective and universal. Therefore, he saw morality as a fair and correct ordering of society applied universally from the top down. In Plato's philosophy, the person is a microcosm of the state, and the state is the macrocosm of the person.

Just as a person must be well ordered, society must be well ordered. Society will be well ordered only when the people within it are well ordered. The goal, then, is to put in place social institutions that will structure society to keep it well ordered. In Plato's *Republic*, he outlines the social structure and institutions he thinks would best ensure a moral society. He admits that his grand plan will probably never be implemented; utopian visions seldom are realized. He offers his plan as a model to which we should aspire, even if we never achieve it.

Plato views the political state as an organism that must find its proper balance, each part playing its proper role and maintaining its proper place. His view of the individual psyche is the same view he has of the society as a whole. A well-ordered society is realized when reason controls the appetites and the spirit. In the case of society, Plato sees groups of people, what we would now call social classes, as representing those three elements.

Plato has the commonsense notion that the functional state relies on a division of labor. Rather than each of us doing everything—from growing food to making shirts to collecting garbage—specializing in particular tasks will allow us to be much more efficient and harmonious. For this reason, Plato thinks society should identify each person's special skills and train people to be skilled workers in fields that best take advantage of those skills. In this strategy, every profession would be filled by people whose skill set enables them to excel in their profession. This includes the leaders of government. Only those exceptionally skilled at making rational political decisions should be in government, just as only those who are exceptionally skilled at making clothes should be tailors. All levels and areas of society would be filled with the best candidates.

Naturally, Plato saw that the skill most essential to leading a state was that of making informed, rational decisions. The political leaders must have knowledge of the Forms and the Good and be able to apply universal knowledge to particular situations. The people with such skills are the philosophers, and yes, Plato wants philosophers and political leaders to be one and the same. Now, don't assume this was self-serving on Plato's part. He's being prudent and consistent with how he saw the world functioning. Just as we would want the physician who would heal the body to possess the skill and experience to make medical decisions, we would want the political leaders who would heal the state to possess the skill and experience to make political decisions. If people trained to be critically thinking, philosophers are the best at making political decisions, then isn't it only reasonable for political leaders to be philosophers? We've certainly seen how disastrous it is when political leaders aren't good at critical thinking.

In Plato's system, the best trained and most rational people should be the political leaders. Unlike what we have seen happen far too often in history, Plato's leaders would not be richer or more privileged than others in society. These leaders would not benefit themselves; instead, they would dedicate their lives to serving the interests of society as a whole, completely forsaking all personal interest. Plato believed that it was impossible for anyone to be a good leader without proper training that began in early youth and continued until one was age 30. These leaders would have known nothing in their lives except training for leadership, having been picked as young as seven years old for their potential in reasoning. Plato didn't even call these people "leaders"; he called them "guardians." They are those who dedicate their lives to guarding society from harm by using their highly trained skills in reason.

The guardians are the personification of the virtue of reason in society, equivalent to reason in the individual person as we saw earlier. What, then, of the appetites and the spirit? The spirit, that willful, dynamic energy with strength of courage, Plato sees as people specially trained and skilled as the police and military. Plato called them "auxiliaries," in the original sense of the word as helpers and supporters. They use their skills to protect society from external threats—invading armies being a harsh reality of Plato's time—and from internal criminal threats. That leaves the appetites, but here, Plato is not as negative as we might think. These people are not at all less valuable to society than are the guardians and auxiliaries.

These people are the producers, the people who, as the name attests, produce all of the material things that people need to survive. These are the farmers, miners, tailors, potters, carpenters, and other craftspeople; merchants; physicians; and other specialists. Obviously, no society could survive without people performing these occupations, and Plato values them accordingly.

Plato's society is a kind of meritocracy—a society based on merit or ability. He proposes that children, regardless of their parentage, be rigorously tested at a young age. Whatever superior abilities and aptitudes they display will determine what occupation they will enter, and they will be trained accordingly. That means that the child of a cobbler could become a baker, soldier, or legislator. The child of a legislator could become a ditch digger if that were the skill that would most benefit society. Plato's ideal society, in this one sense, is without strict class distinctions. The downside to this system is that once one's occupation is identified, one has no social mobility to be or do anything else. Once a cook, always a cook; you can never change professions. Personal ambition would upset the system.

Plato is most concerned with a harmonious well-ordered society. This being the priority, he has a strong bias against individualism and the macro-expression of individualism: democracy. Today, we place a high value on democracy—at least what we take to be a democracy—so his opposition to it sounds bad in our worldview. Right or wrong, Plato had a reason for opposing a government by democracy. He argued that a democracy would ignore the fundamental principle that people should act for the good of society not for themselves. Instead of accepting their social roles, people in a democracy would seek personal advantage over others. Opposing factions would emerge and struggle for power and democracy would "promote [to leadership] anyone who merely call[s] himself the people's friend." (*Republic* 8.558) Plato feared that a person with charisma and guile would grab power by securing the loyalty of enough people to win power. Once in power, that person could become a tyrant and suppress those who might challenge the tyrant's power, and that would result in a state that is far from being just and well ordered. This is Plato's warning against democracy, and history has proven it is not without some legitimacy. However, Plato expresses disdain for the idea that people should have liberty, free speech, and equal rights, so perhaps his opposition to democracy is not entirely for noble reasons. He dismissed such ideas of freedom as giving free reign to the appetites and ignoring the dictates of reason. By equating democracy with unruly passions, he dismissed it as beneath being human.

PLATO'S INFLUENCE

We end the chapter on Plato, but we never entirely leave Plato or his ideas behind. You will see throughout the history of philosophy how Plato's themes and ideas keep returning. Plato's concern with the questions of how we know anything, the nature of reality, and how we can build a better society are the most common fields of inquiry in philosophy to this day. Philosophers have found Plato's answers to these questions to be either an inspiration or a regrettable error.

Plato's idea of intellectual debate in which the truth must be demonstrated by reason and discourse became a model for philosophy. Propositions had to be demonstrated before they could be accepted as truths. Even more, they had to be defended from questioning so they could remain truth. The philosophical tradition of Plato has been one of questioning by using the tools of reason to demonstrate the truth. Attached to that tradition, though, has been the Platonic assumption that philosophical demonstration does not appeal to worldly examples but to higher principles.

Plato's greatest influence is his theory of universal Forms. His conception that there are universals and particulars was accepted by many philosophers. Even when philosophers strongly disagreed with the theory, they remained influenced by Plato's conception in how they structured their own arguments. As we go through the history of philosophy, watch for how varieties of Platonism arise.

REFERENCES

Plato, *Meno*, Project Gutenberg. http://www.gutenberg.org/ebooks/1643. (accessed February 9, 2021)

Plato, *Republic*, Project Gutenberg. http://www.gutenberg.org/ebooks/1497. (accessed February 9, 2021)

CHAPTER 3

ARISTOTLE

Aristotle was a student of Plato. He studied under him for years, but when Plato died in 347 BCE, Aristotle took a different path. With Plato, Aristotle is one of the two main pillars of Western philosophy, but his ideas are quite different from Plato's. He wrote in opposition to Plato only after his death, probably out of respect. Aristotle wrote and taught in his own school, the Lyceum, producing a large body of work, only a fraction of which survived intact. He was an active writer in the years 347-322 BCE.

Aristotle wrote about his break with Plato:

> *We had perhaps better consider the universal good and discuss thoroughly what is meant by it, although such an inquiry is made an uphill one by the fact that the Forms have been introduced by friends of our own. Yet it would perhaps be thought to be better, indeed to be our duty, for the sake of maintaining the truth even to destroy what touches us closely, especially as we are philosophers or lovers of wisdom; for, while both are dear, piety requires us to honor truth above our friends.* (*Nicomachean Ethics*, 1.6.1)

That quote from Aristotle is often paraphrased as "Plato is a friend to me, but the truth is a dearer friend." It was difficult for Aristotle to speak against the ideas of his teacher, but he felt he had to. For centuries after, philosophers chose whether they agreed more with Plato's or Aristotle's approach to philosophy.

Aristotle dealt with many of the same questions that Plato did about how we know things in the world, but Aristotle took an almost diametrically opposed view of them. Plato believed that the objects in the world were only shadows that reflected a higher reality. Accordingly, Plato believed that studying the objects of the world was not fruitful because they were not as they appeared to the senses and less real than the universal Forms. What was needed was not the study of particulars but the study of the universals—this would achieve real knowledge about what was ultimately real. Aristotle believed that the world exists as it seems to exist to our senses. Therefore, anyone with the right training and ability can learn about objects by observing their characteristics. Study of the world achieved real knowledge because Aristotle believed that the physical objects in the world were fully real and that, indeed, they were the only things that fully existed.

That, in a nutshell, is the big difference between Plato and Aristotle. It is why the famous painting by Raphael, "The School of Athens," shows Plato pointing upward and Aristotle gesturing to stay grounded. Plato reasoned from the ideal, the Universals, to the particulars, whereas Aristotle reasoned from the particulars to universal concepts. Aristotle's emphasis on examining the world and cataloging our observations foreshadow modern scientific methods. Medieval protoscience took its inspiration from Aristotle's Categories, and his ideas on potentiality, actuality, and the four causes, which we'll get to a bit later.

Aristotle's philosophy of knowledge can be broken down into three areas: how objects exist, how we know objects, and how objects change. These three areas overlap and are interconnected, but we'll discuss them in that order.

HOW OBJECTS EXIST

Plato argued that particular objects were the way they were because they partook of a universal Form. Aristotle countered that Plato's theory of Forms cannot explain the *existence* of particular objects—literally how objects exist. Aristotle didn't have a problem with the idea that there are particulars and universals, but he objected to the idea that the universals existed separately from the particulars. This ignited a debate that continued for centuries. What came to be known as "the problem of universals" persists to this day.

What is meant by "the problem of universals?" Take the example of a sheet of white paper. It is a particular object. This particular object has a characteristic that we call "whiteness." We say that whiteness is a quality of the sheet of paper. This whiteness is real; it is a real quality in a real object. The question is whether whiteness exists as a universal apart from the object. Another example is baldness. Can baldness exist on its own, aside from being a bald something? We can say that Socrates is bald, and it would be true that Socrates' baldness is real and a real characteristic of Socrates. However, does "baldness" exist outside of Socrates or anyone else?

Plato's theory of Forms says that "whiteness" and "baldness" do exist separate from any objects that are white or bald. Aristotle disagrees. He contends that universals exist *in* objects, not separate from objects. The particular objects in the visible realm are what exist. This means that the objects in the world exist as they appear to exist without connection to a hidden, higher realm. These real objects Aristotle calls "substances" (more on the meaning of substances later)—particulars that we can describe by qualities such as "whiteness." These qualities are in the particulars, not in the observer or a universal; they are objectively present in objects.

Aristotle isn't, strictly speaking, denying universals, but asserts that the universals are not substances (independently existing things) and that only particular objects are substances. Plato had confused universals with substances in concluding that because we can think about a universal, it must therefore exist as a real thing. Thus, Plato concluded there is a realm of the Forms.

To understand objects and the qualities that appear in objects, Aristotle says, we need to study those objects. He developed a system of intellectual inquiry to study and explain objects.

HOW WE KNOW OBJECTS

Aristotle has a quite different view of epistemology (philosophy of knowledge) from Plato. For Plato, we cannot understand the material objects we perceive through our senses because the senses are imperfect and easily mistaken about the changing material realm. Those material objects are less real anyway, so Plato urged his students to study the realm of Forms not the realm of particulars. Aristotle instead says that knowledge begins with a study of particular things. This is the case for material objects and virtues like justice. Being full of theory but lacking experience of the relevant particulars is deficient knowledge. Thus, he thinks it is a mistake to study an abstract quality in isolation from its concrete manifestations. For example, he says that musicalness cannot exist unless there is someone who is musical. Therefore, if we want to study "musicalness" we need to study musicians and what they do. Similarly, what we do with our knowledge is directed at the particular things we deal with in our everyday lives. Aristotle gives the example that a doctor does not try to cure the Form of Man but tries to cure individual men. (Aristotle has very little to say about women.)

However, our study of objects must be comprehensive. Aristotle stressed that wisdom requires going beyond mere appearances or first impressions. Having knowledge is more than sense experiences and more than familiarity with a collection of individual facts. A dog experiences the smells, the textures, and the tastes of things in its experience, but the dog does not have genuine knowledge. Our inquiries need to go beyond knowledge of particular facts to show how these particular facts follow from more fundamental truths. We need to reach beyond appearances to study the true causes of things, so our study of objects is about uncovering fundamental principles of how objects are. For Aristotle, we have knowledge when we understand the first principles and causes of why things are the way they are.

Aristotle developed a method of acquiring knowledge that is a kind of protoscience. Science is a particular way to approach to the world. We can contrast an artist's, a gardener's, and a scientist's interest in a tree. The artist takes in the individuality and particularity of the tree. He is interested in the play of colors in its leaves, the twists and turns of its branches, and the unique textures of its bark. The gardener has more knowledge because she knows what she needs to be done to make trees flourish and increase their fruit. This knowledge has the form of "if you do this action, then this result will happen." The gardener has a knowledge of what works but doesn't necessarily understand why it works. In contrast, when the scientist tries to understand a tree, she is not interested in any particular tree. She tries to gain a general understanding of the universal characteristics of trees. To understand what is essential to being a tree, the scientist sifts out information that is irrelevant and what is unique to this or that particular case. To put it into Aristotle's terms, the scientist is abstracting the essence of the tree from its accidental (nonessential) features. The scientist is not content to know only what helps make trees grow. She wants to account for how each individual fact fits into a system of facts and to understand the causes for each fact. For Aristotle, full knowledge will show us that a particular fact could not be other than it is. That thought of Aristotle's was long influential in European society, as we shall see.

True knowledge is, therefore, not a list of facts. True knowledge inquires into the universal nature of things both in nature and in society and seeks the necessary connections among them. This true knowledge requires knowledge of the ultimate first principles from which particular facts about particular things can be derived. This approach establishes a high goal for how science should be conducted. Too often today, scientists are content with simply collecting observations and the "if you do this action, then this result will happen" level of knowledge, without an understanding of the larger picture and greater connections among all things. To be fair, this contentment with a low level of knowledge is found in most people, and scientists are just people, after all.

What, then, is Aristotle's approach to gathering knowledge? One of Aristotle's fundamental convictions is that the basic structures of human thought are congruent with the structures of reality. This idea explains how our minds can come to understand the things in the world. When we reason from one proposition to another in our mind, we are at the same time moving from one true fact about the world to another true fact about the world. Therefore, Aristotle reasoned, the structure of our language is important because knowledge consists of the ability to inquire and discuss the facts about the world. We need, then, to ensure that our language has the same structure as our thoughts and reality. According to Aristotle, the basic structures of language, thought, and reality are revealed by the kinds of assertions we can make about things. Getting the structures of language correct will reveal not only the categories of our thought but also the categories of reality. This is the first appearance in philosophy of a kind of correspondence theory of truth—that what we believe is true if it corresponds to the way things are in the world—and we will see many philosophers agree with this basic idea.

In his most complete account, Aristotle gives us a list of 10 categories or 10 kinds of questions we can ask about any object or concept. Aristotle proposed them as the 10 irreducible kinds of classification of objects. In other words, if we get the answers for these 10 categories, we have a good and thorough understanding of the object. Here is a table of Aristotle's 10 categories.

Table of the Categories

(1) Essence	What is it?	A tree; a dog
(2) Quantity	What size is it?	10 meters tall; 9 kilograms heavy
(3) Quality	What is it like; what are its capabilities?	Flower-producing; loyal

(4) Relations	How is it related?	Larger than the others
(5) Place	Where is it?	On a hill; in the corner
(6) Time	When is (was) it?	Yesterday; right now
(7) Position	What position is it in?	Standing; lying
(8) Condition	What condition is it in?	Flowering; covered in fur
(9) Action	What is it doing?	Growing; sleeping
(10) Affection	What is acting on it?	Being blown by the wind; being warmed by the fire

The first category of essence differs from the others that follow it. The English word "essence" translates the Greek word *ousia*. Aristotle sees *ousia* as a permanent state of being—the vital core of what a thing is and the ultimate level of being. Aristotle says that essences "are the entities which underlie everything else, and everything else is either predicated of them or present in them" (*Categories* 5.6). What this means is that every individual object has an essence that is what it is. Think of it like we would say today, "The essence of something is…." When we ask, "What kind of object is it?" we answer thinking about its essence, what is essential to it. When we say, "It's a tree," we are saying that the object fits the definition of what a tree is. That definition, the essential qualities of a tree, is true for every tree. Every object has an essence, in other words, that defines the kind of object it is, and this essence has a distinct set of qualities that define this kind of object. We identify an object by its qualities. Every tree has leaves, so we identify an object with leaves as being a tree and understand that having leaves is part of the essence of a tree. But this essence of tree is not a Platonic Form. Plato's mistake, Aristotle is saying, was to think that these similarities of kind indicated the existence of a universal of that kind—in other words, saying that all trees are similar, so therefore there exists "Treeness." Aristotle says that all trees do indeed have similar qualities and share an essence that we can understand by the concept "tree." There's just not a separate Form of Treeness.

The rest of the questions of the Categories help us understand an object beyond the kind of object it is. Categories 2 through 10 are questions we can ask about any object because objects are described by the Categories. We start with a tree and ask quantitative questions like, "How tall is it?" "What shape is it?" and so on. Quality as a category is a bit less obvious. It's asking what an object is like, what its distinct qualities are. That a particular tree can bear flowers distinguishes it from other trees. If a particular tree has lost its leaves, that tells us something about this tree; perhaps it is diseased. Relations compare a particular object to others—it's bigger, smaller, narrower, wider, and so on. Place and time are as straightforward as they seem. They are informative because, for example, the time when we observed a tree is important because trees can be quite different in summer than in winter. Position is different from place. Place is where something is—the tree is on a hill—but position is its disposition within its place—the tree is standing or has fallen down. Condition asks about the object's current state. A tree may be capable of producing flowers but may or may not be flowering right now. A dog may or may not have fur and a person may or may not be clothed. Action is also straightforward: What is the object doing? Finally, affection doesn't mean loving gestures; it means what outside forces are affecting the object. A tree is being blown by the wind or being cut down by a person. Yes, of course, a dog can be petted and loved by a person.

These questions of the Categories can be applied to any object. We can ask, "Where is Phil?" "What is he like?" or "What is he doing?" and so on. The answers to these questions tell us about Phil and any other thing. Anything, whether physical object or social entity, is the locus of myriad qualities and activities, meaning that particular things have general qualities. However, the reverse—that general qualities have things—is not the case. It makes no sense to say "walking is Phil." Furthermore, while Phil would still exist whether or not he was bald or walking, baldness and walking have no separate existence from being present in some thing or another. Therefore, essences are the subjects of statements to which predicates (i.e., the other categories) can be applied. Essences also exist independently, whereas the other categories (i.e., qualities of objects) can exist only when and insofar as they are present in some object.

Immanuel Kant (we'll meet him in Chapter 13) called Aristotle's 10 categories an unsystematic, but brilliant, work of philosophical thinking. When the medieval philosophers (we'll meet them in Chapter 5) discovered Aristotle, they adopted, at least in part, the idea that the Categories can explain the irreducible kinds of qualities that can be described and are present in objects. Aristotle further categorized essences into species and genus. Species were the first order of substances, and genus was the second order, a more general classification. Centuries later, scientists adopted Aristotle's species and genus in the taxonomy of all life.

The Categories help us to see that all of our knowledge is rooted in sense experience of objects. We can go beyond sensory knowledge by using our mental reason and discover the other qualities of objects. The human mind can abstract, generalize, and draw conclusions. Aristotle set forth a method to discipline our mental abilities through his book called *Analytics*, which formed the foundations of logic and greatly influenced medieval thinkers. Aristotle established the idea that we must reason about our sense experiences to be able to achieve knowledge. Sense experience Aristotle called only potentially intelligible, whereas properly applied analysis makes things actually intelligible. Thinking of objects in terms of their essence also helps us see that universals exist in objects but are only fully actualized when understood by the human mind. The mind (reason) can detach the form from the essence, and we can abstract from our sensory experience of particular forms to the universals. These thoughts are crucial to understanding how objects change, which is our next topic.

HOW OBJECTS CHANGE

One of the biggest problems that ancient Greek philosophers dealt with was the problem of change. Why and how do objects change? Plato had agreed with a number of Greek philosophers before him that change was an uncomfortable dilemma. Their reasoning was that Truth was something that was perfect, and perfection is unchanging. Perfect circles are always perfectly circular. Anything that changed was not perfect. Plato's Forms address this—they are perfect and unchanging, and they are what are fully real; the objects that change in the visible realm are less real. Another problem these philosophers had was that change seemed to them to be a movement from nonbeing to being, something being created out of nothing, which was nonsensical. For example, it appears to our senses that an acorn stops being an acorn and an oak tree starts to exist. Some questioned how this can be, that an object of one kind can disappear and another appear. Parmenides went so far as to seem to declare that all appearances of change were illusions. (This is what happens when reasoning is allowed to run free without grounding in experience—much more on that in later chapters.)

Aristotle accepted that objects change. This is consistent with his view that physical objects are fully real and are the only things that fully exist. Change occurs to real things; thus, change is real. We still need an explanation of how objects change. How do acorns seem to disappear and oak trees appear? How does an oak tree have leaves in the summer but not in the winter? Plato's Forms are powerless to explain *changes* in objects, so Aristotle needed to come up with an explanation. His theory is ingenious. He combines several concepts into an account of change that significantly influenced the medieval and early modern world. The concepts he used are form and matter, potential and actuality, and the four causes. We'll discuss each in turn.

FORM AND MATTER

First, let's look at what Aristotle means by form and matter. What Aristotle means by "form" is not at all what Plato means by "Form." We'll capitalize Plato's Form but not Aristotle's form because Aristotle does not see the form of an object as being a higher archetype. It is simply something in objects in the world. Aristotle's form is the answer to the question, "What is it?" It is the answer to what constitutes an object's essence or "whatness." What is it? It's a tree. But what is a tree? A tree is defined by a distinct set of qualities that make it a tree and not something else. This set of qualities is its form. It's perhaps easier to see when we talk about a human-made object like a drinking glass. It's form is cylindrical, about seven centimeters in diameter and twelve centimeters tall; with a solid, closed bottom; and an open top, that is used to drink beverages.

Every object has a form, its "whatness," but, Aristotle says, every object is also made of matter, its "thisness." The drinking glass is made of matter, specifically glass, and more specifically, this particular hunk of glass. I can hold it and say, "this is made of glass," indicating its "thisness." Another object may have some of these qualities, the same shape, perhaps, but if that object's matter was something flimsy or soluble, it can't be used as a drinking glass. It still has a "thisness," but its "whatness" is not the form and essence of a drinking glass.

It's important to remember that for Aristotle, matter is nothing in and of itself. Matter is pure potential but devoid of actuality (we'll talk more about that next). Matter is amorphous and characterless, devoid of form, and only becomes an object when form takes hold of it to create a substance. This is true even though we do not find any matter that has not been formed. Matter in an object can be formed into a new object. In the case of a statue, the sculptor takes matter and changes its form from a hunk of marble into a finished statue. For an oak tree, the matter is changed from the form of an acorn into the form of an oak tree. The oak tree doesn't come from nonbeing into being; it is an acorn that changes form into an oak tree.

Form and matter are the two ingredients of objects, but we still need to know how they change. The next concept is the spectrum of potentiality and actuality.

POTENTIALITY AND ACTUALITY

Change, for Aristotle is a matter of potentiality and actuality. All objects that we perceive in the world have potentiality and actuality. Objects all have actuality because we can perceive them; if they didn't have actuality, then they wouldn't exist for us to perceive them. But every object also has potentiality—the potential to become something more or something else—the potential to change. We only find things that have been actualized into what they are now. They are actualized but also contain the potential to actualize into something else. Only a perfect supreme being with perfect actuality could have no further potential. All the objects we experience are a combination of actual and potential.

Consider an acorn. If I held one up to you and asked you what it is, you'd reply, "It's an acorn." Having had enough experience, you can identify the "whatness" of the object as an acorn. If I then ask you what an acorn does, you'd say that acorns grow into oak trees; an acorn is the seed of an oak tree. Okay. Now I ask you, what is it in the acorn that tells you it is going to be an oak tree? Just looking at the acorn, you can't tell that. If you sliced an acorn open you aren't going to find a tiny oak tree hiding inside just waiting to burst out. Today we can analyze the DNA of an acorn and match it to the DNA of grown oak trees, and thus we can say an acorn can grow into an oak tree because of its genetic makeup. Obviously, though, Aristotle and everyone else in his time didn't have access to DNA information. So how did he explain how acorns changed into oak trees? And what's more, acorns don't turn into anything else. They don't turn into maple trees. They don't turn into cabbages. They don't turn into beavers. Acorns only change into oak trees. How does Aristotle explain that?

Aristotle explains it by saying that every object has a certain potentiality that determines what that object is capable of becoming. An acorn only possesses the potential to become an oak tree. It has no potential to become a maple tree, cabbage, or beaver. Every kind of object has a limited set of potentiality within it, and that's part of the essence of objects. Aristotle's explanation has the same result as our DNA explanation, and you have to give credit to Aristotle for devising an explanation that, based on the information he had to work with, is rather accurate.

Continuing to consider our acorn, the acorn has the potential to become an oak tree, but it can only actualize that potential under certain circumstances. For years, when I've taught this course in person, I've carried in my backpack an acorn, using its potential as a prop for this very philosophy lesson. Clever, huh? Anyway, all the years that this acorn has been in my backpack it has never changed into an oak tree. That acorn still, after all these years, has the potential to become an oak tree, but it's never been able to actualize that potential because some jerk has been carrying it around in his backpack. If instead, that selfish philosophy professor had put the acorn in the ground, given it some water, and let it get some air and sunlight, it could have actualized its potential to become an oak tree. Interestingly, Aristotle seems to imply that an object not only has a certain set of potentials but also the desire to actualize those potentials. Medieval philosophers later picked up on that, and we will get to them in Chapter 5. Whether or not Aristotle believed that an acorn wants to change into an oak tree, we can understand it and every other object as being along a spectrum of potentiality and actuality. But, however much potential an object has, that potential must be actualized. Something has to happen to it.

THE FOUR CAUSES

Aristotle explains how something's potential is actualized with the Four Causes. To understand change in the world, we need to understand that causes affect objects. By "cause," Aristotle meant something different from how we use the word today. Today we mean "cause" strictly in a mechanical sense—what prior event brought about this result. Aristotle used "cause" as the answer to "why" objects are the way they are. So, although we think of a cause as being prior to an effect, Aristotle's thinking is broader. A cause in the Aristotelean sense is a reason why something is the way it is.

Aristotle identifies four different causes, four different aspects that explain objects and change: material cause, formal cause, efficient cause, and final cause. The first cause is the material cause, which is exactly what it sounds like: What is the matter of which an object is composed? An acorn is composed of organic plant matter. A marble statue is made of marble. A person is made of organic animal matter. A wooden table is made of wood. Simple. The second cause of any object is its formal cause. This relates to the form of an object, as discussed earlier. The form and matter describe the object as it currently is. An acorn is a hunk of plant matter in the form of an acorn. An oak tree is a hunk of plant mater in the form of an oak tree. A marble statue of Zeus is marble matter in the form of what it is a statue of—a representation of Zeus.

The third cause is the efficient cause. With this cause, Aristotle is describing the effects that have affected an object. There are many processes in the world that are going on constantly. These processes affect various objects in various ways. We can understand why an object has its current form by understanding what efficient causes have affected that object. This is best understood in objects made by humans. A marble statue of Zeus has the efficient cause of the sculptor who sculpted the marble matter into the form of a representation of Zeus. That sculptor and the act of sculpting are the efficient cause of that statue of Zeus. In terms of efficient causes, it's easy to see how the sculptor creates a statue, but how does the acorn change into an oak tree? For the acorn, the efficient causes are the soil, water, and sun that actualize the acorn's potential. Every acorn has the potential to change into an oak tree but can only reach that potential when the efficient causes operate on it. Same with a block of marble and every other object.

Efficient causes are related to actuality in that every object has its current form because prior causes have affected it, changing it into its current form. An efficient cause can only affect objects that have the potential to be actualized by that cause. For example, fire can be an efficient cause, but it will effect change only on objects that have the potential to be affected by fire. Fire burns a candle but not a metal fork, for instance. The various processes present in the world effect change, with certain efficient causes interacting with certain objects and actualizing certain potentials in them.

Aristotle's fourth cause is the final cause. The efficient causes that affect objects go hand in hand with an object's final cause. This cause is final in the sense of destination. What is the end or purpose for any object? What is the function that it is meant to fill? In Aristotle's writings, there is a strong sense that everything has a purpose, that everything is working toward its own end or goal. The final cause is an object's goal and purpose. An acorn's final cause is to become an oak tree. This is that idea I touched on earlier that an object desires to actualize its potential. Whether it actively desires it or not, there is, in Aristotle's system, only one reason why an acorn exists: to become an oak tree. Acorns either fail in that purpose, or they succeed in that purpose. In the natural world, every seed and every baby animal has the final cause of growing up to become the organism it is meant to be. When we look at human-made objects, the same principle applies. What is the purpose of a statue of Zeus? To be present in a temple dedicated to him. That purpose is why the sculptor sculpted the statue and why every other human decision was made about the statue. Why did the sculptor choose Zeus? Why choose marble? Why hire a sculptor in the first place? All of these questions are answered by the final cause of the statue. The final cause is inherent in the object's essence or form. Essential to being an acorn is the purpose of becoming an oak tree.

In Aristotle's view of the world, everything is working toward its final goal and purpose. Acorns become oak trees; baby beavers become full-grown beavers; blocks of marble becomes statues; wood becomes tables, and so on. Everything is moving toward a purpose. If the efficient cause is there, then the potential that is related to the final cause is actualized and the purpose is fulfilled. Using Aristotle's Four

Causes, we explain an object by answering four questions about it: what it is made of, what made it the form it is, what or who produced it, and what its purpose is.

THE GOOD LIFE

Everything has a final cause, and that includes people. We are to fulfill our purpose; it's part of our essence. Keep in mind, this thought is in the context of 2,300 years ago, so "we should fulfill our purpose" is not the individualized self-actualization we might think it means today. We have to wait another 2,100 years before we start to see people thinking in terms of their individual purpose. Aristotle, and most people after him, thought of the human being as having a singular essence, and each particular human person partakes of that essence. In short, we are all the same. That was the dominant way of thinking until it started to change 200 years ago (see Chapter 17).

Aristotle said that our purpose and goal is to live a certain kind of life, something commentators have called "the good life." For Aristotle, the notion of a good life is intertwined with morality, and morality is based on reason:

> *We state the function of man to be a certain kind of life, and this to be an activity or actions of the soul implying a rational principle, and the function of a good man to be the good and noble performance of these, and if any action is well performed when it is performed in accordance with the appropriate excellence: if this is the case, human good turns out to be activity of soul in accordance with virtue.* (*Nicomachean Ethics* 1.7.5)

That quote is from Aristotle's book on moral philosophy, *Nicomachean Ethics*, in which he summarizes his observations of what constitutes the good. His moral theory is in line with his method of understanding objects, an understanding based on his observations and what he sees as being the objective facts about achieving human excellence. His approach produces a straightforward, grounded ethical philosophy, but it is constrained by the limits of his experience. Being a man of privilege in a hierarchical society, his view of morality included only men of his social status. We'll see more about that in the next subsection on community and government.

For Aristotle, morality is a question of how we achieve the ultimate good. Like all things, human beings have the final cause of fulfilling our nature, and Aristotle says that our final cause is to achieve our human purpose. He argues that the ultimate goal of all people is happiness, but not just happy feelings—a particular state of happiness that he calls *eudaimonia.* To understand *eudaimonia*, don't think of it as pleasures, because those are fleeting, but think of it as the contentment of living well and having a life worth living. What's interesting about what Aristotle is claiming is that everything we do is in one way or another directed toward the goal of this contented well-being. Ask why you are doing anything you do. You are reading this right now; why? To get an A in this course. Why? To get a university degree. Why? To get a good job. Why? To make money. Why? To have a good life. Yes, *eudaimonia* is the ultimate goal.

Some people chase wealth, fame, honor, or other fleeting ways to feel good, but *eudaimonia*, what could also be called "the good life," comes from living a disciplined life of virtue. Aristotle taught that the good life is the life of virtue, and virtue is measured by what helps people to achieve the good life. In other words, you achieve a good life by living a good life. This isn't circular reasoning; it is the nature of virtue ethics. For Aristotle, we must develop our mind and psyche to cultivate the virtues of temperance, justice, and courage that define a good person. We cultivate virtue by practicing virtue. We become just by doing just acts. We become temperate by doing temperate acts. And so on. In living our lives this way, we fulfill our human purpose and achieve the state of *eudaimonia*. Being virtuous brings us the good life.

This is the broad purpose of life, but what about specific ethical decisions? When faced with the decision to do A or B, how do we know which choice is the ethical course of action? Not surprisingly, Aristotle says that the person of virtue will be able to decide on the correct choice by exercising virtue. This is because, Aristotle says:

> *Virtue, then, is a state of character concerned with choice, lying in a mean, i.e. the mean relative to us, this being determined by a rational principle, and by that principle by which the man of practical wisdom would determine it. Now it is a mean between two vices, that which depends on excess and that which depends on defect; and again it is a mean because the vices respectively fall short of or exceed what is right in both passions and actions, while virtue both finds and chooses that which is intermediate.* (*Nicomachean Ethics*, 2.6.6)

This sentence is the heart of Aristotle's ethics, and it holds a lot of meaning.

First, virtue is a state of character. This is the application of practicing virtue previously mentioned—we become just by doing just acts. Being truly virtuous means wanting to make the correct ethical decisions. It is not enough to know what is virtuous; one must live it and act on it. Aristotle says that a virtuous person "delights in virtuous actions and is vexed at vicious ones." (*Nicomachean Ethics*, 9.9.4) The virtuous person makes a choice to act, but the choice must come from a certain character.

The virtuous person makes the virtuous choice by determining the mean course of action relative to the situation. By "mean," Aristotle refers to the course of action that lies between extremes. He explains that "excess is a form of failure, and so is defect, while the intermediate is praised and a form of success." (*Nicomachean Ethics*, 2.6.3) Aristotle's position is that the middle path is always the correct path. Here's an example from Aristotle's time. Let's say your infantry unit is in a battle, and the enemy is charging your position. One extreme reaction to this would be to run away in panic. The opposite extreme would be to abandon your defensive position and charge the enemy. Between the extremes of cowardice and foolhardiness is the mean of standing your ground and meeting the enemy's charge. This simple example is emblematic of how Aristotle wants us to think about every moral decision that confronts us. Thinking is the key because the mean is determined by reason.

The mean is relative to us, to the particular situation that confronts us. That relativity does not imply that we have any leeway to make personal moral choices. Aristotle specifies that the mean relative to us is being determined by a rational principle that any man of practical wisdom would determine. What Aristotle is indicating here is that though every situation is different, every situation has one rationally correct moral answer to it. Every rational man in that situation would reach the same conclusion. And Aristotle does mean men only; he believed women lacked the capacity for reason, a clearly extreme and irrational belief and quite hypocritical. But back to the infantry example: If any man in that unit can keep his head and think rationally about that situation, he will be able to determine the correct prudent action to take.

The bottom line for Aristotle's ethics is the demand that we always practice rationally driven moderation. Aristotle's word for this is *phrónēsis*, which is best translated as "practical wisdom" with a strong sense of prudence. We do not make moral decisions on the basis of emotion or personal preferences; we make moral decisions on the basis of the middle path as determined by rational principles. If we live life in this way, we will develop virtue, and living the virtuous life is the efficient cause of how we reach our final cause of *eudaimonia*. It is important to remember that living the virtuous life is a process; it is not an action we do once and there we are. Acquiring virtue for Aristotle meant developing the habit of *phrónēsis*. Only the person who consistently practices *phrónēsis* can develop moral virtue. Like any good habit, the more we practice it, the easier it becomes. Acting virtuously creates a virtuous character, and a virtuous character will more readily act virtuously. Virtue begets virtue. Aristotle's example is developing courage. You may lack courage at first, but by performing an initial act of courage, you begin a habit. Developing courage is the process of incremental change, small steps of prudent courage taken over time that molds your character.

The person of moral virtue cares not about fame, fortune, or power but rather to act according to the dictates of reason, seeking neither to control others nor to submit to others. He acts with wise, prudent self-control and has the contentment of living well and having a life worth living.

ON COMMUNITY AND GOVERNMENT

Not surprisingly, Aristotle's approach to the political state differed from Plato's in ways similar to how they differed on other topics. Plato had envisioned how the ideal state should be. Aristotle studied existing city-states. His approach was to look at the elements of which states are composed, comparing their similarities and differences, and attempting to identify what worked and what didn't. Unfortunately, the data have been lost that Aristotle and his students had collected about the city-states of their time, but we do have Aristotle's book that came out of that research. That book is called *Politics* from the Greek word *polis* meaning "city."

Strangely and disturbingly, though, Aristotle begins *Politics* with a discussion of the necessity for hierarchies among people. The Greeks should rule over the barbarians, men should rule over women, and masters should rule over slaves. He claimed that this was evident from the natural order of things. I've previously mentioned that he saw women as inferiors (women exist to supply men's everyday needs, he wrote), but he also believed that a large number, probably a majority, were inferior people fit only to serve as slaves (who exist to supply superior men's everyday needs). He declares in *Politics* that there are natural slaves—people whose essence includes being slaves, who from the hour of their birth are marked out for those purposes. This seems evident to Aristotle. "Are there natural slaves? Yes, because we see in the world that some are born enslaved." It is therefore morally acceptable to enslave those people who show, he says, a predilection to servitude.

This shows how even the most intelligent of people can hold prejudiced views and how rational thought can be used to defend ideas that aren't true.

Aristotle's grave flaws aside, he did make several interesting observations about political systems. He said that the two main questions about political systems are "Who rules?" and "On whose behalf?" He identified three forms of "who rules"—a single person (monarchy), a select few (aristocracy), and a large number (polity). To each one, he added the two possibilities of "on whose behalf"—for themselves or for the common good. When any of the three political forms ruled for the common good, they were good, though Aristotle gave preference to polity because it included a larger number in decision-making (not women or slaves of course). But each form could be perverted into benefiting only those in government. Monarchy can descend into tyranny, aristocracy into oligarchy, and polity into democracy. About democracy, Aristotle had similar criticisms as had Plato, seeing it as leading to self-interested tyranny. Aristotle proposed that the state should be governed by a constitution, the rule of law to which all are subject. All citizens would have a voice in decision-making, guided by the state's constitution to act always to do what the common good requires.

AFTER PLATO AND ARISTOTLE

Are we done with Plato and Aristotle? Not at all. Plato and Aristotle form the foundation of Western philosophy. Every philosopher you will meet for the next seven chapters of this course is responding to Plato, Aristotle, or both, and even after that, with a few exceptions, Plato and Aristotle have a strong influence. So keep in mind what you learn about Plato and Aristotle.

REFERENCES

Aristotle, *The Categories*, Project Gutenberg, https://www.gutenberg.org/ebooks/2412. (accessed May 10, 2021)

Aristotle, *Nicomachean Ethics*, translated by D. P. Chase, *Wikisource*, https://en.wikisource.org/wiki/Nicomachean_Ethics_(Chase). (accessed May 10, 2021)

CHAPTER 4

THE HELLENIC AND ROMAN ERAS

Aristotle lived at a time when the Greek world dramatically changed. Aristotle was, for 7 years, a personal tutor of the main agent of that change, Alexander the Great. It's unclear how much influence Aristotle's philosophy had on Alexander, who became a tyrannical ruler, but Alexander respected his teacher enough to assist in the distribution of Aristotle's writings across the empire he established. Alexander's empire, and the states he founded, are known as the "Hellenic world," from what the Greek people then and now call themselves—"Hellenes." The Hellenic era lasted from 335 to 196 BCE when the Romans took over much of Greek territory after defeating the Macedonians.

From 335 to 324 BCE, Alexander's army of Macedonian and Greek mercenaries cut a swath through the eastern Mediterranean, the Levant, Persia, and all the way to India. Alexander died aged only 32, but how Alexander changed the political dynamic had a lasting effect. For centuries, Greeks had seen their world as a collection of isolated city-states. Previously, if one traveled a mere 20 kilometers, one most likely would be in a different country. Aristotle held the opinion that the borders of a city-state should practically extend no further than one can see from a tall hill. Alexander created a large consolidated political state with a homogeneous culture and Greek language.

LATE HELLENIC PHILOSOPHY

Perhaps influenced by Aristotle's philosophy of the mean, a number of Hellenistic thinkers emphasized moderation, which trended toward the denial of worldly things. Several philosophical movements arose, the most significant ones being Cynicism, Epicureanism, Skepticism, and Stoicism. Yes, each of those movements spawned a word still used in our language today.

Cynicism was a broad movement that departed radically from conventionalism in society and philosophy. It was neither a single school of thought nor a carefully defined philosophical system. It was instead a reaction of defiance against the general state of society, largely emotional but informed by intellect. We receive our words "cynic" and "cynicism" from the nickname for this movement—the Latin word *cynicus*, which came from the Greek word *kunikos*, meaning "doglike." That nickname came from Diogenes of Sinope, the prototypical Cynic who abandoned being human and acted like a dog, living in a large barrel on the side of the street, barking in public, and urinating in the street. The Cynics, those who acted like human beings, taught a simple life of rigorous self-control. Like Aristotle, they said that happiness is found in virtue, but added that virtue is attained only by setting oneself free from all worldly possessions and pleasures, because society was hopelessly corrupt. Because of their ridicule of social customs and personal follies, "cynicism" became associated with a negative attitude of defeatism and scorn for others.

Epicurus (341-270 BCE) taught that it was most important to be free from pain in the body and from trouble in the mind. He thought that the main cause of human suffering was not physical pain itself but the fear of possible pain. He believed that the cosmos was ultimately ruled by blind chance—an infinite number of atoms continually colliding in an infinite void. Therefore, he felt that there was little point in trying to control things. He encouraged people to tame their passions and be moderate in all things because prudence frees us from the pains of desire and aversion. He urged restraint from lusts and gluttony and counseled sober reasoning and the banishing of mere opinions. Take pleasure, he advised, in simple food and the presence of friends. Ironically, it was his teaching to take pleasure in food that led to the concept of being an "epicurean," which today means having a love of self-indulgent, high-quality food. Not exactly what Epicurus had in mind.

Skepticism became a formal philosophical system based on the general stance of skepticism about the possibility of knowledge. Plato had been skeptical of trusting sense impressions, saying true knowledge can come only from contemplation of the Forms. The school that Plato had established, the Academy, was eventually run by a group of philosophers, the "Academicians," who were skeptical even of possible knowledge of the Forms. The philosophy of the Skeptics ranged from a more modest claim to an extreme claim. The more modest claim, held by the Academicians, was that knowledge is difficult to attain, so we must suspend judgment and continue to investigate (the Greek word *skepsis* means "investigation"). The more extreme claim, first made by Pyrrho (c. 360-c. 275 BCE), is that because reality is constantly changing, no knowledge is determinate, and accepting that we cannot determine the nature of things leads us to tranquility of mind. Skeptics, most notably Sextus Empiricus, used arguments to discredit claims of knowledge with the aim of steering people away from arguing over false dogmatic beliefs and toward accepting the quietude that comes from suspending judgment. Skepticism in general came to be regarded as holding that nothing can be known except that nothing can be known (see Augustine later in this chapter), though not all skeptics would accept that extreme conclusion.

STOICISM AND THE ROMAN EMPIRE

Stoicism began in Greek times but blossomed in the Roman Empire. The movement started with Zeno of Citium (334-262 BCE) who taught a philosophy of detachment, lecturing in the stoas (covered walkways) of Athens. The school Zeno founded was later led by Cleanthes and Chrysippus, who each helped develop Stoicism into a formal philosophical system. The Stoics followed in Aristotle's footsteps in seeking a systematic approach to knowledge anchored in reason and adopting the virtues of wisdom, justice, courage, and moderation as the core of ethical life. They taught restraint from the satisfaction of lusts and gluttony like Epicurus, but most Stoics rejected Epicurus's beliefs that there is no higher reality, and that the cosmos is random. Most Stoics believed in a higher being that was the source of all goodness, reason, and order.

The Stoics had various beliefs, but all shared the core conviction that emotions, both positive and negative ones, arose from false judgments. A virtuous, wise person would forgo emotions, and this would lead that person to *eudaimonia*, a quiet, resigned contentment. Yes, this is why we get our word "stoic" from these philosophers. The resigned part comes from the Stoic idea that the cosmos is ordered by a higher power, Logos, which is eternal reason (yes, from the same root from which the word "logic" comes), the first principle of the cosmos. All things stem from Logos, which is a kind of divine fire or breath that gives everything its reality and imbues it with logic and morality. We humans can know the Logos, but we are subject to its design, and that we cannot change. The only thing we can change is our attitude toward what is happening. This Stoic story is attributed to Zeno, which I paraphrase as follows:

> *Suppose a dog is leashed to the back of a wagon. If the dog agrees to follow, the wagon will pull it and it follows, so that the dog's own power and necessity unite. If the dog does not agree to follow, it will be required to nonetheless. The same is also true for people. Even if they do not want to follow, they will necessarily be compelled to enter into their fate.*

In other words, the only sensible response to reality is to accept one's fate; indeed, that is the only response of which we are capable.

Stoicism resonated with a common Roman sensibility that the individual is largely powerless in the face of greater forces. The massive political and military machine of the Roman Empire had consolidated power across many lands. The Roman way was the only way. Other cultures were assimilated under Imperial Rome. The Stoic teaching of resignation in the face of more powerful forces offered succor to people at all levels of Roman society. Marcus Aurelius captured this well when he wrote, "When you are grieved about anything external it is not the thing itself which afflicts you, but your judgment about it. This judgment it is in your power to efface." (*Meditations*, VIII.47) Oh, and Marcus Aurelius was Emperor of Rome from 161 to 180 CE. He was a true Stoic in realizing that even occupying the highest position on earth, one is still subject to fate. All that you have control over is your own mind, your own responses to events. The strength of Stoicism is its persistence in the face of any adversity to maintain calm control over oneself.

Epictetus (55-135 CE) is one of the more extreme Stoic philosophers. Born a slave but later freed by his master who thought a man of such intellectual talents should not remain a slave, Epictetus wrote that he wished to return to slavery because it was less taxing than having to fend for oneself as a free man. This feeling was in keeping with his belief that, similar to Marcus Aurelius, people are disturbed not by events but by the views they take of events. Epictetus recommended independence from both the external world and one's own passions. He taught a detached quietism from others:

> *When you see anyone weeping for grief, either that his son has gone abroad or that he has suffered in his affairs, take care not to be overcome by the apparent evil, but discriminate and be ready to say, "What hurts this man is not this occurrence itself—for another man might not be hurt by it—but the view he chooses to take of it." As far as conversation goes,*

however, do not disdain to accommodate yourself to him and, if need be, to groan with him. Take heed, however, not to groan inwardly, too. (*The Enchiridion*, 16)

Do not even feel sympathy for another so as to maintain your own self-control was his harsh teaching.

PHILO

Philo (20 BCE-50 CE) lived in the cosmopolitan city of Alexandria. He must have been a man of some station in that city's Jewish community because he was their principal representative before the Roman emperor Gaius Caligula in 40 CE. Philo had a deep reverence for Plato and referred to him as "the most holy Plato." Philo's own philosophy was an attempt to merge Plato's cosmology with the Jewish scriptures. Philo associated the Jewish creator God with Plato's Good, and he allegorically reinterpreted the Torah to blend with Plato's teachings. He depicted the Stoic concept of Logos as the demiurge (from Plato) or mediator between God and humanity. He described Logos as eternal, but a son of God, neither uncreated—for only God is uncreated—nor created as are humans but existing in some kind of middle form. Logos is God's messenger to the created world because God is beyond time and space and does not interact with the created world. Philo identified Plato's Forms with God's thoughts, which make up Logos and the material world. Philo refers to Logos as the architect's design, God being the architect, and as the receptacle of God's ideas. Logos is distinct from the material world but sustains and permeates it. Logos also is partially in us, as Intellect, our intellect. Philo paved the way for Plotinus.

PLOTINUS

Believe it or not, Plotinus (204-270 CE) is perhaps the single most influential philosopher in European history. Yes, even over Plato and Aristotle. That's because Plotinus was very widely read by scholars starting in the 200s CE, and for more than a thousand years, Plotinus was the chief means by which they understood Plato. Plotinus cosmology of a divine entity above and beyond the world inspired Christian philosophers to synthesize Greek philosophy with their religion.

Plotinus's most influential views are that the source of all is the One and that the divine light of reason emanating from outside of us is what allows us to understand anything. For centuries, Plotinus was known to be a Platonist, and scholars having access only to Plotinus assumed that Plotinus's philosophy was an expression of Plato's. Obviously, he was inspired by Plato, but he took Plato in a new direction. It helped that Plato's writings were lost, allowing Plotinus's cosmology to hold the field, making him so influential.

Plotinus went beyond Plato in dividing reality into three, not two, levels. At the top was the One. The One is Being itself—the immaterial first principle that is self-caused and the cause of all other beings. At times, Plotinus equated it with Plato's Good, and at other times, he suggests that the One preceded the Good. The latter is consistent with Plotinus's view that the One is so fundamental to everything that it is beyond all attributes, and, therefore, calling it "good" would be applying an attribute to it. The One is pure Being. All we can state about the One is that it is. All that we can deduce about it is what it is not. Calling it "the One" is the least inappropriate.

The One is the source of everything. It needs nothing, desires nothing, and thinks nothing, but it is so full of Being that that it overflows and all things are an emanation from the One. An emanation is different from a creation. A creation is an act of will. An artist creates, a builder creates; creation is a product of a deliberate action. An emanation comes out from a source, but the source does not act or will it. A creation occurs in time and space, but the emanations from the One are beyond time and space. If that's difficult to understand, that's because it is beyond human understanding except for the result. We can only point to the reality that all that exists emanates from the One. Plotinus borrows Plato's analogy of the sun to describe the One. It is the eternal light that illuminates everything without being diminished by doing so. The One is behind all the myriad things like white light is behind all the colors of the rainbow.

The first emanation (in terms of Beingness, not in terms of time) from the One is the *Nous*, Intellect, or Divine Mind. Intellect is eternal and immaterial like the One, but it is not the One. It is a perfect overflowing emanation of the One. As Divine Mind, it intuitively—meaning immediately and without effort—knows the One and knows itself. The One cannot know itself because that creates a dichotomy of knower and known, but Intellect can know the One, and Intellect can know itself. In knowing itself, Intellect intuits all of Plato's Forms (see Chapter 2). The Forms have their being from the One, but their identity is from the Divine Mind of Intellect. In other words, the One gives everything being, and Intellect gives the Forms their distinct essence. This is similar to Philo's ideas, but Plotinus adds that Intellect knows not only universal Forms but particular Forms. For example, there is a Form of humanity, but also a Form of Socrates, a Form of Plato, and a Form of every individual human.

The second emanation from the One is Soul. It is also eternal and immaterial, and it stands as a connection between the immaterial and material realms of existence. Soul has a higher aspect that looks to Intellect and contemplates the Forms in the intelligible realm, and the lower aspect descends to the visible realm to replicate the universal Forms in particular objects. Emanating from Soul are also the souls and bodies of all things in the visible realm, and Soul unites the cosmos as one living organism. This lower aspect Plotinus equates with Nature and all of life and movement in it. Soul does not consciously order Nature, but what order there is in Nature flows from the rational order of Intellect.

We people are aspects of Soul, similarly divided into higher and lower aspects. Our higher aspect is our soul (psyche), which mirrors the Intellect, and our lower aspect is our body. Our minds are illuminated by the light of the One, and it is the only source of light; we partially reflect that light in our thinking. For Plotinus, like for Plato, our individual souls existed prior to our material birth, and our souls will survive material death, returning to the One. Our material bodies are, of course, composed of matter. Like Aristotle, Plotinus sees matter as amorphous and characterless, devoid of form. Unlike Aristotle, Plotinus sees matter as deprived of Being. Plotinus justifies this odd characterization with his analogy of the One as the sun. The sun gives off light, but the farther one is from the source of light, the more diminished is that light. The One is Being itself, but the farther one is from the source of Being, the more diminished is that particular being. Matter is removed from the One, further than Soul and Intellect. Again, this is not in terms of time or space but in terms of Beingness. Having also equated the One with Plato's the Good, Plotinus also implies that matter is also deprived of good. It's important to realize that this is not saying that matter is evil. Plotinus didn't believe in evil as a cosmic force. Like darkness is merely the absence of light, what we call evil is merely the absence of good. Matter, like darkness, is absent Being and goodness.

None of the emanations to which Plotinus refers are deliberately willed. They simply happen, emanated like a magnetic field emanates from a magnet. This means that reality is not the conscious products of a creator deity. The world and we as we know them simply are, and they simply are the way they are. The cosmos *is*, though, based on reason. It has a rational order. Part of that order is that we humans are part intellect and part body. Our intellect is from the divine Intellect, and with discipline and focus, we can connect with it. Our material bodies are not evil, but in the order of reality, they have less Being and goodness than our intellect has. In the rational order of reality, we are faced with the choice of whether to focus our attention on our intellect, which is closer to the One, or on our body, which is farther from the One. We want to be closer to the One—the source of all Being and goodness; and it is to the One that we wish to return. The problem is that our material bodies are an impediment to returning to the One. Plotinus says that we have fallen into the lower material realm because of our vanity and desire for independence. Plotinus likens our arrogant ignorance to the prisoners trapped in Plato's allegorical cave (see Chapter 2). If we focus on our bodies and the material world, we are strengthening our own chains and alienating ourselves from the higher realm.

Thus, Plotinus teaches, the more we concentrate on reason, the more we will understand what is real and good and the more we purify ourselves. To not be rational then, is a sin. This is not a religious idea, however, because it is not about needing salvation from a deity or a church—we are our own salvation through our dedication to wisdom and truth. Dedication to reason shall set us free. These ideas inspired religious and nonreligious thinkers, philosophers, writers, poets, and scientists for centuries, and it still reverberates today. Although we will not hear the name Plotinus mentioned often, if you pay attention, you will see this view of the universe holding sway over philosophy, religion, science, and culture into the 1800s.

AUGUSTINE

One philosopher deeply influenced by Plotinus was Augustine (354-430 CE) who also began his philosophy from the assumption that reason was the source of all that is real and good. Of course, Augustine equated reason with the Christian God. Augustine is often misunderstood and dismissed as being merely a theologian. The reality is that he was one of the deepest and most innovative thinkers in the history of philosophy. Augustine delved into questions that no one before him had considered, and he made explorations and fundamental insights not seen again for more than 1,200 years.

Augustine has a bad reputation because, to be honest, his most famous book *Confessions*, though brilliant philosophy in parts, descends toward the end into a maudlin exercise in self-pity. Also, late in his life he became a zealous persecutor of nonconformists, violating their freedom of thought and religion, largely driven by his strange obsession with the doctrine of original sin. Despite all that, his earlier philosophical thought is deep, insightful, and compelling and could easily fill an entire course.

In his young adulthood, Augustine adopted Manichaeism, an ideology that, like Platonism, was highly dualist. Much starker than Platonism, Manichaeism taught that reality was divided between the forces of Good and Evil. Where Plato and Plotinus saw an imperfect realm of material objects, Manichaeism saw a realm under siege from darkness in which good people could be devoured by evil as though by wolves. This ideology seemed to have an influence on some of Augustine's thinking, even though he eventually repudiated Manichaeism. He became a professor of rhetoric and later converted to Christianity.

Augustine was convinced that there is objective truth and that knowledge of that truth is possible. One of his first philosophical writings he titled, *Against the Academicians*, a treatise addressed to the philosophers who ran Plato's Academy (see the earlier subsection) in Augustine's time and who had fallen into a deep philosophical skepticism about knowledge. Ironically, Augustine was more true to Plato than were those who ran the school Plato founded. These skeptics held that nothing can be known and that, therefore, assent should not be given to anything. Instead, they taught, we should suspend judgment on all matters and content ourselves with a life without firm beliefs. Augustine, as both a Platonic philosopher and a Christian, could not abide by such a life.

His argument against the skeptics is elegantly simple. He turns the skeptics' own argument against them. Augustine's argument can be listed as follows:

1. The skeptics claim that there are no truths that can be known.
2. But to deny that we can know truth requires the skeptic to have a definition of truth.
3. Their definition of truth is either true or false.
4. If the definition they give is true, then the skeptics do know at least one truth, refuting their claim in 1.
5. If the definition they give is false, then it is useless and meaningless in the defense of skepticism.

In other words, the skeptics were trying to have it both ways by saying they know that nothing can be known.

Augustine countered with showing not only that the Academicians' argument was fallacious but also that there is at least one truth that we can be certain that we know. If someone argues for an "all" or "never," all you need to do to refute the argument is to find one contrary example. That is what Augustine did.

> *For we both are, and know that we are, and delight in our being, and our knowledge of it. Moreover, in these three things no true-seeming illusion disturbs us; for we do not come into contact with these by some bodily sense, as we perceive the things outside of us,—colours, e.g., by seeing, sounds by hearing, smells by smelling, tastes by tasting, hard and soft objects by touching,—of all which sensible objects it is the images resembling them, but not themselves which we perceive in the mind and hold in the memory... I am most certain that I am, and that I know and delight in this. In respect of these truths, I am not at all afraid of the arguments of the Academicians, who say, "What if you are deceived?" For if I am deceived, I am. For he who is not, cannot be deceived; and if I am deceived, by this same token I am.* (*The City of God*, 11.26)

Augustine's proof of his existence is known as the "*si fallor, sum*" argument, Latin for "if I am mistaken, I exist." It proves that complete skepticism is impossible. It also demonstrates the importance of an individual's power of reason: We *can* know things. Therefore, the quest for knowledge must begin with knowing oneself. That is exactly how Augustine proceeds.

The Inner Teacher and Illumination

Augustine adopts Plotinus's view that the human intellect is endowed with the power of reason. Augustine's idea of learning is that we think for ourselves, but we need the divine light of reason to understand truth. His conception of how our minds see truth is analogous to how we see with our eyes. We can't see physical objects without light. We have the ability to see, but we need help to see. Augustine thinks of understanding in the same way. Our minds are able to understand truths, but we need help. That help is the light of reason. Certainly, Augustine equates reason with God, but in the same way that Plato considers the Good and Plotinus considers the One. Augustine, as a Christian, believes we should love and submit to God, but in matters of philosophy and intellect, his view of God is the God of the philosophers more than it is the God of Christianity.

The idea of divine illumination is a tricky one to understand because it is easy to fall into the mistake of thinking Augustine means that God is doing the thinking for us and we lack free will. Augustine thought the opposite—we will to understand, and our understanding is our doing—with help. Think of it this way: Your eyes see objects, but your eyes can see objects only if there is light available to illuminate the objects so that you can sense them. We are able to see with the help of light. The same is the case, Augustine believed, for your mind. You think about and perceive truth, but your mind can see the truth only if there is light to illuminate that truth. That light is the divine light of reason. So just like the sun shines and we can see physical objects, the divine light of reason shines and we can see truth. Augustine equates that light with the Christian God, but this light shines whether one believes or not. Reason is a part of the universe for all to experience, Christian or pagan. Just like we can close our physical eyes and refuse to look, our minds can be closed and refuse to see truth. On that point, Augustine felt that the pagan is more closed to letting in the divine light of reason.

It remains up to the individual to discover the truth, and at the heart of Augustine's philosophy is the idea that within each of us is an inner teacher. In his book, *The Teacher*, Augustine writes in the style of a Platonic dialogue, portraying a conversation between him and Adeodatus, his son. The opening of the conversation discusses the questions of what is teaching and what is the role of the teacher. Augustine's answers that all communication is teaching because it is the speaker attempting to inform others about what is in the teacher's mind. We communicate in two ways: by saying and by showing. Augustine, in the first ever appearance of a philosophy of language, points out that words are useful only if we already know what the words signify. We first have to learn what words mean, and we must be taught these be shown the connection of words to things. If he says to you the word "walking," but you do not know that word, he has not communicated anything to you. But if he stands up and walks, he is showing you. If he then says the word "walking" and points to what he is doing, you could learn the word "walking" by connecting it to what it signifies. Augustine says this is how we learn language. Because words are learned by showing, Augustine concludes that showing is the only true teaching. He identifies three ways we are shown truths: through our senses; by our memories; and, in the case of concepts (such as mathematics and other truths of reason), by "an inner light of Truth." This inner light is the inner teacher, which Augustine connects with the divine illumination. It is an individual's mind that is doing the thinking, though. The inner teacher is our innate ability to reason that can show us truth, but it is up to us to be open to what it shows us.

Augustine was also the first philosopher to develop what is now called a "philosophy of mind." He saw the human mind as a vast, amazing creation. Augustine says in *Confessions* that his mind is a power of his, and belongs to his nature, but the paradox is that he cannot comprehend all that his mind is. This is from Chapter 10 in *Confessions* (before the book turns to straight devotional utterances) and is part of a wonderful and poetic description of human mental faculty. He writes about "the fields and spacious palaces of my memory." (*Confessions*, 10, 12) He marvels about how we can remember things about our past, how memories are a mysterious mixture of order and chaos. What a gift memory is, he thinks, and what a mystery. He likens memory to a large and boundless chamber, a vast warehouse in which particular memories are stored in wondrous cabinets. Every event that occurs to us, every sensation we experience, gets stored in the warehouse. When we seek to remember something, it is as though we go to the warehouse and ask the keeper to retrieve it for us. Sometimes the keeper returns with the memory immediately, sometimes the keeper is gone a longer time. Sometimes the keeper comes back not with the memory we seek but with related memories. Sometimes the keeper comes back empty-handed. Augustine is correct that we do not have full control of what we remember and when. Memories go somewhere when stored in the mind, and where does a memory go when it is forgotten, Augustine asks.

Here's a good way to think about what Augustine is getting at. Can you remember what you had for breakfast this morning? Certainly. Can you remember what you had for breakfast on this date 11 years ago? Probably not. Try to remember the kid who sat behind you in fifth grade. Unless the kid was noteworthy for some reason, you probably don't remember, though thinking about fifth grade will probably bring to mind other people and events that occurred to you in fifth grade. I remember my fifth grade teacher. He smelled bad. I think you should not be able to smell your teacher when you sit in the third row. Anyway, I remember him because he was distinctive in that way. I have no memory of who sat behind me because there was nothing about that person that stood out. But events like these happened to us and are still stored in our memory even if we do not recall them today. Everything that happened to us was stored in our memory, and those memories, whether now conscious or not, made us who we are.

We are, Augustine points out, completely dependent on our memory. "But what is nearer to me than myself? And lo, the force of mine own memory is not understood by me; though I cannot so much as name myself without it." (*Confessions*, 10, 24) What's your name? You say you know your name, but in truth, you remember your name. It is a truth stored in your memory. Concepts that we have learned are also in memory, Augustine says, from science to words to imagination. We can understand the words of other people because we were once shown what words signify, and we remember that and can apply that memory. When people come to tell us about travels to far-off lands, Augustine says, and describe the rivers and mountains they have seen, we need not have been there to understand basically what they describe. That's because our memory has stored away images of rivers and mountains, and our minds can bring out of the warehouse these memories and apply them as similar to what we are hearing from others. But again, our memory is larger than we can comprehend. Try to remember everything that ever happened to you all at once. You can't; but every one of those memories is who you are. Like Augustine, when you look into your mind, you get a glimpse of an infinite realm of truths, leading to the paradox that you cannot comprehend the totality of what you are.

The Human Will

Augustine was deeply influenced by Greek philosophy, but he broke with the Greek philosophers on a central idea. Greek philosophers believed that reason is primary to the will. Plato and Aristotle both held "to know the good is to do the good." Augustine rejected this, saying that clearly human beings are capable of committing an act even when they know it is wrong. For Augustine, there are three forces in a person: intellect, will, and love. He believed that the will is stronger than the intellect and that the intellect follows the will. No amount of rational argument can convince the will, he claims. Our will is free, but it is pulled in the direction of what a person chooses to love. "My weight, is my love; thereby am I borne." (*Confessions* 8.9) Just as an object's weight pulls it downward if it heavy, or rises if it is light, love is the weight that pulls the will. Wherever we are carried, our love is what carries us. From this, Augustine believes that what we love is ultimately the most important indicator of a person.

A central tension that pervades Augustine's thought is between the power of God and the power of human intellect and will. On the one hand, Augustine wants to give all power to God, who by definition is all-powerful and all-knowing. On the other hand, Augustine cannot help but marvel at and acknowledge the power and freedom of both the human intellect and human will. We saw that Augustine marveled at the power of the human mind and his acknowledgment that its power shows us only what is true when we allow it. The human will must access the power of human intellect.

Augustine's discussion of free will is deeply thoughtful and perceptive. He gives this thought experiment: "Does God know which choices I will make tomorrow?" Augustine agrees that, on the one hand, if God is all-knowing, then yes, God has to know which choices I will make tomorrow. But doesn't that mean that my choices are set in stone? Could I prove God wrong by making a different choice? But if I could, then it would mean my will is more powerful than an all-powerful

God, which is a logical contradiction. To get out of this dilemma, Augustine proposes that God is outside of time, while we are within time. Being outside of time, God sees all events, including my choices, as one—there aren't future or past events. We, inside time, must move from past to future and make choices. God's knowledge of what choices we make in no way interferes with our ability to make those choices. Indeed, we have to make our own choices because we are the time-bound, earth-bound beings that we are. Even if you don't accept the premise of an all-knowing God, Augustine's solution is clever and compatible with both Plotinus and Christianity.

Augustine was passionately Christian, and his philosophy at times is influenced by religious considerations. Augustine believed we have a responsibility to our soul because it was created by God. Self-presentation and self-realization are our recognition of God's love and wisdom. Augustine believed we cannot achieve inner peace without finding God's infinite love and being in relation to God's love. Being the philosopher that he is, Augustine's discussion of love for and devotion to God is steeped in considerations of reason. Augustine never diminished the importance of religious ritual, but he emphasized intellectual understanding in our devotion to God and to ourselves. Being in the Platonic tradition, Augustine saw a difference and even a struggle between body and soul within each of us. Augustine's view of the human soul is a blend of Plotinus's concept of the soul as intellect with the emerging Christian idea of the soul as an object of divine judgment. Augustine did seem to struggle philosophically with the relation between the soul and the mind.

REFERENCES

Augustine, *City of God*, Project Gutenberg, http://www.gutenberg.org/ebooks/45304. (accessed February 24, 2021)

Augustine, *Confessions*, Project Gutenberg, http://www.gutenberg.org/ebooks/3296. (accessed February 24, 2021)

Epictetus, *Enchiridion*, Project Gutenberg. http://www.gutenberg.org/ebooks/45109. (accessed March 14, 2021)

Marcus Aurelius, *Meditations*. (accessed May 11, 2021)

CHAPTER 5

THE NOT-SO-DARK AGES

For centuries, it has been taught that there was a long "dark age" in European history from about 450 CE to sometime between 1250 and 1350 CE. The idea has been repeated so often that it is accepted as truth. This period is denoted by the relative lack of new scholastic material in the sciences, literature, and philosophy. Those who support the myth of a dark age blame as culprits the fall of the Roman Empire and the rise of Christianity.

It is a popular myth that philosophy, if not critical thinking in general, ended sometime in the late third or early fourth centuries, but the evidence belies the myth. The reality is that the method of Christian philosophers was a normal continuation of a philosophical method that emerged in Greek philosophy long before the Christian era. Plato's philosophy was a dualism that saw the higher realm of the Forms as the truer reality. Plotinus followed with the teaching about the One. The fourth and fifth centuries that followed the fall of the Roman Empire and the rise of Christianity saw Christian thought mature as a continuation of long patterns of thought. Christianity did not end philosophy but intertwined with it, largely continuing the concerns and issues present in Greek philosophy.

The myth of a dark age stems from people who looked back in time and did not see previous people performing the quest for understanding in the way that they did it. The epithet of the "Dark Ages" arose during the so-called Enlightenment of the 1600s and 1700s, when people hostile to religion arrogantly dismissed the medieval period as irrelevant. Labeling it the "Dark Ages" was a rhetorical device saying, "We're doing something that is much more important and of much more quality than what people did generations before us." The myth of a Dark Age caused by religion not allowing people to think for themselves and the notion that nothing was really happening of any intellectual depth has stuck with us for the last 300+ years, but it's not really true.

THE TRANSITION FROM ANTIQUITY TO MEDIEVAL

We do see a relative lack of published material in philosophy between 450 and 1250, but Christian, Jewish, and Islamic scholars were, in fact, the only ones who kept philosophy and protoscience alive. What dark age there was was caused by a loss of social cohesion, which was caused by waves of barbarian invasions that caused severe economic and demographic disruption.

The Visigoths sacked Rome in 410 CE—a stunning catastrophe that affected people then far more than 9/11 affects the early 2000s. Rome was literally the center of the known world and had been for more than 500 years. That it would fall to an impoverished, barbarian people was world shattering. Then, in 455 CE, the Vandals sacked Rome even more viciously, an act that gave us the words "vandals" and "vandalism." The military government of the western Roman Empire, rife with corruption and civil strife, finally fell to barbarians in either 476 or 493 CE, depending on whether you consider Odoacer to be the last Roman or the first barbarian ruler of Italy. Then things got worse. Wave after wave of tribes from the north or east devastated the former Roman territory: The Ostrogoths, the Alemanni, the Huns, the Franks, the Bulgars, the Avars, the Suebi, the Magyars, the Lombards, the Goths, the Pechenegs, the Cumans, the Arabs, the Normans, and finally the Vikings all invaded significant swaths of territory over a 500-year period. Some pillaged and disappeared. Others stayed and settled, like the Suebi, Ostrogoths, Bulgars, Magyars, and Lombards. Each generation faced a new barbarian invasion and had to recover and rebuild. Continual outbreaks of plague, often brought by invaders, also contributed to the strife and anarchy.

These violent disruptions affected the Western half of the former Roman Empire more than the Eastern half that was based in Constantinople. As the disruptions continued, western lands were increasingly isolated from the still vibrant political, economic, and cultural centers in what are now Greece, Turkey, and southern Balkans. The political and economic structures of the old Western Empire were swept away or withered away. The loss of social structure meant a loss of education. Schools disappeared. Classical Latin learning did not disappear entirely, but it became limited to prominent families who were well connected and could afford the very few remaining private tutors. These included heads of state, Christian bishops, and the households of dependents and advisers to bishops and secular rulers. Even this education was a limited affair compared to times past and consisted primarily of basic grammar and rhetoric. Philosophy was decreasingly part of that education, even for the elites. This was not because it was banned or frowned on but because it simply was lost to the chaos of the times. The only remaining bastions of learning were isolated Christian monasteries from Ireland in the far West to Persia in the East where the monks kept libraries of ancient scrolls of Greek, Roman, and Christian scholars. The monks' withdrawal from the world was more than a spiritual statement; it was an eminently practical response to the chaos around them.

Compared to what we have today, people in the medieval period had very few of Plato's and Aristotle's writings. Those in the West did not have much at all of Greek philosophy because the great works of the philosophers were lost to them. By the 400s, the only work of Plato available in Latin was *Timaeus*, giving people then an incomplete view of Plato. However, its vision of a perfect heavenly realm and our imperfect world fit well with other ideas that were common, such as those of the Stoics and various religious groups at that time such as the Gnostics.

Aristotle's books fared only slightly better and thanks only to the efforts of Boethius (477–524), who translated into Latin and wrote commentaries on Aristotle's logical works. Thus, the West's supply of Aristotle's genius included only his logic that informed philosophical dialogue, with none of his insights and theories on metaphysics, physics, ethics, politics, and aesthetics. Without knowledge of Aristotle, the student of the natural world, they had a very incomplete view of Aristotle.

The loss of ancient texts meant that scholars did not know about Aristotle's ideas about objects and change. That meant they didn't have a counterexample to the more mystical ideas of Plato and his most notable interpreter—Plotinus (see Chapter 4). The one book of Plato that survived, *Timaeus*, is perhaps the oddest of Plato's books and expresses the most "out there" of his thoughts. *Timaeus* does not feature Socrates as the central character but rather a storyteller, Timaeus, who relates a mythic story that explains why things are the way they are. That story was that the visible world was created by a mystical being, the Demiurge, who crafted the visible realm by copying the Forms. This is why the visible world resembles the Forms but is filled with lesser copies. Armed with Plato's *Timaeus* and Plotinus' thought (inspired by Plato, mostly *Timaeus*), along with some Gnostic ideas about Logos, what scholarship survived the collapse of the Roman civilization developed into philosophy as a study of the mystical Intellect using Aristotle's rigid rules of intellectual reasoning. The whole of Plato and Aristotle, and the rest of Greek philosophy, would not be restored to Western Europe until the 1200s. (See Thomas Aquinas in the later subsection.)

The constant chaos in Western Europe started to calm down by around 1100. Philosophical scholarship gradually returned in the Christian monasteries and seminaries. What emerged was the medieval philosophical movement of Scholasticism: a blend of Catholic theology and ancient philosophy that reopened the unanswered questions left by the Greeks and Romans. Inquiring minds in Scholasticism debated these questions armed with the texts and tools that they had, such as Aristotle's logic.

THE SCHOLASTIC DEBATE OVER FAITH VERSUS REASON

A fundamental issue in Scholasticism was the question of faith versus reason. Now, we have to stop immediately and understand what was meant by the concept of faith. Many people today have the false idea that faith is blind obedience or saying, "I have no reason to believe this, but I'll believe it anyway." That's not faith in the Islamic, Jewish, or Christian tradition. It's also not the definition of faith you will find in a dictionary. Merriam-Webster will tell you that faith is an allegiance to and trust in an authority, either a tradition or a person. Faith, especially in the medieval period, was about loyalty, not irrationality.

So, if faith isn't the opposite of reason, why was the argument in medieval thought framed as "faith versus reason?" The controversy was over the question of from where and how we obtain truth. Remember that we can't be anachronistic, putting today's ideas onto people in the past. What we commonly (and blindly) think of as "faith" today is different. In the medieval tradition, faith means that we get truth from an authoritative source higher than the individual. This sentiment is consistent with the ancient belief in the existence of unchanging, perfect universals. As we saw in Plato and Plotinus, searching for truth meant contemplating the higher universals. The idea that one could come to the truth on one's own was dismissed as a vain and foolish notion. Truth was universal, not particular, and truth was understood by humanity, not by particular individuals. The medievals sought truth from a source higher than the individual—tradition. Obviously, tradition included the church, but it also included the "letters"—the collection of authoritative writings, such as those of the ancient philosophers.

For a long period after the collapse of the Roman Empire, most thinkers in Europe looked back at the Roman period as a golden age superior to the times they currently found themselves in. As the chaos swirled around them, the medieval intelligentsia could not help but look back to earlier times for a sense of stability and wisdom. This admiration for the past encouraged the study of "letters"—the study of ancient texts. The letters went beyond scripture; they included writings of the church fathers and the writings of scholars including Plato, Plotinus, and Aristotle, among others. Still today, we place faith in written authorities: dictionaries, encyclopedias, and textbooks. When you write university papers, you are expected to cite your sources. The medievals had a similar expectation: If you make an argument, you cite your sources.

Scholastic inquiry in the medieval era was a process that began with reading and memorizing the writings of past authorities. Those old writings had to be incorporated into scholarship. This practice is not that far removed from education today. What was different from today was the practice of almost exclusively looking back rather than forward. The attitude in the medieval period was that new thought could not be better than old thought; scholarly writings had to be based on past authority. It is this attitude far more than any religious suppression that discouraged original philosophy. Philosophy, and indeed all learning, was a derivative activity based on conformity to the writings of the old masters who knew more than contemporary thinkers.

The medieval Christian expression of faith, therefore, was the allegiance to and following of the authority of tradition. This included the confession of the Catholic Church and the teaching of the ancient books—the letters. In practical terms, this is applying the inherently philosophical idea that what the ancient authorities said is true and that thinking for yourself is departing from truth. That's where we get the word "heresy." Heresy was not originally a religious thought. The word "heresy" comes from the Greek word *haere* that means "to choose" or "to take." To be a heretic is to choose a path that differs from the authorities of old, forming your own opinions contrary to what is authoritative, accepted truth. The persecution of heretics, which was vile and reprehensible in every respect, was a political persecution of people who thought differently from the prevailing authority. The "heretics" could have been following their own authorities within their subcultural tradition, but they were thinking differently from the established tradition.

Thus, the debate over faith versus reason is about the following question: Must I follow the ancient texts, or can I, as an individual reasoning with my own mind, come to the truth through my own thinking? Most people throughout history both before and long after the medieval period would say no, demanding that others conform to established political and cultural beliefs. If you think for yourself, you might end up disagreeing with what the political leaders teach, and then the political structure is threatened. That is still the case today. There is political pressure to believe that you can't or shouldn't think for yourself.

Separate from politics is the philosophical question of whether an individual mind is capable of coming to truth. If, as the Platonists contended, all truth comes from the Good or Intellect, then the most that individual people can do is open their minds to that truth. Again, largely because of the wide acceptance of the idea of universals, divergence from tradition was seen as deviation from the universal of human reason. If being a good human is defined as sharing qualities with the universal of humanness, then the more one deviates from accepted practice, the less of a good human one is. Most medieval scholars believed in reason guided by the letters and the tradition of interpretation.

Only in the 1000s in the Islamic world and the 1300s in the Christian world did a few bold thinkers start to think outside the box of what everyone assumed scholarship should be. These thinkers argued that through our unaided human reason we can come to understand truths. The philosophical arguments for this rested primarily on the idea that the human mind was created by God and connected to God and that God meant for us to use the rational capacity we have been given. The counterargument is that if we have God-given reason, then we should all be thinking the same, because God is one. Even without the concept of God, the idea of universals suggested that there should be uniformity of thought. Remember that we can't place on the past our present-day ideas of perspectival, relative, and subjective experience—we have to wait centuries for those ideas to take hold. In the medieval period, both Christian and Islamic philosophers struggled with the fundamental issues of guided reason versus unaided reason.

THE CONTROVERSY OVER UNIVERSALS

From Plato on, most philosophers believed that there were such things as universals—Treeness, Greenness, Justice, and so on. The question was whether universal entities are separate from particular objects. As we saw in Chapter 3, Aristotle said no, but because Aristotle's writings on this were lost, and Plato's *Timaeus* and Plotinus' writings were available, medieval scholars adopted the Platonic view that universals are real entities. Aristotle's logic, which these scholars did have, strengthened the position of realism. Aristotle had said that there was a one-to-one correspondence between reason and reality. Medieval scholars concluded that because we can logically reason about universals, universals must be real.

The realist position on universals (universals are real) meant that all objects that shared similarities of kind participated in the same essence. All particular trees participate in the universal essence of Treeness, and their differences as particular objects are accidental (i.e., not what they truly are). Realism worked for scholars who sought to explain Augustine's doctrine of original sin—that we all inherited the sin of Adam and Eve. The argument is that all particular humans participated in the universal essence of humanity. Therefore, when the first people sinned, the essence of humanity was infected by sin, and, therefore, all people are unavoidably infected by that sin. People are inherently sinful, and the only way out of sin is through redemption that changes human essence, which only God can effect.

Peter Abelard (1079–1142) argued against the realist position. He said that if both a human being and a donkey participated in the universal of animal, then the universal essence of animal is both rational and irrational, which is a contradiction. But Abelard also argued that universals couldn't simply be names or "vocal winds," as antirealist Roscelin (c. 1050–1120) had claimed. Yes, Abelard said, universals are nothing more than names; however, a universal name gets its power not from the word but from that which the name stands for as a universal concept. A name like "human" can stand for both a particular human, Plato, and for humans in general. Plato and Aristotle can both be called "human" because they are both humans, but this doesn't need to be explained by appealing to a separate universal thing. All names are universal but also general and derived by us through mental abstractions. We understand universals through observing common qualities in particular objects. If that sounds like Aristotle, it is, but remember that Abelard had no access to Aristotle's writings on universals and particulars. He came to these conclusions independently. Abelard adds that universals refer to objective qualities in things but that those qualities are not independent realities. We mentally apply universal concepts to things and can consider universals separate from things, but they are not actually separate entities. Abelard's position was not accepted by others in his time, though, and wasn't taken up for another two centuries.

THE ISLAMIC RENAISSANCE

Islam had a tremendously positive effect on the Western world in preserving the knowledge of the ancient Greeks. The Islamic world from present-day Uzbekistan in the east, to present-day Spain in the west, had had access to Aristotle going back to as early as the 800s when they discovered ancient Greek manuscripts, all of Aristotle and some more of Plato and other scholars, kept by Christian monasteries in what is now Syria. Islamic philosophy kept alive the tradition of Greek learning. There were several dozen notable Islamic scholars who contributed to an Islamic renaissance of learning in natural philosophy, medicine, mathematics, epistemology, and logic, but we will briefly note four Islamic philosophers who had significant influence on later Western philosophy.

Islamic scholars had access to all of Aristotle, which facilitated their exploration of politics and natural philosophy—the study of the natural world. In a quirk of fate, Plotinus book *Six Enneads* was included in the manuscripts, but it was mislabeled as being a book by Aristotle. Islamic scholars spent a lot of time trying to connect Plotinus and Aristotle, which was a difficult challenge. Islamic scholars also diligently tried to show the compatibility of Islam with the ancient authority of philosophy. They revered Plato and Aristotle as great teachers, and they treated their writings as essential wisdom, similar to the Christian concept of letters.

One of the first attempts to synchronize Islam and Aristotle was undertaken by Abu Yūsuf Al-Kindi (c. 800–c. 870). A native of what is now Iraq, Al-Kindi translated the available Greek philosophical and scientific texts into Arabic, developing new Arabic words to express Greek concepts. He argued that Aristotelian philosophy and science could be incorporated into an Islamic natural theology. It was Al-Kindi who introduced Indian numerals to the Islamic world, which the Christian world later erroneously relabeled as Arabic numerals. He also wrote on astronomy, optics, and chemistry. True to Aristotle, Al-Kindi believed that truth is confirmed by observation, and he adopted Aristotle's theory of potentiality and actuality to describe objects, though he attempted to synchronize Aristotle's theory with Plato's Forms.

Abu Nasr Al-Farabi (c. 872–c. 950) lived most of his life in Baghdad where he wrote extensively on logic, music, mathematics, physics, and of course philosophy. He founded a school of philosophy to build on, but go beyond, the philosophies of Plato and Aristotle. For centuries after, Al-Farabi was referred to as "the Second Teacher," after Aristotle, the First Teacher. Al-Farabi drew on both Plato's theory of the ideal state and Aristotle's writings on biology to create a full picture of life on earth. In multiple books, he adopted Plato's idea of the well-ordered state led by the philosopher king, linking it to the idealized city-state governed by the prophet Muhammad at the beginning of Islam. Understandably, Al-Farabi found the subsequent Islamic governments as falling short of this ideal. He was not, however, as antidemocracy as was Plato because he argued that people had an innate disposition to join together with others to better their society. He advocated for strong leaders guided by the cosmic Intellect, showing he was influenced by Plotinus, whom Al-Farabi and others thought was Aristotle.

Building on Plotinus, Al-Farabi considered the human being as divided between the physical body and the intellect. The human intellect he divided into a potential for thought and the actuality of thought. He portrayed human thinking as the abstraction of universals from sense perceptions retained in memory. Similar to Augustine, he said that thinking requires the light of reason that illuminates the world and concepts about it. Al-Farabi called the light of reason the Agent Intellect, which is an emanation from the First Cause (his Aristotelian term for Plotinus' The One). We cannot comprehend the First Cause except by negative statements: It is uncaused, indivisible, without beginning or end, and so on. However, we can comprehend the emanations of the First Cause that manifest in the world if we act on our potential to think by using our active mind that is part of the Agent Intellect.

Ibn Sina (980–1037), known in Christian Europe by his Latinized name "Avicenna," was from present-day Uzbekistan and trained as a physician but also wrote about astronomy, logic, and philosophy. Much of Ibn Sina's philosophy was a continuation of Al-Farabi's, including the theory of the emanation from the Intellect, but he put more focus on the nature of Being. Central to his theory of Being is the distinction between essence and existence that allows us to discern three modalities of Being. There is a Necessary being (God or The One) whose essence and existence is one—in other words, it necessarily exists, it cannot *not* exist, and so its existence has no external cause. Everything else is either impossible or contingent. Impossible things would be logical contradictions, such as a round square—it cannot exist. Everything else either could or could not exist, and its existence is contingent on an external cause.

Form and matter, Ibn Sina said, cannot interact on their own to create a contingent object; an efficient cause must act to create it. We can contemplate the essence of an object, but reason alone cannot tell us if it exists. To know what exists, we need to know the efficient causes that impart or add existence to essence. Knowing efficient causes is crucial because other than God, nothing has the power to change itself. Only something greater can cause it to change. To cause a change in an attribute of an object, the greater power must already possess the attribute that is then put into the object. For example, for a log to burn, there must be a fire that is burning that puts the attribute of burning onto the log. There is no change into existence from nothing. Following Aristotle and Al-Farabi, Ibn Sina held that God is the First Cause that contains all attributes and therefore is the ultimate source of all change. He isn't suggesting that God is immanently and actively involved in every change (though other Islamic philosophers did believe that). He held instead that God, being pure Intellect and the necessary being, created out of logical necessity. God's perfection is such that creation is a chain of logically necessary events, one efficient cause to the next, from God's creation of the universals to the creation of every particular. We can know about God's creation because thought brings about the generality of forms, meaning that when we think about the world, we identify the universal forms that God used to create everything and we can discern the logical causal chain of events that stem from the necessary being—God.

Ibn Sina is known for his thought experiment of the floating person. He asks us to imagine a person suddenly created who is suspended in midair and deprived of all physical senses. This person would have no awareness of any objects, even their own body, but can perceive their own self-consciousness. The only thing this person could assert is its Self, having no experience of anything else. Ibn Sina concludes from this that we can be sure of the existence of the Self, or soul, and that the Self is something other than the body, something nonbodily. The floating person thought experiment foreshadows a similar one by Descartes that we will discuss in Chapter 7.

Ibn Rushd (1126–1198), known mainly by his Latinized name "Averroes," was the most prolific and famous of all the Islamic philosophers. In both the Islamic world and Christian West, he was known as "The Commentator" because of his meticulous commentaries on every one of Aristotle's many works. He wrote more than 100 books on nearly every subject imaginable in his time, including extensive medical texts. On philosophy, Ibn Rushd was a sharp critic of other philosophers. He thought that earlier philosophers, including Al-Farabi and Ibn Sina, had distorted Aristotle's philosophy by blending in too much of Plato. Rather than attempt to reconcile Plato with Aristotle, Ibn Rushd wrote about the differences between them—most significantly, Aristotle's rejection of Plato's theory of Forms.

Another of Ibn Rushd's books was a point-by-point refutation of al-Ghazali's (1058–1111) *The Incoherence of the Philosophers*, in which the fundamentalist al-Ghazali condemned all Platonist influences as nonbelief in Islam. Despite his own problems with Ibn Sina's Platonism, Ibn Rushd had greater problems with al-Ghazali's attack on philosophy itself and so wrote *The Incoherence of the Incoherence*, quoting the Koran frequently in support of his contention that God wants people to study nature (natural theology) and interpret the revelation of scripture (revealed theology) rooted in knowledge, which Ibn Rushd said referenced philosophy, the highest method of knowledge. Given his background as a judge, he went so far as to issue a *fatwa*, a legal opinion, that philosophy is allowed for Muslims and is even an obligation for those intellectually capable of studying it.

His reference to those capable of philosophy is from his social philosophy, which he used to reconcile religion and philosophy. In a commentary on Plato's theory of an ideal society, Ibn Rushd proposed a three-tiered categorization of human society. His conception at first sounds condescending, but it is a reasonable description of how many people are, and less a proscription of how he thinks people should be. The vast majority of people, he said, are "bronze" people who live by their senses rather than by reason. They can't comprehend higher rational principles, so they need the order provided by the teachings of religion to provide structure to their lives. The people in the next higher level are the "silver" people. They also live by religious teachings, but unlike the bronze people who blindly follow the teachings, the silver people seek rational justification for them. They are the theologians, but their use of reason is only to justify already held beliefs, so they can never attain higher truth, which requires going beyond following orthodoxy. It is only the "gold" people, those blessed with the highest level of intelligence, who can see that religion can't provide all the answers. Gold people are drawn to philosophy, the highest method of knowledge. These people can discover truth directly for themselves, truths that are illuminated by the cosmic Intellect but beyond the ability of the theologians and common people.

Again, this isn't as elitist or condescending as it may at first sound. Ibn Rushd contends that this is how humanity is, created to be so by God, who benevolently has provided religion for those who need it and the Agent Intellect for those who are capable of understanding higher truths. He naturally prefers that gold people be rulers or at least be advisors to rulers, but he stresses that rulers should use persuasion, not coercion, to teach virtue to citizens. He also was one of the first in history to call for women to have full rights equal to men, including women sharing power in government and participating in all professions, even as soldiers and philosophers. It was 600 years before anyone wrote similarly about women's rights in Christian Europe.

MOSES BEN MAIMON (MAIMONIDES)

The greatest Jewish philosopher of all time, Moses ben Maimon (1138–1204), commonly known as Maimonides, was a Jewish scholar in Islamic lands—initially in Spain but for most of his life in Egypt. He was an accomplished physician, even becoming the personal physician of Sultan Saladin. It was a sign of how Jewish people were much more integrated in Islamic states than in Christian states. Maimonides was widely respected as a great man of wisdom across religious communities in his lifetime and to this present day. He is especially revered in Judaism for his *Mishneh Torah*, a code of Jewish law still influential today.

Maimonides was a student of Islamic philosophy, and, like the Islamic philosophers, he sought to reconcile Aristotle's philosophy with his religion. In his book, *Guide for the Perplexed*, he explained how Aristotle's teachings on logic, using observation to learn about the world, and virtuous conduct were the right ways of thinking to understand God and creation. Like Ibn Rushd, who greatly influenced his thinking, Maimonides wrote that some religious teachings are necessary to maintain social order even though they are not the highest truths. In this, he adopted a view of scripture as using metaphors for the nature of God; for example, when the Torah says that God was "angry" with people, it is not meant to be taken that God has human emotions, only that some people need to believe that God can be angry to persuade them to avoid wrongdoing.

Unlike Ibn Rushd, Maimonides was not as pessimistic about people's rational abilities. He believed that all people have free will and can consciously choose to overcome their character failings to practice the opposite virtues. For example, an arrogant person can choose to practice the virtue of humility; an ignorant person can choose to accept teaching. Maimonides wrote that any man or woman, regardless of religion, can through education and virtue, become a prophet. We could say that Maimonides thought that every person has the potential to become a gold person. The flip side of this is that because God has granted all people free will, any person can also choose ignorance and evil.

Maimonides' *Guide for the Perplexed* became a kind of gateway for Christian scholars to accept Aristotle, perhaps because Judaism, on which Christianity is based, was less foreign to Christians than the Islamic faith. Whatever the reason, Maimonides was an important resource for Thomas Aquinas and John Duns (see the following subsections). These Christian scholars understood that *Guide for the Perplexed* pointed to its major influence, Ibn Rushd's commentaries on Aristotle.

The Islamic philosophers' writings, in particular their commentaries on Aristotle, were eventually translated into Latin. These writings were added to the ancient letters that formed the foundation of the Western order. We wouldn't have the culture that we have today without the Islamic philosophers and Islamic culture and civilization keeping alive the ancient Greek traditions of science, philosophy, literature, law, and medicine.

THOMAS AQUINAS AND THE GREAT SYNTHESIS

When Christian armies conquered Islamic lands in southern Spain, they discovered Islamic scholarly texts. Like their Islamic counterparts a few centuries earlier, Christian scholars knew what they had in the Islamic libraries there. Over the period from 1130 to 1240, works by Aristotle (who the Christian scholars knew from his logic books) were eagerly translated into Latin and distributed widely, monastery to monastery to seminary. The spread of the "new" Aristotle and the fascination with these books was so strong that there were reports of monks and priests neglecting their duties because they were busy debating Aristotle.

The problem was simple: The new Aristotle contradicted the Neoplatonic ideas that had held sway for hundreds of years. But Aristotle, despite being non-Christian, could not be dismissed; he was an ancient and venerated authority, a centerpiece of the letters. Some forces in Catholicism tried to ban Aristotle, but the move was unpopular and soundly rejected. The wisdom of Aristotle had to be synthesized with Christian teaching.

Enter the great synthesizer, Thomas Aquinas (1221–1274, Latinized form of "Tommaso d'Aquino" or "Thomas of Aquino"). What made Thomas's great synthesis so great was his willingness to put prejudice aside and learn from Islamic writers. His *Summa Theologica*, published in stages between 1265 and 1274, is filled with the wisdom of Islamic philosophers including Al-Kindi, Al-Farabi, Ibn Sina, and Ibn Rushd. Thomas in particular took important ideas from Islamic philosophers who were trying to synthesize Aristotle with the Islamic faith.

The Passive and Active Intellect

A number of Islamic philosophers had developed the distinction between the passive and active intellect to explain what they saw as major contradictions within Aristotle. They were wrong about the contradictions, but that was not their fault. The problem was that *Timaeus*, Plato's odd book describing a mystical view of the universe created by the Demiurge that influenced Plotinus so much, had become mixed in with scrolls of Aristotle's books. At some point, a scribe appended to *Timaeus* the title "The Theology of Aristotle." Islamic philosophers assumed that this work was also by Aristotle and somehow had to be reconciled with the rest of his works. As we saw in Chapters 2 and 3, Aristotle and Plato differed in how they viewed the world and how we come to gain knowledge of it. How the Islamic philosophers resolved the problem was to make a distinction between passive and active intellect. The active intellect that we all possess is what enables us to reflect on what we sense and think about deeper things such as mathematics and higher concepts such as the universals. Passive intellect is what enables us to use our senses. That division between passive and active corresponds to the division between the physical world and the mental world. Some philosophers referred to the passive intellect as the "material" intellect and the active intellect as the "agent" intellect.

What Ibn Rushd did with these distinctions was chart out a journey of the intellect from fully passive to fully active that fit with Aristotle's methodology of learning about the visible world *and* Plato's view of learning about the intelligible world. In brief, Ibn Rushd said that when we are fully passive all we do is take in sense perception—we are just like the animals. But when we begin to reflect on what we are seeing, we begin to understand the universals that exist in objects (as Aristotle said), and this, Ibn Rushd said, leads us to understand how ideas such as mathematics work. We become in touch with our own personal active intellect. Rather than stop here, we should, he said, continue to reflect on universals across objects, mathematics, and geometry. which allows us to understand objects, their place in the world, the universals apart from objects, and eventually the universals in the mind of God.

Thomas eagerly borrowed these ideas in his synthesis, *Summa Theologica*. He took the next step of making a clear separation between the material world and the spiritual world. He blended in the distinction of existence and essence, which he deftly associated with Aristotle's potentiality and actuality. This allowed him to solve the controversy between faith and reason by placing them into separate spheres of reality and human inquiry.

Thomas began by arguing that truths can be separated into three types. Some truths can be known by reasoning about our sense perceptions, such as the truths of natural philosophy like medicine, optics, and the other protosciences. This fit with Aristotle's writings on observation of the world. Some truths are mysteries that can be known only through divine revelation as recorded in the Scripture, such as the Trinity, the creation of the world, salvation, and the like. This fit with the Church's teachings on scriptural authority and with the Platonic idea that there is a higher realm from which we are separated. These two spheres denote what can be known by reason and what can be known through faith in the tradition of orthodox teaching. Between these two spheres, there are some truths that can be known through either reason or faith, such as the existence of God, the essential attributes of God, the immortality of the soul, and the moral law. This is how

Thomas separated reality itself into natural and spiritual realms and knowledge itself into spheres of reason and faith.

What these philosophical moves allowed him to do was to argue that the Church was the authority on matters of the spiritual world, while philosophy was the authority on matters of the natural world, including universals in objects, natural philosophy (science), and politics. The Church saw this as a great compromise, so much so that they declared Thomas a saint and raised the *Summa Theologica* almost to the level of scripture.

Thomas was certainly philosophically affirming the authority of the Church, but his synthesis was, in practice, curtailing its reach. Yes, the eternal truths that are core doctrines of the Church are above human opinion and debate, but Thomas is also saying that philosophers can legitimately engage in their research as long as they didn't question what the Church said about church matters. It implied that the Church shouldn't interfere in philosophy, opening a door that led to certain consequences (see Chapter 6). Thomas put this in a form that said this is the very nature of reality—a hierarchical universe that is seen as a great chain of being.

The Great Chain of Being

Thomas's synthesis included a synthesis of Plotinus and Aristotle about the hierarchy of being. Thomas brilliantly borrows Aristotle's theory of the potentiality and actuality of objects and combines it with Plotinus' theory of The One, Nous, and Soul. For Thomas, at the top of the hierarchy is, of course, God, who is the possessor of all perfections. Like in Plotinus' system, Thomas's chain moves from the perfection of God down through decreasing perfection as it goes farther away from the divine source. Thomas, employing Aristotle and his Islamic commentators, equates this decrease in perfection with a decrease in actualization. God is perfect, having all potentialities fully actualized, and thus is unchanging. Everything else is created by God and is a dynamic combination of potential and actuality.

At the bottom of the hierarchy is pure matter, which Thomas says is pure potential that God actualizes into the various objects in the world. Above pure matter are lifeless objects, which have some but very little actuality, which, remember, Thomas is equating with perfection. On this hierarchy, plants are higher than lifeless objects, animals higher still, and humans above animals in the level of actuality and closeness to God's perfection. This hierarchy also explains why lifeless objects have very little motion and change, plants slightly more, animals still more, and humans have the greatest ability to move and change in the created world. We humans were created in the image of God and therefore are higher on this great chain of being. We have souls and the ability to reason.

The great chain of being also has an ethical dimension. Every event, Thomas says, whether it is a stone falling or a flower blossoming, occurs because there is an end toward which it is directed. His idea is inspired by Aristotle, but it was easy for him to synthesize it with the sovereignty of the omnipotent Christian God. God has designed the hierarchy of creation with its dynamic of potentialities and actualities with natural ends or purposes. We are the only creatures on earth who have the ability to choose whether we will fulfill our purpose and how. All other objects and life-forms lack free will. Involuntary, natural acts by nonhumans lack ethical meaning because they are not deliberately chosen actions. If a person sneezes, that is an involuntary act and so outside of ethics. Human actions that are deliberately chosen can be judged as ethical or unethical.

Following Aristotle, Thomas said that part of the essence of being human is to will to do what is good, but we need reason to discern what is good. The moral law is written in the creation itself and is evident to our reason if we are not blinded by passions or ignorance. This idea of moral laws inherent in nature was influential for later political philosophers (see Chapter 9). Thomas said that to judge a human action as good or evil we need to consider three factors: the object toward which the action is directed, the circumstances surrounding the act, and the end that the person sought in performing the act. Thomas's example is giving money to the poor, which is a good act; but if the money was stolen, the circumstances of the evil act of theft overshadow the goodness of giving charity. If the act was performed only to gain public acclaim, then that evil overshadows the goodness. A human action can be considered good only if the object, circumstances, and end are all good. The object of the action also takes into account the great chain of being. We can treat animals, plants, and rocks differently from how we can treat fellow people because nonhuman objects are lower beings.

Political Structure

Like Aristotle, Thomas thought that humans by their nature form societies. People will to be good and have the rational capacity to know what is good. Therefore, he argued that governments should act according to reason and in the common good, and that political leaders should be people who care for the community. His division of reality into natural and spiritual realms is reflected in his philosophy of law and government.

He divided law into four kinds. First is the eternal law that is the rational order set down by God at the creation. This law determines the physical laws that govern the movements of nonhuman objects. The second is the natural law that governs human moral behavior. Our material bodies are subject to the eternal laws of nature, but we have the rational capacity to understand the natural moral law and can choose to obey it or not. Similar to Aristotle, Thomas sees following the natural law as a life of virtue, we need to cultivate temperance, courage, justice, and wisdom. The third law he calls the "divine law," which includes the revealed wisdom from God about the mysteries of religion that can be known only through the grace of God's revelation and that corresponds to those truths knowable only through faith in the tradition of Church teaching.

The fourth law is the human law that is instituted by human governments. This was a slightly radical idea for its time because it separated church and state, but this was consistent with Thomas's division of reality and knowledge into natural and spiritual realms. Thomas sees society as a natural expression of human nature, but that same sinful human nature requires a system of government to ensure peace among people. Worldly governments are separate from the Church, though their laws cannot contradict Church doctrine. Beyond that, governments should adopt laws that serve the interests of the people and not interfere with personal freedoms. Monarchs are chosen by God, but they are subject to the will of the people. If a monarch becomes a tyrant, he needs to be replaced, but only if all other people involved can agree. In these ideas, Thomas foreshadows some of the later philosophies about the agreements among people as to who should be political leaders (see Chapter 9).

CHAPTER 6

FROM THE MEDIEVAL ERA TO THE RENAISSANCE

In philosophy, as in life, if you open a door, don't be surprised when other people walk through it. Thomas Aquinas' "Great Synthesis" was a brilliant systemization of philosophical thought up to that time. When Thomas separated truths knowable by reason from truths knowable by faith, he opened a door for philosophy to discuss the things of the world and how we can know them through reason. Enter John and William who not only walked through the door but busted it wide open. John and William led a revolution in philosophy because their new descriptions of universals, particulars, and the primacy of individuals set in motion a chain of reasoning that led to modern science, philosophy, psychology, and culture. In some respects, their ideas were centuries ahead of their time.

JOHN DUNS SCOTUS

John's Latin name means "John from Duns in Scotland." He lived from 1265 to 1308. He agreed with Thomas that there are separate spheres of truths and knowledge, but he believed that the two spheres had no overlap. All matters of the divine cannot be known through reason but only through revelation. This completely separated religion and philosophy. John was not against philosophy, however, and he used philosophical reasoning to arrive at a number of conclusions.

One of John's conclusions is that only individual objects are real, though universals also have objective reality. He deals with this seeming contradiction by arguing that Aristotle was wrong that form and matter define an object. Thomas had adopted that idea, saying that Plato and Socrates both have the form of Humanness and that what separated them was the different collections of matter from which God had made them. John responded that if matter is an indefinite set of potentials, as Thomas said, then it cannot be what differentiates the concrete individualities of Plato and Socrates. Also, if matter is pure potential with no actuality, it cannot be an object of knowledge. We can only know forms, John said, adopting Aristotle's position. That means we can only know a form that constitutes an object; therefore, each particular object has its own unique form or essence. What is Plato? The form of Platoness. What is Socrates? The form of Socraticity. The form of humanness is not separate from individuals, though we can formally consider it. The purpose of John's complicated reasoning is that to understand the world, we must consider the reality of individuals. Our reason can understand the creation because when God created it, God didn't create humanness; God created individual humans. John thought that this way of reasoning was more true to Aristotle and avoids Platonic influences.

John's emphasis on individuals coincided with another important conclusion that he drew. Since the ancient Greeks, philosophers had almost universally held that the intellect was the highest and noblest faculty of the human being. John countered that the will is superior to the intellect, and not just in humans. The intellect provides the will with information, but the will decides what choices to make. The will can move the intellect to think about what the will wants it to think about. Therefore, knowledge is an instrument of the will. The intellect cannot control the will. John said that the only cause of willing is the will itself—the will is completely free to act as it wishes. For John, this has two implications. The first is in morality. Since the ancient Greeks, the dominant assumption had been that to know the good is to will to do the good. Immorality was a product of ignorance or irrationality. John countered that the will can accept or reject whatever is presented to it, and that includes the knowledge of what the morally right choice is. John's position was called "voluntarism," meaning that the voluntary freedom of the will surpasses reason. For John, this meant, that we come to God through loving God—an act of the will. Prioritizing love contradicted Thomas' intellectualism, which said that we come to God through intellectual contemplation of God.

This connected with the other implication of the primacy of the will: voluntarism also applied to God. The Islamic philosophers, Thomas, and their followers believed that God acted only out of reason because God's essence is reason or Intellect. The logically necessary consequence of God being reason is that God must act according to reason. God's Intellect knows what needs to be and what is morally good, and God, being Intellect, cannot act contrary to reason. The positive consequence of that position is that we can use our reason to understand creation and what is morally right. The negative consequence is that because God must think and act according to logical necessity, reason is higher than God. God lacks the freedom to act as God wishes, so God is not omnipotent. John could not accept this. It must instead be the case that God is fully omnipotent and completely free. God's Will is superior to Intellect, and the only cause of God's Will is God's Will. The consequence of John's voluntarist position is that reason will not help us to understand the creation and what is morally right because all facts are contingent on God's Will.

Not surprisingly, the Church took a dim view of John's philosophy. John saw his philosophy as being truer to both Aristotle and Christianity than the Scholastics were being, but his conclusions had serious ramifications. He was not only questioning Thomas' great synthesis but also casting doubt on the long history of Christian philosophy based on ancient Greek philosophy. If God's Will is superior to God's Intellect and God is not limited by logical necessity, then neither are we. Our will makes our choices, our will can move our intellect, and we can choose what we think about and what actions we take. Not that John would endorse an "anything goes" philosophy or morality, but he did further open the door to accepting the active mind and the limits of logic. William took the next step.

WILLIAM—THE FORERUNNER OF MODERN PHILOSOPHY

John was arguably the last prominent medieval scholar, continuing many of their philosophical tendencies. He pushed the envelope, especially with his ideas about the primacy of the will. John blazed a trail for William, who ended up being a transitional philosopher to the modern era.

William (c. 1287–1347) is often called "Ockham" or "Occam." He was born in the village of Ockham, but his name is William so we will call him by his name. William was a radical thinker for his time—so radical he was excommunicated by Pope John XXII. William's philosophy included the principles of voluntarism, like John's, and nominalism—the idea that universals are just names without reality. On the basis of these principles, he concluded that God's omnipotence is fundamental to the universe, everything in God's creation is contingent, and the human mind is active and able to understand the creation through observation rather than through reason.

Theory of Knowledge

William stated that our knowledge begins in experience; nothing is known unless it is known intuitively—meaning directly evident to the mind. By intuitive knowledge, William referred to our sense perceptions of external objects and our awareness of our thoughts and emotions. Any knowledge not directly related to an object of immediate experience is a derivative knowledge, which he also called "abstract knowledge" because this type of knowledge is an abstraction of original experience.

Abstract knowledge is thinking about abstract ideas. William says that abstract ideas seem to be universals because they are indistinct, general representations of qualities or objects of kind (all trees are kinds of tree). These abstract ideas are not universals, William says, because they lack any separate reality. This is similar to John's position, but William goes further. William says that we perceive an object and it causes an image in the mind. We invent names to refer to mental images, and each culture invents its own words. We invent names to refer to specific individuals, like "Plato," and we invent names to refer to abstract ideas like "tree," "circle," and "dog." We abstract from mental images ideas such as greenness. Thomas would say that Greenness is a universal. William says that Greenness is simply a mental image to which we give a name.

When we say, "That tree is green," we are not saying that there is an additional reality beyond that particular tree that is Greenness. The name "green" refers to the mental sign that many experiences of particular objects with that quality have formed in our mind. William's important conclusion to this line of reasoning is that mental images and the names we attach to them are all that we need to explain our thinking about objects. There are no universals, and we have no need to postulate that they exist. This is what leads William to invent the idea that came to be known as "Ockham's razor." The principle of Ockham's razor holds that the simpler of two explanations is more probably true. What William actually said was that we should not needlessly multiply entities. Mental images and names are a simpler explanation for human thinking, and we need not create the idea of universals to explain it. William states that universals do not exist, even in the mind of God. Since universals do not exist, then in the creation, God had in mind individuals, not humanity. God didn't create humanity; God created particular, individual people. Similarly, we think about particulars by using mental signs or names.

The Contingent Universe

It is at this point that William's nominalism connects with his voluntarism. He stresses that the individual is primary because if there were eternal universals as Plato, Plotinus, and others had asserted, then that would limit God's ability to create according to God's will. William accepts John's idea of the primacy of the will applying to both God and humans and freeing them from following logical necessity. William rejects the notion of a logically necessary causal chain of events, meaning that God could not create other than how logic dictated. God created as God wanted to create, so the universe is not governed by logical necessity; everything is contingent.

The contingency of creation forces us to give up hope that we can capture the structure of reality through systems of logical deduction. Even causation—that we see event x followed event y and therefore assume that x causes y—is called into question. William observes that we never experience the supposed causal power in x that causes y and we never see necessity. There may be a cause-and-effect relation, but we cannot know for certain because only probable relationships are visible to us. God maintains the uniformity of the universe, but God can act otherwise and has the power to produce y without it coming from x.

This is no mere theological argument for William. In fact, it has more to do with us than with God. This is because if the universe is not governed by logical necessity, then it cannot be understood logically. Logic is in a separate sphere from the phenomena we observe in the world. Logic tells us *nothing* about the world. Nothing. Logic can only help us construct propositions about our mental signs. The world is contingent; therefore, knowledge of the world can be attained only through experience. You want to understand the world? Get out there! Observe! The Scholastic notion that we can reason to what must be the case is a dead end. The philosopher must instead observe and catalogue facts about the world. Logic and reason can help us order our ideas, but logic can never establish facts, not even about God.

William also rejected the Scholastic tendency to establish logical proofs of God's existence. It may be possible to accept God's existence through experience or through faith, but not through logic. Arguments for the existence of God are empty and worthless. William does admit revelation of Scripture on this question, and on moral rightness or wrongness. Morality is also contingent on God's will; why couldn't God have decreed that murder is righteous? Similarly, William leaves all other questions of theology to revelation. William is completely separating revelation (and faith in it) from reason and experience.

The end-result of William's contingent universe without universals is the separation of natural philosophy from logically necessary causation. This sets observation over logical contemplation, foreshadowing modern philosophy and science. In William's universe, logic tells us nothing; the truth is found by the individual who searches and uses the active mind to understand sense experiences. William, by walking through the door opened by Thomas, opened a new door that led to modern philosophy and modern science.

THE RENAISSANCE

In Chapter 5, we looked at the Islamic Renaissance of 850–1200. Now we turn to what history books and the Western imagination refers to as *the* Renaissance. The period between William and the first "modern" philosophers, Thomas Hobbes and René Descartes—the years 1349 and 1633—was a period of tremendous change. The Black Death (1347–1351) killed more than one-third of the population throughout Europe and set European civilization back for several generations. Tragic though it was, the disastrous loss of life left many lands unowned and positions unfilled, allowing an unprecedented level of social mobility. The resulting economic growth and expansion contributed to changes that helped spark the Renaissance.

Historians have long called the 1400s the "Renaissance" from the French word for "rebirth." Literature, learning, art, and thought all experienced their own transformations that were intertwined with each other. This renaissance of culture and learning in the European world was real and robust and grew out of a series of events that changed how Europeans viewed the world and ultimately themselves and their possibilities. The 1400s saw tremendous changes in Europe. By the end of that century, the world from the European perspective was dramatically different from what it was at the beginning of the century. The seismic shift in perspective of the Renaissance was from one of looking back and copying the past to one of looking forward to creating a better future by rekindling the spark that had given the Greek and Roman eras light. Changes accelerated in the 1500s as momentum from new discoveries and innovations spread across Europe.

There were five broad trends that shaped the Renaissance: trade and exploration, art, philosophy, science, and religious conflict. This chapter will discuss how they spurred the quest for understanding covering the period from 1349 to 1633.

Trade and Exploration

The ancient Silk Road from China, through Central Asia, to ports in Asia Minor, the Levant, and Egypt, had been a major avenue of trade since Roman times. During the 1100s, Venice had grown as a trading power, its merchants establishing trading posts throughout the Middle East and Central Asia. They deftly translated their sea power to military power and for more than two centuries were a dominant naval power in the eastern Mediterranean. Through its dominance over Mediterranean seaways, Venice came to monopolize the silk and spice trades in Europe between 1200 and 1453. The publication in 1299 of Venetian Marco Polo's journeys in Asia opened the eyes of many in Europe to the possibilities of trade with China. Black pepper, cinnamon, cassia, cardamom, ginger, turmeric, nutmeg, and cloves were among the Asian spices increasingly available to Europe in this period. These became luxury items much sought after by those who could afford them, and the Venetians and other traders willingly supplied them—at a profit, of course.

In 1453, the Ottoman Turks captured Constantinople, a city founded in 324 as Roman Emperor Constantine's new Christian capital. Constantinople had been the capital of the Byzantine Empire for centuries, and its fall and the end of the Byzantine Empire profoundly affected Europe in multiple ways. One significant effect was that the Ottoman Empire, now emboldened after consolidating its control of the eastern Mediterranean, forbade Europeans from traversing all trade routes to the Silk Road and levied a large tax on all goods leaving its territory bound for Europe.

The financial incentive to discover an alternative to Ottoman control of lucrative trading routes was perhaps the single most important factor precipitating Europe's age of exploration. Portugal took an early lead, methodically exploring the west coast of Africa. Portuguese navigators charted the route around the southern tip of Africa in 1488 and eventually to India. Portugal's eventual success inspired the other maritime powers in Western Europe to conduct their own explorations.

Giacomo d'Angelo had, in 1406, translated Ptolemy's book, *Geography*, sparking modern mapmaking. The idea that the world was round was widely accepted, partly because rediscovered Greek manuscripts (see "Philosophy" subsection later) described the earth as a globe. The first Renaissance globe was made by

Martin Behaim of Nürnberg in 1490. Coming just before the voyage of Christopher Columbus, the globe did not include the Americas, the Atlantic Ocean instead being bordered on the west by Japan and China. Christopher Columbus believed that conception of the world. On the basis of the Greek manuscripts, which greatly underestimated the size of Earth, he thought that Asia could be reached by sailing due west for 4 or 5 weeks. There was land, right where he expected it, but it wasn't India, as he thought.

People quickly realized that what Columbus had run across was a new world, previously unknown to Europeans (except for Vikings). What happened next had tremendous ramifications for the entire world. A year after Columbus' return from his first voyage, the Portuguese and Spanish crowns signed the Treaty of Tordesillas that set the tone for European exploration. The treaty drew an imaginary north–south line through the Atlantic Ocean halfway between Portuguese territory to the east and the Caribbean islands that Columbus under Spanish patronage discovered to the west. All non-European territory to the east of the line would belong to Portugal, and all non-European territory to the west of the line would belong to Spain. This monumental act of arrogance—the whole rest of the world was not consulted in the making of the treaty—was adhered to by Portugal and Spain, dividing the world between them. Spain considered the Americas its territory, except for Brazil, the east coast of which was to the east of the line, explaining why the official language of Brazil is Portuguese while all other South and Central American countries have Spanish as the official language. Portugal considered Brazil and all of Africa and Asia as its territory. The treaty legalized a European attitude toward the rest of the world as something to be conquered and plundered. This Portugal and Spain did, beginning almost immediately after the Treaty of Tordesillas. France, England, and the Netherlands eventually followed, as the European powers, in a lust for wealth, fought among each other around the world for supremacy over land, resources, and people, a colonial legacy that still stains the world (see Chapter 27).

A more benign effect of the discovery of the "new world" was the expansion of Europeans' perspective. For centuries, the world outside Europe had seemed a forbidding place. To the north, Vikings and extreme cold; to the south, the barren desert of the Sahara; to the east, the fierce barbarians of the steppe; and to the west, an untraversable ocean. After Columbus, the world literally doubled in size, and the door was open to explore new lands. During the 1500s, Europeans started to open their minds to the possibilities of what lay beyond their surroundings; they started to look beyond themselves.

Art

The new wealth of the emerging Italian merchant elites in the early 1400s was a major catalyst for art. The wealthy rulers desired to display their new wealth and status. They built new palaces that had to be filled with paintings, statues, and furniture. Alfonso V of Naples, Cosimo de' Medici of Florence, and Ercole I d'Este of Este were important patrons of the arts in the 1400s.

The robust patronage of the arts allowed artists ample opportunity to experiment. Linear perspective, the attempt to create the illusion of three dimensions on a two-dimensional surface, and the understanding of light and shadow were explored and developed by artists in Italy and in Flanders, which was undergoing similar economic and artistic renaissances. In the 1420s, Florence-based painters Tommaso Masaccio, Masolino da Panicale, and Paolo Uccello developed the technique of perspective, inspired by experiments conducted by the architect Filippo Brunelleschi. Linear perspective revolutionized artistic technique and marked the birth of Renaissance art. Now painters could create realistic scenes that closely resembled what people saw in real life. In Flanders, oil paints were developed, a dramatic improvement in vibrancy and flexibility of color. Oil paints and the techniques developed by Flemish artists were brought to Italy in the middle of the 1400s and greatly influenced the development of Italian art.

Although most art that decorated the homes of wealthy patrons kept to religious themes, their locations in nonreligious settings did encourage nonreligious themes. Influenced by the rediscovery of ancient manuscripts, artists borrowed from Greek and Roman styles and eventually subject matter. Artworks with overtly pagan scenes became common, many of them depicting Greek myths. Before the early 1400s, portraits were rare, but the newly rich merchants and political leaders commissioned artists to paint their portraits. Portraits evolved from simple static depictions of the person to scenes of the person embedded in the world and interacting with it. Increasingly, art transformed from static portraits of the rich to elaborate scenes of daily life depicting ordinary people doing everyday tasks.

The changes in art in the Renaissance had several effects on people's perceptions. The discovery of techniques in perspective and the invention of oil paints allowed artists to create much more realistic paintings. The potential was now there to represent the natural and social worlds realistically. The increasing availability of artwork and the new realism in art encouraged artists and their patrons to capture moments of the everyday. Art no longer was the exclusive territory of churches and noble portraiture. Art connected with life and people. The new forms and methods of art allowed people to view themselves differently.

Philosophy

In Chapter 5, we saw how the rediscovery of Aristotle's manuscripts in the 1200s reinvigorated medieval philosophy. The fall of the Byzantine Empire in 1453 accompanied by the closure of its universities by the Ottoman Turks led to the exodus of many Greek scholars who went to Italy and beyond. Christian monasteries also moved to escape the new Islamic regime. They entered the Christian West bringing their libraries that contained works from ancient Rome. These scholars brought with them texts and knowledge of the classical Greek and Roman civilizations, which had been lost for centuries in the West. Many of the works of classical Greek literature and Roman law that survive to this day did so through the Byzantine Empire. Also, these scholars brought with them the ancient art of exegesis, the critical interpretation of texts. The combination of new material with the method and mindset of critical exegesis was extremely influential. These pre-Christian writings also dealt with themes underdiscussed in medieval times: literature, science, and politics.

The themes and methods of these newly discovered ancient books reinvigorated medieval philosophy in the late 1400s. The ancient writings provided a strong counterpoint to Scholasticism's complicated logical arguments over religious questions. Combined with William's methods of observation, the new exegetical methods of the ancient texts engendered the study of the "humanities," a term we still use today. The original humanities were rhetoric, grammar, moral philosophy, politics, and history. The word "humanism" in the 1400s did not carry the antireligious connotation that it often has today. In the latter part of the 1900s, "humanism" came to stand for an intellectual movement to reject religious and spiritual outlooks in favor of science and logic. In contrast, the humanist thinkers of the Renaissance did not reject religion or belief in a spiritual realm. Their interest was to learn about God's creation through the study of human-centered and world-based subjects as studied via classical authors. Humanism was not an organized school of thought but a perspective that became increasingly popular.

The flavor of classical writings had a tremendous effect on Renaissance scholars. The stories and thoughts were focused on worldly concerns and a broader range of human capacities, talents, problems, and possibilities—not just the moral and devotional were displayed. The rediscovery of Greek mathematics, geometry, and protoscience sparked a rethinking of how the natural world could be viewed. The

Greeks had done what William had talked about: studying the world and using our God-given reason to understand our observations. Now philosophers of the natural world had methodologies and an ancient history to power William's program. Philosophy in the late 1400s and early 1500s led directly to modern science. The rediscovery of more works of Plato also sparked a reaction against Aristotelian Scholasticism. Plato was welcomed as a corrective to the arid and picayune intellectual disputes of the Scholastics who based their methodology on Aristotelian logic. Rather than arguing over meanings and essences, humanist scholarship focused on the human condition and human life.

The rediscovered classics and the new ideas they inspired were spread by the invention of the printing press in about 1450. Paper, cheaper than parchment, had been manufactured since the 1340s. Presses were being used to make woodblock prints in the early 1400s, while at the same time book publishers were experimenting with movable type. It was Johannes Gutenberg who put the pieces together and added two crucial innovations: an efficient means of manufacturing metal movable type characters and the development of oil-based inks ideally suited to printing on paper. The new technology spread quickly; within 50 years there were several hundred printing presses in Europe, and virtually the entire classical canon had been reprinted and made widely available.

The widespread availability of books meant that learning was no longer confined to the nobility and the clergy. Literacy was still predominantly limited to the wealthy, as was the ability to purchase books, but scholarship began to spread beyond strictly theological considerations. Literature began to imitate classical styles; the old became the new. The classical period grew to be idolized and idealized, and classical writers were treated by humanist scholars like church fathers were by the Catholic establishment.

Science

The developments in philosophy stimulated the birth of modern science. Throughout the Renaissance, the studies we now know as physics, chemistry, biology, and so on were known as "natural philosophy." It was so called because people were applying philosophical methods to questions about the natural world.

William developed the theoretical grid that has been labeled "Ockham's razor": "plurality should not be posited without necessity." What that means is that whenever we try to understand anything, we should look for the most direct explanation. It was originally a rationale to reject the belief in universals, but in the new science, it found other applications. An excellent illustration of this was the

Polish astronomer Mikołaj Kopernik (Latinized as "Copernicus") who developed the heliocentric theory in the 1510s to describe planetary motion. Kopernik's system was based less on observations than it was on the intellectual simplicity of an explanation using fewer circles than the prevailing Ptolemaic theory. It was a simpler explanation, plain and simple.

Kopernik assumed the planets could move only in circles because the idea still dominated that the heavens were a realm of perfection. Circles are perfect. Therefore, heavenly bodies must move in circles. This fit with the long appeal of Aristotelian teleological explanations (everything moves toward a final cause) that all motion was to fulfill innate purposes to be perfect. It wasn't until Johannes Kepler's realization in 1609 that planetary orbits are elliptical, not circular, that science had an accurate model of planetary motion. Kepler's theory was based on years of detailed observations made by him and his predecessors. Plus, it was based on the new philosophical approach that was emerging from centuries of Aristotelianism and Platonism.

Here's an example of the philosophical paradigm shift that was occurring in the 1500s. Aristotle had stated that a body's natural state was one of rest. Thus, a body, wanting to be at rest, would cease to move unless continually acted on by an efficient cause that kept it moving. This seems reasonable at first glance, given that we observe objects coming to a stop all the time. If we roll a ball along the ground, it eventually stops, but not for the reason Aristotle thought. Galileo realized through experimentation that a body continues to move at a constant velocity unless a force, like friction, altered its motion. The ball stops because the force of friction is acting on the body to retard its motion. Friction was not visible to an Aristotelian system of causes, but it became apparent through a natural philosophy based on observation.

The heavens gave the observational approach of natural philosophy a big push when in 1572 a bright new star (a "nova") appeared in the sky. It was perhaps the most important astronomical event for human history because it undermined the ancient concept of celestial unchangeability. That the planets moved had always been obvious, but the stellar sphere was thought to be perfect and unchanging—a fixed firmament that divided the visible from a higher realm. The new star, brighter than any object in the sky other than the sun and moon, and visible with the naked eye for several years, was undeniable. The unchanging realm had changed.

Then in 1577, the Great Comet appeared, also bringing into question the concept of celestial unchangeability. This comet was brighter than the moon and for several weeks possessed a tail that crossed a third of the sky. Comets had been known before, but now astronomers had instruments to measure their motion and the philosophical mindset to draw rational conclusions from them. Observations disproved the ancient theory that comets are atmospheric phenomena, similar to high clouds. The observations instead proved that the Great Comet was well beyond the distance of the moon. Some astronomers calculated that the comet must be traveling away from the sun and through the planetary orbits. This shattered, metaphorically if not literally, the idealized notion that the planets moved on celestial spheres of crystal.

Another bright nova in 1604 leant further legitimacy to the new view of a changing heaven. All of these events happened in the middle of the still ongoing debate over the heliocentric theory of planetary motion and pushed the acceptance of it. Kepler's theory of planetary motion published in 1609 and the 1610 publishing of Galileo's telescopic observations of mountains on the moon and moons orbiting Jupiter changed forever the view of the universe.

In 1638, Galileo published the book *Two New Sciences* advancing theories on the motion of objects. It was an inspirational work written in the style of a Platonic dialogue but with the characters in the book discussing scientific experiments they were conducting and what conclusions could be drawn from them. The scientific discipline of physics emerged in the mid-1600s, along with the new sciences of chemistry and biology.

Religious Conflict

What had allowed Spain and Portugal to get a head start on exploration and colonization was that the other European powers were embroiled in a bitter political conflict over religious issues. I say a political conflict because though there were fervent believers on both sides of the religious issues, most of the major players in the conflict were political heads of states fighting over political power. The Catholic Church from the early 900s on had been a political entity, its top clergy and even the popes being selected by monarchies and nobility who openly bought and sold religious offices. The Church was, by the 1200s, a major player in politics and wars, owning vast areas of land as the Papal States and raising and funding armies. With political power, it had become very wealthy and very corrupt.

William was one of the philosophers who argued that the Church's power and wealth should be curtailed. This was the major reason he was excommunicated by the Church. Later, around 1400, a priest-philosopher in Bohemia named Jan Hus also called for the Church to divest itself of its power and wealth. What got Hus into trouble was his philosophy that individual religious communities should have a degree of self-determination in matters of religious practice and that the religious sacraments should be open to the laity. For these ideas, he was executed in 1415 on charges of religious heresy, his teaching being seen as a threat to the balance of power. Hus' arguments were based on the Bible, but his motives were primarily political: religious freedom, equality between clergy and laity, democratic election of leaders, and the end of clerical involvement in secular affairs.

Hus was ahead of time, but with the other trends coming together in the last half of the 1400s, people's thoughts turned increasingly to similar ideas. Around 1500, there were multiple times more political states in Europe than there are today, and their governments and peoples were divided over the questions of increased political freedom. Meanwhile, the Church's role was growing increasingly controversial because of corruption and papal involvement in wars in Italy. Demands for reform and even threats of open rebellion were growing.

Into this environment came Martin Luther, who in 1517 published his *Ninety-Five Theses*, a collection of questions regarding Catholic practices—in particular, the sale of indulgences. Indulgences were a fundraising tool used by the pope and some bishops. The idea was that if you donated money to the Church, you or a departed loved one would be granted forgiveness of sins. Luther correctly pointed out this was a non-Biblical idea. Luther wanted to spark a public debate on his ideas for church reform. In 1518, he published his document in German—so it could be read by those outside the clergy (Church matters were discussed in Latin, which few people knew)—and in 1520, he published several other works, two with the provocative titles of *On the Babylonian Captivity of the Church* and *On the Freedom of a Christian*.

Various doctrinal disputes quickly developed between Luther and the Church, but for our purposes in the history of philosophy, we will focus on two. The first was that Luther's doctrine of salvation by faith alone was a repudiation of the Church's claim of salvation through the sacraments. It meant that the Church was not the middleman, so to speak, of people's relationship with God. That being the case, religion is a matter between the individual and God. Hus had had similar ideas a century earlier, and those ideas had never disappeared. The other trends in Europe at that time had encouraged demands for reform of the feudal power structure and increased personal freedoms. Some took Luther's open intellectual rebellion as a sign that the time for physical rebellion was at hand. When in 1524, peasants violently revolted in three German-speaking states (what is now Germany was then split into dozens of smaller states), they claimed Luther as their inspiration. Luther renounced the revolts, especially when it took the form of mob violence burning monasteries, convents, and bishops' residences. He responded with the second idea we will mention—that though he was calling for resistance against corruption in the Catholic Church, he exhorted people to obey their secular leaders and taught that obedience to secular government was commanded by Jesus. Luther called for the political leaders to put down the rebels like they were insane and devilish. Luther's teaching here furthered the idea of a separation between church and state, a philosophical idea Hus had taught and William had taught, and an idea first suggested by Thomas. This is an example of how philosophy can be a catalyst for change.

The printing press spread Luther's ideas far and wide across Europe. He had lit a match in a gasoline-soaked central Europe. Political leaders chose sides, some declaring they would defend the Catholic Church against this new breed of heretics choosing a new path contrary to tradition. The protesters against the Roman Catholic Church, the "Protestants," came in various denominations, but a number of political states, for a number of reasons, broke with Rome, the first being the Duchy of Prussia, which announced it was no longer a Catholic state in 1525. Europe was plunged into more than a century of turmoil and war, culminating in the Thirty Years' War of 1618–1648. That was the first world war in that every European state at some point was involved on one side or the other as the war raged across central Europe.

The 1678 treaty of the Peace of Westphalia ended that war, and it initiated several changes significant to our story of the quest for philosophical understanding. It established the principle of religious freedom for minorities within a country, though this was too often ignored by governments. It also formally acknowledged the independence of the Dutch Republic, ending their eighty-year war for independence against the Spanish crown. The Peace greatly enhanced the economic power of the Dutch in trade and solidified the Dutch Republic as a haven for intellectual freedom for nonconformist thinkers, like Descartes, who we meet in the next chapter, and John Locke, who we will meet later.

CHAPTER 7

DESCARTES, THE METHODICAL PHILOSOPHER

René Descartes (1596-1650) is one of the few philosophers who is a household name. He is best known for the most famous quote in philosophy: "I think, therefore I am." That quote, and that his most famous book is titled *Meditations*, have created the impression of Descartes as a kind of dreamy thinker detached from the world. This understandable conception is not true.

The real Descartes was thoroughly grounded in the world and the history of scholarship. His concerns were eminently practical, centered on how we can better understand science and mathematics the better to comprehend the world in which we live. Descartes claimed to have found a method of guiding his reason that was highly effective in helping him make significant discoveries in his scientific research. His method, and the philosophical conclusions to which his method led him, were immediately influential and remain so even today.

Descartes' method is often described as a method of doubt. Part of his method is a willingness to doubt that which we take for granted, but in Descartes' method, doubt is only a tool in service of a higher goal. His overarching purpose throughout all of his philosophy was to discover an ultimate truth—a certainty on which he could base all thought. His methodical philosophy was less a method of doubt than it was a method of avoiding error. To doubt methodically is different from a method of doubt. Descartes was not a true Skeptic (see Chapter 4) because he believed that knowledge was possible. In fact, he believed that the human mind, when engaged in the proper method, is incapable of making an error of knowledge.

Descartes has two main assumptions: first, that there is objective truth that can be known; second, that every human is equally well endowed with reason and is capable of knowing the truth. Descartes believed that the essential nature of a human being is to be a rational animal. People have different opinions about the truth not because some people are better equipped with reason than others but because different people have varying degrees of success in applying their reason. Within all people is the power to know the truth; what people need is an effective method by which they can discipline their power of reason and guide it to success.

He proposes his method not as a set of rules that all must follow but as a description of the path, he has followed in the hope that others might similarly profit from it. Descartes' method is a plan for self-instruction, a do-it-yourself method for learning about the world. Descartes firmly believed that not only can individuals think for themselves but also that they should.

THE CARTESIAN METHOD OF PHILOSOPHY

Descartes marks a complete break from the classical-medieval focus on the letters of antiquity (see Chapter 5). He was raised in that Aristotelian–Thomist method of education, and he roundly rejected it.

> *From my childhood, I have been familiar with letters; and as I was given to believe that by their help a clear and certain knowledge of all that is useful in life might be acquired, I was ardently desirous of instruction. But as soon as I had finished the entire course of study, at the close of which it is customary to be admitted into the order of the learned, I completely changed my opinion. For I found myself involved in so many doubts and errors, that I was convinced I had advanced no farther in all my attempts at learning, than the discovery at every turn of my own ignorance.* (*Discourse*, I.4)

Leaving behind the staid education of his time, Descartes resolved to learn instead from "the great book of the world." He decided to travel, choosing the odd method of in the 1620s serving in several armies in the Thirty Years' War. He didn't see much fighting; mostly he had time to think, of which he took full advantage. He wrote *Rules for the Direction of the Mind* sometime in those years, but the manuscript was only published in 1701, years after his death. He published in 1637 an expanded version of his ideas as *Discourse on the Method of Rightly Conducting One's Reason and of Seeking Truth*, known by the shorthand, *Discourse on Method*. That book contained chapters on science and one on philosophy. He then published *Meditations*, a more lyrical version of the philosophical chapter in *Discourse*, in 1641. Also in 1637, he published *Geometry*, in which he set forth the principles of coordinate geometry and algebraic equations for circles and lines (like x + y = 5).

Descartes' interest in geometry inspired his approach to science and philosophy. He saw the continuing disputations among philosophers of his time as accomplishing little more than increasing the level of doubt and confusion. He sought for all knowledge the certainty he found in mathematics and geometry. For example, if I ask you what one plus one equals, you instantly, automatically say, "Two." You didn't require any great reasoning to come up with the answer. You clearly and distinctly knew the answer. That is the type of knowledge Descartes is looking for.

To get to that level of clear and distinct knowledge about the world, Descartes sought to get past arguing over definitions to a more experiential form of cognitive understanding. Descartes' revolution was to construct philosophy based not on any external authority but on the internal authority of the mind.

> *For since God has endowed each of us with some light of reason by which to distinguish truth from error, I could not have believed that I ought for a single moment to rest satisfied with the opinions of another, unless I had resolved to exercise my own judgment in examining these whenever I should be duly qualified for the task.* (*Discourse*, III.5)

Because we have been born with the ability to reason, Descartes urges us to question and withhold assent to all external authorities and even the authorities of our own senses. Once we cast off all of our traditional authorities, we come to the point of accepting the only authority we can trust: our own mind. Our mind can find specific principles on which we can base further knowledge. Descartes believed that our mind is capable of finding and employing a method that makes it incorruptible to all manipulations of outsider sources.

In constructing his method, then, he saw it as more important than all else not to err, even if it meant advancing slowly.

> *But like one walking alone and in the dark, I resolved to proceed so slowly and with such circumspection, that if I did not advance far, I would at least guard against falling. I did not even choose to dismiss summarily any of the opinions that had crept into my belief without having been introduced by reason, but first of all took sufficient time carefully to satisfy myself of the general nature of the task I was setting myself, and ascertain the true method by which to arrive at the knowledge of whatever lay within the compass of my powers.* (*Discourse*, II.5)

The true method must be disciplined, and its guiding principle must, of course, be reason. Nothing should be believed unless it is approved by reason. But on what should we base this rational discipline?

He considers the candidates that were traditionally given by the Scholastics as methods for knowing truth with certainty: logic, geometry, and algebra. He agrees that the true method should use the advantages of these three fields of learning. The advantages are their ability to construct, by means of deduction, knowledge of the truth. Through the operation of deductive reasoning, we can proceed from a self-evident axiom that is known to be certain and proceed step-by-careful-step to a new conclusion that is just as certain as our starting point.

The problem with logic, geometry, and algebra, though, is that they are insufficient in investigations of the unknown. Logic, Descartes says, is valuable mostly in the communication of what we already know (hello, William). Geometry and algebra, Descartes says, are so exclusively restricted to the consideration of figures, that they can exercise understanding only on condition of greatly fatiguing our ability to take in new concepts.

The type of learning Descartes is interested in is the discovery of new knowledge. Science is about exploring the unknown, venturing into uncharted territory to shine the light of reason and separate the true from the false. Descartes' explorations in physics, anatomy, optics, and other hard sciences were to learn about the world and come to understand it. The numerous rules and formulas of geometry and algebra, while valuable to a point, can also hamper the mental faculties and result in confusion and obscurity. In short, logic, geometry, and algebra can't be the basis of a useful method by which we can learn about the world. Rather than the multitude of laws of logic, geometry, and algebra, Descartes said we should have a simple set of rational rules that can be rigidly applied.

DESCARTES' FOUR RULES

To that end, Descartes proposes four rules that he has found perfectly sufficient in his scientific exploration. He sets down four short, simple rules with "the firm and unwavering resolution never in a single instance to fail in observing them."

> *The first was never to accept anything for true which I did not clearly know to be such; that is to say, carefully to avoid precipitancy and prejudice, and to comprise nothing more in my judgement than what was presented to my mind so clearly and distinctly as to exclude all ground of doubt.*
>
> *The second, to divide each of the difficulties under examination into as many parts as possible, and as might be necessary for its adequate solution.*
>
> *The third, to conduct my thoughts in such order that, by commencing with objects the simplest and easiest to know, I might ascend by little and little, and, as it were, step by step, to the knowledge of the more complex; assigning in thought a certain order even to those objects which in their own nature do not stand in a relation of antecedence and sequence.*
>
> *And the last, in every case to make enumerations so complete, and reviews so general, that I might be assured that nothing was omitted.*
>
> *The long chains of simple and easy reasonings by means of which geometers are accustomed to reach the conclusions of their most difficult demonstrations, had led me to imagine that all things, to the knowledge of which man is competent, are mutually connected in the same way, and that there is nothing so far removed from us as to be beyond our reach, or so hidden that we cannot discover it.* (*Discourse*, II.7–11)

What we should notice first about the method is its emphasis on self-discipline. We can summarize his rules as follows and see how the bottom line of each rule is to avoid precipitancy, meaning not rushing to judgment.

Rule one: "Never to accept anything for true which I did not clearly know to be such." Avoid precipitancy and reserve judgement until we have all the facts.

Rule two: Break down whatever we are examining into manageable parts. Avoid the precipitancy of trying to solve the whole problem in one go.

Rule three: Start with the simplest and progress step-by-step through the complex. Avoid precipitancy by methodically gathering and building our knowledge and understanding from simple ideas to more complex ideas.

Rule four: "Make calculations throughout so complete that I might be assured that nothing was omitted." Avoid precipitancy by never jumping ahead in the process. Progress cautiously and thoroughly, leaving no step unconcluded.

We must, Descartes teaches, continually rein in our reasoning. We are all prone to accept ideas as true without weighing all considerations. Often, we are not even consciously aware of this. We accept things without due critical inquiry, and this leads us to error. Instead, we should not too easily accept quick judgments or surface definitions.

Descartes has complete confidence in this methodology because he has complete faith in the power of the human mind. He agrees with the claim that the will controls the intellect, following the views of such philosophers as Augustine and John Duns.

> *Whence, then, spring my errors? They arise from this cause alone, that I do not restrain the will, which is of much wider range than the understanding, within the same limits, but extend it even to things I do not understand, and as the will is of itself indifferent to such, it readily falls into error and sin by choosing the false in room of the true.* (*Meditations* IV.9)

When our will runs ahead of our intellect—which is what he means by precipitancy—we fall into error. Descartes therefore sees controlling the will as the key to discovering truth. Like other philosophers before him and after him, Descartes believes we need to be devoted to reason and follow the dictates of reason. When we explore the world this way, we cannot go wrong. He says as much when he says that when he avoids precipitancy and follows the proper method of reasoning, it is quite impossible for him to go wrong. "As often as I so restrain my will within the limits of my knowledge, that it forms no judgment except regarding objects which are clearly and distinctly represented to it by the understanding, I can never be deceived." (*Meditations*, IV.17) Rigorously following his four rules will make our minds incorruptible and immune to the manipulations and distractions of the world. Or so Descartes claims.

Descartes' project is a method of science to discover all of the truths about the physical world. Descartes had an unbridled optimism about what science with the proper method could accomplish.

> *All things, to the knowledge of which man is competent, are mutually connected ... there is nothing so far removed from us as to be beyond our reach, or so hidden that we cannot discover it, provided only we abstain from accepting the false for the true, and always preserve in our thoughts the order necessary for the deduction of one truth from another.* (*Discourse*, II.19)

Descartes argued that our senses alone cannot lead us to knowledge about the world. Our senses can be deceived and are not beyond doubt, so we need something more to gain knowledge. Descartes, having provided us with the four rules for directing our minds, gives us several thought experiments to demonstrate what applying the rules can do for us.

DOING SCIENCE BESIDE THE FIRE

In his book *Meditations*, Descartes gives us a dramatic reenactment of how he claims to have come to his philosophical methodology. He gave a shorter but more difficult-to-read version in *Discourse*, but in *Meditations* he seems to be trying to reach a more general audience. In *Discourse*, he says he was stuck sitting in a cold barracks in front of a stove (probably a historically accurate portrayal of his time in the army), but in *Meditations* he portrays himself in his own home, in his dressing gown in front of his fireplace. Literary license.

Sitting comfortably by the fire in *Meditations*, he resolves to find the firm and permanent structure in the sciences that can lead us past doubt to certainty. First, he needs to clear away anything that doesn't contribute to this goal. He resolves to doubt anything that can be doubted, because if an idea could be false, then it lacks the certitude to be part of the firm and permanent structure in the sciences. He embarks on a scorched-earth policy toward his beliefs, declaring he will "at length apply myself earnestly and freely to the general overthrow of all my former opinions." (*Meditations*, I.1) By demolishing everything he had believed before, he hopes that what remains will be the unassailable truth of which he can be certain.

He considers in turn some beliefs of which he had felt certain: the existence of the world around him, whether he has a physical body, whether there is a creator God, even whether two and three together always equals five. Perhaps, he wonders, every belief we have is from a long and familiar custom and has deceived us into believing as true what is actually false and imaginary. Or, he wonders, perhaps some evil genius with godlike powers is deceiving him. Descartes can't immediately disprove this fantastic possibility. Every belief he has about the external world could be a false belief caused by a malevolent force.

> *I will suppose that the sky, the air, the earth, colors, figures, sounds, and all external things, are nothing better than the illusions of dreams, by means of which this being has laid snares for my credulity; I will consider myself as without hands, eyes, flesh, blood, or any of the senses, and as falsely believing that I am possessed of these; I will continue resolutely fixed in this belief, and if indeed by this means it be not in my power to arrive at the knowledge of truth, I shall at least do what is in my power, viz., [suspend my judgment], and guard with settled purpose against giving my assent to what is false, and being imposed upon by this deceiver, whatever be his power and artifice.* (*Meditations*, I.12)

As radical as is this program of doubting everything that can be doubted, it is but a temporary suspension of his beliefs. Always for Descartes, the purpose of his doubts is to try to clear the way for more certain beliefs. Anything that has deceived us in the past cannot be trusted. Our senses have deceived us in the past, so we should not trust them completely. He suspends belief in everything he believes because of sense experience.

> *I suppose, accordingly, that all the things which I see are false (fictitious); I believe that none of those objects which my fallacious memory represents ever existed; I suppose that I possess no senses; I believe that body, figure, extension, motion, and place are merely fictions of my mind. What is there, then, that can be esteemed true? Perhaps this only, that there is absolutely nothing certain.* (*Meditations*, II.2)

Where does that leave him? He has to consider the possibility that he alone exists—no external world, no God, no other people. He has to consider that he has no physical body and that he is mistaken to believe that there is anything material. All of these beliefs could be the result of a deceiver, very powerful and very cunning, that employs its great power to deceive him.

At this point, Descartes borrows Augustine's argument against the Skeptics that he exists and knows that he exists (see Chapter 4). Augustine said, "If I am mistaken, I exist." Descartes' formulation is only slightly different: "If I am deceived, I exist."

> *Doubtless, then, I exist, since I am deceived; and, let him deceive me as he may, he can never bring it about that I am nothing, so long as*

I shall be conscious that I am something. So that it must, in fine, be maintained, all things being maturely and carefully considered, that this proposition "I am, I exist," is necessarily true each time it is expressed by me, or conceived in my mind. (*Meditations,* II.3)

WHAT AM I?

But Descartes being a true philosopher, this is not enough for him. He next asks what he is. A person? A body? A thing that senses? All of these could be doubted because perhaps the various sensations he has had came to him when he was dreaming. How can he tell when he is dreaming or awake? But of one thing he can be certain:

> *Thinking is another attribute of the soul; and here I discover what properly belongs to myself. This alone is inseparable from me. I am—I exist: this is certain; but how often? As often as I think; for perhaps it would even happen, if I should wholly cease to think, that I should at the same time altogether cease to be. I now admit nothing that is not necessarily true. I am therefore, precisely speaking, only a thinking thing, that is, a mind, understanding, or reason, terms whose signification was before unknown to me. I am, however, a real thing, and really existent; but what thing? The answer was, a thinking thing.* (*Meditations,* II.6)

He concludes that he is not a body; he is "a thinking thing." "But what is a thinking thing?" he asks. "It is a thing that doubts, understands, [conceives], affirms, denies, wills, refuses; that imagines also, and perceives." (*Meditations*, II.8)

I mentioned at the beginning of this chapter that Descartes is a household name because of his saying, "I think, therefore I am," or in Latin, "*Cogito, ergo sum.*" (*Discourse*, IV.1 and *Principles of Philosophy*, 1.7) It is a common misconception about this statement that his purpose is to prove his existence. Instead, his purpose is to demonstrate what sort of a being he is. Descartes assumes the "I"—his existence—prior to the exercise. "*I* think, therefore I exist." He immediately proceeds from affirming his existence to affirming that "I am therefore, precisely speaking, … a thinking thing." (*Meditations*, II.6)

That is what we are: thinking things. That is what Descartes claims distinguishes us as humans from all other things. The essence of being human is thinking. There is an element of Aristotelianism in Descartes' conclusion. If the essence of being human is to be a thinking thing, then our purpose is to think as excellently as possible. But more important for Descartes' purpose is the conclusion that the essence of what he is is a mind, not a body, whether or not he has a physical body.

THE WAX EXAMPLE

He then turns to the question of corporeal (physical) things. He cannot prevent himself from thinking that there are corporeal things. His bodily senses continually feed him information that such things exist. As he showed before, however, the existence of corporeal things can be doubted despite how real they seem to be. He remarks how strange it is that we say we know and understand more distinctly these corporeal objects the existence of which is dubious. What can we know, and how can we know and understand these objects?

Descartes explains how we are capable of understanding the physical bodies we touch, see, and interact with in his thought experiment, the Wax Example. It's one of the great thought experiments in the history of philosophy.

> *Take, for example, this piece of wax; it is quite fresh, having been but recently taken from the beehive; it has not yet lost the sweetness of the honey it contained; it still retains somewhat of the odor of the flowers from which it was gathered; its color, figure, size, are apparent (to the sight); it is hard, cold, easily handled; and sounds when struck upon with the finger. In fine, all that contributes to make a body as distinctly known as possible, is found in the one before us. But, while I am speaking, let it be placed near the fire—what remained of the taste exhales, the smell evaporates, the color changes, its figure is destroyed, its size increases, it becomes liquid, it grows hot, it can hardly be handled, and, although struck upon, it emits no sound. Does the same wax still remain after this change? It must be admitted that it does remain; no one doubts it, or judges otherwise. What, then, was it I knew with so much distinctness in the piece of wax? Assuredly, it could be nothing of all that I observed by means of the senses, since all the things that fell under taste, smell, sight, touch, and hearing are changed, and yet the same wax remains.* (*Meditations*, II.11)

Think about the problem that Descartes is putting before us. You are sitting by a fireplace, and you have a honeycomb full of honey. (You like your honey the old-fashioned way—straight from the beehive, not from bear-shaped plastic bottles.)

You recognize it as a honeycomb because of the qualities of it: its shape, color, size, smell, feel, taste, and sound. And let's say you decide you'd like a cup of tea, because tea with a touch of honey tastes nice. So you set down your wax honeycomb by the fireplace and go into the kitchen to boil some water for tea.

When you return with your cup of tea, you discover to your horror that your honeycomb is gone. Where you had placed it near the fire, there is no longer your wax honeycomb but a puddle of goo. What is your first thought? Maybe it's, "Egad, someone broke in and stole my honeycomb and left this puddle of goo!" Or maybe it's, "Transporter accident; someone tried to beam up my honeycomb and it went horribly wrong." Or, "Aliens! Aliens abducted my honeycomb and left me this puddle of goo!" No, you don't have any of those reactions. No, your first reaction, without hesitation is, "Damn, my honeycomb melted."

The point is that we automatically assume that the honeycomb and the puddle of goo are the same object; not different objects but the same object that has changed qualities. Descartes' question is: what are we doing when we think this way? How can we make the connection that these two sets of sense impressions with completely different qualities are from the same object? Descartes' answer is that we can make the connection because we understand that the essence of the wax is not the qualities of the sweetness of honey the scent of flowers; its color, shape, or sound but simply a physical body that we perceived first in one form and then in another form. "Let it be attentively considered, and, retrenching all that does not belong to the wax, let us see what remains. There certainly remains nothing, except something extended, flexible, and movable." (*Meditations*, II.12) What we understand, when we recognize that the wax has changed form, is that underlying all of the qualities of the object that we perceive through our senses is something that can be defined only as extension in space. In other words, matter that takes up space has height, depth, and width and is flexible and movable. The piece of wax was the same extended thing when it was a wax honeycomb and when it was a puddle of goo, but, Descartes concludes, we don't comprehend that through an act of vision, touch, or any other physical sense. We are fooled into believing we knew the wax by our senses, but instead, it is through an intuition of the mind that we understand what the wax is.

Descartes' point here is that the physical senses give us information, but it is only with the mind that we understand.

> *[when looking from a window and saying I see people who pass in the street], I do not fail to say that I see the people themselves, just as I say that I see the wax; and yet what do I see from the window beyond hats and cloaks*

that might cover artificial machines, whose motions might be determined by springs? But I judge that there are human beings from these appearances, and thus I comprehend, by the faculty of judgment alone which is in the mind, what I believed I saw with my eyes. (*Meditations*, II.13)

Going back to the Wax Example, if we were capable of knowing only what our senses told us, we could not make the judgment that the honeycomb had melted into the puddle of goo. That's easy to see with the strengthening of Descartes' example that I gave. Left to sense impressions alone, we'd be fooled into thinking they were two different objects, not a single object that had changed. We perceive what objects are because we are a mind, a thinking thing.

THE CLEAR AND DISTINCT IDEA AND THE EXTERNAL WORLD

Using his thought experiment of doubting all that can be doubted, Descartes has affirmed that his mind can know that certain things are true if and only if they are present to his mind clearly and distinctly.

There is nothing that gives me assurance of its truth except the clear and distinct perception of what I affirm...and accordingly it seems to me that I may now take as a general rule, that all that is very clearly and distinctly apprehended (perceived) is true. (*Meditations*, III.2)

Descartes has established his bedrock of certainty: He can accept as true those ideas that are clear and distinct, including the unassailable idea that he exists. He knows that he is a thinking thing who can make mental judgments, but he is aware that he still needs to make the connection between the ideas in his mind and the external world to have a method of science. He cannot deny that he has many ideas about objects existing in the world external to him. These ideas of external objects given to his mind by his senses sometimes seem to be clear but later prove to be false. So, he still needs to solve a big problem before he can reach the experiential form of cognitive understanding that we call "science."

The problem facing Descartes is that the ideas he has about external objects could still be false. That's because what exists in his consciousness are his own ideas and thoughts about external objects, but not what causes those ideas. All ideas are effects; ideas of sense perceptions and thoughts are all effects of causes. Knowledge is a relation between a knower and what is known. Descartes has proven that he can be certain of the knower side of the equation, that he is a thinking thing who has clear and distinct ideas, but what he is less certain of is the cause of any of his ideas. In his thought experiment, he showed that the existence of external objects can be doubted and a deceiver could deceive him about the existence of an external world even though it can't deceive him about his own existence. Descartes needs to get out of the trap of the skepticism called "solipsism"—that the only things he can prove are that he exists and that he has ideas of something. Descartes is not a Skeptic; he believes that there is an objective external world and that we are endowed with reason capable of knowing the truth about that world. Now he has to prove how he can be certain about the external world.

This may seem odd, Descartes returning to the doubt that he may be deceived about the external world after his Wax Example confidently showed that his mind is capable of knowledge. That's his point though. His mind is reliable, but his senses can still be deceived. The wax thought experiment works whether or not there actually are honeycombs and fireplaces in an external world. That's why you can think accurately about the thought experiment without experiencing any honeycombs or fireplaces. The method of doubt he uses is not doubting particular clear and distinct ideas but doubting whether these clear and distinct ideas are ever caused by an external world. Descartes says there are three types of ideas in the mind: ideas innate or inherent to the mind, ideas caused by external forces, and ideas invented by the mind. Innate ideas cannot be doubted, because we cannot think of them without at the same time thinking they are true. That a circle is round is an example. Ideas we invent cannot be doubted because if you imagine a purple unicorn, that idea exists only as *your* idea, so it is neither true nor false. Ideas caused by external forces, what Descartes calls "natural impulses," can be doubted. The natural light of reason, Descartes says, only illuminates innate ideas like that he exists, not natural impulses like "I see a tree." I can be certain of the contents of my thought that I see a tree, but how can I be certain that my idea of what I think I see is an accurate description of what is outside my mind? I can't doubt that I exist or that I can imagine fictitious animals, but how can I believe in an external world beyond doubt?

That's where God comes in for Descartes, and in no way is he meaning a religious God. He uses the idea of God only as a prop in a larger argument. It is his idea of a supreme being that is key. He says he has a clear and distinct idea that there is a sovereign God that is eternal, infinite, all-knowing, and all-powerful; that possesses all perfections; and that is the creator of all things beyond itself. I will make his long argument short: Descartes contends that God, being all-knowing and all-powerful, could be the deceiver (the evil genius he mentioned earlier) who could deceive Descartes into falsely believing that there is an external world. But, because God has all perfections, including being perfectly good, God would not so deceive us; therefore, we can be confident that the natural impulses that cause ideas in our minds about external objects are in truth caused by external objects.

Some have accused Descartes of making a circular argument and, therefore, a fallacious argument. Descartes' argument has often been derided as the "Cartesian Circle." Those who argue the Cartesian Circle position are claiming that Descartes is arguing the following:

1. I have a clear and distinct idea of God as a perfect being.
2. God, a perfect being, is not a deceiver and would not allow me to be mistaken about my clear and distinct ideas.
3. Therefore, I can be certain of the truth of my clear and distinct ideas.

If that was his argument, then he would be assuming his conclusion, and that is circular reasoning and fallacious. The problem is that the so-called Cartesian Circle is a misrepresentation of Descartes' actual argument.

Crucial to understanding Descartes correctly is to realize that he does not begin his argument by asserting God. In fact, God is an afterthought for Descartes. He trots out God only in support of a larger argument that seeks to prove that he can have knowledge about things external to his mind. Descartes first establishes his foundational principle that "ideas that are clear and distinct must be true." Everything else that he argues follows from that proposition. Any idea that can be said to be clear and distinct must be accepted as true; for example, "I think; therefore, I am, I exist." I have a clear and distinct idea that I exist, and this must be accepted as true.

The proposition that clear and distinct ideas must be true is true (or false) independent of God. It is significant that Descartes establishes the proposition of the clear and distinct idea before he turns to the idea of God and then only to counter the possibility that all of his ideas about external objects are placed in his mind by a deliberate deceiver. Descartes knows he exists, but what can he know about the external world? He has ideas that an external world exists, but he could be mistaken, dreaming, or deceived by a powerful being.

Descartes is trying to prove that his ideas about an existent external world aren't completely false. We can portray Descartes' reasoning in this way.

1. Ideas that are clear and distinct must be true.
2. I have a clear and distinct idea of God.
3. Therefore, God must exist.

4. Since my idea of God includes his perfection, God is trustworthy.
5. Therefore, I cannot be deceived about the existence of the external world because God would not allow me to be deceived.

It is important to accept that, as Descartes constructs his argument, premise 1 does not depend on premise 3. The Cartesian Circle accusation incorrectly flips the two premises. The idea of God is a clear and distinct idea thus, God's existence cannot be doubted, just like our own existence and every other clear and distinct idea cannot be doubted.

Descartes introduces the idea of God to meet our general systematic doubts. We can, as Descartes points out, doubt each of our perceptions and beliefs because we know our senses can trick us. More disturbing than our senses being unreliable in particular instances is the possibility, which Descartes establishes earlier in *Meditations*, that an evil deceiver could be tricking us into believing there is an external world when, instead, it's all false images in our mind. Descartes' answer is that God ensures that we are not deceived because the perfectly good God is not a deceiver and the all-powerful God would not allow us to be deceived into believing in a world that does not exist.

Descartes is not saying that he cannot be mistaken about particular propositions such as "that tree looks safe to climb" because he knows his will can overreach and lead him to error. But because he knows he is a thinking thing who can use the power of reason and because he knows God is not an evil deceiver, then knowledge derived from observing an external world is possible. Thus, if he can reason correctly (his four rules for directing the mind), then his mind is incapable of error because he can reason from clear and distinct ideas to truth. We still must be on guard to not make mistakes in our sensory perceptions of the world, but we can rely on the knowledge that an external world does exist more or less as it appears to exist, and that means that science is possible. Establishing the validity of the nascent observational science of the 1600s was Descartes' primary purpose. Descartes's argument can be questioned on several of its premises, but it is not circular reasoning.

DESCARTES' INFLUENCE

Many have said that Bacon (see Chapter 8) and Descartes started two separate branches of philosophy based on two very different theories of how we gain knowledge. Bacon began a trajectory in philosophy known as "empiricism," and Descartes began a trajectory known as "rationalism." The traditional way of portraying this split is to say that the empiricists believe that all knowledge comes from sense experience, whereas the rationalists believe that our rational analysis of propositions reveals truth. There is some truth to this characterization, but it oversimplifies the complexities of the philosophers' ideas. Descartes certainly believes in the value of rational analysis, but he never denies the value of sense experience. We see similarly how the empiricists never deny the value of reason.

Descartes' most enduring influence is what has come to be known as the "Cartesian Subject." This is a reasonable interpretation of what Descartes means by his method of discovering truth. Descartes doesn't appeal to the external authority of the letters or institutions but to the internal authority of the clear and distinct idea. Descartes is seeking mental clarity, not a dogmatic definition but an intuitive (direct) experience of the objects in the world. That means it is his experience and his alone that determines what is true. His method also clearly concludes that he is a mind, not a body. Even though in his thought experiment he concludes that he has a body, his idea remains that what he is is a thinking thing not a bodily thing. This leads to what has come to be known as "Cartesian Dualism"—the idea that a human being has two substances: mental and material. Descartes certainly subscribes to that idea, but it is not his invention, as we saw. The idea that the physical human body is accidental to the immaterial human psyche, soul, or intellect was an old and widely held idea long before Descartes. Nevertheless, it is Descartes' version of mental/material dualism that philosophers still debate today. Predominantly, philosophers today reject the idea of the Cartesian Subject, arguing that it ignores the influences that embodiment and culture have on a person and their perceptions and thinking. In the years between Descartes and today, many philosophers have been influenced by Descartes' ideas and took them into account in their own philosophies, either accepting Descartes or reacting against him.

REFERENCES

René Descartes, *Discourse on the Method of Rightly Conducting One's Reason and of Seeking Truth,* Project Gutenberg, http://www.gutenberg.org/ebooks/59. (accessed February 18, 2021)

René Descartes, *The Method, Meditations, and Selections from the Principles of Descartes.* tr. John Veitch, UK: Blackwood, 1887. (accessed February 18, 2021)

René Descartes, *Principles of Philosophy,* Project Gutenberg, http://www.gutenberg.org/ebooks/4391. (accessed February 19, 2021)

CHAPTER 8

THE "SCIENTIFIC REVOLUTION" AND EPISTEMOLOGY

No doubt you have already encountered the concept of the so-called Scientific Revolution. Like other terms used to describe social movements, it is a little glib and agenda-laden. There was, indeed, in the late 1500s and early 1600s a movement in some circles toward an approach to the world that came to be known as "science." The movement was more philosophical than anything else, and it took place gradually over many decades, not suddenly, as "revolution" implies. Although the movement was not confined to Britain, it was led, as the Brits have ever since been very fond of reminding everyone, by British philosophers.

As you should remember, in Chapter 5, I mentioned that Thomas had opened a door and that when one opens a door, others will walk through it. William walked through it big-time, and his ideas inspired what was then known as "natural philosophy" (the word "science" came later). William had sought to liberate philosophy from Aristotelianism, and for those inspired by his philosophy, replacing Aristotle's approach became a major priority. William gave them important theoretical tools to do just that. William said that we had an active mind that could reason about our sense experiences. He also said that logic tells us nothing about the world, meaning that we can't just sit and contemplate how things should logically be, as the Aristotelian Scholastics had done. The universe cannot be predicted on the basis of logic—we have to go out and observe how God made the world. It doesn't matter if our logic thinks it should be another way. Knowledge comes to those who go into the world and discover what's there, said William and other philosophers. This was the inspiration for observational science. This is why philosophy has always been and remains so important: Philosophy develops ways of thinking that we can use and apply to life that allows us to do everything we do. Even today, science benefits from philosophy.

FRANCIS BACON

In the early 1600s, British scholar Francis Bacon (1561–1626) took up William's ideas, especially the idea that we learn about the world through observing it. Bacon brought to the forefront the empirical method of science. Bacon's goal was to achieve a total reconstruction of sciences, arts, and all human knowledge, raised on the proper foundations. Bacon was a significant creator of the image of science and scientists that persists to this day.

Bacon wanted to replace what he saw as the vain obfuscation of Aristotelian Scholasticism and its contemplative reorganization of long-known eternal truths. Such a conception was largely based on Thomas Aquinas' interpretation of Aristotle, especially the notion that all objects had in their essence a final cause. Scholasticism focused on a more thorough understanding of these final causes. Bacon's alternative was to see science as a discovery of the unknown—science as learning rather than systematizing. He urged his countrymen to sweep away the rubble of medieval tradition and head toward a "new continent" of knowledge, science being the ship that will guide us there. (He was writing in the middle of the Age of Discovery, see Chapter 6.) He saw the emergence of natural philosophy, freed from theology and adopting its own intellectual methodology, as the great hope for humanity.

It may appear to us today that Bacon's program is secular, but it is in fact thoroughly grounded in religious belief. He believed natural philosophy would recover the knowledge humanity had had in the Garden of Eden but had lost because of the Fall. In the Garden, Adam and Eve had dominion over all of the earth. Because of their disobedience, God removed Adam and Eve's dominion over nature and set nature at odds with the children of Adam and Eve who were now required to toil by the sweat of their brows to survive. But by God's grace and providence, humanity was being granted an opportunity to recover this dominion. "The true ends of knowledge," Bacon wrote, are "a restitution and reinvesting of man to the sovereignty and power which he had in his first state of creation." (*New Organum* III, 222) The new natural philosophy was not just a matter of increasing human knowledge and power; it was the means of righting an ancient mistake and partially restoring humanity's rightful relationship with nature. This was not mere lip service by Bacon to keep from running afoul of religious authorities. There is no reason to doubt that Bacon, like nearly all of the intellectuals of his era, sincerely believed the biblical narrative of the creation and fall. Natural philosophy was in no way a threat to the established doctrines of Christianity.

Bacon understood that the way we approach things affects how we perceive them. Knowledge is power, he said. We see what our knowledge tells us we see. Therefore, it is important that we have true knowledge, not false knowledge. Yes, we can have false knowledge if we think we know something is true but it isn't. (We will see later that all we have are beliefs.) False knowledge comes from what Bacon calls the corruption of our minds by idols.

"Idol" was originally a religious term that morphed into a general term for things foolishly worshiped—like pop singers on reality TV. In his book *Novum Organum* (1620), meaning "New Instrument," Bacon observed that people don't think clearly because they are distracted by four types of Idols of the Mind:

1. The Idols of the Tribe. The tribe here refers to humanity, and these idols inhere within human nature itself. Our human tendency is to want the universe to make sense as we think it should make sense (like the Scholastics did). Our human desires affect how we see things, especially how we assume there is more order in the universe than is really there. We all tend to make the facts fit our preferred conclusions. To overcome this idol of wishful thinking, we need a disciplined approach of observation and reasoning about what is. We see what we think we should see, so if we assume that the universe should conform to our expectations, we are distracted by this idol. It is a human tendency we need to overcome, Bacon says, if we are to think clearly.

2. The Idols of the Cave. Bacon uses the metaphor derived from Plato's Allegory. Bacon says that each of us dwells in our own unique little "cave" of beliefs that we think are true. These beliefs, formed by our dispositions, education, experiences, and the authorities we admire, limit our vision of what is. Our philosophy, thus, follows our personal history more than it follows reality. A pessimist sees the cup as half empty; the optimist sees the same cup as half full. Bacon says we need to guard against our natural idiosyncratic prejudices:

And generally let every student of nature take this as a rule,—that whatever his mind seizes and dwells upon with peculiar satisfaction is to be held in suspicion, and that so much the more care is to be taken in dealing with such questions to keep the understanding even and clear. (*Novum Organum,* I.XLII)

3. The Idols of the Marketplace. Today we hear "marketplace" and think of economic activity. Bacon is using the term in the 1600s sense of the market square as the hub of civic life. What you found in the market were people gathering to buy; sell; and talk, talk, talk. The cacophony of voices in the marketplace was Bacon's analogy for the problems of language that interfere with our pursuit of truth. The idols of language are related to the first two idols. We have names for things that do not exist, like "luck," but the name's existence can deceive us into believing in their existence and using their names to explain events incorrectly. More problematic is our use of abstract terms that are full of vagueness and ambiguity. We complain about a "heavy" cell phone even though it weighs less than a "light" backpack. And "heavy" is one of those words that have many different meanings. You can say you have a heavy heart because of your heavy course load, so you listen to heavy metal music, none of which can be measured objectively. The point that Bacon is making is that we need to be careful not to let words distract us from seeing the world clearly.

4. The Idols of the Theater. Bacon's time was the time of Shakespeare. No, Bacon didn't write Shakespeare's plays, but Bacon uses the metaphor: "All the received systems are but so many stage-plays, representing worlds of their own creation after an unreal and scenic fashion." (*Novum Organum,* I.XLIV) In other words, there are various dogmatic systems of philosophy, such as those of Plato and Aristotle. These systems created large internally coherent systems of connected concepts that built a story to describe the universe. But like a world created in a fictional plot, these intellectual worlds have no connection to the real world. We need to hold in suspicion any intellectual system that claims to explain the universe, no matter its origin. Bacon adds that he means not only entire systems but also many of the axioms of science that by tradition, credulity, and negligence have come to be received. The answer is to reject dogmatism and ideology and learn by observing facts in the world.

Bacon, like many before him, assumed the universe had a unified rational order. To learn how that order works, we need to collect facts about the world, properly catalogue those facts, and look for the forms within those data. By "forms," Bacon was thinking in terms of Aristotle's sense of forms or essence. Bacon rejects

Aristotle's theory of final causes but thinks of the material world largely in terms of formal and material causes. We learn about the forms of nature by collecting particular facts and inductively reasoning to discern where forms are present and where they are absent. For example, Bacon says we can learn about the form of heat by observing where heat is present and where it is absent and when heat increases and decreases where it is present; then we correlate those data with other data to find relationships among phenomena. His method leads him to conclude that the form of heat is an expanding notion that travels through bodies, which is an accurate assessment as far as it goes.

Bacon's primary contribution to science was to establish the foundations of a philosophy of science. Bacon placed faith in our ability to gain knowledge through disciplined observation and recording of our sense experiences. Similar to Descartes, Bacon had unrestrained optimism about what science with the proper method could accomplish. He thought that science properly conducted would, in only a short period of time, discover all that could be discovered. He therefore, proposed that society create committees of scientists working to discover the forms of nature. The areas of science would be divided into specialties. He classified 128 particular specialties, from the study of astronomical bodies to the study of machines. For each specialty, he called for two groups of scientists. One group would engage in research, conducting experiments and collecting empirical data. Another group would analyze the data by using induction to identify positive and negative relationships in the data, deriving the forms in nature. Across all specialties, another group of scientists would take the findings of the specialties and use induction to identify positive and negative relationships among the areas of science. Bacon confidently predicted that such a method would lead to "the power and dominion of the human race itself over the universe." (*Novum Organum*, I.CXXIX) Such was Bacon's optimism that, although he never finished it, he wrote a book, *New Atlantis*, in which he imagined the future world as a utopia transformed by science and technology.

Bacon's positive contributions to science were blunted by some serious blind spots in his thinking. He was so enamored with his new empirical method that he rejected as obsolete and unnecessary all theories. He therefore rejected the theories of Kopernik and Kepler on planetary motion, and anything that he saw as reasoning from principles. That type of reasoning he dismissed as medieval Scholasticism. So, though Bacon established the empiricist movement in philosophy and pioneered the idea of systematic science, his failure to appreciate the value of legitimate theorizing in science prevented him from developing a full scientific method.

In 1660, a group of leading British scientists established the Royal Society of London for Improving Natural Knowledge. The Royal Society was based on Bacon's dream of a collaborative science enterprise and was dedicated to acquiring knowledge through experimental investigation. The members of the Royal Society made very clear their inspiration was Bacon's new science. In 1665, they began publication of an academic journal, *Philosophical Transactions of the Royal Society*. For the next 200+ years, the Royal Society was one of the world's leading organizations in promoting science. The Society and its journal are still active today.

THOMAS HOBBES'S MATERIALIST EPISTEMOLOGY

Epistemology is the study of the origins and limits of human perception and knowledge. Philosophers since ancient times had considered some issues pertaining to perception and knowledge, but the dedicated study of epistemology first flowered in 1600s England, mainly from the influence of Bacon. It's important to keep in mind in this chapter and the next three that philosophers in the era of British empiricism were prone to using their own definitions of certain terms. In particular, the term "idea" was used slightly differently by each philosopher. Paying attention to those subtle but important differences is crucial to understanding their theories of epistemology.

Thomas Hobbes (1588–1679) is best known for his political theory (see Chapter 9), but his empirical theory of epistemology is also important in the history of philosophy. Both Hobbes's political and epistemological theories are founded on his belief that there exists nothing but matter. Hobbes was an uncompromising materialist and determinist who insisted that the universe is nothing but material bodies in motion. For this he was and still is often mistakenly considered as an atheist because he said even God was material and subject to material causation. He was not hostile toward God or religion, but he did bring them into line with his radical materialism.

Hobbes's thought was influenced by the emerging science of his time, and he personally knew some of its major actors. He worked as a translator for Bacon, and he met with Galileo in Italy and with a number of French philosophers, perhaps even with Descartes. Hobbes was invited by Descartes to write a reply to *Meditations*. However, Hobbes didn't always share the enthusiasm others had for new methods. He admired Galileo's work on motion and primary and secondary qualities, but he didn't agree with Bacon's empirical and inductive methods, and he tried to steer the new science in a different direction.

Hobbes was, to a fault, a very straightforward, no-nonsense thinker. He believed it was important to reduce the many phenomena in the world to simple, basic principles. He adopted the deductive logic of Euclidean geometry and argued that once we understand the first principles of the visible world, science should be conducted like geometry—by reasoning from first principles. Hobbes took to heart Galileo's conception of the universe as bodies in motion and saw the laws of motion as basic principles that can explain phenomena.

Hobbes's Physics of Knowledge

Hobbes's physics was a natural philosophy of the motion of bodies. Hobbes fought a losing battle with other English scientists of his time over the new observational scientific method of Bacon. Hobbes fervently believed that science must proceed from first principles and that observations made by the easily mistaken senses could not be a foundation for science. He believed that an economy of thought was central to science; therefore, he rejected all extraneous ideas. Hobbes's application of Ockham's razor was to say that nothing existed except matter.

The central idea of Hobbes's physics is that the only things that exist are material bodies. It was an idea compatible with, if not inspired by, the corpuscular (atomic) theory of matter of Pierre Gassendi, a Catholic priest who had embraced the new science. Going further than Gassendi, Hobbes argued that the concept of "immaterial substance" was a contradiction; for something to be a substance, it must be material. If a spiritual thing exists, then it must be made of something material, even if that material is very fine, even finer than a fog. We ourselves are only material. We do not have a separate spiritual substance apart from the material body. What we call a mind or soul would thus be a part of our material existence that is made of finer particles of matter. In turn, all properties of objects are also material. Colors, sounds, and odors are all to be explained as matter in motion. Our perceptions of external objects are caused by particles impinging on our material sense organs. This in turn is a cause of our ideas, which are also particles in motion.

The corpuscular theory of matter seemed to confirm, to Hobbes, the importance of first principles. From this principle that everything is material, he could proceed to the second level of practical science—particular observations of particular bodies, such as the study of planetary bodies or earthly bodies. The world is a world of bodies in motion. Period. Hobbes assumes that nothing moves itself but moves because it has been caused to move by another body. All motion is caused by material contact (collisions) with other bodies; there is no action at a distance (an idea considered by some in Hobbes's time and later confirmed by Isaac Newton in his theory of gravity). All motions and collisions are governed by material laws that exist eternally and unchangingly and presumably were set down by God.

The Basis of Perception

Hobbes insisted that all knowledge comes to us through sensory perception. This means that all of our thoughts have their origin in sense perception and we can only know what comes to us through our senses.

> *There is no conception in a man's mind which hath not first, totally, or by parts, been begotten upon the organs of sense. The rest are derived from that original.* (*Leviathan*, I.2)

This denies notions, such as Plato's, that the human mind has stored within it innate knowledge.

Hobbes derives his conclusion of complete dependence on the senses from his notions that one, everything is causally determined, and two, everything is material. Hobbes understands bodies on macro and micro levels. Although objects may appear to be at rest on the macro level, they are in fact composed of smaller particles at the micro level that are in motion (a truth later confirmed by Albert Einstein). The motion of some micro particles off an object collide with our sense organs, and that is the cause of our sense perception. Particles of light cause vision, particles of sound cause hearing, and so on.

The particles collide with the organs of sense and produce what Hobbes calls a "seeming" or "fancy." If a particle enters our eye, it causes a visual fancy; if a particle enters our ear, it causes an auditory fancy; and so on. By the word "fancy," Hobbes means a kind of conception, like how we would say something is "a flight of fancy." He does not mean that it is something unreal but that it is something that is a mere copy caused by the pressing of external things on the organs of sense. The fancies in our mind are copies, a mere semblance, of the objects in the external world. They are only impressions on our mind—and I'll use the word "impressions" from now on, which sounds less weird today. The total of all of the impressions within a human mind makes up our realm of impressions. This realm of impressions is separate from the external world and the objects themselves. What we directly experience within our mind are different things from the objects that cause them. It is important to remember, however, that the impressions are still real; they are mere semblances, but they are not illusions. All of the impressions are actually material bodies and are caused by material processes. Think of a shadow. We know that a shadow is caused by a material object, and we know that a shadow is not as substantive as the material object that causes it. Nevertheless, we would admit that the shadow is a real thing, not an illusion.

The impressions in the mind are the cause of all other mental processes. To Hobbes, the mind works in a very straightforward manner. Mental events are material motions no different from motions of bodies in the world. The senses produce impressions in the mind, and what we call "thinking" is the associations of those impressions among each other that more or less mirror the associations of bodies in the world. What we call "reason" Hobbes defines as "nothing but reckoning—that is, adding and subtracting—of the consequences of general names agreed upon, for the marking (to our selves) and signifying (to others) of our thoughts." (*Leviathan*, V.2)

Our mental reckonings are dependent on our memories, but Hobbes had a very different view of memory than had Augustine (see Chapter 4). Our memories are what Hobbes calls a "decaying sense" of original impressions. They are like the fading echoes that bounce back the impressions created by sense perception or the fading ripples on the water when a stone is thrown in. Imagination is what arises from the motions of the impressions—just as material objects in the world move and collide, so do the impressions in our mind. The results of these motions and collisions are the new thoughts that we call imagination. However, our imagination can do no more than add or subtract the existing impressions in the mind; it cannot create anything truly original. What we imagine had to first be present in sensation. For example, the idea of a unicorn is simply the combination of the existing impressions of a horse and of a horn added together.

Hobbes's view of the human being is quite unromantic. The universe is nothing but bodies in motion. Our thoughts, feelings, and imagination are nothing but particles in motion. We have no real creativity or self—our beingness is just ripples on the surface of a pond. We will see a very different philosophical perspective in Chapter 13, but between Hobbes's time and then, the notion of a passive mind overshadowed empiricist philosophy.

Hobbes's radical materialism had an interesting effect on his religious beliefs. He believed in God and did not question Christianity, but, like many in his day, he was critical of religious institutions. But his materialism meant that he had to believe that God is made of matter, which he did. He reasoned that either something is matter or it is void. God could not be immaterial because immateriality is nothing. God exists; therefore, God must be material. Of course, God is a different kind of matter than what rocks, plants, trees, and our bodies are made of. Hobbes saw God as a rarefied matter, like a very fine mist, but still matter.

Not surprisingly, Hobbes's theory met with great criticism in his time—not just from religious authorities but from other philosophers and intellectuals. The idea that there is nothing but matter was not intellectually palatable and seemed to contradict common sense, especially the reality of our human mind. The preferred notion was from Hobbes's contemporary, Descartes (see Chapter 7), who reasoned that there were two types of substance—mental and material. Mind and consciousness have no extension in space and thus could not be material. The same argument for a material God would have to be made for a material mind, and, not surprisingly, Hobbes felt that mind was nothing but matter. But if mind is matter, then what is consciousness? Would that lead to us denying the existence of consciousness?

NEWTON CAPTURES THE UNIVERSE

Hobbes's *Leviathan* was published in 1651. Over the next decades, Hobbes saw his political desires fulfilled (we'll cover that in the next chapter) but not his scientific desires. This is because while on the one hand, the corpuscular theory of matter was being widely accepted, he saw being rejected his fervent belief that science must be based on first principles of logic and geometry and not on the new method of experimentation advocated by Bacon and his followers.

To make a long story short, the growing number of observational discoveries greatly increased enthusiasm for the observational method. One significant development was Robert Hooke's book *Micrographia* that detailed his microscopic observations. It opened a window into the unseen world of the microscopic and showed a whole new reality all around and within us. It seemed proof positive to many that truth would be found by increased observation rather than logical speculation (hello, William).

There were some philosophers and other intellectuals who looked for an approach that combined observations with mathematics. One who adopted this approach was Isaac Newton (1642–1726). Science as we know it today began with Newton. Thomas Jefferson wrote, "Bacon, Locke and Newton…I consider them as the three greatest men that have ever lived, without any exception, and as having laid the foundations of those superstructures which have been raised in the Physical &

Moral sciences." ("Thomas Jefferson to John Trumbull") Francis Bacon invented the scientific method and inspired the formation of the Royal Society, the driving force of British science for centuries. John Locke's contributions to epistemology and political philosophy you will see shortly.

Isaac Newton fulfilled the hope that had begun with William of a true natural philosophy—what we now know as "science." Newton brought to science two innovations: Mathematics can explain motion, and reality can be understood through theoretical modeling. Newton didn't discover gravity—people did know that bodies fell to earth—but he gave us a method of describing not only gravity but the motion of all physical bodies. He did this by realizing that the motion of bodies can be modeled mathematically through the use of calculus—which he "borrowed" from German mathematician-philosopher Gottfried Wilhelm Leibniz (1646–1716) and pretended he invented it. Newton's mathematical modeling confirmed the idea that there are rational laws of nature like gravity that govern all material objects and that can be defined by mathematical formulas. Take any set of bodies—real or hypothetical—plug their qualities into the equations that describe natural forces, and you can describe how these bodies have moved in the past and predict how they will move in the future. The Newtonian universe was a clockwork universe that was easily understandable and predictable. All we needed to do was do the math. At least, that was the dream.

JOHN LOCKE'S EPISTEMOLOGY

The earlier Thomas Jefferson quote mentions John Locke (1632–1704) with good reason. Locke was an intellectual giant within his own lifetime and remains one of the most important philosophers. He is equally well known for his political philosophy (see Chapter 9) and his epistemology. Locke talks more about beliefs than knowledge because, as he correctly observes, every idea we have is a belief. Locke was concerned primarily with establishing the limits of human understanding and the grounds of our beliefs. Locke was, therefore, interested in understanding how it is we come to our beliefs.

Locke's philosophical influences were Descartes, Francis Bacon, and Isaac Newton. This is part of why I stressed the importance of Descartes' scientific method. Locke didn't see Descartes as a dreamy meditator. He understood that Descartes' rules for clear thinking and forming justified beliefs was a way forward for science. Locke, like Descartes, was interested in helping clarify and strengthen science.

In trying to understand how it is we come to our beliefs, Locke had the benefit that Descartes had not had of the tremendous innovations of Isaac Newton. Locke wanted to develop a Newtonian view of belief to understand why certain ideas were often found together as though attracted to each other by a kind of mental gravity.

Locke's word for our beliefs is "idea." You need to lose your preconception of what "idea" means to understand fully Locke's use of the term. For Locke, an idea is anything in the human mind—not just something we create, as in "I have an idea—let's order pizza." See? I put the idea of pizza in your mind because you had the experience of reading "pizza," which you associated with your prior experiences of pizza, both past and present experiences becoming ideas in your mind. So now we all have the idea of pizza, which is usually connected with the idea of wanting pizza. I really want pizza now.

Locke insists that we had no innate idea of pizza or of anything else. Innate ideas are ideas that are inherently known by the mind. Knowledge of Plato's Forms is an example. A Platonist would say we recognize a pizza because we have the innate idea of Pizzaness; Locke says we only know about pizza because we have had the experience of delicious, hot, savory, pizza. Okay, I will stop talking about pizza to avert cravings. Other examples of alleged innate ideas are the basic concepts of logic, mathematics, and moral laws. The theory of innate ideas claims that everyone universally has these basic bits of knowledge. Locke counters that even if some ideas are universally known, that doesn't prove they are innate. The ideas could be universal because human experience is universal. He also rejects the idea that logical and moral ideas are universally held by people, pointing to the ample evidence that there are illogical and immoral people.

Locke's claim is that we have ideas only because we have experienced objects in the world. For example, we have the idea of a tree from our experiencing sensations furnished by external objects that we have come to know as "tree." Our minds are like blank sheets of paper, Locke says, on which experiences make their marks. The only ideas in our minds, Locke says, have been put there by our experiences. Locke also likens our minds to a *camera obscura* (Latin for "dark chamber" and, yes, where we get the word "camera" from). The camera obscura was a well-known device in Locke's time, a small hole in a wall through which light would pass and shine an image onto a wall or canvas. It was used primarily by artists as a drawing or painting aid as shown here. The artist could trace the image shown by the light shining on the canvas.

The camera obscura of our mind is a dark box with holes (the senses) through which sensations enter. Inside the dark chamber, the mind begins life as a *tabula rasa* (Latin for "blank slate") on which sensations make their mark. As we have experiences in life, we gather more and more ideas, which Locke calls "simple ideas of sensation." These are ideas like green, flat, smooth, hard, tall, hot, sweet, and so on. That is all our senses give us—simple minute qualities presented to the mind as sensations.

But what happens in the mind to these simple ideas of sensation? Clearly, the human mind is more than a dark box into which simple sensations pour. Locke says that the human mind is also aware of its operations, and this is "the other fountain from which experience furnisheth the understanding with ideas." (*Essay*, II.I.4) This set of ideas is our internal sense. These ideas come not from external objects but from our own "thinking, doubting, believing, reasoning, knowing, willing, and all the different actings of our own minds…[ideas] the mind gets by reflecting on its own operations within itself." (*Essay*, II.I.4) Locke calls ideas of our internal sense "ideas of reflection." For example, the simple ideas that enter our mind of an object that is flat, smooth, and hard are simple ideas of sensation; being aware and thinking about these simple ideas of sensation are simple ideas of reflection.

Locke contends that together with the simple ideas of sensation, the simple ideas of reflection are the only ideas that are ever present in the mind. "External objects furnish the mind with the ideas of sensible qualities, which are all those different perceptions they produce in us; and the mind furnishes the understanding with ideas of its own operations." (*Essay*, II.I.5) That's it. Those are the entire contents of the human mind, and because the mind can reflect only on ideas of sensation furnished to it by external objects, Locke concludes that "the mind thinks in proportion to the matter it gets from experience to think about." (*Essay*, II.I.22) The contents of our minds, then, are strictly products of our experiences—initially of external objects, then by reflecting on our experiences of external objects. Our minds, Locke says, can neither create nor destroy ideas, but they can process them.

Locke says that the mind has the power to repeat, compare, and unite the simple ideas. In so doing, the mind creates complex ideas. Locke identifies three mental operations that we use to process simple ideas into complex ideas: compounding, comparing, and abstracting. For example, if we have the simple ideas of flat, smooth, and hard, we can combine these simple ideas into the complex idea of a tabletop. The simple ideas of green and tall can be combined into the complex idea of a tree. Much of our thinking uses this activity of compounding simple ideas. We don't think "that's flat, smooth, and hard"; we think "that's a tabletop." Our dealings with the world are mostly in terms of complex ideas like "tabletop."

The second activity we use is comparing. Exactly as it seems, we compare ideas. It's hotter today than yesterday, that tree is taller than that one, and so on. Comparing also includes relations such as mother and son, over and under, cause and effect—ideas that you don't experience but determine from comparing relations between things.

The third activity is abstraction, the process that gives us abstract or general ideas. Locke sees these as an important set of ideas. Compounding gives us the complex ideas of a tabletop and a tree, and abstraction gives us the *general* ideas of tabletops and trees. This is Locke's answer to the problem of universals (see Chapter 5). Treeness doesn't exist, either as a Form or in particular objects. The complex idea of trees is a general idea that comes from the process of abstraction. We experience a number of trees, and in thinking about trees in general, we hold in our minds an abstract idea of "tree" without a particular size, color, or other qualities. Our minds abstract all of the qualities that particular trees have in common and ignore individual differences. What remains is the general abstract idea of trees. An abstract idea, therefore, is a vague combination of qualities we have experiences of as external objects. One of the examples Locke gives of an abstract idea is the notion of infinity—a notion others, including Descartes, believed was an innate idea. Locke countered that the idea of finite, in both space and time, is a simple idea. Through the process of compounding, we can mentally observe a repeating without end of a finite length of space or time. This is all the abstract idea of infinity is. Our idea is not innate but determined by a mental process—a faculty of our mind. Our idea of infinity is vague because our minds are finite, but then all of our abstract ideas are vague, not definitive, something to which George Berkeley would respond (see Chapter 11).

Primary and Secondary Qualities

Locke gives us an interesting vision of the human mind, but it leaves out William's concept of the active mind. Locke's concept of the human mind shows the mind to be passive. Experiences happen to it, and external objects cause the mind to form ideas. Therefore, you have nothing in your mind that is not formed by something else, and all we know are our own ideas. This leads to the conundrum of how we can know that what's in our mind corresponds to the external world.

Locke was aware of this problem and tried to solve it by dividing what causes the simple ideas of sensation into two types of qualities. Ideas exist in our mind. By "qualities," Locke refers to a power to produce ideas in our mind. The distinction between ideas and qualities is that we perceive ideas that are caused by qualities in external objects. Primary qualities exist in the objects themselves. Primary qualities include solidity, extension, shape, motion or rest, and quantity—properties found objectively and manifestly in the object. These qualities, such as height or weight, can be objectively measured. Like Galileo and Descartes, Locke sees nature and the motion of bodies as mathematically describable. Primary qualities are entirely independent of the observer, and they are inseparable from the object. Descartes had defined material substance as extension in space, and Locke held the same view. An object has a certain size, shape, motion, and so on whether or not a person is observing it. Primary qualities cause our ideas of them. For Locke, then, the simple ideas of sensation that we have of the primary qualities are representations of the primary qualities themselves. Therefore, we can trust that our ideas of those primary qualities are representations of the objects.

Secondary qualities are powers that external objects have to produce ideas in us, but these qualities do not exist in the objects, and the ideas they produce do not resemble the qualities in objects. That these qualities exist in the perceiver, not in the objects themselves, is shown by the fact that they cannot be objectively measured and can differ subjectively among individuals. Included in secondary qualities are colors, sounds, tastes, odors, warmth, or coldness, all of which are subjectively experienced by individual people. Secondary qualities are mind-dependent—only existing within the mind. Color is a secondary quality, meaning that color is not part of the object but only an idea in our mind. Colors are not part of an object's primary qualities. This can be demonstrated by shining a red light on a red object that makes the color disappear. Also, objects change color on the basis of the light around them and are colorless at night. All of this points to the reality that colors are mind-dependent and do not exist in objects themselves.

Taste is another secondary quality that is not in the object itself but in the experiencing of it. If I detest pickles, but you love pickles, I have two choices in trying to figure out this contradiction. Either you are ignorant, perhaps delusional, or something different is happening when you taste pickles than when I taste pickles. It is easier to believe that taste is a secondary property of an object, meaning that the property exists in the perceiver's experience of the object, not in the object itself. That means that the power of secondary qualities in the food creates different sensations in different people and that explains why some people like a food while other people do not: They are different people whose bodies are experiencing the food differently.

Locke's theory still has some problems. Despite his argument that our ideas of objects' primary qualities are true representations of the object, our mind is still a sealed chamber, and we can never leave that chamber to compare its contents with the object in the world. We can never know how well the contents of our mind correspond to the external world. Also, Locke admits that we do not perceive objects themselves; we perceive only our sense impressions of objects, and we do not ever know for sure if our ideas of objects match the objects in themselves. That we cannot know what lies behind our perceptions does not mean that there is nothing beyond our perceptions. Locke said that there must be material substance that objects are composed of. This substance, he said, this "something-I-know-not-what," must be what has the power to create the simple ideas of sensation in our minds. But we can't confirm that—it is beyond our perceptions. Another problem is that Locke can't explain how the motion of material bodies can cause our subjective experiences of secondary qualities. This remains a problem in philosophy, though Berkeley (see Chapter 13) thought he had the solution.

Locke in Summary

Locke's influential epistemology can be summed up as follows. Sense perceptions furnish simple ideas of sensation to the mind, and the mind's awareness of sensations furnishes simple ideas of reflections. All simple ideas are products of experience of external objects and mental processes. The mind processes simple ideas into complex ideas through compounding, comparing, and abstracting.

Our idea of "tree" is a complex idea that was created in our minds through the Newtonian physics of simple ideas like height, width, color, and so on. Simple ideas of sensation in our mind are connected to primary qualities of shape, size, and color. In other words, when we walk by trees, they produce simple ideas of brown, green, shape, height, and so on, which create the complex idea of "tree" in our minds—no Platonic Forms required. Trees are probably too complex an idea to help easily grasp what is going on here, so try a blank sheet of paper. We have the sensations of whiteness and rectangular shape, which cause the simple ideas of those qualities in our minds. Put together, the simple ideas of white and rectangular form the complex idea of a sheet of paper. Our personal judgments are complex ideas: "It's a nice day." This is a judgment made from the sum of impressions—the sunshine, the warm breeze, the birds singing—it is an idea of reflection based on experience.

Very important for Locke is that every idea we have can be traced to an original sensation and that nothing exists in the mind that cannot be so traced. He thought this conception provides a firm foundation for scientific observation because it describes all activities of the mind in terms of a Newtonian physics of the mind. That physics he describes as the basic activities of compounding, relation, and abstraction that creates complex ideas.

If the qualities in objects cause perceptions in the mind, then we can know only the qualities of the objects, not the reality of the objects themselves. William had said that logic tells us nothing about the world; now Locke was saying that our scientific observations can tell us nothing about the substances behind the objects we perceive. We are not perceiving the objects at all; we are perceiving only the sensations they create in us. We cannot ever step outside the camera obscura of our mind and compare the simple ideas in our minds with the objects themselves.

REFERENCES

Francis Bacon, *Novum Organum*, Translated by James Spedding et al., https://en.wikisource.org/wiki/Novum_Organum/Book_I_(Spedding). (accessed February 28, 2021)

Thomas Hobbes, *Leviathan*, Urbana, Illinois: Project Gutenberg, http://www.gutenberg.org/files/3207/3207-h/3207-h.htm. (accessed February 28, 2021)

Thomas Jefferson, "Thomas Jefferson to John Trumbull," https://www.loc.gov/exhibits/jefferson/18.html. (accessed March 1, 2021)

John Locke, *Essay Concerning Human Understanding*, Project Gutenberg, http://www.gutenberg.org/files/10615/10615-h/10615-h.htm. (accessed March 3, 2021)

CHAPTER 9

THE RISE OF MODERN POLITICAL PHILOSOPHY

We all have a certain sense of what politics means, and it tends to be full of ugly arguments and manipulations. But when we talk about political philosophy, we strangely aren't talking about politics. Political philosophy, like all branches of philosophy, is looking at the deeper, broader issues that lie behind the phenomena that we see in human social interactions. The philosophy of the political is looking at what lies beneath the political phenomena that we see in human societies. Political philosophy is the exploration of the principles on which we can build better communities and a better society at large.

Political philosophy has ancient roots. Both Plato and Aristotle had set forth visions of how they thought society should be structured. Their thinking about society understandably was structured by the time in which they lived. When Aristotle said a state should be no larger than the distance a person can view from atop a hill, he was reflecting the social reality of his time. Ancient Greece was a collection of city-states, like Athens. The Greek word for city, "polis," is the root for our words "political" and "police" and the suffix for the name of a city "-polis," like "metropolis." "Political" has come to mean a number of things, but at its foundation is the idea of community or society. For the ancient Greeks, society meant the city. As society changed over time, philosophers had to develop new political philosophies to reflect new social realities.

After Aristotle, the age of empires began with Alexander the Great. Later came the Roman Empire that dominated the Mediterranean region for centuries. Augustine's political philosophy responded to this new reality of autocratic states with his view of how imperial states should be. His view of the legitimacy of authority, that God moves history and the rules are who God has chosen, came to be known as the "divine right of kings." Augustine's view influenced political thought for centuries to come. The predominant thinking was that the king owned the land and by extension the people who lived on it. A person's identity was as a subject of the king.

In the modern era, society changed with the rise of the nation-state. By the middle of the 1500s, Europe was increasingly consolidating into large, powerful states, and the crown heads of Europe had more power over trade and economic activity. This was, in no small part, the result of colonialism, in which the nations of Europe conquered and exploited other lands and their resources (see Chapter 6). How to acquire, control, and distribute resources had long been a concern of leaders, but in the modern/colonial era, the economic dynamics took on new breadth and dimension as things moved toward a world economy. The rise of the business corporation posed new challenges and opportunities for the crown heads of Europe. Governments were forced to deal with mercantile interests in new ways, and economics itself was changing as raw materials became more diverse, widely available, and cheaper. Economics became far more of a political issue than ever and forced the state to view its political power in new ways. The bureaucracy of the state expanded to deal with the economic changes and needed to develop new means of asserting sovereignty.

Increasingly, people had to deal with the state as a bureaucratic entity, rather than be able to deal directly with a local noble landowner. These trends were consolidated in the Treaty of Westphalia in 1648, which established precedent for the legal notion that a state was defined by discrete territory and that within that territory the state's power is exclusive and absolute. From these changes, in particular the consolidation of national borders, people's identity was increasingly a matter of nationality rather than language or ethnicity. The power of the aristocracy diminished, especially in France, where King Louis XIV (who reigned from 1643 to 1715) declared that the state was him: *L'état, c'est moi*. But what Louis XIV was truly expressing was that he was the absolute leader of the powerful state bureaucracy.

By the middle of the 1600s, the question for philosophers was what the fundamental principles behind the nation-state were. How should the state be governed?

What is the role of the individual within the state? Should the state have absolute authority? In this chapter, we will look at a Hobbesian and a Lockean way of thinking about political society and acting within political society. What they have in common is the realization that governments and nations are human creations rather than having been instituted by divine forces. Beyond that, these two different theories led to two very different answers about how a nation should be.

HOBBES'S SOCIAL BARGAIN

We saw Hobbes's epistemology in Chapter 8. Now we turn to his political philosophy. Hobbes's philosophy of government and society had two major influences. One, understandably, was his own extreme materialism; the other was the political arguments of his time. He combined fundamental principles derived from those two influences into a prescription for how to build a better society: a draconian social bargain to protect the peace. His solution is harsh but, he felt, necessary.

Individual and Political Bodies

Hobbes's political philosophy is consistent with his materialist epistemology. He believed that reality can be divided into two types: natural bodies (people) and political bodies (society, nations). Natural forces act on and determine the behavior of both types of bodies. Hobbes believed that every event in the universe is necessarily determined by prior causes. Societies and nation-states are collections of individual human beings. Each person is like a stone, and a society is like a bag of stones. Just as physical laws of nature govern the movement of stones, those same physical laws of nature govern the movement of human beings. Hobbes hoped to be able to apply the methods of his physics to human society. After all, if a human was a material body that acted in response to physical laws, and a human society was then simply a collection of human bodies, then the laws that govern human social interactions could be formulated the same way Galileo formulated the laws of motion. The more we understand the laws of motion, Hobbes thought, the more predictable are the movements of material bodies, including human beings and societies.

Human bodies may seem to act purposefully and independently, but this is not true, Hobbes says. Humans are governed by two endeavors: desire and aversion. Desire is the compulsion humans have to move toward something, and aversion is the compulsion humans have to move away from something. In short, humans desire pleasurable experiences and are averse to unpleasurable experiences. These two simple endeavors govern all human actions. When humans seem to reason and deliberate between choices of possible actions, what is happening within the human is the conflict between competing desires and aversions. The human is being pulled and pushed, and whichever force is the stronger will prevail and cause the human to move. Every human being is like a cork on the surface of the ocean buffeted by the winds and currents, mechanically determined by all of the forces acting on it.

Because Hobbes believed in this deterministic view of human behavior, he saw all of human society as deterministic. Because he believes that the endeavors of desire and aversion govern all human beings, he sees all of human society as governed by the endeavors. Therefore, to create an orderly society, one needs to control the forces affecting the particular human bodies in it, and that will translate to controlling the body that is society. In terms of politics, Hobbes saw there being two primary endeavors at work. Humans desire peace and stability and are averse to chaos. These two endeavors underlie all of the other many endeavors that act on humans, such as desires for food, water, and shelter and aversions to discomfort and suffering.

The Political Arguments in Hobbes's Time

As we see throughout this book, philosophers respond to the events in their time. Throughout Hobbes's life, English people debated the source of rights and the structure of society. It wasn't always a deeply intellectual, philosophical debate; it too often was an angry argument over power. How much power should the king have over the nobility? What rights do the nobility and freemen of the kingdom have? (Peasants weren't included in this discussion.) The short version of the long story is that the social changes in the 1500s and 1600s increased economic and political tensions between the monarchy and the aristocracy. For centuries, wealth had been a matter of ownership of land. Gold and jewels were nice, but land produced food and other natural resources. Land was the basis of power sharing in much of Europe. The aristocracy were the landowners, often granted rights to the land by the monarch in exchange for pledges of fealty (loyalty with duties attached). It was never an absolute system; the landed nobles were never totally loyal to the monarch, but they did rule almost absolutely over the peasants who were tied to the land and bonded to their noble lord. Colonialism changed the dynamic among the landed nobles and the monarch because the exploitation of natural resources in the colonies changed the sources of wealth and economic power. In the early 1600s, the kings of England and France gained in power and wealth, and they felt emboldened to centralize power and make more demands on their nobility. Some in the nobility, unsurprisingly, resisted. Growing tensions escalated into open warfare in England (1642 against Charles I) and in France (1648 against Louis XIV). Hobbes was a firsthand witness to both rebellions, having been born in England, then having had to flee to France in 1647. Hobbes served a noble family connected to Charles I, who had lost the civil war with the nobles and had been executed. Hobbes and other royalists chose exile in France over suffering probable reprisals in England, which was now ruled by Oliver Cromwell, leader of the revolt. In Paris, Hobbes was mathematics tutor to the son of Charles I—the later king Charles II—and was in the company of other royalist exiles. All of these developments formed the backdrop for Hobbes's political philosophy.

For Hobbes, the conflict between the noble factions in England was proof of the prevailing assumption that social diversity was dangerous. Uniformity of language, ethnicity, social practices, and ideas were necessary for social stability. Difference of any kind was widely felt to be a threat to society. This feeling was particularly strong in religion. We saw in Chapter 5 how the word "heresy" meant to choose a different path, and that root idea was still strong in Hobbes's time. In the early 1600s, as for many years before and after, a prevailing feeling was that a society was best when it was perfectly uniform: one ruler ruling over one homogeneous culture. Again, this extended to all aspects of human society, including the religious loyalty confession, which in the 1600s was to being either Catholic or Protestant. This basic assumption was practiced by all states: If the ruler was Catholic, everyone had to be Catholic. If the ruler was Protestant, everyone had to be Protestant. Diversity was dangerous. England's king was a Protestant; therefore, to not be Protestant was to be suspected as an enemy of the state. Hobbes was Protestant, but mostly out of a sense of loyalty to his monarch. He was not strongly anti-Catholic, as we shall also see in John Locke. For Hobbes, the subject must always be loyal to the sovereign; let's see why he so passionately believed that.

Hobbes's Thought Experiment

To understand how best to govern society, Hobbes thought it best to imagine how life would be if there was no government. This he called the "state of nature," living without any laws or social conventions. In this condition, no one has any rank or status or any of the associated rights, privileges, or restrictions. In the state of nature, there are not the class distinctions that were a given in British society at that time. Hobbes's purpose is to understand what forces are at work on humans prior to social conventions being created. It is important to remember that Hobbes is not necessarily saying that there actually was a "state of nature" from which human society emerged. His is a philosophical thought experiment.

Without social conventions in Hobbes's state of nature thought experiment, everyone is equal, and life consists only of material facts and forces (there are no laws and rules to stop anyone). Everyone has "a right to every thing," Hobbes says, "even to another's body." Hobbes's use of "right" is curious to us today because we think in terms of moral and civil rights. By "right," Hobbes means a "freedom based on power." In other words, if I want your food, I have a right to take it if I have the power to do so. Of course, you have a right to stop me, if you have the power to stop me. The power in question includes physical violence. In the state of nature, there are no laws and no police to stop us from wounding or even killing each other as we struggle to take for ourselves the world's finite resources.

Hobbes's view of human nature is that we are inherently selfish. We have no inherent sentiment for others, and altruism is not natural. Buffeted like corks on the ocean by our own desires and aversions, we think and feel first and foremost about our own needs. In the state of nature, humans are bodies moving and colliding, their desires and needs coming into constant conflict, each particular human compelled by the endeavors to survive by whatever means necessary. Like a postapocalyptic movie, everyone in the state of nature is seeking advantage over others, even dominance. Those with superior physical strength have an advantage, but they have no guarantee of safety because, as Hobbes pointed out, even the strongest person can be overcome when weaker people combine their power to take down the stronger.

No surprise then that the state of nature is a miserable existence dominated by fear and chaos without peace and stability. Hobbes summed it up this way:

> *In such condition, there is no place for Industry; because the fruit thereof is uncertain; and consequently no Culture of the Earth; no Navigation, nor use of the commodities that may be imported by Sea; no commodious Building; no Instruments of moving, and removing such things as require much force; no Knowledge of the face of the Earth; no account of Time; no Arts; no Letters; no Society; and which is worst of all, continual fear, and danger of violent death; And the life of man, solitary, poor, nasty, brutish, and short.* (*Leviathan*, I.XIII.9)

Every person is an enemy to every person. If anyone thinks this portrayal of humanity without laws and conventions is exaggerated, Hobbes points out that we already know this is how people are. We lock our doors at night and lock away our valuables, and this is when we know there are laws and police. This shows our true opinions of our fellow humans, Hobbes says. How much worse would other people be without laws and police? It would create a war of all against all, in which nothing is unjust and thus nothing is off-limits.

Fortunately, there is a way out of the nasty chaos of the state of nature. This is partly why Hobbes engages in the thought experiment about the state of nature: to explain how human society came about. The natural forces of the endeavors led humans to form a society and a government. The first endeavor for all humans is the desire for peace. This, Hobbes says, is the first natural law: to seek the peace and follow it, or, failing that, be prepared to defend oneself by any means necessary. This is true, even for the strongest man, because no human is so powerful that he or she cannot be overcome by others. Peace and safety cannot be ensured by individual strength.

When Hobbes says, "seek the peace," he isn't meaning some flower power love and understanding thing. He's thinking in terms of his theory that people are governed by desires and aversions. We want to be left alone with our food in our shelter. We don't want to have someone break in and steal our food. We certainly don't want to be beaten or killed. We want to be left in peace. Simple as that. Hobbes calls it our desire for ease, and we can understand this. We want things to be easy, and we desire to be at ease, without strife and conflict.

The first law is to seek the peace, and the second law follows from it: To achieve peace, one ought to surrender all of one's rights, provided that everyone else does the same. Remember that this is Hobbes's definition of "rights" as meaning "freedom based on power." I will give up my freedom to do whatever I want if you agree to give up yours. I won't steal your stuff if you won't steal my stuff. I won't kill you if you won't kill me. This way, we can have peace rather than constantly fighting over resources. This agreement, in its essence, is a cease-fire between warring parties. This bargain of necessity is one of self-interest—again desires and aversions.

But what would stop someone from breaking the agreement to surrender his or her rights? There is no honor among thieves, it is said with much truth. If, as Hobbes says, we care only about our own desires and aversions, why would we keep any agreement to limit our freedom? Sure, I can agree to not take your stuff, but I can still do so when your back is turned. Hobbes is aware of this problem, and he provides an answer:

> *There must be some coercive power to compel men equally to the performance of their Covenants, by the terror of some punishment, greater than the benefit they expect by the breach of their Covenant.* (*Leviathan*, I.XV, 3)

People are just bodies in motion for Hobbes. You make them do what you want by exerting force on them. Control the endeavors that compel humans to move a certain way, and you control the situation. Human freedom of action is based on power, so a stronger power needs to control it. Humans are averse to suffering, so put in place a force strong enough to make humans averse to breaking their agreement to limit their freedom. This coercive power, Hobbes says, is a particular form of government that has absolute power.

The only way to compel others to obey their agreement is when everyone agrees

> *to confer all their power and strength upon one man, or upon one assembly of men, that may reduce all their wills, by plurality of voices, unto one will.* (*Leviathan*, II, XVII, 13)

Hobbes takes the old Roman idea of the "body politic" and interprets it literally. A nation is a body made up of all of the particular humans living in it. A human body could not survive if the various organs and bodily parts were at war with each other. The body politic of the nation is the same. Only by reducing all of the wills of all of the humans to a single will personified by one man, the Sovereign, can the nation survive. The Sovereign is the absolute ruler of the nation, who possesses all power and all freedom to act on behalf of all of the humans within the nation. Hobbes takes this quite literally as shown in the title plate of his book *Leviathan*. Looming over a British town and its surroundings is the Sovereign, whose body is made up of the bodies of all his subject humans. Their will and voices are subsumed in his. He speaks and acts for them. His word is law, and he is the coercive power that will compel humans to live up to their agreements.

Hobbes's proposed political arrangement has come to be known as a form of "social contract." The contract is between all particular humans. Everyone gives up all of their rights and freedoms and confers them on the Sovereign. In return, the Sovereign guarantees peace and stability, which, Hobbes thinks, is what everyone wants more than anything. Anyone who acts contrary to the agreement by breaking the laws of the land will be dealt with by the Sovereign who also acts to protect the nation form foreign invaders.

What's to prevent the Sovereign from abusing his power? Hobbes doesn't say. Like Plato long before him, Hobbes believes that those in power will act according to reason and natural laws and, thus, act only in the interests of the nation. Plato understood that people have free will, but believed that no one would choose to do bad deeds if they knew they were bad. Hobbes denied free will, but he seemed to assume that the force of the common power of the social contract would compel the Sovereign to act only to benefit the body politic.

If all of this seems far-fetched to our thinking now, remember that Hobbes is thinking in the 1600s. This was the age, on the one hand, of monarchism and absolute government and, on the other hand, of sectarian violence and rebellion by elements of the aristocracy against the monarchs. Political chaos was a constant threat, and Hobbes, among other like-minded thinkers of his time, thought that the only way to stop the fighting among the aristocracy for power was to concentrate power in one man—the king. Hobbes saw as his model the Kingdom of France. In that nation, Louis XIII had consolidated political power and elevated France to a world power. After a 33-year rule (1610–1643), his son, Louis XIV continued his father's program of absolute monarchy and ruled as Sovereign for an amazing 72 years (1643–1715; his successor, Louis XV ruled another 58 years). Hobbes wrote his political theory in *Leviathan* in France while exiled from England during its civil war. Hobbes's thinking in the early years of Louis XIV's rule was no doubt influenced by experiencing the Kingdom of France on the rise, sheltered from the turmoil in his English homeland.

LOCKE'S THEORY OF A DIVINE RIGHT TO CHANGE KINGS

Government at the consent of the governed—it is a principle we assume today and demand. It was not always so. Hobbes's philosophy of the Sovereign bears strong similarities to the "divine right of kings"—the idea that the monarch held a sacred right to be monarch and was above the law because the monarch was the law. It was the principle held by Charles I. A generation after Hobbes's *Leviathan*, England didn't have the absolute sovereign Hobbes had prescribed as the antidote to political chaos. Charles II had, as Hobbes had hoped, ascended to the English throne in 1660, but it didn't end the strife over who should rule England. There was another removal of a monarch, James II, and another civil war, again over the balance of power in the nation-state between the nobles and the monarch.

John Locke was an ideas person, a kind of a 1600s think tank fellow who supplied advice to politicians and governmental officials. He himself was not a politician or governmental official, but he did work for Lord Ashley, the first Earl of Shaftesbury. His boss was very involved in government and politics, late in life, as a staunch opponent of the king. It was the principle of the right of political opposition that captured Locke's attention. It was the need to justify philosophically the removal of the rightful monarch, James II, that moved Locke to develop his theory of political philosophy. His magnum opus on political philosophy, *Two Treatises of Government*, was likely written while he was evading capture and prosecution for his association with Shaftesbury. Locke had to go into exile in Holland beginning in 1683.

The Political Background for Locke's Philosophy

Locke was writing his political philosophy about 50 years after Hobbes had written his. The political situation was much the same, including the perceived Catholic problem. In 1685, French king Louis XIV revoked the 1598 Edict of Nantes that had granted tolerance and rights to Protestants. Louis—who had been king of France when Hobbes was in France tutoring Charles II and writing *Leviathan*—was a keen proponent of the theory of absolutism. The idea that all citizens of a country were not of the same religious confession (Catholic or Protestant) as their king was disconcerting and disruptive to the unity of the country. Louis' revocation of the Edict made loyalty to the king's views on religion compulsory. The king was Catholic, so the state and you had to be Catholic.

Also in 1685, the openly Catholic brother of Charles II, James, became king, Charles I having no heir on his death. James was not an exclusionary Catholic like Louis, but English fears, real and imagined, of a Catholic king were strong. Earlier, forces in parliament, including nobles such as Shaftesbury, had unsuccessfully tried through legislation to prevent James from becoming king. Anti-Catholic forces attempted several rebellions shortly after James's coronation. James responded with excessive force that, along with his restructuring of the army and local governments, further stirred up distrust among both the English aristocracy and the common people. By 1687, a group of English nobles reached out to the Dutch ruler William of Orange, a Protestant and fierce enemy of Louis XIV. William was married to James's daughter, Mary. The English nobles invited William to become coruler, with Mary, of England if he would raise an army to depose James. William did raise an army to invade England, and James, correctly seeing that he didn't have enough support to stay in power, fled the country. Parliament, members of which plotted the whole thing, declared that James had abdicated the throne, and William and Mary were named co-monarchs. The victors named it "The Glorious Revolution." What the nobles in Parliament also did was restructure English law to decrease the power of the monarch and increase the power of Parliament. It settled the political power struggle that led to so much strife in the 1600s, and the arrangement remains the basic governmental system in the United Kingdom to this day.

Locke's Natural Right of Property

Despite the strife over the Catholic question, Locke was largely unconcerned about religious issues, like Hobbes had been earlier. By all accounts, Locke was motivated by a desire for religious tolerance. He displayed it when he was a university student at Oxford and wrote that most religious disputes were over matters of no great import and should not disturb peaceful coexistence. He displayed it when he published his first major work, *A Letter Concerning Toleration* (1685), in which he argued for restraint from political leaders in trying to dictate the personal religious beliefs of the people. It is certainly possible that Locke's opposition to James II was motivated by a desire for religious peace within England. But in his major work on political philosophy, *Two Treatises of Government* (1689), he didn't present religious tolerance as a major argument.

Instead, Locke's primary concern in the *Two Treatises* is the question of what rights people have, especially in resisting authority. Locke had earlier argued that individuals had the right to believe as they wish on matters of no great import. Certainly, Locke did not extend that idea to who should rule a country, which was clearly a matter of very great import. He felt the people had the power, at least to a degree, to choose who their leader should be. His argument for the right to rebel was made through establishing individual rights within a framework of property rights. At first, that sounds like an odd approach, but Locke's argument is ingenious and takes into account philosophical and political history.

Locke accepted as natural law what almost everyone accepted—that acts such as murder and stealing are wrong. Where Locke broke with the social conventions of his time was on his theory of property, primarily "real" property or land. (Still today we use the idea of "real" property or "real estate.") The prevailing idea about what justified ownership of land in the 1600s was the notion of the divine right of kings. Expressed best philosophically by the Dutch natural law philosopher Hugo Grotius (1583–1645), the argument was that the earth was created by God who granted ownership of various pieces of land to particular rulers. The king thus owned the land and could do what he wanted with it, including granting it to whomever he wanted. It wasn't really biblical, but that wasn't the point, really. It was an explanation of how things had worked for a very long time. It was "natural." The monarchies of both Britain and France operated in this way. The entire realm was considered to be owned by the king, who granted parts of it to various lords and barons, and people who lived on the land effectively belonged to the lord or baron who owned that land. This was how the feudal system worked. Grotius gave the philosophical explanation and defense of this reality, expressing it in terms of natural law.

Locke argued against Grotius that property was, in reality, something that humans earn through their own efforts. Locke made a distinction between natural rights and legal rights. Legal rights are granted by a governmental authority, and the government can take them away. But natural rights are not subject to governmental authority; it would be wrong for a government to try to take away our natural rights. The theory of the divine right of kings and Hobbes's theory of the Sovereign both assume that the monarch possesses the original natural right of use of the land. Locke disagreed. Nature and all of its resources are given to humanity by God, Locke says, repeating a view first proposed by William of Ockham. Locke's innovation is to extend the idea of natural rights to the property held by individuals. Locke's labor theory of property holds that when people mix their labor with the land, they create property that is theirs alone. One's labor, the work of one's own hands, is one's own property, and one acquires a right to it as one's own property. Locke lists hunting, gathering, and cultivating the ground as examples of how a person acquires the right to the material that the person's labor has produced. It makes some sense. God made all the trees in the forest, but if you go into the forest, chop down a tree, drag it back, and build something out of it, your labor gives you the right to the product of that labor. The apples on a tree may belong to everyone, but by going and picking the apples you make them yours. This is the condition of human life, Locke says. To survive, we need to mix our labor with the raw materials in nature to provide ourselves with food and shelter, and this necessarily introduces private possessions.

Earth's natural resources are humanity's common property, free to everyone to use as they need. The king has no inherent entitlement to the land, Locke said. When I mix my labor with a part of nature, it becomes my property. His view was not quite egalitarian. As Locke puts it:

> *Thus the grass my horse has bit; the turfs my servant has cut... become my property, without the assignation or consent of any body. The labour that was mine, removing them out of that common state they were in, hath fixed my property in them.* (*Two Treatises of Government*, II.V.28)

If you are paying any attention at all, something in Locke's passage should jump out at you: "the turfs my servant has cut become my property." Despite Locke's talk about the power of the people, he is operating under 1600s assumptions about who "people" are. He still considers the lord of the manor to be the one who owns the land by virtue of the labor his servants expend on it because the servants belong to the lord. Locke's passage places the horse and the servant on the same level. Nevertheless, for Locke, human labor is what distinguishes what belongs to all from what belongs to one. Obtaining property is, therefore, a natural product of life, and property properly acquired through one's labor is one's own by natural right.

Locke's State of Nature Thought Experiment

Having established property as a natural right, Locke engages in a thought experiment similar to Hobbes's. He also imagines a state of nature without government, but Locke had a very different view of human nature. Hobbes thought we are inherently selfish, and without coercive control, would be in a constant state of war. Locke saw human beings as individuals with free will and rational capacity who also possessed sentiment for their fellow humans and were capable of altruism. From this different view of human nature, Locke saw the state of nature quite differently from Hobbes. He thought a life without government would be one of general peace, goodwill, and mutual assistance. Most humans would act based on reason and benevolent sentiments and get along with each other, respecting each other's property and personal natural rights. The problem would be the minority of people who acted contrary to reason and natural law. To preserve the peace, we would have to deal with those miscreants who ruin it.

How do we deal with those who do harm to others? In a Wild West situation of the state of nature, we'd have to do it ourselves, resorting to vigilante justice. This is possible, but inconvenient and chaotic. Besides, Locke says, even though we could live in the state of nature without society, we humans are naturally inclined toward living in an ordered society. This is Locke's social contract: We agree to form and live within a government that establishes and enforces laws that make our lives better. Locke's idea of government is one based on the principles of natural law, which are written down and enshrined in civil law, to resolve controversies among individuals. From a written law and constitutional government, individual human bias will not enter into judgments concerning individual cases. Rather than force each individual in the state of nature to enact justice and punish wrongdoing, a government can officially appoint indifferent judges who can apply the laws of the land in a manner more equitable than can a person whose interests are at stake.

A crucial element of Locke's social contract is that it is between the citizens of a nation and their government. For Locke, the contract is more like when you hire someone to do work for you. You dictate the terms, and the people hired to do the work perform based on the terms of the contract. Government serves the people in Locke's social contract. We agree to hand over some of our rights and freedoms to the government in exchange for the convenience of having government administer justice and handle the running of daily life on our behalf. The role of government, then, is to defend people's natural rights.

Locke's Right to Revolt

How does this relate to the right to revolt? For Locke, government is a convenience. It is not necessary, and it is not divinely ordained. Rational people established government because they find it preferable to live in a society rather than in a state of nature. Hobbes viewed the social contract as among the people—"I surrender my rights, if you surrender yours, and we hand over all rights to the Sovereign." Locke viewed the social contract as between the people and the government—"we appoint you to rule as long as you serve our interests." This difference in vision explains why Locke can accept revolt against the monarch, but Hobbes cannot. For Locke, if the monarch, or government in general, breaks the terms of the social contract, they have lost any right to remain in government. The people have a right to replace them. In fact, Locke argued that, to preserve society, revolt against tyranny was not only the right but also the duty of every person.

Locke believed that people should obey authority and keep the peace within a society. Nevertheless, he asserts that there is a right to resist unjust authority and in the last resort to rebel against and overthrow that authority. Just as you would fire someone you hired who proved to be corrupt or incompetent, a people should fire rulers who proved to be corrupt or incompetent. The basis of sovereignty is the law. A ruler is not above the law; therefore, a ruler can be fired. People have a right to change rulers when they see fit.

Locke wrote *Two Treatises of Government* in response to the Glorious Revolution of 1688. This revolution was purely political and served the interests of a group of wealthy British landowners. Locke was part of that group, as an employee of Shaftesbury. Locke's primary purpose in his book was to provide philosophical justification for the act of treason committed by his allies. This is why he uses his labor theory of property to explain why the king has no inherent rights to the land but does not extend the right of property to the people lower in social class than the aristocracy. It is also why Locke's formula of the primary law of nature is that no one ought to harm another in his life, liberty, or *possessions*. Only later, in the United States, was this formula changed from "possessions" to "pursuit of happiness."

The government, in Locke's conception, should have a separation of power split into three branches. The legislative branch had supreme power and had the ultimate authority over how the force of the commonwealth should be used. The executive branch was in charge of enforcing law and how it was applied to specific cases. The federative power was to act internationally according to the law of Nature.

Locke's faults and blindness aside, we can't dismiss the importance of his political philosophy. The ideas that there is a social contract between the people and their government, that government exists to serve the people, that government should be divided and limited by a constitution, and that government should enforce the laws on behalf of the powerless are ideas that are now central to our notion of a democratic society. Locke is an example of how terms such as "liberal" and "conservative" are relative to their time and place. Locke's ideas were, for his time, liberal. For our time, because they do not extend rights to the working class, women, and ethnic minorities, his ideas would be considered conservative.

REFERENCES

Thomas Hobbes, *Leviathan*, Urbana, Illinois: Project Gutenberg. http://www.gutenberg.org/files/3207/3207-h/3207-h.htm. (accessed March 9, 2021)

John Locke, *Two Treatises of Government*, *Wikisource*, https://en.wikisource.org/w/index.php?title=Two_Treatises_of_Government&oldid=9693604. (accessed March 10, 2021)

CHAPTER 10

THE RISE OF RADICAL POLITICAL CRITIQUE

The social contract theories of Hobbes and Locke established the template for political philosophy for the next few centuries. That doesn't mean that some philosophers didn't step outside the template to develop philosophies that radically challenged the prevailing assumptions of philosophy and wider society. This chapter looks at two very different philosophers of the 1700s—Jean-Jacques Rousseau and Mary Wollstonecraft—who each in his or her own way fiercely critiqued society. We'll also look at the philosophical issues that underpinned the radical experiment in government known as the United States of America.

JEAN-JACQUES ROUSSEAU'S GENERAL WILL

Jean-Jacques Rousseau (1712–1778) gets short shrift from many, but his philosophy was incredibly influential. His influence was mostly in France, however, which partially explains why he gets little attention in the English-speaking world. The other reason for the lack of attention is that his political philosophy was more or less a disaster when it was put into practice.

Rousseau has been called a "militant lowbrow" because he railed against what we consider "highbrow" culture. Rousseau's targets included science, religion, the arts, education, government—basically everything we would call "civilization." Others, like Thomas Paine who we'll meet later in this chapter, described the 1700s as "The Age of Reason" and "The Enlightenment," denoting their self-satisfaction with what they saw as humanity's progress. Rousseau disagreed and offers us a challenge: Who are we? Why do we assume that our progress in philosophy, science, and technology is an improvement?

The quick version of Rousseau's philosophy is summed up in his book, *The Social Contract* (1762):

> *Man is born free; and everywhere is in chains. One thinks himself the master of others, and still remains a greater slave than they. How did this change come about? I do not know. What can make it legitimate? That question I think I can answer.... But the social order is a sacred right which is the basis of all other rights. Nevertheless, this right does not come from nature, and must therefore be founded on conventions.* (*The Social Contract*, I.I.1-2)

By the "social order," he meant what Hobbes meant by "social conventions": the class structure of society and the many related expectations of how people should behave. France was a hierarchical society in Rousseau's time; a king, an aristocracy, and the common people. Everyone knew their place in the hierarchy because social recognition norms taught people what was expected from them and what to expect from others (we'll talk more about recognition norms in Chapter 24). That set of social relations was what made France a civilized society. But Rousseau saw civilized society as a prison. Its structure of social norms chained people, restricting their true expression.

Rousseau's argument against social norms was that they encouraged people to concentrate on the approval of others to maintain their social status. This social pressure created in people the artificial state of *amour-propre*. Rousseau picked up the concept of *amour-propre* (literally "self-love") from the French moralist François VI, Duc de La Rochefoucauld (1613–1680). François, a contemporary of Descartes, was also raised on letters and was familiar with Augustine, who had condemned love of self, "*amour de soi,*" as the vice of making oneself more important than God. François added to Augustine's *amour de soi* the idea that, motivated by love of self, people seek the approval of others. We are, in fact, so desirous of the approval of others that we put up a public front to cast ourselves in a flattering light, highlighting our positives and hiding our negatives, to win that approval. Being familiar with the French royal court, François saw how courtiers would go to great lengths to gain prestige and status. This pursuit, despite being motivated by self-interest, actually causes people to forget their true nature and misjudge their behavior. "We are so used to disguising ourselves from others that we end by disguising ourselves from ourselves." (François, Duc de La Rochefoucauld, *Maxims*, Maxim 11). This desire for esteem, François terms "*amour-propre*." The concept helps him explain why we behave as we do and why we are blind to why we behave as we do.

Rousseau took the concept further and defined *amour propre* as approval and esteem that must come from others. This, he argued, was not natural self-love, or *amour de soi*, which Rousseau, in sharp contrast to Augustine, saw as positive. Rousseau claimed that *amour-propre* was an artificial creation of civilization that caused individuals to compare themselves with one another to gain social status. He claimed that *amour de soi* was compatible with happiness but that *amour-propre* corrupted individuals and led to misery and vice. Rousseau saw *amour de soi* as difficult, if not impossible, within civilized society, which is dominated by the pressure to conform to social norms.

Civilized man is born and dies a slave, Rousseau wrote in his novel, *Emile*. All his life, man is imprisoned by institutions. Man is naturally good, and in the state of nature we can live organically in unity with each other and ourselves. In nature, we are savage but noble, happy and with goodwill toward others. Civilization is harmful; its nature is corrupt. Imprisoned within it, we are forced to compete with others for esteem and status. We are deceitful to each other and to ourselves, alienated from our true nature. Our greatest evils, Rousseau says, flow from ourselves. Trapped together in society, alienated and confused, we are all in chains.

You may ask (as you should), how does this convert into a political philosophy? Well, that was the problem. As much as he'd like to see civilization swept away and ended, he understood it was not that simple. He settled for a lesser evil. The short version is that Rousseau, like Hobbes and Locke, adopted the concept of a social contract. Rousseau, however, had no tangible concept by which he could unite society under a contractual bond. So, in his book, *The Social Contract* (1762), he put forward the tenuous concept of the "general will"—a difficult combination of total political freedom with strong authoritarianism. Rousseau believed that in the state of nature, which he meant more literally than did Hobbes and Locke, an individual's will would be allowed to express itself freely. Society was a prison; nature was freedom. Rousseau pointed to an idealized vision of the indigenous populations of North America, whom the French had come to know in their explorations of what is now Canada. Indigenous societies seemed to the French explorers to be less rigidly structured than was French society, its people more at peace with the land and with themselves. It was the myth of the "noble savage," a person of dignity free from the social constraints of class hierarchy and war. If we were more free, as the indigenous peoples of North America are, Rousseau thought, we would be happier. This was his rough idea of the state of nature.

Rousseau's general will is the combination of the necessary evil of society and the good individual will found in the state of nature. The general will is the abstract expression of what is best for all, as if the society were one individual. The idea is similar to Hobbes's Sovereign as the embodiment of all. Rousseau, however, does not reduce the will of all to one man but considers the body politic as the Sovereign (*The Social Contract,* I.VII.3). Also like Hobbes's Sovereign, the collective general will is the sole source of sovereignty to which each individual must subjugate himself or herself. Because the general will is not one man, as Hobbes proposed, Rousseau adds that the general will is determined by individual participation. He believed that everyone should be required to vote directly on the laws of the land—no elected representatives. Good laws make for good citizens, but good laws can be willed only by good citizens, and laws are legitimate only if they are agreed on by the common assembly of citizens. Rousseau believed that through public debate and voting, disagreements that arose from individual opinions would cancel each other out. What is left is the general will. Everyone was required to obey that general will as the law of the land. In this way, everyone develops within a framework of equality under the law.

It did not work. Rousseau's basic idea of the general will was implemented in the early years of the French Revolution. The idea of who decided what the general will of the people was slid into a morass of self-serving petty disputes. A bloodbath ensued, which came to be known as the "Reign of Terror" (1793–1794). In a few years, Napoleon grabbed power and plunged all of Europe and most of the world into decades of total war. It would be unfair to blame it all on Rousseau, but the American Revolution was philosophically based on Locke's version of the social contract, and that turned out a bit better (see below). These revolutions weren't entirely about philosophy, but philosophy did have a part in them both.

MARY WOLLSTONECRAFT AND THE BIRTH OF FEMINISM

A woman! Yes, finally we are discussing a female philosopher. Not because we are now censoring female philosophers but because women were censored back then. In many countries, prior to the 2000s, women were legally forbidden from publishing books. So, although women were every bit as intelligent and thoughtful as men (perhaps more so), we do not know about them. Women's voices were silenced.

Mary Wollstonecraft (1759–1797) was vividly aware of these facts. She refused to accept the secondary status to which society had relegated women. Wollstonecraft's central idea was that all human beings have God-given abilities and rights and, *very* importantly, that these abilities and rights are shared by *both* men and women. Yes, feminism is the radical idea that women are human beings (see Chapter 25). And I am not being funny. That is an accurate description of what Wollstonecraft was doing with her 1792 book, *A Vindication of the Rights of Woman*. The dominant idea then and since the beginning of civilization had been that women lacked the capacity to be rational and therefore could not do philosophy or be leaders. Aristotle was a big believer in this idea—women were lesser humans too weak-minded to reason. One of the few philosophers who thought otherwise was Descartes, who had a long intellectual correspondence with Princess Elisabeth of Bohemia, and he supported her efforts to publish her ideas on philosophy, which she did. (Elisabeth made no significant contributions to the history of philosophy, so she is not included in this book—we can only cover so many—and hundreds of male philosophers are left out for the same reason.) Wollstonecraft was adamant that women have every bit the rational capacity that men have.

Wollstonecraft's political philosophy matches well with Locke's, and she was greatly influenced by him. Locke wasn't as anti-woman as most philosophers were, but he was no feminist. Neither was Edmund Burke (1729–1797), who was also influenced by Locke but took a different direction to which Wollstonecraft objected. Burke is known as the father of conservatism as a political philosophy because he believed in natural law, like Locke and Wollstonecraft. What Burke did with natural law, though, is to say that what happens in the world is an expression of how things should be. One of Burke's arguments is that we should not question tradition because if society has been doing things a certain way for many years it must be because people long ago figured out that is the best way to do things. In other words, be quiet and follow along with how things are; if you disagree, you are going against natural law. That is basically why Burke opposed the French Revolution and its efforts to change society.

Wollstonecraft's fame and reputation in her time began with her 1790 book, *A Vindication of the Rights of Men*, a critical response to Edmund Burke's *Reflections on the Revolution*. Burke had launched a conservative attack on the French Revolution and its calls for radical social and political change. He defended social tradition and custom in general, and specifically the institutions of the monarchy and aristocracy. Wollstonecraft was of exactly the opposite opinion about the French Revolution, mainly because of its idea that women should be equal to men. Wollstonecraft saw the French Revolution as a necessary rational response to the corruption of the French absolute monarchy. Wollstonecraft embraced the new ideals of progress and social reform. She turned Burke's arguments back on him and exposed the inconsistencies in his position. For example, she pointed out that logically, because Burke is such a staunch defender of tradition, he should be opposed to Jesus, a radical who broke with Jewish tradition. Similarly, she noted that Burke, a Protestant, should oppose the Protestant Reformation that rebelled against Catholicism. Furthermore, she observes that the American war for independence, which Burke supported, could not be supported if he was true to his stated principles.

Wollstonecraft adopted the then emerging view that humans have natural, God-given rights:

> *It is necessary emphatically to repeat, that there are rights which men inherit at their birth as rational creatures, who were raised above the brute creation by their improvable faculties; and that, in receiving these, not from their forefathers but, from God, prescription can never undermine natural rights.* (*A Vindication of the Rights of Men*, ¶31)

These natural rights precede the social conventions of rights obtained through inheritance or the privileges of one's place in the social structure.

Throughout *Rights of Men*, Wollstonecraft condemns the tradition of hereditary privilege and the inequalities of the class system and social structure of England. She argues that people should be judged on their individual merits rather than on who their family is. Following Locke's labor theory of property (that ownership of land and products is acquired through one's own labor) and against Burke's justification of inherited wealth, Wollstonecraft says,

> *The only security of property that nature authorizes and reason sanctions is, the right a man has to enjoy the acquisitions which his talents and industry have acquired; and to bequeath them to whom he chooses.* (*A Vindication of the Rights of Men*, 62)

Burke's central argument was that political traditions of England had been tested for centuries and thus should be accepted and that radical social and political change should be rejected. Wollstonecraft countered that no government or constitution was above rational reassessment because all human institutions are unavoidably imperfect.

Wollstonecraft followed up in 1792 with her most famous book, *A Vindication of the Rights of Woman*. This book extended her ideas and responded to Rousseau's. One of Rousseau's themes is the question of nature versus nurture: How much of our character and behavior are produced by nature and is inherent to us versus how much of our character and behavior are nurtured and learned through our upbringing and socialization? Pretty much everyone in the 1700s believed that there were fundamental, inherent differences between men and women. This assumption, coupled with the concept of natural law, presupposed that it was simply natural for women to be kept in a status subordinate to men.

This assumption of a natural order of the sexes is the object of Wollstonecraft's strongest ire. She argues that women have the same human nature as men and that women should aspire to the same standard of virtue.

> *But I still insist that not only the virtue, but the knowledge of the two sexes should be the same in nature, if not in degree, and that women, considered not only as moral, but rational creatures, ought to endeavor to acquire human virtues (or perfections) by the same means as men, instead of being educated like a fanciful kind of half being.* (*A Vindication of the Rights of Woman*, 3.4)

Wollstonecraft argues that the differences between men and women are strictly the artificial result of men keeping women subordinated and preventing women from fulfilling their potential, a potential that was the same as that of men. The issue was how women are socialized and deprived of education and opportunities. Wollstonecraft condemns the view of Rousseau and others as believing that woman "was created to be the toy of man, his rattle, and it must jingle in his ears whenever, dismissing reason, he chooses to be amused." (*A Vindication of the Rights of Woman*, 2.58) She also chastises women for accepting the male-created false ideal of femininity that dictates who and how women are supposed to be. Wollstonecraft decries how "Gentleness, docility, and a spaniel-like affection are...consistently recommended as the cardinal virtues of the [female] sex." (*A Vindication of the Rights of Woman*, 2.58) Girls are from birth indoctrinated to embrace these ideals, even by older women: "The civilized women of the present century, with a few exceptions, are only anxious to inspire love, when they ought to cherish a nobler ambition, and by their abilities and virtues exact respect." (*A Vindication of the Rights of Woman*, Introduction.1) Women, Wollstonecraft said, are the equals of men in their natural capacities and should claim that as their God-given right.

Wollstonecraft sees reason as what defines human beings. On this point, she agreed with most philosophers, but in sharp contrast to them, she sees women and men as possessing equal capacity for reason. Since men and women have the same natural human nature, any social structure that prevents women from fully and freely developing their talents is unreasonable and unjust. Wollstonecraft declares that women deserve full equality and that society harms itself by depriving women of equality in education. She points out that women are the primary educators of children and, therefore, it is important to educate all mothers. She further calls for a reform of marriage. Women, she says, should not be mere ornaments or property of men. Educated women should be equal companions of their husbands, and, in this, both spouses would benefit.

One of Wollstonecraft's ideas was to challenge everyone that if we as a society treated girls the way we treat boys—teach girls like we teach boys that they can reason—women would equal or surpass men. Wollstonecraft argued that women should not be restricted to particular professions; with proper education, women can contribute to society in traditionally male professions such as medicine, business, politics, or farming. This issue of occupational fairness is a challenge that even today our society has not fully met. For example, less than one-quarter of philosophy faculty in the United States are women. It is better in Europe, but women are still underrepresented. It is worse in many areas of science and engineering with women constituting as low as one-tenth of faculty. It is because, as Wollstonecraft said more than 200 years ago, we raised girls differently than we raised boys. In the language of today, we raise everyone to be sexist.

Alas, not surprisingly, Wollstonecraft's arguments were rejected by the men who dominated society. Nevertheless, her arguments on the social benefits of the rights of women were taken up years later by John Stuart Mill and his wife Harriet (see Chapter 16). Oh, and worth mentioning: Mary Wollstonecraft had a daughter, Mary, who became the author of a famous novel called *Frankenstein*.

THE AMERICAN EXPERIMENT

Hobbes and Locke had considered the question of whether it was acceptable to rebel against the monarch. Hobbes had said almost never, and Locke had said yes, if the circumstances justified it. Locke's position was known to a number of well-to-do intellectuals in the American colonies, and they took it to heart. Locke provided an intellectual justification for the colonies' rebellion against the British Empire, its monarch, and its parliament.

The movement toward independence of the United States of America from the British Empire had multiple influences, but we can pick out, in addition to Locke, two major philosophical influences and one significant philosopher who directly inspired the revolution. Chapter 8 mentioned how colonialism had altered the economic dynamic and resulted in increased tensions between nobles and monarchs and the growing importance of trade between the colonies and the home nations. These changes were intensified in the North American colonies for two reasons. These colonies were far removed from the seat of empire, and they were far more populated than other colonies with European, mostly British, settlers who took not just resources but land from the natives. These two factors developed in the colonial settlers an attitude that eventually was called "Manifest Destiny"—the idea that providence had ordained that all of North America should become the property of European settlers. The attitude of destiny fueling settler colonialism tied in with the second philosophical influence. We have seen in previous chapters the gradual move toward accepting the ability of individuals to reason to truth independently. By the 1700s, this acceptance was commonplace among the learned middle class, which was growing as a result of the economic changes. The idea grew of the "self-taught man" (women were still excluded) who could learn for himself, think for himself, and rule himself.

Thomas Paine (1737–1809) had his finger on the pulse of these changes. A strong advocate for American independence and a sharp-witted writer, he wrote "Common Sense," an appeal to individuals to reason for themselves. His assumption was that anyone who could think clearly could realize that the colonies should be independent from England. In "Common Sense," Paine presented philosophical arguments directed at the common person. Paine was clearly influenced by Locke's political theory and similarly argued that government was a convenience established by rational people who find it preferable to live in a society than in a state of nature. He also adopted Locke's notion that people had a right to rebel against the government if the situation justified it. Given these two notions, Paine's task was to show that the situation justified the colonies rebelling against England. Simply stated, he portrayed George III and the English nobility as rulers who contributed nothing to the people. The very idea of a monarchy is false, he argued, because all men are created equal (as long as they were white). The colonies must declare independence and elect their own government that would serve the common interests of the people. The American revolt against England came about predominantly for economic reasons, but there is no denying the philosophical underpinning for the movement for greater self-determination, which reached back to at least Jan Hus (see Chapter 6). These three philosophers inspired not only their eras, but political philosophers in more recent times (see Chapters 24 and 26).

REFERENCES

François, Duc de La Rochefoucauld, *Reflections; or Sentences and Moral Maxims*, Project Gutenberg, https://www.gutenberg.org/ebooks/9105. (accessed March 8, 2021)

Jean-Jacques Rousseau, *The Social Contract*, Project Gutenberg, http://www.gutenberg.org/files/46333/46333-h/46333-h.htm. (accessed March 9, 2021)

Mary Wollstonecraft, *A Vindication of the Rights of Men, Wikisource,* https://en.wikisource.org/w/index.php?title=A_Vindication_of_the_Rights_of_Men/Letter_to_the_Right_Honourable_Edmund_Burke&oldid=2235002. (accessed March 9, 2021)

Mary Wollstonecraft, *A Vindication of the Rights of Woman,* Project Gutenberg, http://www.gutenberg.org/ebooks/3420. (accessed March 9, 2021)

CHAPTER 11

BERKELEY: MATTER DOESN'T MATTER

As you are reading this, are you sitting down? On what are you sitting? A chair, probably. Of what is the chair made? Wood? Plastic? Metal? A combination? And what does science, and common sense, tell us that these things we call wood, plastic, and metal are? We say all of these things are matter. Wood, plastic, metal, and things like chairs that are made from them, we say are all made of matter. Since Aristotle and on through Locke, everyone has believed in matter, and not just philosophers; everyone assumes that the objects of the world are made of matter. George Berkeley (1685–1753) asks a simple and surprising question: Why do we assume matter exists?

The philosophy of George Berkeley (pronounced BARK-lee) is often misunderstood and unfairly mischaracterized. Because he was a cleric, eventually a bishop, some people who are hostile to religion irrationally dismiss Berkeley's argument as religious nonsense. Such dismissal is intellectually dishonest. Berkeley's argument is solid and important philosophy that presents us with a dilemma that we cannot easily dismiss. His argument strikes at the core of our assumptions, calling into question how we perceive the universe and what it actually is.

EXPOSING OUR UNTHINKING ASSUMPTIONS

Berkeley took Descartes' method of questioning and turned it on Locke's empirical philosophy. His first target was Locke's theory of general ideas. Berkeley agrees with Locke that all of our knowledge comes from ideas that come from experience. As mentioned in Chapter 8, British empiricist philosophers used terms slightly differently. Berkeley uses the term "ideas" similarly to how Locke used it, but because Berkeley's focus was on what lay behind our experiences, "ideas" in his writing refers to experiences not concepts. For example, when Berkeley writes about our idea of fire, he refers to our experience of the light and warmth of fire not our concept of fire. That's important, as we shall soon see.

In the introduction to his book, Treatise Concerning the Principles of Human Knowledge (1710), Berkeley takes on Locke's concept that we have abstract ideas, such as the idea of the color green.

> *It is agreed on all hands, that the qualities or modes of things do never really exist each of them apart by itself, and separated from all others, but are mixed, as it were, and blended together, several in the same object.* (*Principles*, Introduction, 7)

Berkeley is dismissing the Platonic idea that Forms exist separate from objects and goes on to explain how we've heard from a number of philosophers that we can hold in our minds the quality "green" or "motion" abstracted from any particular object.

> *But we are told, the mind being able to consider each quality singly, or abstracted from those other qualities with which it is united, does by that means frame to itself abstract ideas....Not that it is possible for color or motion to exist without extension: but only that the mind can frame to itself by abstraction the idea of color exclusive of extension, and of motion exclusive of both color and extension.* (*Treatise*, Introduction, 7)

We saw Locke make this argument that qualities exist only in, not separate from, objects but that we can think about them as abstract ideas. Locke claimed that we experience a number of green objects and abstract from those experiences the idea of "green." Similarly, we experience a number of dogs, and in thinking about dogs in general, we hold in our minds an abstract idea of "dog" without a particular size, color, or other qualities. Locke's mistake, Berkeley said, was in deriving the objective existence of primary qualities through a principle of abstraction. This principle, Berkeley argued, was bogus.

Berkeley critiques Locke's account of abstract ideas in two arguments: We can't do it and we don't need to do it. The first argument, that you can't think of an abstract idea, is simple: Try thinking of the abstract idea of "dog." If you are honest with yourself, what comes to your mind is not an abstract dog of no particular size, color, and so on, as Locke had said. What comes to mind when you think of "dog" is a particular dog; maybe a dog you have or once had or one you saw recently. What you did was focus on an image of a particular dog, which stood as a general idea for all dogs. This may seem a subtle distinction, but a general idea is not the same as an abstract idea. A general idea is a particular idea that stands as an example of a type of object. Whenever we think of such concepts as "tree," "dog," "person," or "green," Berkeley said, we have in our minds a particular idea that stands for all other similar objects.

We can really see this when we think of big concepts like "animal" or "color." We can't hold in our minds an idea of an animal that abstracts all of the qualities that particular birds, fish, lizards, insects, mammals, and so on have in common and ignore individual differences. How many wings and legs would this abstract animal have and what size would it be? Similarly, how can we think of color as having no particular color? We can't; We think of a particular animal or a particular color. Berkeley points out that the very idea of an abstract idea is inconsistent. He quotes Locke's abstract idea of a triangle, an idea that "must be neither oblique nor rectangle, neither equilateral, isosceles, nor scalene, but all and none of these at once" (Locke, *Essay*, II.IV.7). Berkeley counters that such a thing is inconceivable because it is contradictory. A triangle is equilateral, isosceles, or scalene. It can't be all of them. It can't be none of them. Where Berkeley seems to make a mistake is to assume that if we have an idea that does not specify a particular quality—such as the idea of an animal of no specific color—that means we are thinking of an object that lacks that quality—an animal with no color. True, an animal with no color is nonsensical, but is that what we are doing when we think of what is common among all animals? Are we ever denying that animals have color? What Berkeley doesn't take into account is that we can have a concept about objects that are separate from a particular idea of a particular object.

Berkeley's stronger second argument, that we don't need abstract ideas, harkens back to William's nominalism. Locke believed that only particulars exist, not universals, as almost everyone did by that time, Platonic Forms having been dismissed. Berkeley says that we only ever encounter particular entities, never abstract entities. As he showed in his first argument, we think in terms of particular ideas. These particular ideas can function as general ideas, but they are always particulars. What, then, are words? Berkeley says that "it seems that a word becomes general by being made the sign, not of an abstract general idea but, of several particular ideas, any one of which it indifferently suggests to the mind" (*Treatise,* Introduction 11). Words like "tree" or "dog" stand in general for all the particular ideas we have for trees or dogs in general. The principle of Ockham's razor holds that the simpler of two explanations is more probably true. Following this principle, Berkeley holds, as William had, that words are signs that we use to denote objects or kinds of objects; they are not entities that exist outside our minds. There is no need to postulate that there are abstract ideas.

RETHINKING PRIMARY AND SECONDARY QUALITIES

Armed with his disproof of abstract ideas, Berkeley turned his sights on Locke's theory of primary and secondary qualities. Locke had said that primary qualities exist in objects themselves, whereas secondary qualities are powers that external objects possess to produce ideas that reside in us. This, Berkeley argued, was a fiction. Berkeley offered multiple arguments demonstrating that both primary and secondary qualities exist only within the perceiving mind. For brevity, we'll look only at two: the perceptions of pain and of color.

Locke had argued that pain and pleasure were secondary qualities because these sensations existed in the perceiver, not in the objects. A fire can cause us pain if we stick our hand in it, but we would not say that the pain is in the fire; the pain is in us. Pleasure is the same. Food gives us feelings of pleasure, but we wouldn't say those feelings are present in the food, only within us. Berkeley answers that pain and pleasure must exist only when they are perceived, only when they are experienced by a mind. That means that every quality that is experienced as a pain or pleasure (temperature, smells, tastes) exists only when it is perceived. You can reply with the reasonable objection that heat exists in the external object and that this causes pain in us. Berkeley's equally reasonable response is that we have only one distinct sensation of intense heat *as* pain and it is artificial to separate them. Temperature is experienced in a range of sensations corresponding to a range of pain and pleasure—too hot, too cold, and just right.

Berkeley also examines our perceptions of color, which Locke and others had labeled a secondary property. Berkeley uses color to argue that we cannot separate our ideas of primary and secondary qualities because we always perceived them together.

We never perceive green all by itself. We perceive green grass, green leaves, green shirts, and other green things. If, as Locke says, color and other secondary qualities are mind dependent and do not inhere in objects themselves, then so must be the primary qualities we perceive like size and shape. Here's an example:

How wide is this black circle? Width is a primary quality, right? You can measure it, and it is an objective quality of the object, yes? So how would you measure the width of the circle? You'd need a measuring device—a ruler, but how would you use that ruler to measure the circle's width? You say you would place the zero mark on your ruler at one edge of the circle and measure to the other edge, yes? Great! So how do you know where the edge of the circle is? The edge would be where the color changes, correct? The edge is where the black stops. But color is a secondary quality. It's mind dependent, Locke says. But if the only way we can perceive the width of the circle is by the secondary quality of color, how is width not also mind dependent? This is true of every object we perceive through the sense of sight. Look at the walls of the room you are in. This example has long worked well for me in classrooms, which invariably are painted a dull off-white. I ask the students where the corners of the room are. You can perceive where one wall ends and another begins by the subtle differences in shading of the off-white colors. Even if we accept Locke's argument that those differences are caused by the different ways light reflects off objects, we still know only the simple ideas of sensation in our minds. Our experiences of colors and, thus, of walls and ceilings, and circles, and everything are mind-dependent secondary qualities. At least, that's Berkeley's argument, and it is difficult to say he's incorrect.

When we analyze our concepts in our minds and our language, Berkeley argued, we will see that the "curtain of words" deceives us. Like Bacon did (see Chapter 8), Berkeley holds that we put too much faith in our language and that our words obscure what is going on behind them. In the case of Locke's abstract ideas, the words used to stand for them, like "color" and "texture," seem to indicate a reality. Berkeley counters that when we remove the idol of the words, we see that there are really no distinctions between primary and secondary qualities and no such things as abstract ideas.

Well, if we accept Berkley's claim that there is no distinction between primary and secondary qualities, we can still trust that our ideas of primary qualities are representations of the objects, right? Here, too, Berkeley has a strong argument to refute Locke. It's actually Locke's argument, or rather Locke's admission, that Berkeley justifiably leverages against Locke. We saw in Chapter 8 that we can't leave the sealed chamber of our mind to compare our ideas with objects in the world. Berkeley correctly points out that if we can perceive only our own ideas, then Locke has no basis for claiming that our ideas resemble the primary qualities of objects because he can't compare the two.

MATTER DOESN'T MATTER

George Berkeley asks a simple question. Why do we assume matter exists? Matter had always been assumed in philosophy, and by everyone actually. Locke equated matter with the abstract idea of substance. Substance is a definite weak spot in Locke's philosophy, and Locke was aware of it. He said that objects must be composed of a "something-I-know-not-what" that must be what has the power to create the simple ideas of sensation in our minds. Locke assumed this "I know not what" was matter. Locke had to concede that we never have an experience of matter but only of the effects of matter on us.

As we've seen, Berkeley argued that both primary and secondary qualities exist only when they are perceived. Not surprisingly, then, Berkeley also argues that all external objects that people assume to be composed of matter exist only when they are perceived.

> *It is indeed an opinion* ***strangely*** *prevailing amongst men, that houses, mountains, rivers, and in a word all sensible objects have an existence natural or real, distinct from their being perceived by the understanding. But with how great an assurance and acquiescence soever this principle may be entertained in the world; yet whoever shall find in his heart to call it in question, may, if I mistake not, perceive it to involve a manifest contradiction. For what are the forementioned objects but the things we perceive by sense, and what do we* ***perceive besides our own ideas or sensations****; and is it not plainly repugnant that any one of these or any combination of them should exist unperceived?* (*Treatise* 4; emphasis his)

Yes, the only things we perceive are our own ideas. Locke said as much. Berkeley is willing to accept the full consequences of this, even though they lead to an extreme conclusion: Matter does not exist.

Berkeley argued that Locke's idea of substance was a conclusion relying on an abstraction that close scrutiny would reveal to be a mistake. Again, Locke held that there is a "real" tree with primary qualities and material substance that cause simple ideas of sensation in us. Berkeley responds that if substance is a "something-I-know-not-what," then why should we assume its existence? We can't say that our sensations of the tree correspond to a "real" tree because we can't compare our ideas with external objects. Instead, Berkeley states that our experiences of a tree are not caused by a "real" tree beneath appearances. Our experiences of the tree *are* the real tree.

Where does our idea of matter come from? Berkeley asks. We have no sensation of matter, something to which Locke has to agree. We also have to agree. Samuel Johnson, a learned man of the time, said he refuted Berkeley by kicking a rock, making the assumption that his material foot kicked a material rock thus proving matter exists. But that's a specious objection. Johnson can say no more than that he has an idea of a foot and an idea of a rock and an idea that they interacted. If you kick a stone, what does that prove? You experience the idea of solidity of the stone in your foot and the idea of the stone moving. Ideas. A series of sensations. It doesn't at all disprove Berkeley's philosophy. All we have are ideas and beliefs about our ideas. We can't demonstrate otherwise.

We never, ever experience matter, and, in fact, we have no need to assume that matter exists. Nowhere is Berkeley suggesting that there is no mind-independent reality. He is questioning the philosophical conception of matter, not the existence of a world outside our mind. However, Berkeley says the idea of substance is a mistake as are the ideas of universals. You probably dismissed Plato's idea that universals exist, right? So, here's why we should dismiss the idea of matter. Berkeley argues that the essence of objects is that they are perceived.

> *Attend to what is meant by the term "exist," when applied to sensible things. The table I write on I say exists, that is, I see and feel it; and if I were out of my study I should say it existed—meaning thereby that if I was in my study I might perceive it, or that some other spirit actually does perceive it. There was an odor, that is, it was smelt; there was a sound, that is, it was heard; a color or figure, and it was perceived by sight or touch. This is all that I can understand by these and the like expressions. For as to what is said of the absolute existence of unthinking things without any relation to their being perceived, that seems perfectly unintelligible. Their ESSE is PERCIPI (their essence is being perceived), nor is it possible they should have any existence out of the minds or [of the] thinking things which perceive them.* (*Treatise* 3)

The essence of any object is not material substance, as Aristotle had said and everyone since had gone along with. The essence of any object is to be perceived or known. "All those bodies which compose the mighty frame of the world, have not any subsistence without a mind, that their BEING (ESSE) is to be perceived or known." (*Treatise* 6) Think about this. If you are in a classroom, think about your bed at home. If you are at home, think about your classroom. If you are not in a place, why do you think this place and the things in it exist? What basis do you have to believe that any particular thing exists if you are not perceiving it? You are tempted to reply, "because other people perceive those things when I don't." That's correct, and you prove Berkeley's point. We believe that something exists only if someone perceives it. (Yes, even nonmaterial things, but that's another topic.) You go home because you believe that you will perceive home once you get there. You come back to a classroom because you believe you will be able to perceive what is in that room once you are there. The essence of existence is being perceived. Matter doesn't matter; being perceived does.

WHAT CAUSES OUR IDEAS? BERKELEY'S SIMPLE SOLUTION

Here's the thing. If matter doesn't actually exist, but something nonmaterial is causing these impressions we have of objects, how would our experiences be different? The answer is—not at all. You are reading this, either as a paper book or as an e-book on a screen. Either way, all you have is your perception of these words. All that exists for you are your ideas about these words. You have no idea about what is behind those words. The same is true for everything. Take a table or desk. Why do you believe it exists? Well, to simplify things, let's take the top of a table. You believe it's a tabletop because when you perceive your hand touching it you perceive qualities like flatness and hardness. But that is *all* you perceive—those qualities. You don't perceive what causes those ideas. What that cause is does not matter; the sensations you experience would be the same.

Interestingly, Berkeley believes in the active mind, unlike Hobbes and Locke. One knows that one causes some of one's own ideas, Berkeley says (*Treatise* 28), and that's important for Berkeley: Minds create ideas. However, the mind is also passive when perceiving external objects, so there are ideas that one's own mind does not cause. Therefore, Berkeley concludes, only another mind can be a cause. "There is therefore some other will or spirit that produces them" (*Treatise* 29). This, for Berkeley, is where God comes in. It's not an argument like Descartes using the idea of God as a prop for a larger argument. It's more akin to the arguments of Plato, Plotinus, and Augustine—God as the source of all existence and understanding. Everything that exists is ideas in the cosmic mind. Berkeley's basic principle of "*esse est percipi*" ("to be is to be perceived") requires a "first perceiver" or cosmic mind to be the cause of all existing objects that we can experience. It oversimplifies things a bit to say that we are all living inside the mind of God, but that's not too far off. Berkeley's idealism (everything is thought) perhaps sounds weird, but it shares the same foundation with quantum mechanics in that reality is dependent on the observer. We'll see a similar philosophy from Fichte in Chapter 14.

It's important to remember that Berkeley is not at all denying that there is an external reality. His theory is an attempt not to multiply entities needlessly, according to Ockham's razor. Berkeley sees the prevailing assumption of our perception as needlessly complex. He argues that Locke's view theorizes that there is an immaterial God who created material objects that are perceived by a material human body and understood by an immaterial human mind. If we apply the principle of Ockham's Razor, Berkeley's theory of perception is simpler. There is an immaterial God who created immaterial objects that are perceived and understood by an immaterial human mind. There is still an external reality that causes our perceptions of ideas; Berkeley just offers a more elegant explanation for it.

The science of Berkeley's time was based on the assumption of matter, and Berkeley was upending the basis of that science. And yet, Berkeley is not denying science. His books, *Essay Towards a New Theory of Vision* (1709) and *The Analyst* (1734), were scientific works of high quality. Whether it is matter or a cosmic mind that causes our perceptions, everything about our science remains the same. Scientific experimentation and observation are nothing more than our perceptions—ideas in our minds. Scientific instruments don't alter this fact because, again, their measurements and readings are simply perceptions—ideas in our minds. Again, matter doesn't matter. Our ideas or perceptions are all we have.

All of this contradicts our commonsense assumptions of matter, so it's difficult to take in. If you think Berkeley is being irrational, keep in mind that we see a seemingly opposite but actually quite similar reasoning by materialists today. Whereas Berkeley assumes ideas, the materialists assume matter. Any criticism you have of Berkeley's argument applies equally to anyone who argues for matter.

Regardless, we can't disprove Berkeley's theory. No one has. We can correctly say that Berkeley is making an assumption that he can't prove, and Berkeley admits this. His motive is not to prove God but to challenge our assumptions, though Berkeley certainly wouldn't mind if you accepted that God creates everything.

REFERENCES

George Berkeley, *A Treatise Concerning the Principles of Human Knowledge*, Project Gutenberg, http://www.gutenberg.org/ebooks/4723. (accessed March 12, 2021).

John Locke, *Essay Concerning Human Understanding*, Project Gutenberg, http://www.gutenberg.org/files/10615/10615-h/10615-h.htm. (accessed March 12, 2021).

CHAPTER 12

HUME: THE END OF PHILOSOPHY?

David Hume's (1711–1776) philosophy was the culmination of the trajectory of British empiricism (see Chapters 8 and 11). Hume's shocking conclusion was that the long quest for understanding had reached no true understanding at all. Descartes was not a true skeptic because he believed that knowledge is possible. Hume was a true skeptic in that he genuinely doubted that real knowledge was possible. Is scientific and philosophical knowledge possible? Does it make a difference in our lives? Yes and no, is what Hume's philosophy tells us.

In Hume's time, science was rebuilding the structures of knowledge, but he was disturbed by the looseness he saw in these structures. Similar to Descartes, Hume thought that all was not well with the foundations of science and knowledge:

> *There is nothing which is not the subject of debate, and in which men of learning are not of contrary opinions. The most trivial question escapes not our controversy, and in the most momentous we are not able to give any certain decision. Disputes are multiplied, as if every thing was uncertain; and these disputes are managed with the greatest warmth,*

as if every thing was certain. Amidst all this bustle 'tis not reason, which carries the prize, but eloquence; and no man needs ever despair of gaining proselytes to the most extravagant hypothesis, who has art enough to represent it in any favorable colors. (Treatise of Human Nature, Introduction 2)

Hume's claim is that debates in science and philosophy are based on flowery language more than on reason, something that perhaps is still the case today. Hume equates this situation with the reality that all of the sciences are related to human nature but that we have little understanding of human nature. Rather than wading into the lingering, tedious scholastic skirmishes at the periphery, he resolved to march to the center of all the sciences—human nature. Hume decided that philosophy needed to establish the foundations for all other disciplines, the science of humanity being the foundation of all other sciences, and the application of experimental philosophy being the only method of understanding human nature. Hume sought to lay down the foundations of the physical sciences, but he ended up destroying all hope for certain scientific knowledge.

HUME'S EPISTEMOLOGY

Hume, being Scottish, was educated in the British empiricist tradition, so it is no surprise that his exploration of human nature begins in epistemology. He respected Locke's epistemology, but because he took seriously Berkeley's critique of Locke, Hume felt he needed to begin again with an analysis of our perceptions and consciousness. Hume uses terms differently than philosophers before him did, though the concepts are largely the same. You need to keep straight his particular usage of terms. The main term that is difficult is Hume's use of "ideas," a term he said we wanted to restore to its original sense, "from which Mr. Locke had perverted it, in making it stand for all our perceptions." (*Treatise*, I.I.I, fn 1)

Hume said that introspection shows us that our perceptions of the world fall into two classes: impressions and ideas.

By the term "impression," then, I mean all our more lively perceptions, when we hear, or see, or feel, or love, or hate, or desire, or will. And impressions are distinguished from ideas, which are the less lively perceptions, of which we are conscious, when we reflect on any of those sensations or movements above mentioned. (*Enquiry*, II.12)

Locke talks about simple ideas of sensation and reflection, but Hume labels the former "impressions" and the latter "ideas." Take that into account, and Hume and Locke are similar in their epistemology. They agree that everything in the mind comes from sense experience and every idea in the mind is a representation of impressions.

In Hume's epistemology, impressions may be either sensations (seeing a tree) or the immediate and original contents of our own psychological states (I feel happy). For Hume, when we experience anything, either an object or our own thoughts or feelings, those are impressions, but they immediately become ideas or memories. Our ideas are copies of impressions that become increasingly faint over time. There is a direct one-to-one correspondence between impressions and ideas. Every one of our ideas directly comes from an impression. Hume says:

> *Every idea which we examine is copied from a similar impression. Those who would assert that this position is not universally true nor without exception, have only one, and that an easy method of refuting it; by producing that idea, which, in their opinion, is not derived from this source.* (*Enquiry*, II.14)

Our thinking, Hume says, is a processing of ideas that come only from original impressions.

Hume is more pessimistic than Locke is about the powers of the human mind. Hume adopts the model of the passive mind. For him, the creative power of the mind amounts to no more than combining, resizing, and switching around ideas provided by ideas. For Hume, all ideas originate from impressions, each of which is distinct and exists only for a brief moment, disconnected from any other. The human mind is just a kind of theater where ideas come and go. As we shall soon see, this belief of Hume's has serious consequences.

A SCIENCE OF THE MIND

On the basis of his conception of impressions and ideas, Hume wanted to create a science of the mind. Locke had offered one, but Hume believed that Locke had failed to explain fully how simple ideas became complex ideas. Hume sought to identify the "bond of union" or a "gentle force" that constituted a kind of mental gravity that brought together particular ideas into association. For example, the idea of touching fire is associated with the idea of pain, not pleasure. A certain shade of green is associated with grass but not cows and so on. Hume thought that because particular sets of ideas introduce each other with a certain degree of method and regularity, it was evident that we could identify three principles of the association of ideas: (1) resemblance, (2) contiguity, and (3) cause and effect.

Hume's first principle is resemblance. Ideas with similar features tend to be associated with each other. A cartoon caricature reminds you of someone real because they share similarities. Different particular trees resemble each other, and you can compare and contrast their appearances. Second is the principle of contiguity. If you look at a building, you see the rows of windows, and these impressions lead to ideas that behind the windows are rooms that are connected to other rooms in the building. We frequently move from one idea to another in this way, just as we would bodily move from one room to another. The third principle, and one that will become especially important for Hume, is causation, or cause and effect. Certain pairs of impressions follow one another frequently. Whenever we touch fire, we shortly afterward feel pain. When one impression regularly succeeds another, we associate the former with causing the latter.

These "gentle forces" of association operate entirely without any conscious willing on our part. It is not something that we control, like natural objects are controlled by the force of gravity. Hume does not quite go to the extreme of saying we entirely lack free will, but he implies it. Hume sees our minds being like a cork in the ocean, bobbed about by the waves around us. This is why he sees there being no evidence that we have a self, but more on that later.

REASONING ABOUT OUR IDEAS

Hume adopted the conception that there are two types of reasoning. He took the concepts from Gottfried Leibniz, the German polymath who invented calculus. Leibniz's labels of "analytic" and "synthetic" for these two types of reasoning are what survive, thanks to Kant, as we will see in Chapter 13, but Hume's labels describe the same concepts.

> *All the objects of human reason or enquiry may naturally be divided into two kinds, to wit, relations of ideas, and matters of fact. Of the first kind are the sciences of geometry, algebra, and arithmetic; and in short, every affirmation which is either intuitively or demonstratively*

certain. That the square of the hypothenuse is equal to the square of the two sides, is a proposition which expresses a relation between these figures....Matters of fact, which are the second objects of human reason, are not ascertained in the same manner; nor is our evidence of their truth, however great, of a like nature with the foregoing. The contrary of every matter of fact is still possible; because it can never imply a contradiction, and is conceived by the mind with the same facility and distinctness, as if ever so conformable to reality. That the sun will not rise to-morrow is no less intelligible a proposition, and implies no more contradiction than the affirmation, that it will rise. We should in vain, therefore, attempt to demonstrate its falsehood. Were it demonstratively false, it would imply a contradiction, and could never be distinctly conceived by the mind. (*Enquiry*, IV.20-21)

Relations of ideas are propositions that must be true because their negation leads to a contradiction. An example of that is the proposition "all unmarried men are bachelors" whose negation "all unmarried men are not bachelors" is a contradiction of the two ideas, unmarried men and bachelors. In the same way, all of the propositions of logic, geometry, and algebra are necessarily true relations of ideas. We can be absolutely certain of the truth of relations of ideas.

Unlike relations of ideas, matters of fact are not ascertained through reason but are based on our past observations of the world. Matters of fact are propositions the contrary of which are still possible because they can never imply a contradiction. Hume's example is this: "*That the sun will not rise to-morrow* is no less intelligible a proposition, and implies no more contradiction than the affirmation, *that it will rise.*" (*Enquiry*, IV.21) If the sun does not rise tomorrow, though it may surprise you, it would not be a logical contradiction. Matters of fact are very different kinds of propositions from relations of ideas in that we can't be absolutely certain of any matter of fact. A good litmus test is this. If you can imagine the opposite of a proposition, it is a matter of fact; if you can't, it is a relation of ideas. You can't imagine a triangle without three sides, so the proposition "triangles have three sides" is a relation of ideas. You can imagine the sun not rising tomorrow, so the proposition "the sun will rise tomorrow" is a matter of presumed fact.

Another example might clarify what is going on here. There is a table in this room. It is a fact because of the impression we have in our mind of the presence of a table. But the opposite possible fact, that there is no table in this room is not logically impossible. Of course a room could be without a table. No amount of logic can determine whether there is a table in the room because there is no logical necessity for there to be a table in the room. You have to observe the world to gain knowledge of the facts. Will the sun rise tomorrow? You don't know! You have to wait to find out. And as we shall see Hume tell us, your thought, "but of course the sun will rise again because it has always happened before," is not a guarantee that it will happen again.

The point is that it is not *logic* that tells us about tables and sunrises. Hume completely agrees with William's contention that logic tells us nothing about the world. Matters of fact have to be discovered through observation and experience. Hume used the literary example of the first human, Adam, to illustrate the need for experience.

> *Adam, though his rational faculties be supposed, at the very first, entirely perfect, could not have inferred from the fluidity and transparency of water that it would suffocate him, or from the light and warmth of fire that it would consume him. No object ever discovers, by the qualities which appear to the senses, either the causes which produced it, or the effects which will arise from it; nor can our reason, unassisted by experience, ever draw any inference concerning real existence and matter of fact.* (*Enquiry*, IV.I.23)

We know that water drowns people only because humans have drowned in water. Thinking based on experience can explain this association of the ideas of water and drowning, but it could not have told us prior to experience what effect it will have on us. Hume's point is that there is a gulf between the realm of reason and the realm of experience. Proof of his point that reality does not conform to the ideas in our reason is that since Hume's time, scientists have learned that euclidean geometry does not always work to explain facts of the universe (and let's not even start on quantum mechanics).

Hume's empiricism states that impressions are the strong and vivid originals of experience and therefore have priority in our knowledge. Impressions literally force themselves on us. Sights and sounds happen to us, and Locke was correct that we passively receive them. Ideas are different in two ways. First, they are feeble and derivative copies of impressions, but, second, we seem to have at least some control over them—we actively think about ideas. Hume wants to establish the rule that every one of our ideas must be tied to a corresponding original impression for it to be valid. Any idea, and especially any philosophical term, that cannot be traced to an original impression is empty and useless. It does not have even the faint content of a legitimate idea. Using this rule, we can "banish all that jargon which has so long taken possession of metaphysical reasonings and drawn disgrace upon them." (*Enquiry*, II.17)

TWO EMPTY IDEAS

Hume says we need to consider every idea as to whether it is a relation of ideas or a matter of fact. This may seem a simply academic enterprise, but Hume's fork (the fork in the road between relations of ideas and matters of fact), as it has come to be known, reveals some very interesting things. The first target of Hume's fork is the long-held philosophical idea of substance. Locke had argued that substance must be assumed, even though we could not experience it, because there must be something, we know not what it is, to which the properties of objects inhere. But this idea failed Hume's rule: The notion of substance could not be tied to an original impression or found as necessary in logic, so substance was neither a reaction of ideas nor a matter of fact. Hume accepted Berkeley's critique of Locke's primary and secondary qualities distinction and agreed with Berkeley that the idea of material substance has no basis in our experience. Therefore, Locke the empiricist is believing in something his empiricism forbids him from believing. Hume is also an empiricist in that he argues that we know anything only through experience, but Hume thinks that to be consistent, he needs to reject the idea of substance. All that we can know about the world is the flow of impressions we receive. We have impressions but never any perception of what causes those impressions. Again, we perceive no proper identity that we can ascribe to anything that could be substance. Hume is not denying that there is an external world, only that we have no evidence to justify that belief fully.

Also falling to Hume's rule is the idea that we have a self. This is the most difficult of Hume's ideas to grasp, but he is on solid ground. Hume writes that, "It is certain there is no question in philosophy more abstruse than that concerning identity, and the nature of the uniting principle, which constitutes a person"; however, "it is evident these ideas of self and person are never very fixed nor determinate. It is absurd, therefore, to imagine the senses can ever distinguish betwixt ourselves and external objects." (*Enquiry*, IV.II.6) This is another way that Hume shows that he took Berkeley's philosophy seriously.

Why do you think you are a self? A self, meaning a distinctive "I." This is a different question from "why do you think you exist?" Descartes—well, Augustine before him—had conclusively proven that if thinking is happening then that thinking thing exists. Hume is giving us a different conundrum: Awareness of impressions and thinking about ideas is happening, but why do we think this means there is an "I," an enduring self underneath these impressions and ideas? Hume correctly states that "there are some philosophers who imagine we are every moment intimately conscious of what we call our SELF; that we feel its existence and its continuance in existence." (*Enquiry*, IV.VI.1) Descartes and Berkeley are two of those philosophers, and almost everyone would tend to agree that we think we are conscious of a self that is the "I."

Hume concludes that there is no self, no "I," because he has no impression of it. "I never can catch myself at any time without a perception, and never can observe any thing but the perception" (*Enquiry*, IV.VI.1). Oddly, Hume here is taking Descartes' "I think, therefore, I am a thinking being" more literally than Descartes did, for Hume is saying that our existence is simply the collections of perceptions and we never perceive a self that is connected to those perceptions. We are *nothing* but perceptions:

> *[We perceive] nothing but a bundle or collection of different perceptions, which succeed each other with an inconceivable rapidity, and are in a perpetual flux and movement. Our eyes cannot turn in their sockets without varying our perceptions. Our thought is still more variable than our sight; and all our other senses and faculties contribute to this change; nor is there any single power of the soul, which remains unalterably the same, perhaps for one moment. The mind is a kind of theatre, where several perceptions successively make their appearance; pass, re-pass, glide away, and mingle in an infinite variety of postures and situations. There is properly no simplicity in it at one time, nor identity in different; whatever natural propension we may have to imagine that simplicity and identity. The comparison of the theatre must not mislead us. They are the successive perceptions only, that constitute the mind; nor have we the most distant notion of the place, where these scenes are represented, or of the materials, of which it is composed.* (Enquiry, IV.VI.1)

Let what Hume is claiming sink in. Your mind is a series of impressions and ideas, but there is no "you" behind them; your mind isn't even a stage on which these impressions and ideas occur. There are only the flickering of images or shadows. This constant variation and interruption of perceptions means, he says, that there is no proper identity that we can ascribe to anything that could be called a self. Thoughts happen, and there isn't even an "I" to which they happen; they simply happen like so many other motions in the world. That is what Hume is claiming.

If we reject the idea of material substance because we can't tie it to an original impression of it, so too must we reject the idea of a self, whether or not we call it a mental or spiritual substance or simply a human "me." Your first instinct is to say that of course you have a self. Well, when do you ever experience a self? Oh, sure, you have impressions of confusion (like now), feeling disturbed (also like now), and all the other emotions and thoughts you have, but analyze deeply every one of those thoughts and feelings and you will not find a self. You experience only those surface impressions just like you experience only the surface impressions of the properties of objects. You never experience the objects themselves, and you never experience a self itself. Hume's theory of the mind says that there is no coherent self that underlies the stream of consciousness, which is itself just a bundle of impressions. And you never experience a "me" that is having these impressions. Or at least that is Hume's claim.

The third victim of Hume's fork is our idea of causation, a critique that strikes at the foundation of science and knowledge.

CAUSALITY AND SCIENCE

Hume's most challenging arguments are against science. He was in no way against science, but he became aware that science makes assumptions that are on shaky ground. Like Berkeley's argument against matter, Hume's arguments against scientific reasoning have no easy refutation.

Hume says that there are three main assumptions of science: that the present and future behave like the past, that we have impressions of causation, and that we can reason from effect to cause. On the first assumption, our default, unthinking way of dealing with the world is to assume that if the impression of the table in a room today is identical to the impression of the table the last time we saw it in the room, that it is the same table. Hume points out that we have no solid rational reason for our assumption that similarity of impression equals similarity of identity. Someone could have switched tables that look the same. This may seem a silly argument, but science is based on such an assumption, and Hume points out that it has no rational basis. The problem for science is that all scientific beliefs in laws assume that the objects and forces operated the same in the past as they do now and will continue to operate the same in the future. What if this is not the case? Hume points out that if gravity started operating differently tomorrow, this would not violate logic. Much of Hume's arguments in the mid-1700s is directed at academia's still lingering belief in the logical approach of Scholasticism (see Chapter 5).

Science's second assumption is the target of Hume's most devastating critique: causation. We never have an impression of causation, Hume points out. Hume's argument is that the reason that you concluded the hammer caused the pain in your thumb is because you had an impression of the hammer hitting your thumb and immediately afterward you felt an impression of pain in your thumb. But this is correlation not causation. We have not experienced the actual causation of the impression of the hammer on the impression of pain. This can be seen if we conditioned someone by shining a light before we secretly flipped a switch opening a door. The person, not seeing us flip the switch, would come to conclude that the light switching on is what caused the door to open, but this would be an incorrect assumption.

Here's an example that Hume uses that I will describe more fully. Consider a game of billiards. In the game, we see a white ball moving in a straight line across the billiard table toward a red ball. Then we see the white ball appear to come in contact with the red ball. Then we see the red ball move. We experience three separate impressions. But we assume that the white ball has caused the red ball to move. Why? Hume asks where we find the impression of *causality*. That the red ball moved is not the question; *why* the red ball moved is. It is an imagined assumption on our part that the white ball caused the red ball to move, and it is no more than the influence of custom, Hume said, to believe with certainty that it will do so again.

This is a difficult argument to grasp, but work with me here. Let's briefly return to Hume's earlier sun example. Hume says we have observed the sun rise every day, so we have come to expect that the sun will rise tomorrow. But the relation between the fact "the sunrise has always happened" and the proposition "the sun will rise tomorrow" is not a necessarily true relation of ideas. That is because the proposition "the sun will not rise tomorrow" is not a contradiction. It would not be contrary to reason if the sunrise did not happen tomorrow. Obviously that would be a surprise to us, but that is Hume's eventual point.

Back to the billiard balls. If we saw the white ball come in contact with the red ball and the red ball did not move, would that be a logical contradiction? Well, remember our litmus test. Can we imagine the red ball staying still when the moving white ball comes in contact with it? Of course; therefore, it is not logically *necessary* that the white ball will make the red ball move. We will find the same to be true about every single cause-and-effect relation in which we believe.

"Wait a minute," you might say, "we can demonstrate that white balls striking red balls will cause the red ball to move." Hume would say you are making a mistake of reasoning. You appeal to science, thinking, "Can't we prove this scientifically?" Well, let's construct a scientific experiment. We'll conduct 100 trials of white balls striking red balls and record the results. We do this, and we record the data that 100 times the white ball struck the red ball and 100 times the red ball moved, and you feel this vindicates your proposition that white balls striking red balls causes red balls to move. All right, I say, what if we did a 101st trial. Would you say the red ball will move again? "Of course!" you reply. Can you imagine the red ball not moving? Yes, you can. It is not logically impossible for the red ball not to move when the white ball strikes it. Therefore, our experiment has not established a *necessary* causal connection. We have only recorded a pattern of past behavior. Nor have we ever observed causation, or a cause-and-effect relationship. In each trial, we saw only three separate impressions. We saw a white ball moving toward a red ball; we saw the white ball come in contact with the red ball; we saw the red ball move. That's all we observed. We did not observe the necessary connection between these separate impressions that establishes causation.

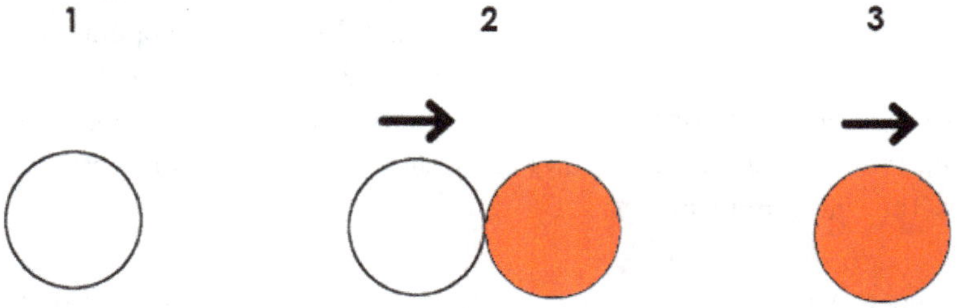

Hume said that we imagine causation on the basis of our experiences. We imagine causality because we experience contiguity between certain events; in this case, the white and red balls appear contiguous in space. We also experience priority in time. We experience impressions in a certain order; in this case, we always experience the order as 1, 2, and then 3 in our graphic, never another order. We also experience them in constant conjunction, meaning that we have witnessed the impressions 1, 2, and 3 conjoined repeatedly. These are real matters of fact, we have experienced them, and Hume says we add to these impressions the further idea that there is a necessary connection between these events. We observe X followed by Y, so we infer that all similar occurrences of X will be followed by similar occurrences of Y. We infer it, but we cannot *prove* it as a certain relation of ideas. It is at most a probable correlation, but as any good scientist should know, correlation is not causation.

Hume's argument about causation has enormous implications for science. Everything in science is predicated on cause-and-effect relations, from the motions of the planets to the workings of cells. But if we never have an impression of causation, what faith can we place in our science? Is our faith in physics, chemistry, biology, and all of the others misplaced?

This is a big problem because, as we can see in Hume's arguments, science not only assumes causation without a rational basis but most of its arguments depend on assuming that from effects we can reason to causes. This is science's third assumption. For example, when a paleontologist finds fossil bones, he or she tries to determine what caused the bones. The paleontologist looks at other bones, including from animals alive today, and tries to infer what animal in the past created the fossil bones. The paleontologist is doing science and is relying on three assumptions: causation (that we can know that a particular something caused these bones), that the past behaved like the present (that we can reason from present examples to what happened in the past), and that we can reason from an effect to a cause (that we can infer from this bone [the effect] what caused the bone). All other sciences make the same assumptions and operate similarly. Intertwined within that reasoning from effect to cause is science's assumption that the future will operate as it has in the past. We've touched on this point previously, but it is worth mentioning that there is absolutely no reason to believe, on the basis of either reason or experience, that even the most fundamental laws of physics will continue to operate in the future as they have in the past.

Hume is not suggesting that we give up on science. He is suggesting that our science is based on assumptions born of *habit*, not reason, and that this should concern us. Reason cannot prove our most fundamental beliefs about how the universe operates. We must give up the pretension that our reason and science give us perfect knowledge. Instead, we must accept that human knowledge is inference based on inexact ideas of fleeting impressions molded by social customs and personal habits.

THE SOURCE OF MORALITY

Hume also applies the primacy of our habits to an explanation of moral philosophy, a field he remarked was even less developed than geometry or physics. One's morality is a reflection of how one thinks the world is, and this is definitely the case for Hume. His moral theory applies his thoughts on perception and reason discussed earlier. He asks whether moral judgments are relations of ideas—in other words, can they be determined through reason alone? He rejects the long-held tradition that moral laws are as evident to reason as are the rules of geometry. He counters that reason is wholly inactive in being a source of a sense of morals. Reason can tell us what is true, but it can't answer moral questions about what we ought to do. A merchant can use reason to tally the business's accounts accurately, but reason cannot tell the merchant not to cheat customers. Reason can never produce an action, Hume says. That is the province of the will, and Hume takes the same position as did John Duns Scotus (see Chapter 6) that the will is superior to the intellect. Hume connects the will with Hobbes's idea (see Chapter 9) that people are moved by aversions to pains and desires for pleasures, so it is not our reason but our will, acting on the prospects of pain and pleasure, that chooses our actions.

If moral judgments are made by personal will rather than reason, does that mean that they are matters of fact that can be derived from experience? No, said Hume, and we can show this by examining willful murder. Imagine you are walking along a sidewalk and you see a human body lying face down under some nearby bushes. You approach to see what has happened, and you notice the body is lifeless, covered in blood, with a large knife handle sticking out from the back. You can induce from the impressions before you that this person has been murdered. But, Hume asks, examine it as you will, and see if you can find the moral wrong in the sense impressions of the scene before you. If you are honest, you can never see, hear, smell, touch, or taste moral wrongness. It is not a matter of fact discoverable through observation.

If we can't reason to moral truths or discover them in the world, then are we without any sense of morality? No, Hume says, morality is within us:

> *The vice [of murder] entirely escapes you, as long as you consider the object. You never can find it, till you turn your reflection into your own breast, and find a sentiment of disapprobation, which arises in you, towards this action. Here is a matter of fact; but it is the object of feeling, not of reason. It lies in yourself, not in the object. So that when you pronounce any action or character to be vicious, you mean nothing, but that from the constitution of your nature you have a feeling or sentiment of blame from the contemplation of it. (Treatise,* III.I.I.25)

When you look at the murdered person, the wrongness is not something you observe in the external objects; it is something you *feel* within you. Feelings are not subject to reason; they are passions that are part of our will. That is why Hume makes the astonishing statement that "It is not contrary to reason to prefer the destruction of the whole world to the scratching of my finger" (*Treatise*, II.III.VI.6). We are moved to avoid pain, and reason alone doesn't tell us that I shouldn't prefer everyone else be destroyed to my suffering a cut to my finger. Human society survives, Hume said, because most of us feel positive sentiments and sympathy for others, and these desires incline us to work together for our mutual benefit. Sentiment for our fellow human beings is the source of morality, Hume concludes, and we need not look further than that. We desire good for each other, and we are averse to the suffering of others. Obviously, this is not universally the case, as we know all too well from the examples of atrocities that people commit. Hume acknowledges this and observes that people feel more sentiment for those close to them than for those distant from them, but even then we are capable of feeling moral approval and disapproval for acts thousands of miles away or hundreds of years ago. We are feeling beings, and that is what makes us moral beings.

THE DEAD END FOR PHILOSOPHY AND SCIENCE?

Let's tally what Hume has done. In seeking a science of the mind, he has instead found that reason tells us nothing about the world, we are nothing but a collection of customs and habits based on fleeting impressions, we have no basis for believing in material substance or mental substance, we have no basis for believing we are a self, we have no basis for believing in causation, and therefore all of science is without foundation. Oh, and moral philosophy cannot be established by reason or experience.

Perhaps philosophy is at a dead end. Hume seems to think so, as he writes in the conclusion of his *Treatise*:

> *The intense view of these manifold contradictions and imperfections in human reason has so wrought upon me, and heated my brain, that I am ready to reject all belief and reasoning, and can look upon no opinion even as more probable or likely than another.... I am confounded with all these questions, and begin to fancy myself in the most deplorable condition imaginable, invironed with the deepest darkness, and utterly deprived of the use of every member and faculty.*
>
> *Most fortunately it happens, that since reason is incapable of dispelling these clouds, nature herself suffices to that purpose, and cures me of this philosophical melancholy and delirium, either by relaxing this bent of mind, or by some avocation, and lively impression of my senses, which obliterate all these chimeras. I dine, I play a game of backgammon, I converse, and am merry with my friends; and when after three or four*

hours' amusement, I would return to these speculations, they appear so cold, and strained, and ridiculous, that I cannot find in my heart to enter into them any farther. (*Treatise*, VII.9)

Give up philosophy and play backgammon? Well, that's not exactly Hume's answer, but he is admitting he sees no way out. Rational philosophy and empirical philosophy have both reached dead ends. Science, too.

We can't just dismiss Hume's conclusions, because his arguments are valid. He took the quest for understanding seriously, he took earlier philosophers seriously, and he drew their work to their rational conclusions. A philosopher who took Hume seriously was Immanuel Kant, who we will discuss at length in the next chapter.

REFERENCES

David Hume, *A Treatise of Human Nature,* Project Gutenberg, http://www.gutenberg.org/ebooks/4705. (accessed March 15, 2021)

David Hume, *An Enquiry Concerning Human Understanding,* Project Gutenberg, http://www.gutenberg.org/ebooks/9662. (accessed March 15, 2021)

CHAPTER 13

KANT

Immanuel Kant (1724–1804, rhymes with "want") is the single most influential philosopher in history, even though you have probably never heard of him. How we think of ourselves and how we think about how we perceive the world is from Kant's philosophy. Philosophy is a long conversation. Immanuel Kant formed a significant turning point in that conversation. And Kant was inspired by Hume, who was inspired by Berkeley, who was inspired by Locke, who was inspired by Descartes, who was inspired by Augustine, who was inspired by Plotinus, who was inspired by Plato. It really was a long conversation.

There are two eras of philosophy: before Kant and after Kant. Again, and I can't emphasize this enough, how we think about human perception is based on Kant's philosophy. All subsequent continental philosophy is based on Kant, and he inspired the field of psychology. You'll see why as we explore his insights into the structure of the human mind.

Now, if Kant's philosophy confuses you, that shows you are paying attention. Kant is notoriously difficult to understand. That's an indication of how fundamental the level of his insights is. That's because Kant is revealing the foundations of our perceptions and thinking, concepts so fundamental that they are difficult to put into words. Kant's more complicated ideas are off-the-charts complex and obtuse. We won't deal with those here. You're welcome. But we will deal with Kant's basic philosophy, which is still complicated, but you've made it this far, so you can grasp this too.

KANT'S WAY OUT OF HUME'S DEAD END

Kant became so influential because he listened to and took part in the long conversation of philosophy that preceded him. Kant was educated in Prussia, which is significant, because that meant he was taught 1700s German language rationalist philosophy. That school of thought, which rejected the British empiricism of Locke, took no small amount of inspiration from Plotinus and was dominated by the grand system of Gottfried Leibniz (1646–1716) and philosophers who extended his system. In a nutshell, Leibniz's system that claimed to explain all of reality was based on the assumption that all truths can be known through applying the basic logical principles of mathematics. Philosophy, he claimed, was the project of reducing all truths to elementary units that would serve as a logical language that would correspond to the logical structure of the world (we'll see more of that approach in Chapter 19).

Leibniz pointed out a mistake that Locke and the other empiricists had made. Leibniz said that, yes, there's nothing in the intellect that was not put there by the senses except for the intellect itself. This meant that the mind's ability to process sensations of the external world must be present in the mind prior to experience. However, Leibniz assumed that this meant that all the eternal laws of logic were innate within the mind and that learning was a process of awakening those innate ideas, a throwback to Plato (see Chapter 2). Leibniz further reasoned that the only truths that exist are necessary truths, which means that everything that is the case must necessarily be the case. What's more, he claimed that everything that is the case must be the best it could possibly be because God, who created out of logical necessity, would create only the best of all possible worlds. Therefore, what we call evil is just an unavoidable imperfection of no real consequence. Oh, and Leibniz said all of reality is made out of fundamental particles he called "monads," which are like little atoms of perception, each unique but mirroring the entire universe; which are not located in physical space or time; and which do not interact with each other but are made to appear to interact with each other because everything was preordained by God to act the way it does—the best of all possible worlds. Leibniz was the most famous philosopher of the rationalist tradition and was completely devoted to the notion that if a proposition makes rational sense to us within our minds it therefore must be true. Like monads and evil being an illusion.

Kant was trained in the Leibnizian rationalist system but somehow managed to get ahold of Hume's books. Kant wrote that Hume "interrupted my dogmatic slumber, and gave my investigations in the field of speculative philosophy quite a new direction" (*Prolegomena*, Introduction). He referred to Hume's critiques as the most decisive to date for philosophy, and though Hume's investigations were incomplete, they deserved further concentrated attention. Kant explained how seriously he took Hume's critique of causation:

> *(Hume) demonstrated irrefutably that it was perfectly impossible for reason to think a priori and by means of concepts a combination involving necessity. We cannot at all see why in consequence of the existence of one thing another must necessarily exist, or how the concept of such a combination can arise a priori. Hence he inferred that reason was altogether deluded with reference to this concept, which she erroneously considered as one of her children, whereas in reality it was nothing but a bastard of imagination, impregnated by experience, which subsumed certain representations under the law of association, and mistook the subjective necessity of habit for an objective necessity arising from insight.* (*Prolegomena, Introduction*, 9)

What Kant means is that Hume was correct: We have only the belief that causation exists, but we never actually witness it. We believe in cause and effect only because we have developed habits from our experience to believe that certain events are connected. For example, we have developed a belief that flipping a light switch turns lights on or off because we have experienced the sensations of flipping the switch and the lights turning on or off. Habitually, we now believe that switches turn lights on and off, but we do not *know* that this is the case. In fact, we do not know that anything causes anything. We have just developed the habit of believing that certain things we do create certain results, and we believe that causation exists. Kant agreed with Hume that this calls all of our knowledge and science into question.

Like Hume, Kant was talking about the justification for believing in causation, not whether it exists or not. Key to Kant's philosophy is the understanding that we think *in terms of* causation and that no amount of reason or experience proves causation. This doesn't mean we completely ignore the idea that certain actions cause certain effects, but it does demand that we not blindly assume our theoretical beliefs are full understanding. This insight requires us to look into how our own minds are contributing to our experiences of the world.

KANT'S COPERNICAN REVOLUTION

Hume cast doubt on the possibility that the ideas in our mind are accurate representations of objects in the world. Kant's solution to the doubts Hume raised was to revive the idea of the active mind, something that was adopted by William but that Hobbes, Locke, and Hume had abandoned. Now, be sure not to misunderstand: Kant does NOT say that we create ideas or knowledge out of nothing. To have the foundation for understanding Kant, understand this sentence:

> *That all our knowledge begins with experience there can be no doubt.... But, though all our knowledge begins with experience, it by no means follows that all arises out of experience. (Critique of Pure Reason,* Introduction.I.1-2)

What Kant is saying is that both empiricism (all knowledge comes from sense experience) and rationalism (all knowledge comes from reason) are wrong. Neither alone provides us with an understanding of the world, but both have a grain of truth in how they approach philosophy and the world. Everything in our minds begins with experience, **but** our minds contribute to our understanding. Kant's Copernican Revolution is that he shifts the center of epistemology from external objects to the human mind. Our minds are not completely blank prior to experience, as Locke had assumed. Our minds come with abilities to process sense perceptions into knowledge, as Leibniz had said. Kant also connected with William on the latter's teaching that logic tells us nothing about the world—only experience does. Kant agreed but also understood that experience alone cannot tell us about objects in the world.

Plato, Plotinus, and everyone inspired by them separated reality into two realms: the intelligible and sensible realms. The problem was that if these two realms are separate, how can we intelligent beings have knowledge of the sensible realm? Kant realized that the sensible world is not completely separate from the human mind; therefore, the human mind can have *a priori* (prior to experience) knowledge about the structure of the sensible world. Kant realized, what Hume and others had not, that what we have in our minds are depictions of objects, not copies of objects in the world. Since Plato, the unanimous assumption in philosophy had been that our senses create copies, impressions, of external objects. Thus, philosophers also unanimously had to answer the question of how well the impressions in our minds connect with how external objects actually are.

Instead of the passive mind theory of perception (Hobbes, Locke, and Hume) that says that the mind conforms to the objects, Kant's active mind theory says that objects conform to the mind's rational structure. What that rational structure is and what it does will take a lot to explain in this chapter, but at its most basic, Kant is saying that the human mind imposes a form on the contents of sense experience that enables knowledge about objects. Locke had said that we can never step out of our mind to compare its contents with the objects in the world. What Kant is saying is that we can never have an experience that has not been processed by our mind's rational structure.

Kant's theory is that the human mind constructs the world of appearances by combining impressions provided by the senses with *a priori* concepts supplied by our mental faculties. This faculty of the human mind does not give us absolute knowledge of the sensible world. Kant says that we experience things only within a form or structure and that our mind contributes to our experience of them (*Critique of Pure Reason*, Preface, 11). But because our mind does contribute to the structure of the world as we perceive it, we can have real knowledge about the sensible world, and we aren't left with Hume's dead end.

THE VARIETIES OF JUDGMENTS

Kant's goal was to identify the necessary conditions for understanding. Kant is convinced that we do have knowledge of the world and that reason does have power, but speculative rationalism is not knowledge, and Hume had shown that passive empiricism can't explain how we can know anything about the external world. To explain how we can know the world, Kant first needs to show what power reason does and does not have to gain understanding and, specifically, what concepts in the mind can extend our understanding of the world.

Knowledge is a judgment about a belief or proposition. To say that a proposition is true or is false is a judgment. Kant clarifies the varieties of knowledge judgments that are possible by identifying two types of judgments.

Analytic judgments, Kant says, are when a predicate B belongs to the subject A. His example is from Descartes: "All bodies are extended." The quality of extension (B) belongs to the definition of bodies (A). In other words, the meaning of bodies includes that they are extended. Analytical reasoning is the analysis of the meaning of terms that we already know. They are mostly empty tautologies, though they may clarify propositions by confirming the relations of terms, but this type of reasoning tells us nothing about the world.

Synthetic judgments are when a predicate B can be connected to, but lies outside, the subject A. Kant's example is "All bodies are heavy." The quality of heavy (B) does not belong to the definition of bodies (A) because a body could also be light. A synthetic judgment combines (synthesizes) two different concepts. "That particular body is heavy" combines the concept of body and the concept of heavy into a judgment about that particular body. Synthetic judgments do tell us something about the world, because instead of just linking terms we already know, we gain new connections beyond what we already knew.

Kant also identifies two types of knowledge: *a priori* and *a posteriori*, both terms from medieval Latin, literally meaning "prior to" and "after," respectively. Knowledge that is *a priori* is known by us prior to any experience; these are innate ideas or ideas that are self-evident to analysis. All analytical judgments are *a priori* knowledge independent of experience. Knowledge that is *a posteriori* is learned through experience—our observations of the world. *A priori* judgments are justified by reason and need not be verified by experience; we know them independent of our experience. *A posteriori* judgments cannot be verified by reason; they can be verified only by experience., thus "after experience." Most of our knowledge is of this type, that we learn through experience, such as "that is a tree" and "the Twins won the World Series in 2001."

Kant combines the two types of judgments and the two types of knowledge into four kinds of propositions, shown here:

Kant's Four Propositions

	Analytic Judgments	Synthetic Judgments
A priori knowledge (independent of experience)	Logic/Math/Geometry	?
A posteriori knowledge (derived from experience)	Impossible	Science

We are already familiar with two types. Analytic *a priori* propositions are what Hume called "relations of ideas"—propositions that are intuitively or demonstratively certain based on an analysis of terms. Synthetic *a posteriori* propositions are what Hume called "matters of fact"—propositions learned through observations of the world. Analytic *a posteriori* propositions are impossible; if a judgment is analytic, it is not based on experience, and if it was derived from experience, then it is synthetic, not analytic.

That leaves the fourth type of proposition, synthetic *a priori* judgments. Everyone before Kant believed such propositions were impossible contradictions as are analytic *a posteriori* propositions. But Kant claimed that there are propositions that are independent of experience *and* that give us certain knowledge about the world. His example is "All events have a cause." We don't derive this proposition from experience; we bring this knowledge to our perceptions. Hume pointed out that the concept of cause does not belong to the concept of event and that we do not perceive causation in experience. Kant agrees but counters that universal causation is a synthetic *a priori* proposition that gives us knowledge by structuring our perceptions. We perceive events *in terms of* the proposition. Propositions like these give us a kind of knowledge that goes beyond the analysis of terms or the collection of experiences. *A priori* propositions can explain how the ideas in our mind can be accurate representations of objects in the world.

THE TRANSCENDENTAL METHOD

The challenge for Kant is demonstrating how synthetic *a priori* propositions are possible. To accomplish this, Kant engages in what he calls the "transcendental method." It's *transcendental* in that the method explores the universal nature of experience to uncover the universal and necessary conditions for understanding. If we cannot imagine experiences without a certain feature, then that feature must be a universal and necessary condition of our experiences. This was Kant's method to identify the concepts in the mind that can extend our understanding of the world. His method is possible because he accepts that our experiences are mental depictions of external objects, not copies of them. Our active minds contribute to our experiences and our understanding.

Time and Space

The transcendental method uncovers the most fundamental structure of our experiences: space and time. Grasping time and space is so difficult because we never actually experience them but we never experience anything without them. Kant writes:

> *Space is not a conception which has been derived from outward experiences. For, in order that certain sensations may relate to something [external to me]...the representation of space must already exist as a foundation. Consequently, the representation of space cannot be borrowed from the relations of external phenomena through experience; but, on the*

> *contrary, this external experience is itself only possible through the said antecedent representation. Space then is a necessary representation à priori, which serves for the foundation of all external intuitions. We never can imagine or make a representation to ourselves of the non-existence of space, though we may easily enough think that no objects are found in it. It must, therefore, be considered as the condition of the possibility of phenomena, and by no means as a determination dependent on them, and is a representation à priori, which necessarily supplies the basis for external phenomena. (Critique of Pure Reason,* I.I.2.2-3)

We do not perceive space—we perceive things *in terms of* space. The same is true with time.

> *Time is not an empirical conception. For neither coexistence nor succession would be perceived by us, if the representation of time did not exist as a foundation à priori. Without this presupposition we could not represent to ourselves that things exist together at one and the same time, or at different times, that is, contemporaneously, or in succession. Time is a necessary representation, lying at the foundation of all our intuitions. With regard to phenomena in general, we cannot think away time from them, and represent them to ourselves as out of and unconnected with time, but we can quite well represent to ourselves time void of phenomena. Time is therefore given à priori. In it alone is all reality of phenomena possible. These may all be annihilated in thought, but time itself, as the universal condition of their possibility, cannot be so annulled.* (*Critique of Pure Reason,* I.II.5.1-2)

Space and time are the intuitions that make our understanding of objects possible. They are the conditions by which all of our experiences conform. Try to imagine the color green. You cannot image "just" green, but a green something that has qualities of both space and time. Remember Berkeley's argument that we can't conceive of abstract ideas? We can add to it that we cannot imagine green in the abstract, and we cannot imagine it outside of space and time.

Kant refers to space and time as "the pure elementary notions of the Sensibility." (*Prolegomena*, 39.4) Time and space are forms of inner sense that structure our depictions of objects. Without that structure, the contents of our minds would be no more than what Hume called the flux of impressions. Time and space are synthetic *a priori* judgments that structure our perceptions and allow us to have sensible experiences. We do not experience space or time in and of themselves—

only objects in space and time. Space and time are intuitions that make experiences possible, but we do not learn them through experience; they are always there. Human perception is impossible without them.

The Categories of Understanding

Space and time are just the beginning of what the transcendental method uncovers. Kant also says that our mind has a set of further categories that structure our mental depictions of external objects. He calls them Pure Conceptions of the Understanding, or Categories. The Categories are, like space and time, conditions by which our understanding is possible. Our mind's depictions of objects are structured and made sensible in space and time, and the Categories do what Kant describes as a synthesis

> *by which alone the elements of our cognitions are collected and united into a certain content.... a blind but indispensable function of the soul, without which we should have no cognition whatever, but of the working of which we are seldom even conscious." (Critique of Pure Reason, I.III.6.1)*

The Categories are what turn mere collections of sensations into depictions of things. We never experience the Categories because they are *a priori*—they are independent of experience because they are a necessary precondition of experience. We don't experience what the Categories do; we experience only their effects.

Kant's bold claim is that the Categories are synonymous with all possible logical functions and judgments. In other words, they are how we think, and we cannot think otherwise than through their *a priori* synthesis. Kant says he calls these pure conceptions "Categories" after Aristotle's Categories because, Kant says, his purpose is identical with Aristotle's, but executed differently.

Kant's Table of the Categories of Understanding

Quantity	Quality	Relation	Modality
Unity (Measure)	Reality	Inherence and Substance	Possibility—Impossibility
Plurality (Quantity)	Negation	Causality and Dependence	Existence—Nonexistence
Totality (Whole)	Limitation	Community and Interaction	Necessity—Contingence

(*Critique of Pure Reason*, I.III.6.8; *Prolegomena* 21, 2)

The concepts in this table are what the human mind contains *a priori*. They are literally how we think about and make sense of our mental depictions that we perceive in terms of space and time. They are not what we think about; they are *how* we think. They are thinking at the most basic level, the logical *a priori* synthetic judgments by which we understand anything and everything. Kant said that space and time are the faculty of *Sensibility* and the Categories are the faculty of *Understanding*. Knowledge is the product of these two faculties of the mind.

Kant's discussion of how the Categories give us understanding is complex—so complex he had to write a second book (the *Prolegomena*) to explain his first book (*Critique of Pure Reason*) on the subject. Suffice it to say for our purposes here that a simple example can show how the Categories unite our depictions into one conscious understanding of objects.

Imagine a dot. Just one dot. Right away you are using the logical judgments of the Categories, starting with Unity to understand that you are considering one dot. You didn't need to think hard at all; your mind is predisposed with that capability. Now imagine a second dot. That's using Plurality to go beyond one dot to a plurality of dots. If I draw seven dots and ask you how many dots there are, you can answer because you can Measure the Quantity of dots as a Whole as equaling seven. If I then ask you to draw a circle around three of the seven dots, you can do that because you logically Limit the Reality of the dots, choosing three while Negating the other four dots. If this sounds very simplistic, that's the point. This is *the* most basic level of human thought. We don't learn this—we know this *a priori*—but we can use these judgments to gain knowledge of the world, so these propositions are synthetic propositions.

The Categories of Modality are also basic forms of thought. They are logical modes by which we judge objects and ideas. They come in pairs, and each pair of modalities underlies substantial questions that philosophers have debated for centuries. We never learned these modalities through experience; we think in terms of them. To think that something is possible or impossible, that it exists or does not exist, that it is a necessary or contingent occurrence means to think in terms of synthetic *a priori* judgments of the Categories.

The Categories of Relation deserves special attention because they answer Hume's serious objections. Kant agrees that we do not have sense experience of substance or causality, but the Category of Inherence and Substance forms a unity out of our various perceptions of qualities that enables us to form concepts such as "tree," "dog," and "human." True, we cannot say what the reality beneath these qualities is, but that's not the point. Substance is a logical function and judgment that orders the flow of sensations into coherent objects in our mind. Perhaps the idea of "tree" is, as a skeptic could say, nothing but an idea in our mind, but that is all we have to work with, and it is how we think about our sensations. Hume said our idea of necessary causality is simply a product of habit. Kant replied that causality is a logical *a priori* synthetic judgment by which we understand the succession of events that we perceive. In the billiard ball example, Hume said that we do not witness causation; we witness only three impressions. Kant agrees and said that our mind contributes the concept of Causation and Interaction to the sense impressions to make sense of the events that we witness. We cannot imagine a world in which there is no causal order, no interaction between objects (Leibniz's bizarre theory aside), but these *a priori* concepts structure our experiences and enable understanding. The Categories are how the human mind is structured. Kant says that God or horseflies may experience the world differently because they may have different Categories, but all human beings have the same Categories and thus experience the world in the same basic way.

Kant's Active Mind

Kant therefore views the human mind as an active mind. The intuitions of space and time and the Categories of Understanding provide structure to our thoughts, but we do actively think thoughts through that structure. We perceive what Kant calls a "manifold of phenomena" always in succession; but though we passively perceive that manifold in a particular order of succession, we can actively think about it in different ways.

To illustrate what Kant said about the mind being capable, imagine listening to a piece of music. Music is a succession of notes that your mind perceives as a succession of perceptions. Your mind is performing multiple tasks as you do this. First, you are separating the notes of the music from all other sounds in the background, isolating the notes as the concept of a song. Kant refers to this with the clunky term, "synthesis of apprehension in intuition," which means that your mind is synthesizing out of the manifold sensations a particular thread of phenomena and considering them together as one experience. As you listen to the succession of notes, you can remember the previous notes in the sequence. To switch the thought experiment briefly—if I said a sequence of numbers to you and then asked you what the second number was, you can, using your memory (what Kant called the "reproduction in imagination") repeat what that second number was. Back to the piece of music. You are more than simply a perceiver; you can think about the music to which you are listening, and using what Kant calls the "synthesis of recognition in a concept," you can think about the piece of music in terms of its melody, its rhythm, its genre, what instruments are being played, and so on. These examples of how our mind works are possible because of the intuitions of space and time and the Categories of Understanding, but you are actively thinking about what you experience, and objects conform to your mind.

THE THREE TRANSCENDENTAL IDEAS OF PURE REASON

Kant considers the mind as having a faculty of *pure* reason, which produces its own concepts different from those produced by the intuitions of space and time and the Categories of Understanding. The concepts of pure reason relate to the most difficult problems of the nature of reality that transcend all possible experience. They are, Kant said, questions, that human reason must necessarily encounter. Kant discussed three concepts of pure reason: self, cosmos, and God. We have no experience of these concepts, but they are important because, Kant argued, we must hold these concepts to make sense of the universe.

Self

Hume said that we never experience a self (see Chapter 12), which is a very challenging concept. Basically, what Hume means is that we have no impression of the self within our sense impressions but only the sense data themselves. Kant agrees with Hume that we never experience the self in our thoughts just as the eye never sees itself in visual perception. But does not Hume make a mistake here? Do we believe we do not have eyes because we do not see the eye when the eye sees? And what is seeing without an eye? What is gathering sense impressions and having ideas if not a self? Finally, and most damning to Hume's argument—if he is correct that we have no idea that is not linked to an original impression, from where, then, does the idea of a self come?

Kant said that the self is not a something we experience but is another necessary condition for experiences to exist. Kant is not agreeing with Descartes and Berkeley that the self is a substance because Kant sees substance as a Category of Understanding within experience. Concepts of pure reason stand behind experience. The self is transcendental to all experience and underlies all experience. We can't experience the transcendental self just like the eye can't see itself, but we do think of our experiences as being experienced by a unified self, the subject of all our experiences. Hume unwittingly showed this in his objections to the idea of a self. He said, "I never can catch myself at any time without a perception." He can't construct that sentence without the words and concepts of "I" and "myself." We always assume the self and need the concept of self, even when we try to deny the self. The self is a logically necessary idea for us to be able constitute our past experiences and believe they are our experiences.

Cosmos

The ancient Greek word "cosmos" meant the entirety of everything. The school of speculative philosophy in which Kant was educated made bold dogmatic claims about the nature of the cosmos and statements about it such as "the world has a beginning in time, and is also limited in regard to space." This seems like a reasonable claim to knowledge, but as Kant points out, the opposite contradiction, "the world has no beginning, and no limits in space, but is, in relation both to time and space, infinite," is equally reasonable. He brings forward these conflicting propositions, and three other similar pairs, to demonstrate that reason can go beyond what it can prove and can go into dogmatic propositions that are nonsense. What he means by "nonsense" is that the propositions have an opposite proposition and that these pairs of contradictory propositions cannot both be true, but neither side of the antinomy can be proven true or false. The proposition and its opposite can be held only dogmatically, without evidence or rational argument, and that is nonsense.

Kant's purpose in stating the antinomies is that reason has certain proper bounds within which it must stay. We cannot reason to propositions about the cosmos as though it were a finite object. Synthetic *a priori* judgments are acceptable in mathematics and physics because they make sense of our experience. But the entirety of the cosmos is beyond our experience and beyond our reason. We do not and cannot experience the totality of everything.

To help understand what Kant is getting at, consider the more finite example of the same basic idea. Our knowledge of the world is limited by what we can perceive in space and time; therefore, there is a limit to our sense experience and our reason. There is a phenomenal world (a world of phenomena) that contains objects we can perceive and with which we can interact. There is also a noumenal world, meaning a world independent of our sense of it. When we perceive an object, we can perceive the object as it appears to us, but we cannot perceive the thing-in-itself, the noumenon that is beyond our perception, and that is not structured by the Categories of Understanding. Accepting the reality of the noumena seems to be a logical necessity. If there are limits to our capabilities of perception and understanding, then there must be a realm of reality beyond the reach of our knowledge. The noumenon is that which is beyond what we can perceive. Kant agreed with the British empiricists that we don't really see the tree-in-itself; we see sense impressions caused by the tree. Kant postulates the noumena as a logically necessary reality because we do not and cannot experience the things-in-themselves.

Similarly, the cosmos, the entirety of everything, is independent of our sense of it but is a logically necessary reality. However, it makes sense to assume that there is a cosmos and that all that we can perceive is within it. We need to restrain our reason within its proper limits and not engage in dogmatic propositions beyond those limits. The cosmos is a logically necessary idea for us to believe that there is a reality.

God

I have said nothing in this book about the various rational "proofs" for the existence of God. Even when I teach philosophy of religion (a very enjoyable course because human thinking about God and religion is beautiful), I leave out the so-called proofs. That's because I take seriously Kant's admonition that God is neither provable nor disprovable. Kant believed in a supreme creator, but he thought that attempts to argue for it rationally are nonsense, for the same reasons he thought propositions about the cosmos are nonsense. Kant systematically refutes the well-known arguments that allegedly demonstrate God's existence—ontological, teleological, and cosmological—exposing them as the dogmatic assertions without basis that they are. Similarly, any and all arguments against the existence of God are also nonsense. Atheism is just as dogmatic an assertion as is theism. Interestingly, Kant does not say that God's existence is a matter of faith. He's not against that, but that's not the conclusion at which he aimed. What he states is that like the concept of self and cosmos, the concept of God is a logically necessary idea for us to think about why there is something we can call morality (see Chapter 16). We can say nothing more about God.

Kant's rejection of the dogmatic propositions of speculative philosophy serve the purpose of, on the one hand, keeping reason within its proper limits, and on the other hand, establishing a positive role in philosophy for these unprovable concepts of self, cosmos, and God. We cannot prove that we have a self; that there is a coherent, enduring cosmos beyond our perceptions; or that there is a God, but it is helpful if not essential to think that they are true. They are important regulative concepts that give us reference points to help us make sense of what we can experience. One quick example is that it is only because we think that there is a coherent, enduring cosmos beyond our perceptions that we can explore new territory or plan for the future. After all, if we assume that all that exists is what we have already perceived, how could we discover new things? What reason would we have to think tomorrow will come?

KANT'S LEGACY

In a real sense, the whole of the rest of this book (save one chapter, as we shall see) is Kant's legacy. Most philosophers since Kant have adopted Kant's admonition against dogmatic rational speculation and his realization that the mind actively contributes to perception. Kant changed everything in philosophy and by extension in all of the sciences. The poet Heinrich Heine (1797–1856) said that Kant's philosophy was world destroying, world crushing. It's difficult for us to understand that today because we grew up in the Kantian world. Every way that we look at our world and every way in which we understand our world as Westerners is Kantian.

One huge implication of Kant's philosophy is that our minds are not purely perceivers. Think of a motion-sensitive spotlight that simply reacts. It has no consciousness of what it is doing; it turns on only in response to stimulus. Locke and others had more or less reduced the human mind to that level of mere passive response. Locke would reply that he did believe we are aware of our ideas of sensation, but that's just a second layer of passivity—sensations cause ideas of reflection. Hume agreed with that model of the passive mind—objects cause impressions; impressions cause ideas; there is no self. Kant's realization that the human mind is active in structuring perceptions solved some of the problems present in the epistemologies of Locke and Hume. Our minds join different depictions one to another, and we comprehend their diversity in our understanding. We can have knowledge. There does remain the issue that the phenomena in our minds are not copies of the objects themselves, so there remains the issue of the noumenon—the thing-in-itself that is beyond our perception.

Kant's philosophy increased the contribution of the human mind to our understanding but at the same time limited its reach. On the one hand, Kant believed in human free will, that that the will is in its every action a law to itself, and we can freely use our reason to make decisions, though mostly in the realm of moral decisions, as we shall see in Chapter 16. On the other hand, Kant also said that the Categories of Understanding are how all human beings perceive the universe and that all human beings have the same mental structure. Perception and understanding, therefore, are determined by a one-size-fits-all structure. He also said that we can't go beyond the Categories of Understanding—they determine how we can perceive and think about our perceptions. A group of philosophers disagreed with Kant's restrictions on human possibilities but accepted Kant's idea that the mind is active in perception. We meet them next in Chapter 14.

REFERENCES

Immanuel Kant, *Critique of Pure Reason.* Urbana, Illinois: Project Gutenberg, http://www.gutenberg.org/ebooks/4280. (accessed March 18, 2021).

Immanuel Kant, *Prolegomena to Any Future Metaphysics.* Project Gutenberg, http://www.gutenberg.org/ebooks/52821. (accessed March 18, 2021).

CHAPTER 14

GERMAN IDEALISM AND HEGEL

German idealism was a philosophical movement in the early 1800s. It was a direct reaction to Immanuel Kant's philosophical system. We call the movement "German" because it was discussed by a circle of German philosophers and artists, and we call it "idealism" because the movement argued that everything must be understood as being dependent on mental or spiritual reality. The German idealists developed a unique philosophical movement that synthesized multiple earlier ideas into an approach to the universe that greatly influenced the arts and, by extension, much of human society.

I've mentioned that at certain points in philosophical history, when someone opens a door, others will walk through it. Kant opened a new door with his revolutionary insight that our perceptions conform to our mental structure, which he described through the Categories of Understanding. This means that reality conforms to our minds and our minds aren't purely passive perceivers. Instead, our minds are active in our experiences, and the structure of our minds structures our experiences. This worldview places the human mind at the center of philosophy. Even more important to the German idealists, this worldview positioned human individuals as the engines of creativity.

BEYOND KANT

Kant opened a door, and the German idealists barged through it with glee. In the late 1700s and early 1800s, the German-speaking lands were awakening to a fresh view of human expression inspired by the writer Johann Wolfgang von Goethe, who was opening up new possibilities for literature. The thinkers in the German idealist movement were also open to new possibilities, and they were willing to take Kant's insights about human understanding and reassess everything in human experience. They asked a number of penetrating questions. If the mind is active in experience, as Kant showed, then the question is how active? If our perceptions conform to our mental structure, then can we change that structure? Do people in different cultures have different mental structures? Kant said we can't go beyond the Categories of Understanding, but is perception outside their limits really impossible? Are the categories really the same for every human being, as Kant says? What if we can change the way we experience the universe by changing our approach to it? The German idealists, each in his own way, explored these fundamental questions about the way we approach the universe.

The German idealists crafted a new philosophical approach to the questions of what the universe is and what we can know about it. The fundamental theme within German idealism is the claim that reality is dependent on the mind of the perceiver; therefore, when the perceiver changes his or her approach to the universe, that changes his or her understanding and perhaps even his or her reality. This opens us up to the big question of what approach to reality will best reveal reality to us.

Common to all of the German idealists was their rejection of what they saw as the limits that Kant placed on human knowledge. The first limit I already mentioned—Kant's belief that all human beings are limited to the unchanging Categories of Understanding. The second limit rejected by the German idealists is Kant's idea of the noumena (see Chapter 13), that the ultimate reality is beyond our knowledge. Kant's reasoning about the noumena is sound because if there are limits to our capabilities of perception and understanding, then there must be a realm of reality beyond our knowledge. The only way around this limitation is to believe instead that human perception and understanding are, at least in theory, unlimited. That argument is probably impossible to maintain, but the German idealists flirted with it.

There is a large territory between the limits of scientific knowledge and perfect knowledge and the German idealists each staked their own claim in that territory.

The German idealists believed that our minds have a power of intuition that can transcend the limitations of science and reason and reveal the deeper reality that we can experience. They argued that Kant and those who followed his system were limiting their understanding, believing they were cut off from reality beyond sense perception.

To varying degrees, the German idealists also rejected the scientific and rationalist approaches to the universe and instead adopted an intuitive, passionate, and artistic approach. The artistic movement, known as "Romanticism," was burgeoning in the 1790s, and armed with Kant, the German idealists gave it intellectual power. Romanticism and German idealism both celebrated personal experience and supplemented, if not supplanted, rationality with emotions. They combined the emphasis on personal experiences with a spiritual view of nature as a living force to be experienced with a sense of wonder rather than dispassionately as does science. It is easy to see how this approach encouraged creativity and personal expression.

JOHANN GOTTLIEB FICHTE

Johann Gottlieb Fichte (1762–1814) led the charge of the German idealists through the door that Kant had opened. Fichte and several other German philosophers were impressed with Kant's approach to knowledge as being structured by the mind but thought it incomplete. Fichte's conviction was that Kant has only indicated the truth but had neither fully explained it nor proved it. Fichte certainly had great respect for Kant as a person who had the power for divining truth, but he also felt that Kant was not conscious of the grounds on which he stood. Yet again, we see in Fichte a philosopher who sought to discover the foundations of human knowledge. In his quest for understanding, Fichte applied Kant's critical philosophy to the contents of the human mind and its ideas.

Kant's philosophy is critical in that he says that all of our beliefs are open to analysis. You should be responding to that sentence with the thought, "but wasn't every philosopher before Kant also analyzing our beliefs?" Yes, but what Kant changed in philosophy (and our culture) was realizing that our minds actively contribute to our perceptions and beliefs. Look back at Locke for a second. He saw the mind as completely passive—sensations happened to the mind. Hume, too, saw the mind as no more than a "stage" on which ideas moved around, caused by the outside world. Kant said that not only does the human mind actively structure its sense impressions by means of the Categories of Understanding, the human mind is active and thus capable of being critical about its perceptions and ideas by focusing its critical capability on particular ideas. Fichte and the other German idealists took that idea and ran with it.

Kant held that there is only one set of categories that structured human understanding that is universal to all people in all times and places. Fichte questioned this assumption. What if we could change the categories through which we understand the world? Fichte argued that there is more than one way to perceive and make sense of the world. Kant had made the human mind the new center of epistemology by declaring that objects conform to the mind's rational structure. Fichte went further than Kant's Copernican revolution by saying that the categories employed by the individual are what make the world meaningful. The world is my world. My values structure my experience. Philosophy, Fichte said, was not a dead piece of furniture but something animated by the soul of the person who wields it.

Fichte unfolded the insights of Kant by centering his philosophy on the idea of freedom. Both philosophers were concerned with the question of how to reconcile freely willing human agents with the seemingly deterministic world of material objects. Kant had placed freedom as a fact of reason at the base of moral decision-making (see Chapter 16), but Fichte moved freedom to the center of everything. Our experiences of the world are accompanied by the feeling of necessity, Fichte said, but there is also always the practical certainty of human freedom. In Fichte's view, freedom is a presupposition not only of moral action but also of human cognition.

Fichte asks, "What is the ground and meaning of experience?" He postulates that there are two alternatives. The first he calls "dogmatism," an approach to the universe that sets the foundation of experience in an independent external reality (the Kantian noumena). This approach interprets inner experience as being determined by the outer world. This approach is assumed by the scientist and by both the rationalist and empiricist philosophers. In sharp contrast, Fichte advocates "idealism," which finds the ground of experience in our own nature, our own self. This approach interprets the outer world in terms of our inner experience. If we limit ourselves to scientific knowledge, as the dogmatist does, we will see ourselves only as passive objects subject to the deterministic necessity of the material world. Kant showed that we become conscious of the moral law through our intellectual intuition, which requires us to think of ourselves and each other as freely self-determining agents pursuing moral ends (see Chapter 16). Fichte shows that this same intellectual intuition operates in all areas of life; therefore, we are required to think of ourselves as free, self-determining agents in all aspects of life.

How we should view ourselves and our world is, for Fichte, an intensely important and practical question. Like the later American pragmatists whom he influenced (see Chapter 18), Fichte thought that our beliefs cannot be proven by rational arguments. He said that what makes a belief viable is whether it positively affects our lives and our interests. The scientific method is not a given, and "facts" are not beyond interpretation. Yes, people can choose to approach the universe scientifically, but those who choose this approach are doing so because they believe it serves their interests and makes the world meaningful to them. Even science is based on subjective commitments and acts of practical faith. The world I live in is always a world structured by the way I approach it.

Fichte argues that the self is the foundation of experience. We have to begin with the self because we know the inner world better than the outer one. Exactly the opposite of Hume's argument, Fichte's argument is that the objects of perception come and go, but behind all of your impressions is the constant activity of the self that stands behind all impressions of the world. Fichte is recorded to have once said to his students, "Gentlemen, think the wall," then, "Gentlemen, think him who thought the wall." Meaning, behind every object that appears to you is your individual self that grounds those appearances. The world that you experience is not a collection of meaningless bits of sense data that you take in passively like a camera obscura. Quite the contrary—the world you experience is structured by your interests and values. Your world is a dynamic place in which you make choices. Our philosophy, thus, must move from understanding our self to an understanding of the outer world. Only if we begin with our inner experience of being a unified, creative self will we then have the basis for giving meaning to everything else. If instead we start, as the dogmatist does, in approaching the universe as being nothing more than a plurality of matter in motion, we will never be able to discern our unified mind and consciousness.

According to Fichte,

> *The Nature on which I have to act is not a foreign element, called into existence without reference to me, into which I cannot penetrate. It is molded by my own laws of thought, and must be in harmony with them; it must be thoroughly transparent, knowable and penetrable to me, even to its inmost recesses. In all its phenomena it expresses nothing but the connections and relations of my own being to myself, and as surely as I may hope to know myself, so surely may I expect to comprehend it.* (*The Vocation of Man,* 125)

Thus, the "external world" is not so external after all. Through sense perception, you encounter many sensations that make up your experiences. However, you will encounter meaningful objects only when you creatively make those objects a part of your world. Any way that you experience the world, it is always a world you have made in your own image. The world is not a world of dead objects but is a dynamic, spiritual process in which we participate.

Late in Fichte's philosophical career, his philosophy morphed into a transcendental speculation that came to be known as "subjective idealism." Fichte taught that all of our individual thoughts are avatars of a universal intellect he called the "Absolute Idea." There are shades of Plotinus in Fichte's later view, though it is also strongly reminiscent of Berkeley's philosophy. Fichte said that we *are* experience and that we cannot raise ourselves above experience. He therefore rejects Kant's idea of the noumena because the idea of the thing-in-itself beyond experience is, Fichte claimed, a pure invention with no reality whatsoever. For an object to be objectively real, Fichte said, means it possesses possible experiences. In other words, a tree is real because it can be perceived by a potential observer who can interact with the tree in many ways: look at it, sit under it, paint a picture of it, cut it down, and so on. Those experiences are what the tree is, and its reality is summed up by all possible experiences of it. In Fichte's philosophy of idealism, all of these interactions are thoughts because thought is an interactive act, not a passive reflection on something apart. In this way, everything is thought, and everything is mind dependent, like in Berkeley's philosophy. This idealism perhaps sounds weird, but it shares the same foundation with quantum mechanics in that reality is dependent on the observer.

GERMAN IDEALISM AND ROMANTICISM

Contemporary with, and stimulated by the philosophy of German idealism, was the artistic movement of Romanticism. This movement was an artistic expression of the active mind and Kant's idea that the will is, in its every action, a law to itself. At the heart of Romanticism was the vital importance of the artist's free expression. This was not a rational expression but an emotional one. The artist's feelings are a law to themselves, and artistic creation should be free from rules dictating art's content or form.

The nucleus of the Romantic movement was two brothers in Jena, Germany: August Wilhelm von Schlegel and Friedrich von Schlegel. Beginning in 1798, they published the philosophy of literature journal, *Athenaeum*, which, though it only published six issues over three years, was influential in establishing Romanticism as an intellectual movement. *Athenaeum* was the centerpiece of a circle of philosophers and artists in Jena, many of whom were professors at the city's university, who discussed and wrote about philosophy, religion, science, literature, and art. Notable members of the circle include Fichte; natural philosopher Friedrich Wilhelm Joseph Schelling; philosopher of religion, Friedrich Schleiermacher; poet and philosopher Friedrich Hölderlin; Georg Wilhelm Friedrich Hegel (discussed at length later in this chapter); and literary critic Caroline Schlegel, who was married to August Schlegel until she divorced him in 1803 to marry Schelling when she became Caroline Schelling.

After the circle in Jena dispersed in 1804, the center of the Romantic movement shifted to Coppet Castle, Switzerland, where Germaine de Staël (1766–1817), commonly referred to as Madame de Staël, held court. Madame de Staël had been educated in the writings of Rousseau (see Chapter 9) and legal theorist Baron de Montesquieu (1689–1755) by her mother who hosted an influential Parisian salon (a regular gathering of intellectuals). She followed in her mother's footsteps, holding her own salon and writing about political philosophy. She used her social and political connections (her father was the French Minister of Finance and her husband the Swiss ambassador to France) to urge dialogue and moderation among the adversaries in the years of chaos (1794–1799) after the French Revolution. She opposed Napoleon, publishing a book of political philosophy and then a novel that argued against his absolutist ideology. Napoleon responded in late 1803 by banishing de Staël from France. That was the impetus for her setting up a new salon at Coppet Castle, where she conversed with many dozens of intellectuals and politicians (including Napoleon's brother), many of whom were or became leaders in academia, literature, or government. In her Coppet salon, she learned about German idealism and Romanticism, and became a patron and disseminator of both. She published *De l'Allemagne* ("On Germany") in 1810, coining the term "Romanticism," which we still use today. The first printing of the book was destroyed by the order of Napoleon, who objected to de Staël's philosophical theories, but she managed to get it republished in London in 1813, after which it became popular. In the book, de Staël introduced German idealism and Romanticism to the rest of Europe, and she advanced a progressive vision of society combining Lockean limited government, individual expression and freedom (á la German idealism and Romanticism), and liberal Christianity. Her views influenced modern ideas of religious liberty and tolerance within a secular society.

Romanticism found natural expression in literature and music. Poets William Wordsworth, Lord Byron, Samuel Taylor Coleridge, and John Keats were among the writers who immersed themselves in Romanticism. Many people are not aware that Ludwig van Beethoven's tremendous musical innovation was in part influenced by the incredible innovation occurring in German philosophy at that time. Beethoven knew several German idealist philosophers and corresponded with them. That is not to say that Beethoven was himself a philosopher. He produced no philosophical literature, preferring to do his communicating through music. Nevertheless, he was certainly influenced by the philosophers whom he knew and read. The cool thing about Beethoven is that he was the punk rock of his day. Yes, really. His *Fifth Symphony* is famous not only because of its sublime beauty but because it shattered previous musical forms. In this and other compositions, Beethoven willfully disregarded convention and wrote music that expressed his emotions. In this, he captured the spirit of German Romanticism and German idealism. Beethoven is known for his fierceness, personified in such quotes as, "I will seize fate by the throat," but this side of his personality is often exaggerated. The last movement of his *Ninth Symphony* is a musical version of playwright Friedrich Schiller's poem, "An die Freude" ("Ode to Joy").

HEGEL AND THE GRAND SYSTEM

It is a bit of an exaggeration to say that in the last 200 or so years there has been a war in philosophy. But if we can describe the long "analytical/continental" divide in philosophy as a war, it was Georg Wilhelm Friedrich Hegel (1770–1831) who started it. That was not Hegel's intention, but he produced an all-encompassing system that still incites passion among philosophers. To call someone a "Hegelian" is, depending on who is saying it, high praise or an insult. Few, if any, today are true followers of Hegel's system, but his philosophy has influenced much of what is called "continental" philosophy. Understanding Hegel helps understand some of the issues in continental philosophy that developed in response to Hegel.

Hegel was a Prussian philosopher who followed in the footsteps of Kant but took Kant's ideas in a different direction. Some say Hegel is even more difficult to understand than Kant. I don't agree with that, which is not to say that Hegel is a walk in the park. If you break Hegel's philosophy down into three main components, it is more manageable. The first part is to see his epistemology as an extension of Kant's. The second is to understand Hegel's philosophy as a system to understand human freedom in terms of history and the political state. The third part is his theory of interpersonal relations, centered on the concept of recognition.

Hegel's Approach to Knowledge: Philosophy in Context

As early as 1797, Friedrich von Schlegel (1772–1829) was lecturing at Jena on the idea of historicism, the idea that philosophy should stress historical development and, in particular, how historical and cultural context affects ideas. This approach is in keeping with German idealism's idea that people's structures of perception differ, as opposed to Kant's idea that all people have the same, unchanging Categories of Understanding. This approach also reflected the growing belief in the reality of cultural, if not biological, evolution, meaning that ideas are products of their time and place. People in the 1790s could see that a new era was upon them. The medieval era was long gone, the so-called Enlightenment had happened, and society was now morphing into something else. The United States had rebelled against England, and the French Revolution had toppled the long-standing French monarchy. James Watt's new steam engine was igniting an industrial revolution. Change was happening. More than change, there seemed to be progress. The growing belief was that an old era was being replaced by a new, better era, just as the previous era was better than the one before it.

Almost hand in hand with German idealism was the idea of progress as a historical inevitability. The new era was progress over the Enlightenment, which was progress over the Renaissance, medieval, and classical periods. The challenge for philosophers and indeed all intellectuals was to understand earlier writers and their works in their historical contexts. Increasingly in the 1800s, writers portrayed human civilization in terms of historical progress and interpreted past writings according to their place within the unfolding development of humankind—how those writers fit within the greater totality of progress. One of the biggest proponents of historicism and progress was Karl Marx, whom we meet in Chapter 15. He was a follower of Hegel, although, as Marx said, he turned Hegel on his head. First we need to understand Hegel's approach.

Hegel's goal was to encapsulate in a philosophical system the unified totality of everything. He saw all of history as a unified, rational process; therefore, he believed that to understand any particular thing, we need to understand it within its place in the rational historical process. Hegel was a rationalist in that he believed that the universe had a rational order that could be understood through human reason. He was Kantian, however, in also believing that reason alone cannot bring us knowledge. Our reason needs sense experience to provide us with details about reality. Hegel's program is to gather information about the world, put that information into context, and then use reason to discern patterns and synchronicities in the information to understand the rational order of the universe.

Hegel was also Kantian in that he believed the human mind is structured by "concepts"—the term he preferred over Kant's Categories. Different from Kant, Hegel portrayed human understanding as a much more dynamic process that differed among people. He rejected Kant's theory that all humans had the same set of Categories and said there are a variety of ways that people can experience the world. To learn about human understanding, Hegel employs a method he calls "phenomenology." He means the study of the phenomena of the mind, which is not an entirely new approach (we've seen it before), but Hegel places it at the center of philosophy as a full-fledged approach and discipline. He believed that we learn about ourselves and the universe best by starting with an analysis of the phenomena we perceive within our mind. Hegel's phenomenological approach inspired a new school of philosophy, which we will discuss in Chapter 21.

Hegel's phenomenology reveals human understanding as a three-step process. The first is sense perception, which provides direct sensory information. This level of perception he calls "sense certainty" because it is direct experience without the mind contributing any content or concepts. This is a level of experience Kant would say is not possible, but Hegel says that it is not only possible but that this pure but empty and abstract experience shows us our need for concepts to interpret it. The conscious mind must take the information given by sense certainty and place it under universal concepts. This second level, which Hegel calls "perception," shows that our minds are actively interpreting sense information about objects. We begin to see patterns and connections in our experiences, but we still do not have knowledge. That requires the third level, "understanding," in which we conceive of objects in the context of the logical physical forces of the universe—specifically for Hegel, Newton's physical laws. At this level, we understand the unity of the object and how its properties can change or endure. These three levels of consciousness work in sequence to give us conscious understanding of objects.

Continuing the phenomenological study of the mind, Hegel says that the next mental activity is self-consciousness, the level of awareness that the physical laws within understanding are imputed by our own minds. The mind is actively co-creating our understanding. This is similar to Kant's idea of the Categories, but for Hegel, this is a more conscious and dynamic process. Hegel sees the theories and models of science as products of the mind that are internal mental concepts by which we understand objects at the level of perception. When we aren't self-conscious, we mistakenly think these laws are external to us. When, using the phenomenological approach, we are self-conscious (that is, conscious of ourselves), we can see how we are creating the structures of theory, formulas, and interpretation by which we understand objects.

The level of understanding and how it works is especially important in comprehending Hegel's philosophy. He is saying two things. The first is that our theories about the universe are the framework by which we understand the universe. Our knowledge tells us what we perceive. The second is that the framework we have right now is the product of many centuries of human development. Humanity is evolving and has been doing so for a very long time, and the mental framework of the understanding is a product of that evolution. This is one aspect of Hegel's historicism. Philosophy and science have evolved as humanity has evolved. Of course Kant had a more advanced epistemology than did Aristotle. Of course Newton had a more advanced science than did any of the ancient Greeks. Later scholars built on the achievements of the past. All ideas are products of their time and place and need to be viewed within their historical setting. The larger point is that human understanding is evolving and growing as it interacts with the world and with previous understandings. Hegel's idea that understanding is a result of active cocreation also applies to an individual's consciousness. We learn through experience and by applying reason to our perceptions, learning from the experiences of others and ourselves. What we understand today is a better understanding than we had in the past.

Hegel's acknowledgment that human thinking and perception are relative to time and place and his call for a contextual study of ideas compose much of the foundation of what is now known as "continental philosophy." This approach to philosophy accepts that the ideas of philosophy and science are not eternal objects but are expressions of people living within historical and cultural contexts. The continental approach is similar to Hegel's levels of understanding: gathering sense information, placing it in context, and employing reason to identify the physical and social forces at work. We'll see several branches of continental philosophy in the rest of this book. It's quite different from the approach of analytical philosophy (see Chapter 22), which focuses on logical analysis of language and scientific data, largely separated from their context.

Another of Hegel's ideas that has been generally adopted by continental, but not analytical, philosophers is that we cannot discover a perfectly correct criterion for truth. Hegel noted that much of philosophy's history has been spent arguing about the correct criterion or method on which we must base all of our reasoning. Hegel says this is the wrong approach. We must begin where we are, not wait to find the perfect method. Hegel says that in starting to try to understand the universe, we find that our own consciousness provides the criteria we need. Hegel's dialectical view of knowledge is that it is through the act of investigating and reasoning that we learn. We begin with a partial understanding of what we investigate, and as we gather more and more information, we develop greater and greater understanding. Thinking, for Hegel, is a continuing process of self-correction, progressing from limited to more complete understanding. This is true no matter what we investigate, including the operation of our own minds.

Few continental philosophers follow Hegel's next step in his version of historicism. Hegel believed that (1) the human framework of thought was a true expression of the objective reality and (2) the evolutionary progress of human thinking was connected to the evolutionary progress of the divine Intellect, which he called *Geist*, a concept I will explain shortly. His philosophical system was his phenomenology of the march of reason through history as the expression of *Geist*.

Hegel's Historicist System

The second part of Hegel's philosophy is his system that attempts to show how people find freedom within the march of reason through history. One way of looking at what Hegel is doing is that he is telling a story about human history. As we explore this story of history, it will seem difficult to see that his focus is on freedom. It is, but not in the way we understand freedom today. Perhaps we have evolved further? We'll see.

Hegel's historicist system has four main ideas that we will go through in rational sequence.

1. **History is the dialectical process by which *Geist* comes to know Itself and realize Its Idea.** Yes, *Geist*. It's a German word that has no exact translation into English (this is a problem especially in German-language philosophy), so I will leave it untranslated, as I will do for several of Hegel's terms. *Geist*, as Hegel uses it means mind, spirit, and culture simultaneously. Remember when I said that Plotinus is the most influential philosopher in history? Here is part of the reason why. *Geist* is Hegel's name for what Plotinus had called *Nous*. Hegel sees *Geist* as Intellect that is active in the world, and the world is an expression of *Geist*. Hegel thinks that everything, and I do mean everything, is *Geist* trying to understand itself. Don't mistake *Geist* for the monotheistic conception of a God with whom we interact and who cares about us. *Geist* is doing its own thing and is not a knowable deity. However, we are living in *Geist*'s universe. Berkeley's philosophy made it seem as though we are living in the mind of God. Hegel's philosophy is that the universe *is* the rational mind of *Geist* manifesting its thought in a material and spiritual reality. For Hegel, "God" or "Intellect" is not an entity separate from the universe; it *is* the universe, and the universe *is Geist*. We are all parts of a cosmic

matrix that is a mind trying to understand itself. As *Geist* engages in its rational process of understanding, it literally creates the universe, and the evolution of *Geist's* understanding creates the evolution of rationality in the world in which we live. Hegel's philosophy of history is based on the idea that *Geist's* reason directs the world through universal rational laws, and when we look back at history, we can discern this march of reason through history as the development of rationality. The purpose of the universe is *Geist* trying to understand its Idea, Itself. We are part of that purpose.

2. **Freedom is the idea of *Geist*, and *Geist* is reason in and for itself.** *Geist* is Intellect; it is rationality. Because *Geist*'s rational activity is the cause of everything, rationality is what is real, and all that is real is rational. Freedom was the final cause (in the Aristotelean sense) for Kant. Everything in Kant's philosophy was to try to establish the importance and reality of human freedom (see Chapter 13). The same for Hegel, except Hegel didn't believe in individual freedom as we would understand it. The final cause of the universe is for *Geist* to realize Itself as reason itself, and this realization gives it freedom. That's freedom for *Geist*, and we can only find our own freedom within that because...

3. **The realization of freedom is the passionate individual as subject and object of history, and Its expression is the state.** This is a very interesting aspect of Hegel's thought and is less "out there" than the previous two ideas. You are the subject and object of history. This is true whether or not you agree with the existence of *Geist*. You are the subject because you are an active participant in history. Your actions contribute to the unfolding of events. You are the object of history in that history happens to you and you are a part of that matrix of historical events that, in Hegel's opinion, is *Geist* trying to realize its Idea. Like *Geist*, we all have a drive for self-realization—to understand who we are and our greatest potential. Self-realization is true freedom. For Hegel, realizing your role as a cog in the machine is the realization of your freedom, and the fullest realization of this is understanding your role in the state. Yes, Hegel means the political nation-state. Your freedom is realized in the state; if you are an American, your freedom is being a good American. That's about culture, not politics.

Hegel wrote that "the I is a we and the we is an I." You are who you are in the context of your society. This makes sense when you think about it, because although you are an individual with your own mind and thoughts and feelings, you are defined more than anything else by your relations with others and the society around you. Your life history of friends, family, community, and learning and your reactions to them define who you are. This idea from Hegel, inspired by Kant (inspired by Hume, inspired by Berkeley, and so on...) is accepted today by every academic worth anything. What is distinctive about Hegel is that he takes this interconnectedness as primarily expressed as the nation-state. Your freedom and identity are realized in being a good patriotic member of your nation.

4. **The national *Zeitgeist* is a moment in history as world *Geist*.** The German word "*Zeitgeist*" is best translated as "the spirit of the time." Hegel applied the concept of *Zeitgeist* to the nation-state as a whole, and he believed we can discern its *Volksgeist*, or "national spirit." Hegel accepted the idea that the human mind was active in cocreating its experiences, but he placed individual human minds within the nation-state, which is within the absolute mind of *Geist*. We aren't exactly cogs in the machine, but we are parts of a whole, and the whole is what is significant. Hegel believed that nations are the only real individuals in history. You are insignificant. The nation is significant. And *Geist* works out its Idea on the grand stage of interactions of nations. History is the progressive working out of that idea. What Hegel called "the march of reason" through history is *Geist* learning and developing through history as it manifests its reason through nation-states. Hegel further said that on earth at any given time, there is one nation that most exemplifies *Geist* and its Idea. That nation's *Volksgeist* ("national spirit"), was the greatest current flowering of culture and reason. It once was ancient Greece, then the Roman Empire, and so on. In Hegel's time, he saw the Prussian Empire as that manifestation of *Geist*.

Recognition

All of that fits well with the third component of Hegel's philosophy: recognition. Hegel uses a German word, *Anerkennung*, that does not have an exact match in English but is translated as "recognition." In English, recognition has two meanings: to identify something—"I recognize that object is a tree" (*Erkennen* in German)—and to acknowledge, value, and respect something—"I recognize you as a student and treat you as a student deserves to be treated" (*Anerkennung* in German). It is this latter definition, to respect and value something, that is the sense Hegel means.

Hegel realized that recognition is crucial in social life. You are defined by your relations with others. To have successful, healthy relations with others, you need the acknowledgment and approval of others. Hegel realized that we are all dependent on recognition from others. Think about any label or idea by which you can identify yourself: friend, student, citizen, and so on. You cannot meaningfully be that unless others acknowledge you as that; therefore, you are dependent on them for your identity. You are not a friend unless someone recognizes you as a friend. You cannot say, "I am a student at State University" unless the university recognizes you as such. You are not a citizen of a country unless that country legally recognizes you as one. Every single relation you have, every social identity you have, has a similar requirement. This includes even simple things like being a nice person or being attractive. You are not such unless others think you are. That is why we stress out so much about how we appear to others.

The positive side of recognition is that when we receive it, we become part of a community. The negative side of recognition is that because people need it, they compete for it. Remember François VI, duc de La Rochefoucauld and Rousseau's discussion of *amour propre* in Chapter 10. People become obsessed with the need for approval and recognition from others. This obsession drives them to act according to how society tells them to act, and people end up being untrue to themselves in order to curry favor with others. Hegel doesn't share Rousseau's antisociety position—he sees social norms as positives. We are members of a society, and that society has a system of social norms that inform people how to act and how to treat others. When we act in accordance with those norms, we receive recognition from others, including social authority. Hegel believed that recognition is essential for providing the conditions under which individual people can form an identity. Hegel said that an individual develops as a person through the guidance of recognition norms. Through our actions, some successful, some not so, we receive approval and disapproval, and we learn how to behave and be a part of our society. Recognition also gives us social roles and responsibilities by which we come to the self-realization of who we are as a passionate individual and member of our society. Recognition is the means by which we actualize our various freedoms through becoming a good member of our social community and of society as a whole.

Hegel does acknowledge that recognition can be a negative burden. His position is that recognition is more of a problem in interpersonal relations. Because we are defined by others and need recognition from them to know how we are and thus be autonomous, Hegel thought that we will fight against another person to affirm our own freedom by proving that our status is of more importance than that of the other person. We are trying to express our autonomy through elevating ourselves over another, but this conflict cannot achieve the mutual recognition that is essential to our autonomy. Hegel's example is the master–slave relation, which needs to be interpreted more as an analogy than as literal. Someone is a master only if a slave acknowledges that mastery. So, Hegel says, the master is actually dependent on the slave for his own autonomous identity. This creates a conflict that neither can ever win. In Hegel's harsh assessment, the conflict ends only when one of them dies. The master–slave analogy illustrates that the irony of freedom is that we cannot be free except in terms of our relations with others and our place in a society. The theory of recognition based on Hegel's ideas became a topic in social philosophy, as we will see in Chapter 24.

REFERENCE

Johann Gottlieb Fichte, *The Vocation of Man*, trans. William Smith, Public Domain, *Wikisource*, https://en.wikisource.org/wiki/The_Vocation_of_Man/. (accessed May 13, 2021)

CHAPTER 15

KARL MARX, THE MISUNDERSTOOD DIAGNOSTICIAN

Karl Marx (1818–1883) is not that difficult to understand, but a century of misinformation about what Marx actually wrote and advocated for has given people false impressions. Much of that false information about Marx came from those who claimed to be instituting his ideas but, in fact, were not. There has never been a truly Marxist society. No, the Communism of the Soviet Union and China were not true to Marx's philosophy. Another huge chunk of that false information about Marx came from the capitalists whom Marx opposed and who wanted to stamp our Marx's critique of capitalism.

The path to understanding Marx begins by understanding this excerpt from *The Communist Manifesto*:

> *A spectre is haunting Europe—the spectre of Communism. All the Powers of old Europe have entered into a holy alliance to exorcise this spectre...*
>
> *Where is the party in opposition that has not been decried as Communistic by its opponents in power?...*
>
> *The Communists disdain to conceal their views and aims. They openly declare that*

their ends can be attained only by the forcible overthrow of all existing social conditions. Let the ruling classes tremble at a Communistic revolution. The proletarians have nothing to lose but their chains. They have a world to win.

WORKING [PEOPLE] OF ALL COUNTRIES, UNITE! (*The Communist Manifesto*)

Whoa, dudes, that's intense. Marx, with Friedrich Engels, wrote *The Communist Manifesto* in 1848. In it, they famously predicted a worldwide workers' revolution. They were incorrect, but they had good reason to believe that what they predicted would transpire. That very year, 1848, came to be known as "The Year of Revolutions" because, across Europe, six different peasant or worker revolts took place against local or national aristocratic rulers. Everything seemed to be coming to a head. For Marx, it seemed to be the case that workers were realizing their state of alienation and were rising up against their oppression. He applauded this because he saw revolution as the only possible response to the alienation caused by capitalism.

THE ERA OF REVOLUTIONS?

As the manifesto's text shows, the idea of communism already existed—Marx didn't invent it. "Communism," after all, comes from the Latin *communis*, which means "community," so the idea of communism is the idea of communal society, variously interpreted, in contradistinction to a hierarchical society dominated by an elite class. Marx and Engels were discussing an emerging philosophical idea that, on the basis of contemporary events, they thought was about to become the major political philosophy in Europe. Marx's goal was to understand both the movement he thought he saw coming and the broken sociopolitical system that the movement was opposing.

How did Marx and Engels come to the conclusion that revolution was inevitable? They based it not only on then current events but also on then current philosophy. The dominant philosopher in Europe in the 1840s was Hegel. A split had developed among Hegel's followers into a conservative, or right-wing, interpretation of Hegel, and a radical, or left-wing, interpretation of Hegel. The split was predominantly based on whether the followers focused on the transcendent or the earthly interpretation of Hegel's system. Here is the central example. Hegel had written that the real is the rational and the rational is the real, by which he meant that rationality is reality and vice versa. Right-wingers linked this concept to the hierarchical philosophical systems of the past. "The real is the rational" harkened back to Platonic ideas of the Good and Aristotelian ideas of final causes and essences. These Right Hegelians saw the Hegelian system as a fulfillment of that tradition of human thought. It is certainly a reasonable interpretation of Hegel, who saw human progress in terms of a march of reason through history (only European history and thought, of course).

Marx was part of a group of left-wing Young Hegelians who agreed with the Hegelian idea of historicism (the notion that there is a pattern to historical development) but who believed that human society is not rational, and if the "rational is the real," then history is still evolving and not yet fully real. In brief, Marx saw the central contradiction of European society as, on the one hand, thinking it embodied the ideal of individual reason and liberty but, on the other hand, the lived reality of irrationality and the lack of freedom caused by industrialization and poverty. Marx believed that working people were waking up to these contradictions and were rebelling against the elite class that was oppressing them.

THE MARCH OF CLASS STRUGGLE

Armed with the Hegelian notion that history has a pattern and that history is developing along rational lines, Marx believed he saw that pattern.

> *The history of all hitherto existing societies is the history of class struggles. Freeman and slave, patrician and plebeian, lord and serf, guild-master and journeyman, in a word, oppressor and oppressed, stood in constant opposition to one another, carried on an uninterrupted, now hidden, now open fight, a fight that each time ended, either in a revolutionary re-constitution of society at large, or in the common ruin of the contending classes.* (*The Communist Manifesto*)

In short, Marx and Engels claim the rich exploit the poor. Always have. Society has always been divided into a small wealthy elite and the poorer masses. In Marx's time, that divide was between the capitalists who owned the means of industrial production and the workers who owned nothing. The capitalists profited from the labor of the workers—the rich exploited the poor.

Similar to Hegel, Marx thought that when we look back at history, we can discern a rational evolution through successive epochs. These epochs rise and fall as a result of "economic determinism," a concept Marx invented, indicating that all human activity is determined by inescapable economic necessities. Marx said that he had turned Hegel on his head, replacing Hegel's *Geist* with economic determinism as the force that drives the world. Individual humans are powerless to escape or affect these material macroeconomic forces that determine our lives. Human history is, therefore, economic history for Marx. Humans need to satisfy their material needs; therefore, they are dependent on the forces of production that satisfy those needs. As history evolves, the forces of production are altered by economic necessities and technological changes. What never changes are human material needs and the struggle over control of the forces of production. History is, therefore, the history of the class struggle.

In the economic epochs of history, there was first the epoch of slavery when the elite owned other people, then the epoch of feudalism when the elite tied the people to the land, and now the epoch of capitalism when the elite tie the people to the industries. In each epoch, the elite own and control the means of production, including farm fields, mines, and factories from small to big. In each epoch, the system of economic exploitation grew until its rational contradictions became unsustainable and circumstances forced an evolutionary change to a new system. So, slavery morphed into feudalism and feudalism morphed into capitalism. Next, capitalism will collapse from the weight of its rational contradictions, which make it unsustainable. This collapse of capitalism will usher in the next epoch—communism—when the class divide will finally end and society will be without rational contradictions. At least, that's what Marx predicted.

THE PROBLEM WITH THE BOURGEOIS CLASS

Why will capitalism collapse? What did Marx see as its rational contradictions? Capitalism is an economic system defined by bourgeois property. Marx and Engels write in *The Communist Manifesto* that "modern bourgeois private property is the final and most complete expression of the system of producing and appropriating products, that is based on class antagonisms, on the exploitation of the many by the few." It's crucial to understand what Marx and Engels do *not* mean by bourgeois private property. They say:

> *We Communists have been reproached with the desire of abolishing the right of personally acquiring property as the fruit of a man's own*

> *labor, which property is alleged to be the groundwork of all personal freedom, activity and independence. Hard-won, self-acquired, self-earned property! Do you mean the property of the petty artisan and of the small peasant, a form of property that preceded the bourgeois form? There is no need to abolish that; the development of industry has to a great extent already destroyed it, and is still destroying it daily. Or do you mean modern bourgeois private property? But does wage-labor create any property for the laborer? Not a bit. It creates capital.* (*The Communist Manifesto*)

Bourgeois society ("bourgeois" from Middle French, roughly meaning "merchant class") creates capital. Capital is not a personal but a social power. The problem with bourgeois society is that its private property is capital. Capital is independent and has individuality, while the living person is dependent and has no individuality. Marx and Engels refer here to the corporation, a social institution that developed in the 1600s with the express purpose of creating capital for its investors. Corporations proliferated in the early 1800s, and Marx and Engels were prescient in their description of capital having individuality because 18 years later in 1866, the United States recognized a corporation as a "natural person," giving this social power as many rights as, if not more rights than, individual people naturally have. Today, corporations dominate economic, social, and political life.

The bourgeois system is the private ownership of the means of production that splits society into the classes of bourgeois and proletariat (from the Latin meaning "propertyless"). Members of the bourgeois capitalist class own the means of production at which workers produce commodities to be sold for the personal profit of the bourgeois class. Driven by the combination of greed and competitive pressures from other capitalists, the capitalists need to keep costs low, and labor is the biggest cost to production. Yes, there are fixed costs, such as the costs for raw materials and the running of a factory, but the lower the wages the capitalist can pay the worker, the more profit the capitalist makes. Capitalism has an inherent need to keep wages low.

Regardless of the level of wages, the capitalist business model is inherently corrupt and exploitative, said Marx. All profits, Marx argues in *Das Capital* (1867), are made by exploiting wage labor. Marx's argument is simple and eloquent and shows one of the differences between capitalism and free enterprise. Capitalism is the exploitation of the surplus value produced by labor. Here's what that means. In free enterprise, where the worker—for example a blacksmith or a tailor—owns the means of his or her own production, the worker also owns the goods that are the products of his or her own labor and can sell those products and keep all of the revenue. In capitalism, the bourgeois capitalist owns the means of production but does not work, hiring others to perform the labor needed to produce goods. The workers do not own the products of their labor, the capitalist does, who then sells the product and keeps all of the revenue. But to make a profit, after subtracting other fixed costs, the capitalist has to pay the workers less than the value of their labor. In a twelve-hour workday (common in the 1800s), the worker is paid wages, but only the equivalent value of 8 hours of work. The value of the other 4 hours of work is pocketed by the capitalist as profit.

Marx argues that instead of working only for yourself, because you don't own the means of production, you work only partially for yourself. You work to make profits for the capitalist. The wages you receive are not a fair exchange for the value of your labor. Because you do not own the means of production, your only way of surviving is to sell your labor to the capitalist. This is why the capitalist work relationship is not equal. The capitalist holds much more power in the labor-for-wages transaction. The worker doesn't receive a fair wage for his or her labor, and in the capitalist system, never will. This is one principal corruption of the capitalist system, and why capitalism is doomed to failure, Marx said.

HUMAN ALIENATION: CAPITALISM'S GREATEST HARM

For Marx, the injustice of capitalism is far deeper than "I don't get paid enough." The capitalist system harms human beings. Even the capitalist, who benefits from the exploitation of the proletariat, is harmed. The capitalist is trapped by the system, Marx says. The capitalist is in continual competition with other capitalists and is driven to make more profits so that the profits can be invested to grow the means of production to make more profit to grow more, and so on, and so on. "Accumulation for the sake of accumulation, production for the sake of production," characterizes the bourgeois capitalist, Marx says. This, along with its inherent need to exploit labor, is why Marx sees capitalism as an irrational system.

But, of course, it is the worker who suffers the most.

> *It is true that labor produces for the rich wonderful things, but for the worker it produces poverty. It produces mansions, but for the worker, shacks. It produces beauty, but for the worker, deformity. It replaces labor*

> *by machines, but it throws one section of the workers back into barbarous types of labor and it turns the other section into a machine. It produces intelligence, but for the worker, stupidity, ignorance.* ("Economic and Philosophic Manuscripts of 1844")

For Marx, the central question is the relationship of workers to production. Among other things, capitalism is a particular system of production, and all production is dependent on labor, so capitalism has a particular relationship of workers to production. Workers suffer not just economic deprivation but also a kind of spiritual alienation. In writings now known as the "Economic and Philosophic Manuscripts of 1844," Marx explains the forms of alienation suffered by the proletariat. It is unfortunate that Marx did not publish these manuscripts (they were found years later) because they show another side of his philosophy about which few people know.

Marx said that the irrational nature of the capitalist system causes estrangement or alienation for the worker in four ways, all of which stem from the fact that in capitalism, labor is *external* to the worker. When one works for oneself, one's work is a personal expression. Marx, more than 150 years ago, was much more familiar than we are with independent craftspeople who owned their own workshops, producing their own goods to sell. Marx said such people's work belongs to their intrinsic nature and their work affirms who they are. The opposite is true in capitalism. Work is a job that is external to one's intrinsic nature. You go to your job at which you are unhappy because the labor is neither an expression of who you are nor an activity that develops you mentally or physically. These facts cause the first two forms of alienation.

Workers are alienated from the product of their labor. We've covered much of this idea already, and it's central to Marx's philosophy. Craftspeople, because they own their means of production, own the products they produce. Workers in capitalism don't own the means of production. They work at the bourgeois property owner's factory, producing goods that are owned by the factory owner. The products of the workers' labors are controlled by the factory owner, who is free to sell and profit from it. Yes, the worker receives a wage, but as Marx explained earlier, that wage is not fair compensation for the worker's labors.

Workers are alienated from the process of production. Workers have no say in the process of production; they are merely used by it. The process is fully external to them. Factories require the commodities of raw materials, the commodities of the machinery that processes the material, and the commodity of workers to run the machines. On the job, workers are not people; they are interchangeable parts. Still today, companies refer to "human resources," showing that workers are just so much fungible raw material to be used by the company as it sees fit and for its sole benefit.

Workers are alienated from their own human nature. Workers are human beings, but capitalism does not treat them as human beings. Marx says that the nature of human beings is to be free and consciously active. As other philosophers have said, we each have our own will, and Marx says that our conscious life activity distinguishes us from the animals. Animals act only to satisfy their own immediate needs, but we humans can create for purposes beyond our immediate needs, and we see ourselves in the world we create. The capitalist system strips this creative activity away from workers. The capitalist system objectifies workers, turning them into mere beasts of burden, but actually lower than beasts of burden because the capitalists spend no effort to care and feed the workers. Workers are forced to work to sustain their physical bodies—they work to eat. Work, therefore, is forced labor that is merely a means to satisfy needs external to that work. The height of the workers' servitude is that it is only as workers that they can maintain themselves as material beings and that it is only as material beings that they are workers. They are no longer human beings.

Workers are alienated from each other. Workers are not only degraded below being human but they are forced to see other workers as degraded. In their servitude, they are alienated from their employers, but they are also alienated from their fellow workers. Because capitalism reduces them to fungible commodities, they don't see their fellow workers as allies but as competitors for the finite number of jobs available.

THE STRUCTURE OF SOCIETY

Marx defined three large-scale structures in society. These structures delineate capitalist society, but similar structures can also be found in precapitalist epochs. The first is the forces of production, which are the means of production—industry and the raw materials, machinery, and labor it consumes. The second is the relations of production—the social institutions and practices that regulate the forces of production. Marx refers to these first two structures as the combined economic substructure, to differentiate them from the third structure. At a social level above the economic substructure is what Marx calls the superstructure—the social institutions and norms engaged in the production of ideas. Marx's use of "ideas" is not the epistemologist's limited uses but the broader sense of the term common to us today. The superstructure contains all of our social ideas: moral, political, legal, cultural, philosophical, religious, and linguistic.

Marx believed that the superstructure rose out of the economic substructures. The superstructure is an expression of the economic substructure and, therefore, changes over historical epochs subject to economic determinism. But while the superstructure's foundation is the economic forces to which it corresponds, it affects society. The superstructure is the way in which people think about themselves and their world. From this point on, Marx's philosophy gets complex and even more controversial. Marx claims that because society is defined by class struggle, the ideas produced by the superstructure serve the interests of the ruling class. Those who control the economic substructure also control the superstructure, and they use the superstructure to rationalize the current social system. The ruling class creates a false consciousness that hides or justifies the irrationalities and injustices of the exploitation of workers. Marx calls this illusionary consciousness "ideology." In the capitalist system, the superstructure pushes the ideology that creates the false consciousness that capitalism is rational and good.

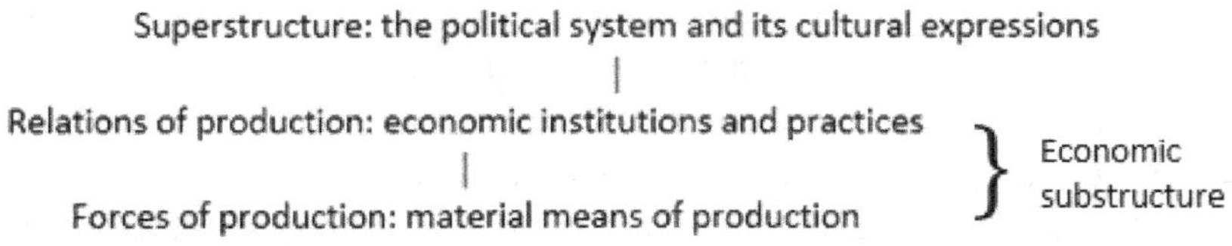

Marx claims that in every epoch of history, every society is ruled by the ideology created by the ruling class. This is Marx's most influential and controversial idea. The debate is not whether he has identified a real feature in human society but how complete the reach of ideology in societal and individual thinking is. Marx and a large cadre of his followers claim that reach is complete—that ideology inescapably permeates every aspect of human life. All social institutions are tools of the ruling power structure, and the primary purpose of all social expressions is to perpetuate the class structure. Marx also claims that ideology is always false and therefore always harmful. All ideology deceives people into seeing their circumstances as upside down from how they really are. Ideology justifies social and economic inequities as natural and even beneficial to exploited people. Examples of these false ideological justifications are such ideas as "colonization benefited the primitive colonized people" and "capitalism serves the interests of the working class." Even philosophers and scientists, who think they are discerning truth and leading the way to positive social change, are active ideologists, Marx says. All social institutions and all human consciousness are social products that have no history and no development aside from being tools of ideology.

Working People of the World Unite?

We come full circle to where we began this chapter. The working class has nothing to lose but its chains, Marx and Engels claim. Workers of the world must unite and rebel against the ruling capitalists. Marx, for all his analytical skill, is very black-and-white in his conception of how to deal with the inequalities and injustices of capitalism. There is only one solution: Capitalism must be ended because capitalism dominates every aspect of both the superstructure and the economic substructure; therefore, it cannot be reformed. All of society must be upended to destroy capitalism. Many small-minded, bitter people have ever since latched onto that idea and acted accordingly. Much hate-filled violence has been rationalized by appealing to Marx.

Marx thought that the workers' revolution was inevitable. As mentioned earlier, he had some good reasons for thinking that, but his primary reason was theoretical. His economic determinism told him that change happens when the material forces of social development come into conflict with existing relations of production. The resulting tensions within that society eventually spark a social revolution and usher in a new epoch. He thought this had happened before when slavery changed to feudalism and when feudalism changed to capitalism. Marx didn't describe how and when these changes happened, probably because there are no clear signs of exactly when and where these changes occurred. Nevertheless, Marx was certain that economic determinism would force the next social revolution to happen soon, sweeping away capitalism and ushering in a new postcapitalist epoch.

Marx's vision of the workers' revolution has much in common with religious eschatological predictions of a final judgment. Evil is in control of the world, but the die is cast that the great evil will be destroyed and humanity liberated. First though, the current epoch must run its full course until a breaking point is reached. In its simplest terms, Marx predicted that capitalism was doomed because of its inextricable needs to exploit labor and have competing companies engage in cutthroat struggles with each other. Capitalism would run its full course as competition eliminates less efficient companies, increasing the consolidation of economic power. Having fewer companies gives more economic power to the surviving capitalists and throws more workers (including new workers from the now bankrupt capitalist companies) into competition for wages. This further drives down wages in addition to capitalism's inherent pressures to keep wages low. As the numbers of the working class increase, and as their misery increases, they will reach a breaking point, and workers will explode into revolution. Marx describes this no differently than a chemist would describe a reaction of ingredients because Marx thought this entire process was governed by economic determinism.

So what happens after the breaking point, according to Marx? Violence will ensue because the only way to end capitalism is through the forceful elimination of capitalism—what Marx ominously calls "the dictatorship of the proletariat." Chaos is inevitable but will be contained when leaders of the revolution form a temporary state to take over the means of production. This intermediate stage Marx called "socialism," meaning a political state dedicated to serving the interests of all of society, not just the interests of the ruling class. The state's only purpose in this stage is to manage the redistribution of the means of production to the workers. After this redistribution is effected, the leaders of the state will willingly dissolve the state and work for themselves alongside the other workers. The revolution having eliminated class divisions, there remains only the people. Working for themselves rather than for others, they are no longer alienated from their labor and the products of their labor. No longer being exploited by capitalists, they are no longer alienated from their own human nature and each other, so they have no cause for struggle and can express themselves freely. All people are now equal and free, and the people can collectively control the political and economic life of society. This is the final stage of the epochs of human history, which Marx calls "communism," which means simply a communal society.

Obviously, there are multiple problems with this vision. The overarching optimism of the sequence of events, for starters. Marx, like Rousseau, believes that greed and selfishness are not a part of human nature but are emotions created by society. When capitalism is destroyed, human behavior will change, and people will naturally work together for the greater good. This is why Marx assumes that after the revolution has finished eliminating capitalism, the temporary state will efficiently perform its tasks of redistributing all ownership of the means of production back to the workers and will dissolve itself. History shows us that human nature is not as communally minded as Marx hoped. The world has never seen a communist society. Those revolutions that claimed to communist—in the Soviet Union, China, Cuba—were quickly hijacked by leaders who remained permanently stuck in the stage of the temporary state. They called their states "socialist," but they were never dedicated to the good of society. They clung to power continually claiming the revolution was not yet over so they had to keep control of the means of production a little longer. The fault in these failed states wasn't communism or socialism because those states never got to those points;

they were ironically more capitalist than anything in their exploitation of workers. Marx didn't seem to consider this a possibility.

Another problem is Marx never explains how communism will actually work. Marx said the motto of the communist society will be "from each according to his ability, to each according to his needs," but he doesn't explain how we determine individual abilities and needs or how we prioritize conflicting abilities and needs. His other basic principle of the new communal society is that workers control the means of production. Okay. How? To say that workers will now make political and economic decisions doesn't explain the mechanism by which they do so. Marx seems to be relying on his assumption that absent class struggle, everyone will be eager to cooperate. Soviet propaganda films played heavily on the theme of happy peasants joyously working, but these expressions of ideology never dealt with the realities of life. How do worker-run farms, mines, and factories govern themselves? How do they conduct business? How do these separate communities work together? Worker ownership is a good idea, but how does the communal society not slip into the mode of businesses competing against each other that is part of capitalism? How can these worker-owned businesses avoid being taken over by selfish and exploitative people? We need not be as pessimistic as Hobbes was about human nature to realize that people are capable of selfishness and hostility. Locke was correct that some form of government is necessary to preserve the peace. Marx claims that communism is the solution to the riddle of history and the salvation of humanity, but his conception of a communal society is poorly defined. This is surprising, considering how impressively detailed and thoughtful his historical critique of capitalism is in *Das Capital.*

Evaluating Marx

Some philosophers argue that the concept of alienation outlined in his 1844 writings is the driving force behind Marx's thought. Their reading of Marx (the psychological reading) is that the plight of the worker is his central concern and that understanding workers' alienation is the key to understanding the rest of Marx's ideas about capitalism, revolution, and communism.

The other primary reading of Marx (the scientific reading) is that Marx's primary concern is macroeconomics. This reading by analytical Marxist philosophers (see Chapter 22) focuses on Marx's later book *Das Kapital* (published in three parts from 1867 to 1883) that details the excesses of capitalism in the mid-1800s and his theory of economic determinism throughout history. The scientific economic reading sees Marx as interested in detailing the evils of capitalism and the need to fight against its ideology and oppressive superstructure. Advocates of the psychological reading counter that the economic and political content of *Das Kapital* is best understood in terms of human alienation.

The primary reason for this divergence in readings of Marx is that his views on alienation are contained in the 1844 manuscripts and not explicitly referred to in *Das Kapital*. The 1844 manuscripts were not rediscovered until the 1930s, and by then many people had entrenched ideas about what Marxism is; they were not open to reassessing it. The Soviets had, in their gross expropriation of Marx, poisoned generations against Marx's ideas. Decades of relentless anti-Marx propaganda by capitalists didn't help. Academic study of Marx was all but censored in the United States, and it's only been in the past few decades that there has been a rational, objective study of his philosophy. Not that any consensus has yet emerged about how to think about Marx's philosophy, good or bad.

So what should we think about Marx and his ideas? I have long felt that Marx was a brilliant diagnostician but a lousy prescriber. He knew what was wrong with society but had a wrong idea about how to fix it. His analysis of the alienation of labor in capitalism remains incredibly accurate today. Anyone who has ever held a job working for a company rather than for himself or herself can relate to the four alienations. Marx's accounts of the excesses of capitalism in the mid-1800s are also accurate, pulled as they were from official government records. Marx's conclusions about how capitalism has distorted society, creating an ideological superstructure that maintains the status quo of the class structure, is arguably accurate and highly influential for a wide range of scholarship (see Chapters 24–26).

No matter how accurately Marx may have described our world, his predictions and preferred solutions fell well short. One reason that Marx focused only on those facts that supported his preferred narrative and ignored historical facts that contradicted his theory. Another reason is that Marx assumed that human actions are fully determined by external forces and that all external forces boiled down to economic issues. He failed to take into account that individual people could act contrary to the dictates of their class expectations and the ideological teachings of their society. He also failed to consider that people could act for reasons other than economic ones. These omissions are glaring given the time and place in which he lived and learned—influenced by German idealism among other individualistic and passionate expressions of thought and culture.

Marx's predicted rise of the proletariat never occurred. No, the Russian Revolution was not Marxist, despite the propaganda they used to justify it. Marx's insistence that the complete destruction of capitalism was necessary to improve the plight of the working class was also wrong. Marx could not foresee, because he was a determinist, that workers and capitalists could come to agreements to improve working conditions and pay. Marx believed that economic determinism forced an eternal conflict between the bourgeoisie and the proletariat. Marx did not foresee the possibility of organized labor unions that could take actions to better their lives short of a violent overthrow of governments. Marx also could not imagine some capitalists having concerns for workers' well-being and being willing to work together with their employees. Rather than war, cooperation is possible. Marx did not understand that, and neither today do some of his hard-core followers.

REFERENCES

Karl Marx and Friedrich Engels, *Communist Manifesto.* Project Gutenberg, http://www.gutenberg.org/ebooks/61/. (accessed April 1, 2021)

Karl Marx, "Economic and Philosophic Manuscripts of 1844," in *Classical Sociological Theory and Foundations of American Sociology*, ed. Allison Hurst, https://open.oregonstate.education/sociologicaltheory/chapter/economic-and-philosophic-manuscripts-of-1844/, licensed under a Creative Commons Attribution-ShareAlike 4.0 International License. No modifications made. (accessed April 3, 2021)

CHAPTER 16

MORAL PHILOSOPHY

We won't be discussing moral philosophy in great detail because it is usually covered in depth in other courses. To tell the story of philosophy's long conversation, it's necessary to have a short chapter on the subject at this point in the book. A new early 1800s movement in thinking about morality—the fundamental principles of how we should act toward others—had major effects on the rest of philosophy. That movement is utilitarianism, and it broke from a long tradition of seeing morality as obedience to transcendent rules. First, though, we need to mention another major movement in moral philosophy against which utilitarianism set itself.

KANT'S MORAL LAW

We discussed Kant's epistemology in Chapter 13. His moral theory in some ways connects with the rest of his philosophy but mainly stands apart from it. Kant took seriously Hume's critique of epistemology, but he dismissed Hume's contention that morality is based on feeling. For Kant, everything is about reason, and that includes morality. His basic assumption about all morality is that there is a rational, universal moral law. Kant put forward a moral system centered on the concept of moral duty. In some respects, Kant's system can be understood as a post-Enlightenment version of the ancient command to obey the moral law.

Kant did recognize what Hume meant by saying that we have an internal moral sense. For Kant, our inherent moral law is within us. Morality is not a matter of following a rule book like the Ten Commandments or the do's and don'ts of etiquette. There is a moral law that we sense, but through reason not through emotion. The moral law is a transcendent, universal, objective part of reality. If someone violates the moral law, that does not affect the law. The universality lies in the law itself and not in a sense that all humans always act on it. Kant thus believed that there is a pure practical rationality for a science of morality just like there is a pure practical rationality for science and perception. People can sense the moral law and make pure rational moral judgments.

How do we know what is morally right and wrong? Kant said we cannot give a law that is true for each and every instance, but we can identify a basic axiom for moral behavior. The argument he gives makes sense; it's internally consistent, tough, long, and complicated, like everything in Kant's thought. It begins with a basic principle, an axiom that can be the ultimate principle of morality: the good will. Kant wrote that nothing can possibly be conceived in the world that can be called good without qualification except a good will. Every other positive aspect of humanity can contribute to the good, but the only thing that can be truly purely good is a good will. All of our other moral virtues, like courage, moderation, perseverance, and other qualities of the human psyche, could be good or bad only if they are so because it is the will that makes them good or bad. It is the will that makes use of other virtues and that constitutes the human character. The good will is good not because of what it performs or creates, nor by its aptness to attain some proposed end, but simply by virtue of the volition that is the good in itself and considered by itself. When we look at the coldness of a villain, what makes the villain so dangerous to us and abominable in our eyes is that that villain lacks good will. It is not so much what the villain does as it is that lack of good will, that lack of sensing the moral law, that is evil.

Kant says that the good will must always be directed toward doing one's moral duty to the moral law. Kant's morality is usually referred to as a "deontological" system, from the Greek word *dion*, which means "duty." This proposition is not in addition to the good will because it is in no way separate from the concept of the good will. We have, Kant says, a universal moral duty. We have many specific moral duties; for example, we have a duty to preserve life, including our own life. Kant said it is wrong to commit suicide because it is a duty to preserve your own life no matter what the circumstances. That type of thinking is an example of the duty we have to the moral law that is at the heart and core of being moral. Will and duty are inseparable within Kant's system. It is only willingly acting out of duty and respect for the moral law that makes an act good, not the consequences of an act.

Respect for the moral law is a rational necessity. We know there's a moral law. We know we have a duty to the moral law. We know that the moral worth of any action is because we act out of duty. There is no other rational choice but to respect and follow the moral law. Kant combines all of these ideas into the categorical imperative. That imperative can be expressed as follows: "I am never to act otherwise than so that I could also will that my maxim should become a universal law." (*Metaphysic of Morals*, 1.19) What Kant is arguing is that if there is a universal moral law, and of course there is, then I should act not just according to that moral law but I should respect the moral law in such a way that my will and my duty combine so that I will that my maxim is a universal law. This looks a little bit like circular reasoning, but sometimes circular reasoning isn't a logical fallacy; sometimes it's because the concepts are connected with each other. The ideas in Kant of a moral law, a good will, and a sense of duty combine into the categorical imperative of *always* acting so that will, duty, and universality are all one.

The main reason Kant is arguing this way is to get away from what he calls the "hypothetical imperative." We're very used to the hypothetical imperative even if we're not really aware of how aware we are of the hypothetical imperative. The hypothetical imperative is the if–then statement. If I can get away with it, I will break the rules; or if other people don't obey the rules, I won't either; or if it doesn't do too much harm, I will bend the rules a little. It's a very human way of thinking, but it's a very wrong way of human thinking, according to Kant. If morality has any meaning, it should be something that we respect and to which we feel a duty. Our entire will should be behind following the moral law. Kant thinks that hypotheticals lack respect because they are about making excuses, trying to find a way around the moral law. Or it's saying that I have an inclination to follow the law and sometimes do what's morally right. Kant is calling your bluff on this. He's saying something like this: "Look, if it's a universal moral law, then it universally applies; that's what "universal" means. Your will should follow the universal law *always*." That is why Kant says it's a *categorical* imperative not a hypothetical imperative.

We also have a duty to other people in terms of treating them always as an end in themselves and never as only a means to another end. The plain language version of this is to not use other people. Slavery is wrong because what you're doing is using other human beings to gain something from them. We all know about manipulating or tricking people, and we all have a sense that that is wrong. Kant says that you should never use a person as a means to an end because human beings are moral agents. They are rational beings with a soul. They are human beings, not inanimate objects, so it's morally wrong to use or manipulate people for your own ends. That doesn't forbid us from interacting with other people to accomplish our own goals. For example, we interact with a cashier at the store to purchase our goods, but that's not using them *only* as a means. We need to recognize that the cashier is a person who deserves our respect, who is a moral actor just like we are. So when you're doing a transaction, be kind, be generous; that's your duty anyway. Kant says that we have a duty to act lovingly toward each other. If the only reason you are kind to other people is because you want to get something out of it, that is not moral. Morality is the good will plus duty to the moral law, so if you are acting kind to someone simply because you want something in return, or because you want to be recognized as a kind person, or for some sort of heavenly or earthly reward, then that's not acting out of a sense of duty.

Kant believes that we are moral legislators and moral agents, and that means we have autonomy. We are most free and autonomous when we are acting in a sense of moral duty and our will is united to the moral law. When you unite your will with the moral law, then you are contributing to the moral law, and you can see yourself as the author of the moral law. This isn't just a mental trick. When we act from duty and respect for the moral law, then we are fully existing as an autonomous being. Kant is not a Stoic (see Chapter 4), but he is expressing a similar idea that when we unite our will with how things are, then our will and necessity are united, and we are free.

JEREMY BENTHAM'S UTILITARIANISM

Happiness. Who doesn't want more happiness? Everyone wants happiness, Jeremy Bentham (1748–1832) thought, and that's not a bad assumption. Aristotle said that everyone wanted to attain *eudaimonia*, a state of contentment of living well and having a life worth living. Bentham's idea was similar but far less lofty. Like Hobbes (see Chapter 9), Bentham believed that the basic human reality was pain and pleasure. He begins his book on his theory with this definitive statement:

> *Nature has placed mankind under the governance of two sovereign masters, pain and pleasure. It is for them alone to point out what we ought to do, as well as to determine what we shall do. On the one hand the standard of right and wrong, on the other the chain of causes and effects, are fastened to their throne. They govern us in all we do, in all we say, in*

all we think: every effort we can make to throw off our subjection, will serve but to demonstrate and confirm it. In words a man may pretend to abjure their empire: but in reality he will remain subject to it all the while. (*An Introduction to the Principles of Morals and Legislation*, I)

He shares Hobbes's theory of endeavors. Bentham was also, like Hobbes, a determinist. Therefore, Bentham considered morals and politics to be a kind of physics that just needed to be solved through equations. We just want to be happy, and any pleasure will do, he thought. Greater happiness could also simply be a lessening of pain and suffering. If there's a pain-to-pleasure scale of −10 to 10, lessening pain from −4 to −2 is good, just like increasing happiness from 2 to 4 is good.

Bentham set out to change moral philosophy, which he thought was empty. He took a very different approach to moral decision-making by focusing on the consequences of actions. In some respects, Bentham, who grew up wealthy and never knew anything but privilege, was expressing the bourgeois sentiments that Marx later condemned. His moral theory is correctly described as a form of hedonism: Pleasure means moral good. Bentham saw moral systems based on universal laws (like Kant's) and rights (like Locke and Wollstonecraft's) to be denying the reality of pain and pleasure. To counter what he thought were the absurdities of those systems, he introduces what he coins the "principle of utility."

The principle of utility recognizes this subjection, and assumes it for the foundation of that system, the object of which is to rear the fabric of felicity by the hands of reason and of law. Systems which attempt to question it, deal in sounds instead of sense, in caprice instead of reason, in darkness instead of light. (*An Introduction to the Principles of Morals and Legislation*, I)

Utility, for Bentham, was a quality within any object whereby it tends to produce benefit, advantage, pleasure, good, or happiness or to prevent the happening of mischief, pain, evil, or unhappiness to people. Just as the objects in the world can produce impressions of sight and sound in us, they can produce pain and pleasure in us. Obviously, Bentham observes, we prefer pleasure to pain. Everything we do as individuals, and everything our governmental, social, political, and legal institutions do, should follow the principle of choosing that course of action that results in the greatest happiness for the greatest number of people.

This principle of producing the greatest happiness for the greatest number of people, which he called the "principle of utility," he proposes to be the guiding principle of all human activity. In adopting the principle, Bentham is rejecting any consideration of human rights, virtue, motive, or goals. All that matters are the consequences of an action. If an action increases total happiness, it is good; if it doesn't, it's not good. It was that simple for him.

Bentham genuinely believed the principle of utility was a universal truth that can be objectively, rationally quantified and scientifically measured. He developed an equation to measure happiness that he believed could be used to solve moral and political issues. He called this a "felicific calculus" meaning "a calculation to produce happiness." He didn't provide us with any kind of happimeter or specific ways by which we could measure units of happiness. He did leave us with the basic principle of the felicific calculus to guide our thinking about social policy. He proposed that we measure the utility of any proposed action on seven scales:

1. The intensity of pleasure produced
2. The duration of that pleasure
3. The certainty the action will actually produce pleasure
4. How soon the pleasurable result will occur
5. How likely the action will produce more pleasures of the same kind
6. Whether the pleasure will be followed by sensations of the opposite kind (pain followed by pleasure or pleasure followed by pain)
7. How many other people will be affected by the action

Even though we lack a happimeter, we can analyze any proposed course of action by using these seven scales, as Bentham would want us to do.

Bentham believed that the English legal system was founded on unscientific principles—that it was a confused muddle of historical prejudices and superstitions. He was most critical of the prevailing theory at the time of inalienable human rights. Bentham attacked the French revolutionary "Declaration of the Rights of Man and the Citizen" (1789) as "rhetorical nonsense—nonsense upon stilts." Condescending though he was, Bentham was not arguing that people should not have rights; he was taking issue with the presumed source of those rights. Bentham was arguing that rights do not exist in nature but are willfully created by human institutions. They are not absolutes but are matters for debate. In this way, Bentham was taking Locke's vision of the social contract one step further: Not only is government created by humans to serve human needs but the concept of rights is likewise created by humans to serve human needs. But Locke had believed that the need government served was the inalienable human rights of life, liberty, and property. Bentham believed the need government served was the need to ensure the greatest happiness for the greatest number of people.

Bentham walked the walk of the principles he set forth. He spent decades advocating for social reform. He is particularly known for his proposals for criminal justice reform. He proposed that the focus shift from retribution against criminals to reforming them to create greater social happiness. Punishment causes pain, Bentham argued, which is bad; therefore, criminals should be punished only enough to deter criminal acts but no more. He focused on one common aspect of punishment in his time—locking prisoners in solitary dark cells. His proposal was a new form of prison architecture, the panopticon, from the Greek for "all seeing." In this architectural plan, prison cells are built in a circle with a central observation platform. Bentham's idea was that instead of rows in which each prisoner is isolated and out of sight, the prison guards could more easily watch all of the prisoners. The design followed Bentham's belief that power should be visible, but he added that the guards in the central tower should be behind blinds or other means of concealment. From this, Bentham said, prisoners had the sentiment of a sort of invisible omnipresence of authority; whether they were being watched and held to account was unverifiable. If prisoners knew that at every moment they could be watched, they would behave, and if they increasingly behaved, they could increasingly be reformed to become better citizens. Obviously, this idea of invisible, all-seeing authority has chilling implications. But Bentham said the utility of unverifiable authority also applied to the guards and the managers of the prison. Their positions in the prison would be visible to passersby, so they did not know whether they were being watched by the larger public and, therefore, would be less inclined to abuse their power over the prisoners. Bentham did not abandon the idea that fear of punishment would increase utility.

All was not oppressive in Bentham's plan. His architectural plan included skylights in the central area of the prison that would allow sunlight and air into the prison. He extended the panopticon idea to factories. In this area also, he thought that decreasing isolation and the sentiment of a sort of invisible omnipresence of authority would encourage workers to behave. We can't deny that we behave better at work when the boss is around. He did not champion the individual as did the German idealists or Kierkegaard and Nietzsche whom we will meet in Chapter 17. Bentham thought that the aggregate happiness in society was what matters and that utilitarianism requires everyone to be impartial and a disinterested spectator as to who specifically experiences happiness.

JOHN STUART MILL'S UTILITARIANISM

John Stuart Mill (1806–1873) was also British but lived two generations after Bentham. He was strongly influenced by Bentham, adopting utilitarianism, but giving it a strongly different emphasis. Mill made his mark in philosophy with his 1843 book *A System of Logic*. Mill cowrote several essays with his wife, Harriet Taylor, whom he considered his friend and equal, though everyone else ignored her because she was a woman working in a very sexist time.

Central to Mill's philosophy was that "over himself, over his own body and mind, the individual is sovereign" but that political philosophy should be guided by what is good for society as a whole. There is a slight tension in Mill between the individual and the commons. Mill does not think like Hobbes and Hegel that the individual should give his or her all to the state, but Mill also does not think like Rousseau or Marx that the state and the individual are at odds. Instead, Mill believed that the state should be interested primarily in ensuring the welfare of its citizens, especially their liberty. In 1859, he wrote *On Liberty*, in which he advocated for all people to have complete freedom as long as they acted responsibly toward other people.

In his major work on moral theory, *Utilitarianism* (1863), Mill says that morality is implicitly utilitarian, that people naturally act to maximize happiness. Bentham had advocated increasing "utility," but Mill opted for the more direct term of the "greatest happiness principle." In a number of respects, Mill's version was more down-to-earth and practical than Bentham's abstract conception.

Mill recognized several flaws in Bentham's formulation. One was that there was no real incentive for people to contribute to the happiness of others. Mill countered that the firm foundation of morality was our social feelings for each other and the desire to be in unity with them. Another problem was that Bentham was not recognizing that some pleasures were ultimately better than others. Mill thought that intellectual pleasures were more valuable than mindless physical pleasures. Bentham had famously said that a child's game was as good as poetry if they both produced happiness. Mill famously replied that:

> *It is better to be a human being dissatisfied than a pig satisfied; better to be Socrates dissatisfied than a fool satisfied. And if the fool, or the pig, are of a different opinion, it is because they only know their own side of the question. The other party to the comparison knows both sides.* (*Utilitarianism*, 3.7)

Not any pleasure would do, Mill said. Pleasures that edified the mind and spirit were more valuable than empty, fleeting pleasures. In other words, put down the video game and read a book.

A third concern of Mill's was that Bentham's felicific calculus was without compassion and sentiment; it reduced people to mere objects. Mill saw that Bentham's principle of utility could be used to force people to do things they do not want to do. Bentham said that individuals should be impartial to their own happiness and look instead to the aggregate happiness of all. Mill was aware that this could be interpreted to permit the suffering of a small number of people if that suffering caused happiness for a larger number. One of Mill's concerns was eliminating poverty, which caused disease, a sense of worthlessness, unkindness, and other forms of suffering. He could not agree with the logic that poverty and inequality could be justified if the happiness of the wealthy was greater than the unhappiness of the poor. He insisted that greatest happiness principle should not be calculated to rationalize individual suffering.

Although Mill believed in the crux of Bentham's utilitarianism, he worried that it would almost certainly lead to a tyranny of the majority. If the majority comes to believe that they can be happy through the harsh treatment and exploitation of minority groups, then they could argue that the government is obligated to do that. Bentham's utilitarianism denies individual human rights; consequently, the majority could use the power of government to oppress minority groups. Mill believed there was more to morality than majority rule—that the state has to consider the happiness and rights of all.

To protect those people in the minority, Mill introduced the "harm principle."

> *The only purpose for which power can be rightfully exercised over any member of a civilised community, against his will, is to prevent harm to others. His own good, either physical or moral, is not a sufficient warrant.* (*On Liberty*, p. 17)

By establishing this principle, Mill is prohibiting the exploitation of the few by the many. The harm principle denies the utility of slavery, which a strict utilitarian could argue is justifiable if the pain caused by the enslavement of some is less than the pleasure of those who benefit from the products of slavery. The harm principle also expressed Mill's strong belief in personal freedom. One's personal tastes and habits are the concern of that individual. As long as one doesn't harm anyone else, the public has no business interfering. This has led to the concept of the "victimless crime," the usual examples being drug use and prostitution. Mill was not endorsing these practices but simply making the point that social morality has bigger, better concerns.

Writing in the midst of the industrial revolution, Mill declared that people are people, not machines. It was society's obligation not simply to give people pleasure but to facilitate their personal growth that would cultivate lasting happiness, similar to Aristotle's *eudaimonia*.

> *Human nature is not a machine to be built after a model, and set to do exactly the work prescribed for it, but a tree, which requires to grow and develop itself on all sides, according to the tendency of the inward forces which make it a living thing.* (*On Liberty*, p. 111)

Mill thought that combining the basic idea of utilitarianism with a concept of human rights would retain respect for human dignity while accepting the value of human happiness.

Mill was a leading influence on what has come to be known as "social democracy." As Mill put it, the role of the government is to represent the public interest, serve society, and be answerable to it. The government should not exert any power of coercion on people, even when the public opinion calls for such coercion. This is another expression of Mill's caution against the "tyranny of the majority." Mill emphasized the preventative and supportive roles of the government. To protect the innocent, the government must take precautions against crimes before they have been committed and must detect and punish criminals afterward. He agreed with the death penalty for aggravated murder but said that the legal system must be constrained to following the harm principle.

Mill became a well-known and respected author and statesman, and he leveraged his fame to argue for the rights of women in his book, *The Subjection of Women* (1869). His arguments were similar to Mary Wollstonecraft's arguments (see Chapter 10) decades earlier, but Mill's book, because he was a man and famous, was more widely read and respected. Mill took up Wollstonecraft's observations that society systematically discriminates against women, subjecting them to a lower status. All people should be accorded the same rights and opportunities, Mill argued, and the legal subordination of one sex to the other should be abolished.

Mill walked his talk even more than did Bentham. Bentham stayed aloof from politics, but Mill ran for public office and served a term as a member of the British parliament. During his tenure there, he was a leading progressive voice, most notably being the first member of parliament to advocate for women's suffrage.

REFERENCES

Jeremy Bentham, *An Introduction to the Principles of Morals and Legislation.* Clarendon Press, 1907. Public Domain.

Immanuel Kant, *Fundamental Principles of the Metaphysic of Morals*, Project Gutenberg, https://www.gutenberg.org/ebooks/5682. (accessed January 22, 2021)

John Stuart Mill, *On Liberty,* Project Gutenberg. http://www.gutenberg.org/ebooks/34901. (accessed January 21, 2021)

John Stuart Mill, *Utilitarianism*, Project Gutenberg, http://www.gutenberg.org/ebooks/11224. (accessed April 6, 2021)

CHAPTER 17

THE EXPLOSION OF INDIVIDUALISM

The German idealists inaugurated a new method of philosophy, opening the discussion about what the individual contributes to his or her experiences and ideas. Hegel had adopted idealism but had woven it into an absolute system in which everything is explained in terms of the one Spirit or mind. Hegelianism quickly became the dominant philosophy of Europe, especially in German-speaking countries. People like the concept of a monist philosophical system that explains everything through one foundational idea: knowledge, morality, perception, the structure of the universe, society, and history.

Into this environment strode Søren Kierkegaard (1813–1855, pronounced *"sorn KEER-ke-go"*) and Friedrich Nietzsche (1844–1900, pronounced "*NEE-tjeh*"). On the one hand, these two philosophers are drastically different, but on the other hand, they share a fundamental approach to the world, and it is that philosophical approach that is their important contribution to philosophy. Today, we know this approach as "existentialism," though neither of them used that term. It was Jean-Paul Sartre (see Chapter 21) who coined the term because he, inspired by Kierkegaard and Nietzsche, defined the approach as existence preceding essence. Existentialism is the approach that puts the nature of our existence as a conscious being at the center of philosophical inquiry. It is similar to phenomenology in its emphasis on the contents of consciousness, but existentialism reaches beyond the analysis of the contents of consciousness to the questions of what it means to be a consciousness in a world. Problem one: One exists as a particular, individual being.

Since Plato and Aristotle, philosophy, and to an extent all of Western culture, had thought of things in terms of their universal essences. Whether it was a tree or a human, a thing was defined as a type of thing; therefore, it must have the characteristics that defined that type of thing. In practice, this meant that all things are basically the same and do not vary or change much if at all. So, if you understand the universal essence of a type of thing, then you understand all particular things of that type. That approach looks at everything in the world from the top down: We understand universal essences, and from those standard types we consider particulars.

This top-down approach to the world through essences is particularly problematic when it comes to humans. It encourages stereotypes about humans in general and groups of humans. This type of thinking says that all women are alike, all blacks are alike, all Germans, and so on. It leaves little room for individuality because individuality is assumed to be an aberration; to be distinctive is to go against type. If you look at human history, you will see how much that approach has affected human interactions. Remember our discussion of the word "heresy" in Chapter 5.

Kierkegaard and Nietzsche turned that approach on its head. They each said that we are not defined by some universal definition. We are all individuals. We are free to make choices, and our choices define who we are. Kierkegaard and Nietzsche thought of this primarily in terms of values. Sartre, who considered values to be some kind of imperialist tool of oppression, thought of it only in terms of the nature of existence. Sartre also thought that freedom was something fearful—a horrible burden on us. That says more about Sartre than anything else. Kierkegaard and Nietzsche thought that freedom was a positive thing, though certainly not always easy. We are individuals, and we are free to make choices, and the biggest choice we have to make is what moral system we will follow. These are the main themes of their philosophies.

Kierkegaard was philosophy's first great rebel, and Nietzsche was its second. They ushered in philosophy as an expression of the personal rather than an attempt to capture objective rationality. In that, they took things further than did the German idealists like Fichte and Schelling. The idealists had talked about how individuals experience things differently. Kierkegaard and Nietzsche contemplated the full implications of that realization.

KIERKEGAARD

Søren Kierkegaard, a Dane, was a brilliant thinker who could take any question and look at it multiple different ways. Unlike most philosophers, he tried to reach nonacademic people. He was also a clever writer who used words to try to encourage people to reflect on who they are and change their way of being.

Primary to Kierkegaard's philosophy is the place of the individual. Hegelianism taught that humans are nothing more than a part of a historical process. That rankled him. It went against every fiber of his being. Kierkegaard saw some value in Hegel's philosophy, but he brought Hegel's philosophy of progress in consciousness from the level of nations down to the level of the individual. We do inherit the value system of the society into which we are born, but unlike the Hegelians, Kierkegaard said we are free to choose whether to accept this system or not. What's more, we are free to make our own moral choices all the time. We do not have to conform to what we are told. This is a very important issue for Kierkegaard because our decisions shape who we are.

Kierkegaard chose to reject much of what his society taught him, especially the Hegelian system. While the fervent followers of Hegel reveled in the perception of human progress, Kierkegaard vehemently dissented. The Hegelians were proclaiming a golden age; Kierkegaard was warning of a coming collapse. Kierkegaard saw himself as a kind of gadfly trying to wake up his people. His master's dissertation was *On the Concept of Irony* with constant reference to Socrates. In it, he analyzed the conversational method Socrates used to steer people into questioning their own assumptions. Kierkegaard's interpretation was that Socrates was trying to birth in them their subjectivity by forcing them to take responsibility for their thinking and beliefs. Kierkegaard was attempting to follow this path, and he used his written words, quite often laden with irony—intentional ambiguities to motivate people to think beyond what they were taught and think for themselves. Like Socrates, he was irreverent toward authority and tradition, and Kierkegaard was at times deliberately shocking to try to jolt people out of their passive obedience to tradition and force them to look inward and reflect on who and what they are.

Now, people bigoted against religion reject Kierkegaard because he was Christian, despite the fact that very few Christians would ever accept Kierkegaard as one of their own (and Kierkegaard would agree he wasn't). That's the problem rebels have—so few want to be associated with them. All that said, Kierkegaard is fun but agonizing at the same time. He is like that friend who makes us laugh at times but also often makes us cringe at how darkly negative he or she is.

We Are Beings Who Must Choose and Act

Kierkegaard saw human beings as alienated from their own nature. He came to this conclusion around the time, the 1840s, that Marx was coming to a similar conclusion about human alienation. Also like Marx, Kierkegaard saw the purpose of philosophy in general, and his life purpose in particular, to be to change the world for the better. After that, the similarity between Kierkegaard and Marx ends. Marx saw economics as the driving force of history and to a large extent denied human free will. Kierkegaard saw human choices as the driving force of history and stressed above all the vital importance of our free will. Marx said capitalism is the cause of our alienation; Kierkegaard said we are the cause of our alienation.

Like Kant and Hegel, Kierkegaard had as his main concern the concept of freedom, but Kierkegaard railed against the empty freedom about which previous philosophers talked. Fichte and Schelling were closer to what Kierkegaard had in mind—the concept of freedom as personal expression. But Kierkegaard realized that freedom was more than expression. Freedom was a beingness.

Beingness. Existence. We exist. Obviously, you say? Maybe. Kierkegaard would reply that your existence is so obvious that you never think about it or the implications of it. Existence means you have the freedom to choose who you are, and this means having a life of commitment. Most people usually ignore questions about the meaning of their lives and prefer to escape into some kind of anonymous routine. Today, people blame television, the Internet, and video games, but people have always found various meaningless tasks to occupy themselves to avoid dealing with the questions of who they are and what their lives mean. People—including you, yes, you—prefer meaningless routine and immersing themselves in the objective environment around them that we call society. You—yes, you—do this to avoid your own subjectivity and freedom and the need to commit to them. Everyone does this, Kierkegaard says. This goes way back, he says, and only a few brave souls fight against it. In *On the Concept of Irony*, he argued that Socrates used irony to force people to abandon their pat answers to Socrates' annoying questions. They had to begin to think for themselves and to take individual responsibility for their claims about knowledge and value.

Hegel had placed individual human minds within the absolute mind of *Geist*. In the Hegelian system, we can and should actively engage in reasoning about philosophical questions, but the goal of our critical reflection is to understand the mind of *Geist*, which is the logical structure of the universe. Kierkegaard rejected this totalizing narrative that through logic we can understand the cosmic mind and everything in it. He saw it as hubris. He understood the limits of human knowledge and felt it our duty to accept the reality that there are things that we cannot understand. And, as is always present in Kierkegaard, he wants the emphasis to be always on the individual, something he noted was sorely lacking in Hegelianism.

Kierkegaard dismissed Hegelianism as being futile and irrelevant to the concrete real-life issues that all individuals must face. For Kierkegaard, philosophy was about life and how to live it. One analogy he uses is that seeking life guidance from Hegelianism is like traveling in Denmark with a tiny map of Europe that shows Denmark only as a dot. In other words, it's impossible. No abstract system, no matter how logical, can address the concrete features of my life. Only I can do that.

In following the traditions and systems of the world, we are avoiding the reality that we humans are beings who must choose and act. Our day-to-day lives are filled with dilemmas that require us to make decisions. Some of these dilemmas are relatively insignificant—what will I have for dinner tonight? Others are life changing. We agonize over these decisions, worried we will make the wrong choice. Kierkegaard wrote in his book *Either/Or* (1843) that if you marry, you will regret it; if you do not marry, you will also regret it. What he means is that we are always capable of seeing the negatives of any choice we make. The point is that we should not reduce our lives to a series of binary choices because life is more dynamic than that. Part of that dynamic is that we will always be aware that we could have made different choices. We could have lived our lives differently.

> *It is really true what philosophy tells us, that life must be understood backwards. But with this, one forgets the second proposition, that it must be lived forwards. A proposition which, the more it is subjected to careful thought, the more it ends up concluding precisely that life at any given moment cannot really ever be fully understood; exactly because there is no single moment where time stops completely in order for me to take position [to do this]: going backwards.* (*Journalen* JJ: 167, volume 18, page 306.)

Objective Knowing Versus Subjective Knowing

Throughout history, philosophers believed that the primary problem of epistemology was how to rise above individual subjectivity to acquire objective truth. Kierkegaard completely reverses this. For him, the primary task in our life is how to become more aware of our own subjective life. He proposed the radical notion that our natural tendency is to hide within the cover of objectivity. We do this, he says, to avoid the difficult crisis of making our own decisions. He makes the stark distinction between following the crowd and being self-directed. We can come to truth only when we arrive at it through our own experiences and decisions.

Kierkegaard declared that truth is subjectivity. He does not deny the possibility of objective truth, but any objective facts are *truth* only when they are taken in and *owned* by an individual. The word "subjective" has two meanings. Most philosophers, and people, focus on the bad kind of subjectivity when personal interests corrupt one's ability to perceive and judge matters correctly. In many matters, for example, grading students' assignments, we want people to make objective decisions rather than biased ones. We often associate "objective" with "fair" and "subjective" with "unfair."

The word "subjective" also means "related to a subject," and philosophers often use the word "subject" to refer to a human as a being who perceives and acts. This is how Kierkegaard uses "subjectivity"—related to a subject, or person. An objective fact becomes truth when it becomes related to a person by that person's decisions and actions. The statement "2 + 2 = 4" is an objective fact, but you can be forgiven for saying, "yeah, so?" The statement "someone got an F in the philosophy class" may be another objective fact, but it would be a very different fact if the statement was "you got an F in the philosophy class." The difference is whether a fact is related to you in a manner that means something to you. Facts such as "2 + 2 = 4" and "České Budějovice is the administrative seat of the South Bohemian region of the Czech Republic" probably have little direct relation to you, so they don't mean much to you.

When facts do relate to you and you care about them, they become subjective facts and a part of your conscious being. Consider the difference between hearing someone say "I love you" to someone else and hearing someone say "I love you" to you. These are different facts and different experiences. Consider also the difference between understanding that cheating is wrong and actually deciding "I will not cheat." Someone can objectively know a moral truth but not be subjectively living in that truth. However, someone could be without a grand rational moral theory but still have empathy for others. A large part of Kierkegaard's philosophy was his shift away from philosophy's focus on objective rationality to focus instead on the importance of individuals living their beliefs.

Kierkegaard's Christianity was in keeping with this sentiment. He didn't care at all about objective doctrine. Genuine Christianity was subjective being—living a life of passionate inwardness. When Kierkegaard talks about inwardness, he is not at all meaning selfishness. He means a kind of freedom. His conception of freedom is not that far off from that of the German idealists who inspired him. For him, an individual is free when he or she chooses his or her own path in life. The free individual expresses his or her self-activated self in who he or she is and what he or she does. In this context, when Kierkegaard talks about inwardness, he means focusing on one's self-activation of one's potential voluntarily to choose and to act.

Philosopher Isaiah Berlin explained that there are two concepts of liberty ("Two Concepts of Liberty," 1958). There is "negative liberty," which means the absence of constraint and coercion, and "positive liberty," which means the ability to pursue and accomplish one's goals. Kierkegaard's view of freedom has both of these concepts. On negative liberty, he saw the institution of Christendom as a source of constraint and coercion. He targeted the People's Church of Denmark, which functioned as a state religion in his time. He saw the church as effectively dead, mired in dogma and ritual, made all the worse by its leaders enthusiastically adopting Hegelianism. Doctrine was a constraint and coercion on individual freedom, Kierkegaard argued. Foreshadowing the discussion of indoctrination in recent political philosophy (see Chapter 24), he called doctrine the way to power for the teacher but indolent aping and mimicking for the learner.

Social institutions provide people with valuable ethical guidelines, Kierkegaard said, but institutions also serve to normalize people into stereotyped social identities, which produces the crowd of pseudo-individuals. Social stereotypes constrain the ability to realize and actualize one's genuine self. Kierkegaard's critique was primarily directed at Christendom, but he clearly included all social and political institutions. His consistent theme throughout his writings was to champion the individual in the face of forces that constrained the individual.

Kierkegaard also was consistent on the individual's need to cultivate positive liberty through passionate inwardness. This inwardness for Kierkegaard is not an abstract concept; the more passionately subjective one is about one's own path, the more free one is. He calls for us to engage in a deeply subjective focus on the discovery and activation of who we are meant to be. Rational contemplation about doctrine or philosophical universals cannot tell us who we should be. You are not the universal human; Kierkegaard exhorts you never to forget that you are an existing individual. You are you, and you are in the continual process of becoming. Objective truth is, he says, a chimera of abstraction (echoes of Hume, there). Subjective truth is what is true for you, and you need to win an understanding of who you are meant to be.

And that is where Kierkegaard sees Christianity as vital. Again, not Christendom and its artificial doctrines and rituals, but *Christianity* and its passionate inwardness of coming to know who we are meant to be. That is because Kierkegaard sees God as the source of who we are each meant to be. He wrote that he sought to understand himself and to see what God really wished for him to do. That is the truth that is true for him and the idea for which he could live and die. Like many philosophers before him, Kierkegaard equated God with Truth. Unlike most philosophers before him, he didn't equate Truth with systems or logic. Truth was subjectivity. The individual exists, so the individual must understand what is true for himself or herself. God was the source of all things, so he reasoned that God must also be the source of what we are meant to be. That truth becomes actualized when we hold it with passionate inwardness.

Previously, I have talked about how our every thought is a belief. Kierkegaard challenges you not to rationalize your belief with conformity to what others are doing but to *own* your beliefs. Yes, you can believe the same as others do, but if you believe and do things only because you are supposed to, that is false belief. True belief is when you are committed to that belief as *yours*. You have to experience things for yourself, relate those experiences to the values you have chosen, and make those experiences and beliefs yours.

This is where Kierkegaard perhaps goes a bit overboard, talking about owning your beliefs to the point of it being the only type of act that matters and the need to be willing to die for your beliefs in fear and trembling, reflecting on what God may require of us. He called for subjectivity at all costs. His passion scares some people off. Well, it scares almost everyone off. He was intense. But he was correct. If you do not feel and own your own subjective existence, if you do not contemplate the meaning of your life and are not willing to leap into that continual struggle to know who you are and what your purpose is, how meaningful is your life? Ultimately, you cannot escape the freedom and responsibility that Kierkegaard is talking about. Everything that happens to you is interpreted through your beliefs and values, and your beliefs and values are chosen by you—whether or not you consciously and actively chose them. So, your life and who you are is your creation and, therefore, your responsibility.

The Spheres of Life

Which leads us to Kierkegaard's spheres of life. Life must be lived; it can't be understood through abstract philosophy. Kierkegaard saw life as a journey that is traveled in terms of one's commitments. He taught that every individual chooses, mostly subconsciously, between three fundamental kinds of commitments. He placed these commitments into three spheres of life: the aesthetic, the ethical, and the religious. That last is very inappropriately named, as we shall see. He variously refers to these spheres as "existential categories"; "modes of existing"; "stages on life's way"; and, most illustratively, "existence-spheres." Kierkegaard says we are unavoidably in one of the three spheres, though we can move between them. Each sphere of existence is a way of life based on the fundamental commitment we have to life and others. One is either an aesthetic, ethical, or "religious" person, depending on which sphere one is living within.

Kierkegaard's first existence-sphere is the aesthetic. He uses the word "aesthetic" to describe people being driven by their senses. This is a person who lives based on sense experiences and animal impulses and emotions. The aesthetic person is similar to how Hobbes described all human beings—ruled by endeavors of desire and aversion. For such a person, things are either interesting or boring. They are driven to go from one vicarious sensation to the next, like the person mindlessly flipping through Instagram, searching for a mindlessly, mildly interesting picture, until they are bored with it and swipe to the next mindless picture. Our age of memes, social media, and short videos capture Kierkegaard's concept of the aesthetic sphere in ways he could never have imagined. The aesthetic person believes he or she is pursuing pleasure, but Kierkegaard says they are simply staving off boredom. They are trapped in an ongoing cycle of looking for the next cheap thrill. Their life is no more than a collection of fragmentary, spasmodic moments. Aesthetic people do not have a self. Their choices are determined by their environment, which feeds them sense experiences to which they can only react according to their fleeting moods and impulses. They constantly need more stimulation, driven by the restless urges to consume more. They have no real values, no real self.

If the aesthetic person wakes up to this predicament and listens to an inner knowing that he or she can be more, this person can choose to move to the ethical sphere of life. It is in this sphere when one can begin to make choices. The aesthetic person is like an addict, addicted to drugs, video games, or the need to fit in with a group of pseudo-friends, but because they are determined by their environment, they have no commitments and, therefore, no self. Kierkegaard taught that when a person decides to make commitments to others and live according to an ethical code, that person achieves the possibility of gaining a history. For example (feel free to insert your own preferred gender labels into this example), a womanizer jumps from one woman to another, constantly seeking the next interesting sexual encounter. This man has no real history because he has no actual commitment to anyone. When this man stops using women for his own pleasure and forms a committed relationship with a particular woman, he develops a history with her and a lasting mutually fulfilling relationship that enhances his life and his self. Kierkegaard says it is only in the existence-sphere of living within ethical commitments that one can become a self. One now interacts with the world and other people in it through ethical considerations—recognizing others as full human beings who deserve respect and consideration. Others are no longer just things to be used for pleasure. Similarly, the ethical person can have real pleasure because he or she interacts with the world in terms of what is edifying to himself or herself, not simply in terms of base sensual pleasure.

Kierkegaard said that, although the ethical sphere is a welcome improvement to the senselessness of the aesthetic sphere, the ethical sphere is still empty. The ethical person is summed up by the series of universals that clothe him or her. The ethical person is no more than a set of social roles and corresponding social commitments. These people are no longer ruled by endeavors of desire and aversion, but their choices are still determined by their environment. They are now ruled by social ethical constraints. They are defined by society as a man, woman, mother, father, student, citizen, and so on, and on, and on. The ethical person is comfortably situated within the ethical sphere and is content to do only what is morally required. Because of this, such a person is still not a fully self-aware individual. When one realizes that, one can make the difficult but deeply meaningful leap to a new existence-sphere where self-authenticity is possible.

This is why Kierkegaard's label of this existence-sphere as the "religious" sphere is so strange and unhelpful. Kierkegaard, who rejected all forms of religiosity as being trapped within the ethical sphere, should have found a different label—"spiritual" perhaps, because he steeps this existence-sphere in the language of spiritual communion with God and the universe. Better would be the self-actualizing sphere, similar to what psychologist Abraham Maslow (1908–1970) discussed. For Kierkegaard, even the most fully developed ethical person, who clearly perceives the ethical ideal, will, paradoxically, be painfully aware of his or her ethical shortcomings.

The realization of one's chronic inadequacy to live up to social ethical demands produces a despair that must be resolved. Kierkegaard taught that fully pursuing the ethical produces a tension that leads one to the existence-sphere beyond it. The only escape from the tension of the ethical sphere is through a leap to another stage of existence. The religious or self-actualizing sphere is described by Kierkegaard in the religious language of his time. He uses the following example.

In his book, *Fear and Trembling* (1843), Kierkegaard explores the scriptural story of Abraham, who hears the voice of God calling on him to sacrifice Isaac, his son. Kierkegaard retells the story from multiple perspectives to get at the heart of Abraham's experience. Abraham's dilemma is that murdering his son is obviously an ethical wrong, but disobeying an order from God is also wrong. He is caught between choosing to obey the demands of the ethical norms or to serve God. He chooses to believe there has to be a higher purpose for God's command beyond the universal ethical law. Kierkegaard uses the story to show the sharp contrast between the ethical and religious spheres. Abraham must choose and act, but he can't follow the universal, ethical law (Kierkegaard was aware of Kant's Categorical Imperative, see Chapter 16), which tells him to love and protect his child. He must instead take on what Kierkegaard calls the "teleological suspension of the ethical." He must suspend his commitment to the universal ethical sphere for the sake of a higher goal—specifically, his individual relationship to God. There is an existence-sphere higher than the ethical laws of the world.

We need not resort to biblical language to understand what Kierkegaard is getting at with the "teleological suspension of the ethical." "Teleological" means to be goal oriented. To suspend the ethical teleologically means to go beyond social ethical constraints in pursuit of a higher purpose. We can understand this as the movement a person makes when he or she refuses to obey an unjust law or refuses to conform to social pressures to do what he or she believes is correct and life-affirming. Kant declared that the ethical and the religious never conflict—that reason makes plain the commands that are binding upon us and that there are no higher goals than duty to those commands of reason. But Kierkegaard's view of both God and us is akin to John and William's philosophy that the will guides the intellect (see Chapter 6). Kierkegaard wants us to reject Kant's idea that God's will and the moral law can be collapsed into one. By giving us an example where the two are in tension, Kierkegaard is pointing out that the individual's relationship to God is a higher priority than a rationally based universal ethics.

The religious or self-actualizing sphere is, for Kierkegaard, the existence-sphere in which an individual is willing not to be determined by his or her environment and to do what he or she knows is right. This person is willing to be an individual, willing to find the type of person he or she is meant to be and *be* that person.

NIETZSCHE

Nietzsche is one of the few philosophers frequently mentioned in popular culture. And as with most things, popular culture gets Nietzsche wrong. Nietzsche was not a nihilistic antimorality monster, as some portray him, and he wasn't the hostile bigot as others portray him. He was cynical, yes, but his was the cynicism of the idealist, of one who believes that life and society can be better than they are. Nietzsche's negativity was primarily a despair over how people throw their lives away on false and harmful beliefs.

Toward a New Concept of Truth

Nietzsche thought about beliefs in a manner similar to Kierkegaard. He downplayed the importance of rational objective truth and elevated the personal and subjective. Nietzsche went beyond Kierkegaard in stating that what was important was subjective interpretation, not just subjective experience. We put our own personal stamp on things. This is what is real—not "facts." As he said:

> *In opposition to Positivism* (see Chapter 19), *which halts at phenomena and says, "These are only facts and nothing more," I would say: No, facts are precisely what is lacking, all that exists consists of interpretations. We cannot establish any fact "in itself": it may even be nonsense to desire to do such a thing.* (*Will to Power* §481)

Nietzsche would say that uninterpreted "facts" or "truths" are a fantasy. We never encounter such things. What we do encounter is our interpretation of experiences because everything we experience is seen from one perspective or another. Nietzsche calls this his theory of "perspectivism." Perspectives are unavoidable because they are all we have. All of our perspectives are false, compared to the phantasms of objective truths, yet these "false" perspectives are highly useful.

Here is how it works in Nietzsche's conception. He says that "there is only a perspective seeing, only a perspective 'knowing.'" Each individual, because he or she is each an individual, has a different perspective on things, and as we have learned from previous philosophers, all that individuals have are their ideas in their minds caused by their sense impressions. So what each individual thinks about and communicates to others are their own ideas, all of which, Nietzsche points out, are ideas influenced by each individual's own past experiences, circumstances, values, and purposes. When he says, "there are no 'facts-in-themselves,'" he means that an interpretation must always be projected onto ideas before they can be facts. Individuals are thus creators of their own facts. They can't help it. It is what human minds do, and we can see here how Nietzsche is influenced by Kant.

But these "facts" created by individuals may or may not be true depictions of the world. Actually, they almost certainly aren't, Nietzsche would say, because what an individual thinks and feels is a product of his or her mind. So, by the age-old standard of objective truth, all we think and speak are false ideas. Nietzsche at one point says that all words are lies because they express how we think and feel, not how things are. Furthermore, once spoken or written down, words are no longer part of us but exist outside of us, and everyone, including ourselves, view these words through perspectives and the words must be reinterpreted. We suffer the delusion that we capture reality through our words, but we don't. Everything is perspective, even science. Physics, too, is only an interpretation and explanation of the world, Nietzsche insists.

Despite our ideas being inherently "false," they are useful. Loosely speaking, how that works is like this. To make sense of our experiences and ideas, we compare them to similar experiences and ideas and apply labels to these groupings of concepts. These labels become words that stand for universal concepts (hello, William). We use these words to communicate with each other, and these words become grounds for our interpretations of the world. Nietzsche considers interpreting the world by means of a perspective the basic condition of all life. Our ideas are false and our words are lies because they are perspectives that do not perfectly depict reality itself. Regardless, our ideas are needed and useful because they are all we have. Our perspectives create a world that is calculable, simplified, and comprehensible for us. Here again, we see Nietzsche employing Kant, this time Kant's response to Hume that the human mind imposes order on the jumble of impressions the senses give to it. But while Kant thought this gave us a kind of knowledge about the world, Nietzsche takes Kant's insight of the active, ordering mind into an entirely other direction.

Truth, Nietzsche insists, is not defined by our ideas corresponding to the world. Instead:

> *Truth is that kind of error without which a certain species of living being cannot exist. The value for Life is ultimately decisive.* (*Will to Power* §493)

To any idea anyone has, Nietzsche asks, "Is it useful to us?" It does not really matter if a belief is true, if it is useful. A belief can be a condition of life and nonetheless be false, Nietzsche says. If a false story protects people from harm, then it serves a useful purpose. All of our human ideas are just that, anyway—fictions that are useful. The most useful fictions become widely adopted and part of our common wisdom. As long as a belief continues to be useful, it survives within society. When a belief is no longer useful, it often, but not always, is replaced by new, more useful, beliefs. If this sounds weird, it shouldn't. This is, after all, how science works. Scientific theories are created by individuals imposing their perspectives to create ideas that are calculable, simplified, and comprehensible. Scientific theories are accepted until they are no longer useful. Scientists then create a new theory that is more useful.

Toward a New Humanity

Armed with this new perspective on truth and how it functions, Nietzsche called for us to move beyond tradition and forge a new path. Whether we want to or not, Nietzsche says, we must forge that new path because the old ways are dead. He is infamous for declaring that "God is dead" in his book *The Gay Science* (1882). Often quoted, but almost never in context, this is not a declaration about the existence of God but about something he found much more relevant. Nietzsche understood that whatever truth Christianity may hold, its tradition was integral to European culture. What he was announcing as being dead was everything that was built on and sustained by this Christian tradition, *including* and especially the whole of European morality. This moral system was his real target, and this system, he was convinced, was destined for collapse. Worse, Nietzsche claimed, the Christian moral system that had evolved in Europe was harmful to human beings. Humanity must abandon the old foundation, leave the dead and crumbling structures built on it, and create a new morality that is beyond the old categories of good and evil.

Yes, beyond good and evil is where we must go. Nietzsche's philosophy is primarily a moral philosophy. His philosophy touches on many other topics because he correctly understands that morality is foundational to and intertwined with all other aspects of how we are and what we do. He saw European culture and society in crisis and that was because the European moral system was dead; it just did not realize it. Therefore, his critique of European culture had to be a critique of European morality.

What exactly was so wrong about European morality? Nietzsche argues in his book, *Beyond Good and Evil* (1886), that the prevailing moral law based on good and evil is an artificial creation that replaced a more natural morality. We lie to ourselves through our philosophy, laws, and religion that our definitions of good and evil are objective, universal realities. They aren't. We invented a moral law to constrain ourselves and others—a moral law, he claimed, that was born out of resentment.

Nietzsche's radical argument is that in humanity's distant past, a social order emerged with a higher class and a lower class. This arrangement spawned a pair of evaluative terms: "good" and "bad." Over time, he argues, the idea of goodness came to be associated with character traits that those of the privileged higher class saw in themselves and by which they distinguished themselves as superior to the masses, who were "bad." Traits such as strength, power, courage, pride, willfulness, and wealth were good and noble virtues. Traits such as weakness, cowardice, timidity, pettiness, and humility, associated with the lower class, were considered bad. The rulers of the ancient Mediterranean societies, Nietzsche claims, were self-directed, their only justification for their actions being their own judgment. They practiced self-mastery and thus mastered their domains and others. This is why Nietzsche, in *Beyond Good and Evil,* calls good/bad "master morality." Nietzsche is oversimplifying, but ancient history, a field he knew quite well, does support his basic idea.

The good/bad evaluative terms were gradually replaced with the concepts of "good" and "evil." This pairing focuses on judging as evil violations of the well-being of others and, therefore, judging as good altruism for others. Nietzsche grants that altruism has some common sense to it, and he is not against feeling love and care for others. Nietzsche's problem with good/evil thinking is its focus on evil to the exclusion of good.

What Nietzsche thinks happened is that people who lost out when the noble higher classes exerted their power came to resent those with power and wealth. Feeling powerless, downtrodden, and uncertain of themselves, and having no value within good/bad thinking, they revolted against that morality. They engaged in what Nietzsche, in *Beyond Good and Evil,* provocatively calls "slave morality." Weaker people feared and resented stronger people; to express their bitterness, they invented the moral concept of evil. The values that the higher class had called "good," the slave morality now condemned as "evil." The values that the higher class had called "bad," the slave morality now called "good." The qualities of charity, humility, abstinence, compassion, patience, resignation, and submissiveness were now considered virtuous.

Nietzsche argues that demanding that no one be made lesser condemns anyone who expresses self-interest. All of the traits that are good in the good/bad evaluative pairing—strength, power, courage, pride, willfulness, wealth, and so on—are condemned as evil in the good/evil evaluative pairing. That means that the good/evil evaluative pairing declares as being morally good traits such as weakness, cowardice, timidity, poverty, and humility. It is a reversal of the original social order, and this Nietzsche saw as the problem.

Historical evidence for Nietzsche's theorized sea change in morality is sketchy, but he points to a reasonable target: Christianity. He saw the Christian morality of "turn the other cheek" and "the meek shall inherit the earth" as a slave morality. Lacking tangible power, the slaves revolted in the only way they could—through telling and retelling the story of good and evil. This was the revolt and revenge of the slaves—to condemn their masters as evil. The Christian good/evil morality has the appearance of gentleness, kindness, and goodness, Nietzsche claims, but it is a mask for bitter resentment and antipathy for the strong and successful. Nietzsche's summation of slave morality is as follows: "I dislike him."—Why?—"I am not a match for him" (*Beyond Good and Evil*, IV.§185). Because most people lack tangible power in the world, the slave morality of good and evil has enjoyed popularity. When stronger or superior people grab what they want, we can condemn them as evil. We have created the categories of good and evil and use them to judge people and actions.

Okay, so how do we forge a new path beyond good and evil? A good first step, Nietzsche says, is to acknowledge that our primary interaction with the world is in terms of our likes, dislikes, experiences, and lack of experiences, all driven by our instincts. The high-minded notion of the philosophers, theologians, and scientists—that we interact with the world through reason—is a big lie. We are human animals, Nietzsche says, and instinct, not reason, is at the center of human behavior. We have drives, but not so much a drive to knowledge as the learned want to believe. "The greater part of the conscious thinking of a philosopher is secretly influenced by his instincts," Nietzsche says (*Beyond Good and Evil*, I.3). That human instinct is another drive that is disguising itself. That drive, a centerpiece of Nietzsche's philosophy, is the will to power.

Nietzsche's concept of the will to power has been horribly misunderstood. This is partially because the Nazis misappropriated the concept to justify their murderous regime. For example, the infamous 1935 propaganda film *Triumph of the Will* glorified Adolf Hitler as the personification of the will to power. The Nazis shamelessly misappropriated Nietzsche as though he were a protofascist, despite the fact that Nietzsche would have vehemently opposed the Nazis and their bigotry.

The truth is that Nietzsche's will to power is not a will to dominate others. Nietzsche is not Hobbesian in thinking that we are driven by selfish desires. Yes, we are attracted to pleasure and averse to pain, but not in a brutish and destructive way as Hobbes thought. The will to power is a different truth.

> *From a moral standpoint* the world is false. *But inasmuch as morality itself is a part of this world, morality also is false. The will to truth is a process of* establishing things, *it is a process of* making *things true and lasting, a total elimination of that* false *character, a transvaluation of it into being. Thus, "truth" is not something which is present and which has to be found and discovered; it is something* which has to be created *and which* gives *its name* to a process, *or, better still, to the Will to overpower, which in itself has no purpose: to introduce truth is a* processus in infinitum, *an active determining—it is not a process of becoming conscious of something, which in itself is fixed and determined. It is merely a word for "The Will to Power."* (*Will to Power* §552, emphasis his)

For Nietzsche, the will to power is about rejecting determinism, both material and cultural, in favor of believing in our own power to make and preserve our being. As long as we believe that something other than ourselves is responsible for our happiness, we corrupt our ability to establish our own truth and become ourselves for ourselves. Life itself is the will to power, he says, the will to create and the will to self-preservation. Our basic drive is to overcome obstacles and discomforts and create truth—a truth for us. Yes, we are averse to pain, so we want to overcome it and be free from pain. It can be as simple as we don't like to be uncomfortable, so we are driven to soothe our discomfort. If we are cold, we turn up the heat. That's the will to power, not lusting for political power over others. We don't like not to know or understand things, so we are driven to create beliefs and meaning to feel more at ease. We are our beliefs, and we are driven to create beliefs that are useful to us. In the same way, Nietzsche saw the slave morality and its idea that morality is based on good and evil as a useful facade. Underneath, it was the slaves' will to power. But now, instead of hiding behind the veneer of Christian European morality, we need to rise up and master ourselves.

What is so radical about Nietzsche's will to power is that he doesn't just think that we do create our own truths but that we *should* create our own truths. This requires, as Nietzsche fully understood, the destruction of all dogmas. ALL dogmas. People bigoted against religion love Nietzsche because he was so antireligion. Nietzsche didn't hate religion, as some atheists do; he even believed that Jesus really existed. True to Nietzsche's belief in the will to power, he called Jesus the only true Christian and said that everyone who follows Jesus is a sheep. Don't follow anyone, Nietzsche would say. Do what Jesus did and forge your own path. "What have we Sons of God to do with morals" (*Beyond Good and Evil*, IV.§164). Return to the master morality. Strength, accomplishment, and pride are good; timidity and weakness are bad. The will to power is spontaneous, aggressive, and expansive, giving us new interpretations and directions to our lives.

Nietzsche saw the ideas and words of Christianity (similar to Kierkegaard's conception of Christendom) to be no longer useful—so many archaic dogmas and social traditions that needed to be discarded, just as the dogmas of science and philosophy must be discarded. Nietzsche wanted to tear down everything, literally everything, and start anew. In this, he was similar to Marx in calling for the radical restructuring of society that humanity desperately needed.

This is where Nietzsche is cynical—he believes very few people have the courage to master themselves, much less restructure society. Very few people have the courage to create their own truths. Nietzsche was a person filled with optimism of what people could be but despairs at how little people actually achieve. This is Nietzsche's cynicism. He thinks he sees a brilliant, positive future beyond our current humanity when we accept our will to power and express our perspectives. We then can create new beliefs, share them with others, and work together to find life-affirming truths that are useful to us.

Nietzsche calls a person with the courage to participate in this process an "Übermensch," which literally means "over man." Not "superman" as has been widely misinterpreted, but a man who overcomes. (Yes, "man" because Nietzsche was still in the sexism of his time.) What the Übermensch overcomes is not others, but himself and his human tendency lazily to accept the dogmas given to him. The Übermensch accepts his will to power and joyfully creates new beliefs and new truths. Those who lack the courage to accept their will to power Nietzsche derides as "little gray people" and "shallow ponds" of humanity. They remain stuck in being "all too human." But Nietzsche was confident that the time of the Übermensch was coming, because the old European morality was dead and humanity was evolving beyond it.

TRANSCENDENTALISM

A rather different take on individualism came from a circle of American writers in the mid-1800s. They were also inspired by German idealism and the Romantic movement in literature. They emphasized intuitive understanding of the world through subjectively experiencing it. Like Kierkegaard and Nietzsche, the transcendentalists exalted individualism and feeling over rationality. The transcendentalists' distinctive idea was the possibility for individuals to achieve intellectual and spiritual enlightenment, a possibility they were very optimistic would be achieved.

The definitive start of American transcendentalism was 1836 when a group of intellectuals founded the Transcendental Club in Cambridge, Massachusetts. Its most famous members were authors Ralph Waldo Emerson (1803–1882) and Henry David Thoreau (1817–1862), educators Elizabeth Peabody (1804–1894) and Amos Bronson Alcott (1799–1888, father of poet Louisa May Alcott), and feminist Margaret Fuller (1810–1850, see Chapter 25). Similar to the circle in Jena (see Chapter 14), the Transcendental Club published a literary and philosophical journal, *The Dial*. They accepted Kant's Categories, but like the German idealists, they thought that individuals could extend their knowledge beyond those mental structures. They adopted the name "transcendental" because their philosophy focused on the individual transcending the restrictions of social institutions and understanding the whole of humanity and the universe. Each person can find within himself or herself a piece of the greater whole.

One strong influence on the transcendentalists was Friedrich Schleiermacher (1768–1834), a member of the Jena circle who sought to reform Christianity by prioritizing individual feeling, similar to Kierkegaard's thought. Schleiermacher accepted Kant's Categories as the foundation of human knowledge but emphasized the need for individuals to extend their consciousness beyond intellect into an active holistic perception and experience of nature, humanity, and the universe. Another strong influence on the transcendentalists was new English translations of scriptures from Indian religions. The approach of Indian philosophers, highly rational but displaying a different set of assumptions and concerns, encouraged the transcendentalists to look at philosophical questions from perspectives beyond the Western tradition.

The individualism of the transcendentalists led them to advocate for the abolition of slavery and for women's rights. Their philosophy of feelings over rationality led them to urge a reconnection with nature. Fuller and Thoreau wrote essays against industrialization and its exploitation of the environment. Thoreau and Emerson wrote passionately about the good that comes from finding truth and psychological grounding in the natural world. The strong spiritual component of transcendentalist philosophy inspired new forms of religion and spiritualism in the United States, and transcendentalist writings on the importance of nature inspired the environmental movement.

REFERENCES

Søren Kierkegaard, *Journalen* JJ:167 (1843), *Søren Kierkegaards Skrifter*, Søren Kierkegaard Research Center, Copenhagen, 1997, Public Domain. http://sks.dk/forside/indhold.asp. (accessed April 10, 2021)

Friedrich Nietzsche, *Will to Power: An Attempted Transvaluation of All Values. Books III and IV*, trans. by Anthony Ludovici, Project Gutenberg, https://www.gutenberg.org/ebooks/52915. (accessed May 15, 2021)

Friedrich Nietzsche, *Beyond Good and Evil*, tr. by Helen Zimmern, Project Gutenberg, https://www.gutenberg.org/ebooks/4363. (accessed May 15, 2021)

CHAPTER 18

AMERICAN PRAGMATISM

Philosophy's long conversation reached the United States fairly early in the nation's history. The European settlers in the United States understandably brought with them European ideas. Any early openness in the 1700s to the ideas of America's indigenous people soon dissipated amidst the rush to expel the native populations to expand territory for more European settlers. It took a while before the United States developed any of its own movements in philosophy, but in the last decades of the 1800s, a distinctively American philosophy emerged—pragmatism. Influenced by the Kantian ideas of the Categories of Understanding and the active mind (see Chapter 13) and the emerging sense of historicism (see Chapter 14), the core ideas of pragmatism are that knowledge is an ongoing activity and that truth emerges from the practical utility of ideas. In other words, we engage with the world to develop useful ideas with which we can do things in the world; successful and useful ideas become true ideas. Pragmatism is aptly named.

Some romanticize pragmatism, portraying it as expressing the American spirit of individualism and its can-do attitude of technology and innovation. That's fair enough. There is a certain ruggedness to pragmatism, and it does prize individual thought and initiative as long as individuals take into account collective knowledge and understanding. The bigger picture, though, is that what pragmatism does more than anything else is ground philosophy in practical human concerns. We do philosophy to solve problems in our daily lives. Charles Sanders Peirce (pronounced "purs"), who invented the philosophy of pragmatism, turned Descartes' use of doubt into a practical and important part of learning for individuals and humanity as a whole. William James built on Peirce's ideas by showing how we develop habitual beliefs and call that knowledge (hello, Hume), but that is okay, James said, because that *is* what knowledge is for the most part. We develop habits because they work for us and therefore the ideas on which those habits are based become true. Kant and Fichte inspired the field of psychology. James is the one who put those ideas together and invented the science of psychology. Everything in James's philosophy is based on his notion of individual psychology—the individual who engages in freewill choices according to that individual's subjective situation. John Dewey further developed James's ideas and applied them to the scientific method and education. If you are a psychology major, most of what you learn traces back in some way to James. If you are an education major, most of what you learn traces back in some way to Dewey.

Pragmatism is less concerned with the truth of a proposition than it is concerned with the practical effects in the real world of that proposition. This shift in emphasis has a profound effect on the meaning of the concept of truth. For starters, it means that truth is a concept in our minds, not something metaphysically transcendent to it. Furthermore, it means that knowledge means having valid explanations for what we experience. Knowledge is not a matter of certainty about a transcendent truth but evolving explanations for phenomena we experience, and we adjust explanations when they are no longer valid or useful. This conception of truth and knowledge—that they adapt to new information—is one of the core elements of pragmatism and its greatest influence on philosophy and society. It's a shift similar to Kant's Copernican revolution. The pragmatists are saying that we contribute to what is true. Truth is not a fact out there but something that we create, structured by our own thoughts, beliefs, and activities. This is all similar to Nietzsche's ideas, which we saw in Chapter 17.

CHARLES SANDERS PEIRCE

Peirce's father was a mathematician on faculty at Harvard University. This enabled the younger Peirce (1839–1914) to get his own education at Harvard and to meet a number of important and interesting people. He did poorly in his university courses, graduated last in his class, but clearly the hierarchical grading system of

Harvard at that time did not accurately correspond to intellectual ability. Peirce's innovative philosophical method created a new school of philosophy. He was, first and foremost, a physical scientist, spending more than 30 years studying minute differences in Earth's gravitational field. The importance of exact measurements and rigorous interpretation of data motivated his philosophy.

Peirce approached in multiple ways the question of what truth is. His first approach is to renew the old idea that words are signs. The first to discuss words as signs was John Duns Scotus (see Chapter 6), who inspired William of Ockham's nominalism. Peirce, informed by John, William, and Kant, takes the idea of signs further and uses the term "semiotics" to refer to the study of the formal usage of signs. Signs were traditionally seen in a dyadic formula of signifier (the word) and signified (that to which the word refers) as seen by John, William, and even Augustine before them, and in Peirce's time, by linguist Ferdinand de Saussure (1857–1913). Peirce added to this the "interpretant"—the social set of meanings that interpret signifiers. Signs succeed as symbols standing for things because interpretants relate them to those things. A sign itself is a brute fact. It is the social system of meanings that makes the symbol meaningful. A flag is just a piece of cloth, but the interpretants of the social habits and feelings that the flag are meant to elicit in people relate the piece of cloth to what it signifies. All signs generate further signs to interpret the use of signs. To make sense of this, consider the dictionary. It uses words to interpret the meaning of words. Our universe is perfused with signs, Peirce says, and the elaborate system of signs makes up the world and makes up our individual and collective consciousness. A society is a web of signs, words symbols, meanings, significances, and interpretations that combine and interact in an ongoing process of interpretation of objects and ideas. Our language of signs is not inert but is in constant motion as we reinterpret what is true. This portrayal of how signs work informed Peirce's pragmatist definition of truth.

Another way Peirce explored the concept of truth was to argue that we need to consider what practical effects our conception of an object has because our conception of these effects is the whole of our conception of the object. What Peirce means by this is that what we believe an object does or what we can do with it defines for us what we think that object is. In other words, our idea of an object is our idea of its sensible effects. On the one hand, this is a rejection of speculative philosophy, as Kant and others had done. On the other hand, it is an affirmation that our words and ideas must be testable. Peirce said that if a quality or idea of an object cannot be tested, then our idea and word for that quality is meaningless. This idea is much of what Peirce means by pragmatism. As philosophers and scientists, we need to focus on the practical, testable effects of objects. Anything other than that is meaningless.

Peirce understood that what we call "truths" are really beliefs. A list of what we think is true and a list of our beliefs would be the same. He defined beliefs as something that we are aware of, that mollifies the irritation of doubt, and that produces habits in us. This is reminiscent of Hume (see Chapter 12), but Peirce emphasizes that our beliefs, being habits, are tied to physical actions or psychological expectations. Our habits predispose us to respond in certain ways to certain situations, and the essence of belief is the establishment of habits. Despite his scientific orientation, Peirce recognized that all we have are beliefs about the world. Peirce was focused on mathematics and hard science, so he did not explore the full social implications of how society produces and depends on habits and the signs that signify beliefs. He did, however, provide an excellent basic start on how we come to develop and maintain certain beliefs.

The Fixation of Belief

In his article, "The Fixation of Belief" (1877), Peirce identifies the ways that we develop habitual beliefs and how they become fixated in our minds. First, however, he explains how beliefs work. Our beliefs, he says, guide our desires and shape our actions; they create in us psychological states from which we act. Believing something or believing in someone instills in us habits that will condition us to behave in certain ways. Like Hume, Peirce has no problem with our truths being formed by habits; Peirce sees our habits as good for us, as long as they lead to positive practical effects. We believe a leader, so we have the habit or inclination to obey that leader because we believe that obedience will yield us positive effects. Belief, Peirce says, is a calm and satisfactory state that we enjoy and want to hold onto.

Doubt, Peirce says, is very different from belief. "Doubt is an uneasy and dissatisfied state from which we struggle to free ourselves and pass into the state of belief" ("Fixation of Belief," III.3). A way to think about what Peirce is saying is this. If we have a comfortable pair of shoes, then we enjoy walking in them; but if something breaks in our shoe and makes walking uncomfortable, we will stop and repair our shoe or get new shoes. The irritation that doubt causes is an important part of learning. Descartes used doubt as a way toward certain knowledge. Peirce didn't have certain knowledge, but more useful knowledge, as the goal, so he viewed doubt in that context. Peirce said that doubt spurs us to reflect on our beliefs, reject beliefs that are not satisfactory, and struggle to attain new beliefs that ensure better habits and better results.

At least, that's how we should behave, Peirce says. We don't always, though. Peirce identifies four different methods by which we eliminate the irritation of doubt and fix our beliefs. He discusses the four methods from most undesirable to most desirable and begins with a common behavior caused by the nature of belief itself.

> *The instinctive dislike of an undecided state of mind, exaggerated into a vague dread of doubt, makes men [sic] cling spasmodically to the views they already take. The man feels that, if he only holds to his belief without wavering, it will be entirely satisfactory.... [He] hides the danger, and then calmly says there is no danger; and, if [he] feels perfectly sure there is none, why should [he] raise its head to see? A man may go through life, systematically keeping out of view all that might cause a change in his opinions.* ("Fixation of Belief," V.1)

This behavior, Piece labels "the method of tenacity." He says it is unstable because those who use this method to fix their beliefs continually run up against evidence to the contrary and people who think differently. We frequently see people employing this method. Such people attempt to eliminate doubt by ignoring all evidence and reasoning that could call their belief into question.

The method of tenacity is at the level of the individual person. Peirce identifies a second similar doubt suppression method that works at the level of a community or social institution. This is "the method of authority" that Peirce says has been used by all great civilizations in which each established a set of correct doctrines and taught them to its people. Peirce acknowledges the method of authority brings about greater consistency of belief in a community by producing a comfortable, communal belief system. The problem with this method is that it effectively raises the method of tenacity to the level of a community or whole society. It also is unsustainable because an institution cannot control every opinion of every person. Peirce says, as had ibn Rushd (see Chapter 5), that the method of authority will always govern the mass of people who have no higher impulse than to be intellectual slaves. But there are also people who possess a wider social feeling and become aware of other beliefs, which causes doubts to emerge.

A third method of eliminating doubt and fixing belief is simply to hold opinions that are agreeable to reason. Peirce calls this "the *a priori* method," after the common philosophical belief in knowledge separate from experience (see Chapter 13). These are just opinions, though, Peirce says, opinions that are not based on evidence but on that which we find ourselves inclined to believe. Peirce correctly charges many philosophers with using this method. This method is more intellectual than the methods of tenacity and authority, but it turns inquiry into something similar to a matter of taste. What is agreeable to reason is a subjective issue that reflects one's personal sentiments and experiences. Peirce rejects speculative rationality because, in his opinion, the field is a warring collection of opinions, with philosophers expressing their personal preferences. The *a priori* method ends up being simply intellectual prejudices.

The shortcomings of the three methods show that the proper method of finding belief is important. We will have beliefs—we can't operate without them—the question is how to find ones that produce good tangible results. What we need is a method of fixing belief in which our beliefs may be caused by nothing personal but rather by some external permanency—by something beyond our personal thinking. Peirce is not calling for our minds to be passive but to be responsive to the world and to the evidence it shows us. What he calls "the method of science" is when we use our active minds to follow a disciplined method of observing the real things in the world that are independent of our minds. We start with known and observable facts and proceed to the unknown. We let the evidence, not our feelings, show us what to believe. We are using the method correctly when new information throws our beliefs into doubt. If you are not open to being puzzled or questioning your beliefs, you are not capable of the kind of inquiry that will lead to knowledge. The force of habit and the desire for comfortable conclusions will always tempt us, but reflection on the facts will overcome these temptations. The method of science is an open-ended method that lets the evidence guide our thinking. With this method, our beliefs are a response to the world, not to our personal prejudices. We learn what experience has to teach us.

Science as Public Meaning

Peirce said that the meanings of our beliefs are defined in terms of our interactions with the world. Those interactions are publicly observable, and it is the actions that people perform that give us the meanings of signs and beliefs. Meaning is performative and public. The public aspect of Peirce's definition is important. All we have are our beliefs, but we can't say that whatever we believe is real and true because, as we saw earlier, people can fix their beliefs on reasons contrary to evidence. Our beliefs are meaningful when they can be shown to connect with what is real—what is the case independent of our beliefs.

But how do we determine what is real? What brings meaning, truth, and reality together for Peirce is science. The beliefs of any particular person do not determine what is real, but people collectively can determine what is real. Science, broadly construed, is about collecting information through observations. Peirce is not overly concerned with a particular correct method of conducting science; as a scientist himself, he knew that experimenting with different methods was a good approach. He was confident that different scientists using different methods of observation will initially yield different results, but that,

> *as each perfects his method and his processes, the results will move steadily together toward a destined center. So with all scientific research. Different minds may set out with the most antagonistic views, but the progress of investigation carries them by a force outside of themselves to one and the same conclusion.* ("How to Make Our Ideas Clear," 300)

Peirce places his faith in an objective reality that is discernable by a community of dedicated humans. One person, or even a number of people, can be mistaken in their beliefs, but through concerted effort, humanity as a whole will come to understand reality. People collectively determine truth.

> *The opinion which is fated to be ultimately agreed to by all who investigate is what we mean by the truth, and the object represented in this opinion is the real. That is the way I would explain reality.* ("How to Make Our Ideas Clear," 300)

Peirce's conception is similar to Hegel's in the basic idea that knowledge progresses from incomplete to more complete understandings (see Chapter 14). Also like Hegel, Peirce is optimistic that humanity will in time solve all questions. Peirce was far more oriented toward science and observation than Hegel was and didn't have Hegel's notion of *Geist*. Peirce had little direct influence on the methods of science, as he had hoped, but he did have a strong influence on his friend, William James.

WILLIAM JAMES

William James (1842–1910), brother of novelist Henry James (1843–1916), was a medical doctor turned philosopher. William James literally wrote the book on psychology—*The Principles of Psychology* (1890)—establishing the field as a bona fide science. On philosophy, he was a pragmatist who followed Peirce and built on his work, bringing pragmatism into everyday life. The purpose of philosophy, James wrote, was to find out what definite difference various beliefs will make to us and our lives. His most notable works in philosophy are *The Will to Believe* (1897) and *Pragmatism: A New Name for Some Old Ways of Thinking* (1907).

The Cash Value of Beliefs

Like Peirce, James said that truth is a matter of whether a belief is useful to us. Truth *happens* to an idea, he said, when it succeeds in predicting new sense experiences. Also like Peirce, he was a staunch empiricist, seeing all of our knowledge coming from sense experience. But while Peirce emphasized the public and collective aspect of empiricism, James argued it was the right of the individual to understand the consequences of beliefs in his or her own personal life. Truth is what works for each person. The individual determines the practical and satisfactory consequences of a belief.

It may seem that James is saying that anything goes—if we like a belief we can say it's true—but this is misunderstanding him. It is up to the individual to decide what is true, but this decision is not arbitrary; this decision is based on solid empirical evidence. James understood that the notion that truth was a rarified objective reality was nonsense. Truth is a tool by which we do things, or, to use James's bold analogy, truth has a practical cash value. Whether a belief is useful or valuable can be determined only by the individual. That's because knowledge comes only from experience, and experience is always subjectively experienced by the individual. We share many circumstances in common, but many particular circumstances differ from person to person. A belief is true if it works *for me* in my particular circumstances, though it is incumbent on me to be sensible in deciding what works; it is not a matter of whim. I should be able to demonstrate that my beliefs are responding to evidence.

Everything in James's philosophy rests on practical usefulness. Truth *happens* to an idea, not because we want it to, but because we *make* it true through our actions. A scientific hypothesis is true only after we have tested it sufficiently. Our personal goals are true only after we have taken action to accomplish them. James understood that truth is pluralistic, meaning that a particular belief could work in practical terms for one person but not another, meaning it is true for the first person but not a second person. Also, different beliefs work in different situations; there are multiple ways to do any task, so there are multiple truths.

What James was doing generated controversy. He was attacked by critics for being too subjective and relativistic. It was a seismic shift to measure truth not by it being universal but by it being useful. This went against most of what was held by philosophy and all of the political, scientific, and cultural expressions that stemmed from philosophy. But as James noted in the title of his book, *Pragmatism: A New Name for Some Old Ways of Thinking*, he was pointing out the way people behave in their everyday lives. Truth is a matter of usefulness, and if an idea is useful, it is true—that's how we act. More than that, he said, truth is merely the expedient in the way of our thinking. Interestingly, these ideas are similar to what Nietzsche had said a few years earlier (see Chapter 17), but there was zero chance that James saw Nietzsche's writings, which had not yet been translated.

Like Peirce, James's pragmatism was subjective but grounded in objective human experience. His critics were mistaken in thinking he meant that willful belief alone makes something true. He stressed that when we say a belief works for us, we don't mean that it simply feels good to us. We mean that we have tangible experience that it works: "Experience, as we know, has ways of BOILING OVER and making us correct our present formula" (*Pragmatism*, VI.44, emphasis his). There is no absolute truth, James goes on to say, but we are still wise, even obligated, to strive continually to ensure that our beliefs are in harmony with the evidence before us, and we need to adjust our beliefs in accordance with new experiences.

> *Meanwhile we have to live to-day by what truth we can get to-day, and be ready to-morrow to call it falsehood. Ptolemaic astronomy, Euclidean space, Aristotelian logic, scholastic metaphysics, were expedient for centuries, but human experience has boiled over those limits, and we now call these things only relatively true, or true within those borders of experience.* (*Pragmatism*, VI.45)

Truth is the expedient in our way of thinking—expedient in the sense of the most direct path to what works. This is how we learn and grow from childhood on, and this is how science operates. Truth is dynamic in always growing and changing.

A Right to Believe

James applied the realization that there is no absolute truth, only our best attempts at it, in *The Will to Believe*, in which he responded to a paper by mathematician William K. Clifford (1845–1879). Clifford asserted that it is morally wrong, everywhere and for anyone, to believe something on insufficient evidence. Clifford meant this as an attack on religious belief, and he had written other essays hostile to religion. James rightly called out Clifford's bigotry, but identified the larger issue that if we followed what Clifford demands, we would end up not being able to believe anything, anywhere.

Having read this far in this book, you should have realized that absolute, certain knowledge is impossible. Beyond this reality ignored by Clifford and other positivist philosophers (see Chapter 19), James observed that generating beliefs is a process and that we can identify multiple dimensions to that process. We must make choices about what to believe and how we will act, James said, similar to what Kierkegaard had said (see Chapter 17). Affecting our freewill choices are the dimensions of the options among which we must choose. Options can be living or dead, forced or avoidable, momentous or trivial. A live option is one you can put your will behind; a forced option is one for which there is no possibility of not choosing; and a momentous option is one that is unique, irreversible, and/or has significant effects on you. Those are genuine options, and I list those sides of the dichotomies because dead options are irrelevant, avoidable ones are just that, and trivial options are of no consequence. Therefore, James says, our decisions on dead, irrelevant, and trivial matters are of no great import, so we can concede to Clifford's demand to withhold belief and action without sufficient evidence.

However, only options that are of the forced, living, and momentous kind can be called genuine options for us. With these genuine options, we have a right to believe what we see as the practical decision, even when the evidence could be considered insufficient. When options are forced, these are decisions that we have to make, and we have a right, even the duty, to make decisions even though we do not have complete evidence. Plus, James reminds us that some beliefs can become true only when we first place faith in their possibility. He gives as an example cultivating a friendship: "Do you like me or not?" he asks. There is little chance of you coming to like me if I do not act toward you with the faith of believing you are worth trusting and capable of liking me. But, he says, "if I stand aloof, and refuse to budge an inch until I have objective evidence, until you shall have done something apt, as the absolutists say,...ten to one your liking never comes" (*The Will to Believe*, IX, 2). On religious beliefs, which Clifford attacked, James says that these are clearly live options. We will live our lives either with or without a religious perspective, so it is a forced option. Undeniably, it is a momentous option because the choice to live with a religious mindset or not affects us in profound ways, James says. Therefore, on pragmatic principles, if the hypothesis of God works for us satisfactorily—if it has cash value—it is true.

We Have Free Will

One truly genuine option is whether we have free will. It's a simple hypothesis: I have the ability to choose freely what actions I will take. Whether that hypothesis is correct—or its opposite, that our choices are determined by external forces—is impossible to prove by reason or experience. This is, undeniably, a living and momentous option to believe we have free will, and James says we are forced to make a choice. Therefore, he said, we have a right to choose the option that works for us. James emphatically chooses to believe that he has free will—and not only to believe it but to act with it and believe in his individual reality and creative power.

Not content with his freewill choice to believe he has free will, James wrote an essay entitled "The Dilemma of Determinism" (1884) in which he refuted the deterministic hypothesis. We've seen several versions of determinism already in this book, when philosophers in their quest for understanding assumed that believing in determinism was understanding how the world works. James refutes that belief with the following argument:

1. Many actions that people perform are later regretted (murder or cruelty, for example).
2. Determinism professes that it is impossible for anything in the universe to be otherwise than it is.
3. Determinism claims that everything is the inevitable result of previous causes, but that implies that judgments of regret are in error. To regret something is to believe that things could have been different from the way they are.
4. Determinism is the pessimistic position that evil and cruel actions are necessary and unavoidable and therefore should not be regretted but accepted.
5. The only way a determinist can avoid this fatalistic pessimism is to say that acts of cruelty are actually good and rationally necessary and that regret is irrational and bad. (This was a position of some Stoics, see Chapter 4.) We are left with the dilemma that either regret is good and cruelty is bad or that cruelty is good and regret is bad. But determinism says that both cruelty and regret are necessary and unavoidable events. This is a contradiction.
6. Therefore, James concludes, if determinism is true, then "something must be fatally unreasonable, absurd, and wrong in the world" ("The Dilemma of Determinism," 164).

Belief in determinism suppresses the reality of our moral and practical lives. If, instead, we believe in indeterminism (free will), then, James says, we open ourselves up to the reality that our choices and actions make a difference.

The best way to sum up James is to understand that everything in his philosophy is based on his notion of individual psychology. The individual engages in freewill choices according to his or her subjective situation. We are beings who must choose and act; to act, we create beliefs that have value to us. Each one of us maintains our beliefs as long as they work for us.

JOHN DEWEY

John Dewey (1859–1952) was the next generation of pragmatist philosopher. He combined the scientific orientation of Peirce with the individual psychology of James. Dewey's scientific orientation was biology, and he was influenced by the developments in evolutionary biology. His philosophical starting point was the fact that people exist within a biological environment. We create beliefs to adapt to our environment. Dewey created the term "instrumentalism" to describe the human activity of developing and using beliefs as tools or instruments for solving problems and altering our environment to meet our needs and desires. One of Dewey's primary aims was to reform education to help children develop problem-solving skills—instruments to solve problems.

Instrumentalism and Truth

We exist in a world, and we must react to it and try to navigate within it to accomplish our goals. Our intellectual abilities, Dewey said, are developed in response to our world. The world places demands on us, and we are beings who must make choices and act (hello, Kierkegaard). The implication of this for Dewey was to understand human intelligence as the continual activity of developing more profitable relations with the objects we encounter. This view rejects the passive mind of Locke and Hume and adopts James's "cash value" theory of beliefs. Dewey said that our thinking doesn't make copies of the objects in our environment but that we think about how to interact with and use them better. Dewey intentionally speaks of "intelligence" rather than "mind" to focus on mental activity rather than on an entity.

Dewey sought to promote human inquiry, which he saw as the core of successful instrumentalism. Very similar to Peirce, Dewey saw doubt as an unsettled and confused state from which we seek to free ourselves by attaining a unified and resolved situation. Dewey, as he consistently did throughout his philosophy, spoke of doubt as a response to the environment—we are doubtful because the situation is doubtful—rather than an intellectual exercise, á la Descartes. In this way, Dewey is not talking about academic doubt but practical and functional doubt. We are thinking about real life rather than conducting thought experiments. Here is one of the examples of inquiry that Dewey gives:

> *A man traveling in an unfamiliar region comes to a branching of the roads. Having no sure knowledge to fall back upon, he is brought to a*

standstill of hesitation and suspense. Which road is right? And how shall perplexity be resolved? There are but two alternatives: he must either blindly and arbitrarily take his course, trusting to luck for the outcome, or he must discover grounds for the conclusion that a given road is right. Any attempt to decide the matter by thinking will involve inquiry into other facts, whether brought out by memory or by further observation, or by both. The perplexed wayfarer must carefully scrutinize what is before him and he must cudgel his memory. He looks for evidence that will support belief in favor of either of the roads—for evidence that will weight down one suggestion. He may climb a tree; he may go first in this direction, then in that, looking, in either case, for signs, clues, indications. He wants something in the nature of a signboard or a map, and his reflection is aimed at the discovery of facts that will serve this purpose. (*How We Think*, 10–11)

This forked road situation is analogous to how we deal with every problem we face, from deciding what to have for dinner to solving complex scientific or moral problems. We are confronted with a question; we gather information; we try a solution; and if that doesn't work, we seek another, and so on until we come to a satisfactory conclusion.

Dewey's idea of truth is essentially the same as for Peirce and James. His notion of instrumentalism focused the idea of practicality onto specific tasks. The tool analogy is quite apt. Dewey said that the question is not, "Is a hammer adequate?" That's too general to be meaningful. The question is, "Is a hammer adequate for pounding in nails?" The answer is, "Yes." The answer is, "No," to the question, "Is a hammer adequate for dividing a board in two?" We understand that we use different tools for different tasks, and Dewey asks us to think of beliefs in the same way. Which belief or idea is adequate to solve the situation before me? That's what thinking is, what ideas are, and what truth is. Dewey says, "Ideas are not then genuine ideas unless they are tools in a reflective examination which tends to solve a problem" (*How We Think*, 109).

Peirce had ignored moral philosophy, and James spoke of it only when he discussed moral decisions as being made in the same process of expediency that we use to come to truth. Dewey thought along similar lines as James but spent more effort on thinking about moral problems. He rejected the happiness principle of Mill's utilitarianism (see Chapter 16), contending that it doesn't explain *why* something is desired. A moral act is genuinely valuable when our inquiry identifies it as helping us flourish in the long run. Dewey argued that, like the scientist begins with observations and tests theories until a satisfactory hypothesis is reached, we should make moral value judgments in the same way. Dewey is consistent with the rest of his philosophy in thinking that moral laws, like scientific laws, are ways that we respond to our environment that need to change when circumstances change.

Education

Education was Dewey's prime concern because it is through education that we learn how to solve problems and this is the way we can improve society as a whole for the long term. Students are individual people and should be cultivated as such. Education should not be taught by rote or en masse. Dewey thought that, in schools, students were seen as theoretical spectators who were under the instruction of experts. Dewey criticized education and academia itself as not perceiving the uniqueness of individuals. Individuals have an infinite diversity of active tendencies, and education, and society as a whole, must account for this. Dewey thought that education is best when it is active involvement, not passive seeing or hearing. Central to his educational reforms was the need to get away from rote memorization of facts and instead adopt processes of open inquiry. Good education, he thought, teaches individuals how to solve problems and engage better with their society. Students need to be active questioners—hands-on in both practices and dialogue. Discussion is an important part of education, and the students need to be able to ask questions of their teachers, discuss among themselves, and discover truths for themselves. Dewey's proposed reforms along these principles, far lengthier and more detailed than we can hope to discuss here, have inspired many educators since. Sadly, some educators, including those with advanced degrees, still insist on requiring "teaching to the test" and treating students as passive vessels to be force-fed facts that they must memorize and regurgitate back to receive a grade. Education still has not achieved Dewey's vision of a learning process of problem-solving and creative thinking.

REFERENCES

John Dewey. *How We Think*, D.C. Heath & Co. Not in Copyright. Internet Archive. https://archive.org/details/howwethink02dewegoog/. (accessed April 8, 2021)

William James. "The Dilemma of Determinism" in *The Will to Believe, and Other Essays in Popular Philosophy*, Project Gutenberg. http://www.gutenberg.org/ebooks/26659. (accessed April 7, 2021)

William James. *Pragmatism: A New Name for Some Old Ways of Thinking*. Project Gutenberg. http://www.gutenberg.org/ebooks/5116. (accessed April 6, 2021)

William James. "The Dilemma of Determinism," in *The Will to Believe, and Other Essays in Popular Philosophy*, Project Gutenberg. http://www.gutenberg.org/ebooks/26659. (accessed April 7, 2021)

William James. "The Will to Believe," in *The Will to Believe, and Other Essays in Popular Philosophy*, Project Gutenberg. http://www.gutenberg.org/ebooks/26659. (accessed April 7, 2021)

Charles Sanders Peirce, "How to Make Our Ideas Clear," *Wikisource*, https://en.wikisource.org/wiki/Popular_Science_Monthly/Volume_12/January_1878/Illustrations_of_the_Logic_of_Science_II. (accessed April 6, 2021)

Charles Sanders Peirce, "The Fixation of Belief," *Wikisource*, https://en.wikisource.org/wiki/The_Fixation_of_Belief. (accessed April 6, 2021)

CHAPTER 19

PROCESS VERSUS POSITIVISM: PHILOSOPHY'S GREAT DIVIDE

In Chapter 14, I mentioned the divide between continental philosophy and analytical philosophy. The rest of this book deals with these two different major trajectories of philosophy. In this chapter, we will look at the beginning of that divide as the difference between focusing on ongoing processes (continental philosophy) and applying a logical positivist paradigm (analytical philosophy). There are specific schools of philosophy that went by the names "process philosophy" and "logical positivism," but we will see how the terms can be more broadly applied.

POSITIVISM: THE BIRTH OF ANALYTICAL PHILOSOPHY

We have seen several philosophers who sought to find a solid foundation for science in philosophy. Positivism is the attempt to turn that relation around and find a solid foundation for philosophy in science. The term "positivism" was invented by French philosopher Auguste Comte (1798–1857) to describe that to which he thought philosophy should aspire: positive knowledge completely devoid of speculation and superstition. In itself, this wasn't a new idea, but Comte's conception of a positivist philosophy was colored by his deep hostility toward religion. He viewed human history as a matter of historical progress, but unlike Hegel (see Chapter 14), Comte saw history as humanity's journey of overcoming religion's pernicious influence. He rejected every idea that could not be reduced to logic or scientific observation as "superstition." This credo was taken up by the later "logical positivists," discussed later in this chapter. Comte rejected all speculation about causes, even within the sciences. He said we should not ask what gravity is but simply account for the phenomenon in the experiences of objects falling. In other words, even scientific theory and modeling, such as what Newton had used (see Chapter 8), was to be rejected. Comte suggested that beyond the "hard" sciences of mathematics, physics, chemistry, and so on, there should be a further science he called "sociology" that analyzed phenomena in human society to uncover the materialist laws that govern human behavior. He inspired the field of "sociology" and a common materialist method of doing social sciences. Comte also proposed a scientific religion that would set down the ethical laws for human interactions. He condemned the idea of God, but he correctly pointed out that atheism was an equally dogmatic position. Rather than waste time on debates between theism and atheism, a scientific religion would seek to aid human beings, a sentiment he admitted was a positive value found in traditional religions.

BERTRAND RUSSELL

Positivist philosophy didn't follow the strict regimen Comte had laid out, but it found a new foundation in the work of Bertrand Russell (1872–1970). The core of this new foundation was logic and mathematics and the idea that they were one and the same. Russell could rightfully be called the first analytical philosopher from his method of mathematical-logical analysis of philosophical problems.

Russell was a very British philosopher, a member of the aristocracy and House of Lords. His wealthy family had been one of the leading political families in England for the 350 years prior to his birth, his grandfather even being British prime minister. They had long been staunchly liberal politically, and Bertie (as he preferred to be known) followed in that tradition, being very active and outspoken in progressive political causes, especially antiwar and anti-imperialist causes. Strangely, he never wrote any political philosophy, it being just about the only field of philosophy he didn't address in one way or another.

Russell's great love was mathematics, and he used the word "love" to describe his lifelong fascination with it. His first book was on a philosophy of geometry based on Kantian ideas, but he later rejected Kant and his own book. Russell wanted to identify the foundation of mathematics, which he came to see as an extension of logic. He abandoned Kant and embraced the mathematical ideas of Italian Giuseppe Peano (1858–1932), the founder of set theory, and of German Gottlob Frege (1848–1925). Frege was a then unknown scholar who Russell, as he became well known, came to champion. Frege had invented a new system of logic that used quantified variables to convert propositions into symbolic logic. He then argued that mathematics was not a separate entity but an extension of logic and, thus, mathematical laws and proofs are understood to be pure logic. Russell took inspiration from Frege and Peano; with his professor, Alfred North Whitehead (1861–1947), Russell wrote a formal system of the logical foundations of mathematics. Their *Principia Mathematica* was published in three volumes from 1910 to 1913. It is a contender for the most dense book ever written. For example, here is their proof that 1 + 1 = 2:

***54·43.** $\vdash :.\, \alpha, \beta \in 1 \,.\supset :\, \alpha \cap \beta = \Lambda \,.\equiv .\, \alpha \cup \beta \in 2$

Dem.

$$\vdash .\, *54{\cdot}26 \,.\supset \vdash :.\, \alpha = \iota`x \,.\, \beta = \iota`y \,.\supset :\, \alpha \cup \beta \in 2 \,.\equiv .\, x \neq y \,.$$

$$[*51{\cdot}231] \qquad \equiv .\, \iota`x \cap \iota`y = \Lambda \,.$$

$$[*13{\cdot}12] \qquad \equiv .\, \alpha \cap \beta = \Lambda \qquad (1)$$

$$\vdash .\, (1) \,.\, *11{\cdot}11{\cdot}35 \,.\supset$$

$$\vdash :.\, (\exists x, y) \,.\, \alpha = \iota`x \,.\, \beta = \iota`y \,.\supset :\, \alpha \cup \beta \in 2 \,.\equiv .\, \alpha \cap \beta = \Lambda \qquad (2)$$

$$\vdash .\, (2) \,.\, *11{\cdot}54 \,.\, *52{\cdot}1 \,.\supset \vdash .\, \text{Prop}$$

From this proposition it will follow, when arithmetical addition has been defined, that $1 + 1 = 2$.

Proof 54-43 in *Principia Mathematica, Volume I, 1st edition,* p. 379.

It's okay, I don't understand it either. The point of this proof, and of all of *Principia Mathematica*, is to get mathematics away from intuition. Remember that in the discussion of previous philosophers, we used the example that we simply know that 1 + 1 = 2. That's an appeal to intuition, and Russell isn't comfortable with that. His contention was that we understand 1 + 1 = 2 because we think logically.

Russell then turned to the idea that if all of mathematics can be reduced to logic, then all language expressions could also be reduced to logic. There was a growing sense in the late 1800s and early 1900s across philosophy that the role of language in knowledge needed to be addressed. How we express our ideas and how we understand ideas depend on the language we use. Surprisingly, philosophy had done little work on the nature of language. John and William (see Chapter 6) had written a little bit about the need to be clearer on the names we use to construct philosophical arguments. Kierkegaard (see Chapter 17) had mentioned that philosophy needed to take heed of the significant role of language in philosophy. He observed that language is partly something given to people, but also something that people develop freely, a realization that foreshadowed the later Wittgenstein (see Chapter 20).

Russell's dream was to show that all language can be expressed with a logical syntax that can accurately and with certainty describe the world. Obviously, not all language expressions make logical sense, but that, Russell said, is because the syntax we use in our ordinary language is problematic. Here is an often used example of the problem with ordinary language that Russell identified:

Argument 1	Argument 2
a) There is a fire in my kitchen.	a) There is a pain in my foot.
b) My kitchen is in my house.	b) My foot is in my shoe.
c) Therefore, there is a fire in my house.	c) Therefore, there is a pain in my shoe.

Both arguments have the same grammatical structure, but Argument 1 makes sense as written, and Argument 2 does not. The problem is with the word "in," which has a spatial meaning in Argument 1 that it does not have in Argument 2. Our syntax can disguise and distort the underlying logical forms of arguments, leading us to incorrect conclusions. Russell was confident that the tools he developed in *Principia Mathematica* could be applied to reformulate ordinary language into logical language.

Russell's quest for a logical language was inspired by, but ultimately doomed by, his assumption that because language describes the world, there is a necessary link between language and the world. Russell believed that every word has a factual meaning—namely, the basic entity to which it refers. This is his theory of "logical atomism"; by "atom" he means the original Greek sense of irreducible entities, not necessarily literal material atoms. In logical atomism, all truths ultimately depend on a layer of atomic facts, which consist either of a simple particular exhibiting a quality or multiple simple particulars standing in a relation. Russell assumed that we can attain certain knowledge about the world's logical structure if we can clear up the muddle of our ordinary language. If the world is composed of a finite number of basic entities, our language should be composed of a finite number of basic linguistic units. Match every entity in the world with a corresponding linguistic unit, and we have a logically perfect language that we can use to describe everything.

The methodology of logical atomism is a process of analysis, whereby one attempts to define or reconstruct more complex notions or vocabularies in terms of simpler ones. According to Russell, such an analysis would lead to a language containing only words representing simple particulars; the simple properties and relations thereof; and logical constants, which, despite its limited vocabulary, could adequately capture all truths.

With the tools of a logically perfect language, Russell believed we could construct arguments in which every proposition corresponds directly to a fact in the world. For example, we have the atomic proposition "this is taller than that," which corresponds to the atomic fact that a particular tree is taller than another particular object. Atomic propositions can be combined to create molecular propositions—for example, "this is green, and that is brown." The tools of the logical language would be the collection of atomic propositions and the logical operators such as "and," "or," "not," "if…then." This process often reveals that what we take to be brute necessities are instead purely logical. Such a logical language would clear up illogical arguments like Argument 2 and, Russell felt, would solve most philosophical problems.

The problem with logical atomism is that though it's a great dream, it doesn't work in real life. In Russell's quest for the simple, fundamental units of the world and our language, he ran into multiple problems. He realized that, on the one hand, we experience hard data that are unreasonable to doubt and that, on the other hand, we have beliefs containing soft data about which we are less certain and we need to infer what we are experiencing. He wanted to be able to be certain about every bit of sense data, so he needed to reinterpret soft data as logical constructions based on hard data. This leads him down a difficult path. When you walk toward an object, in your visual field are the shifting sense data of blocks of color of particular sizes and shapes. You can be certain of those bits of sense of data; they are hard data. Russell said that out of habit (like Hume said in Chapter 12), you group together these bits of sense data and treat them as belonging to a class you have learned to call "table." But he has to admit that this general idea "table" is soft data that can't be converted to hard data. Words like "table" refer to an inferred entity of which we cannot be absolutely certain. Russell can be certain only that "table" is a class term that refers to a collection of hard sense data. By extension, all of our words are actually logical constructions with an uncertain relation to our sense data; thus, so are all of our ideas about external objects. But this seems to defeat the whole project of logical atomism that sought to make certain connections between our language and objects in the world.

To make a long story short, Russell's path leads him to the very skepticism he wanted to avoid. He ends up having to admit that we can state with certainty only such propositions as "redness is here." About entities in the world, he can say only that "if I have tablelike sense data at one moment, I can reasonably expect similar tablelike sense data in the next moment," but he can justify those propositions only by appealing to human habit. (Hume would be chuckling at this point.)

It took his famous student Ludwig Wittgenstein to find ways out of these conundrums of language. It upset Russell greatly, but Wittgenstein rejected the project of logical atomism in favor of ordinary language. We'll see how in Chapter 20. As a short side note, one has to feel sympathy for Bertie who devoted his life to a project, helped by both his favorite professor, Whitehead, and his favorite student, Wittgenstein, only to see them both reject his project and go in very different directions, as we will soon discuss.

THE LOGICAL POSITIVISTS

In the 1930s, two decades before Russell reached a dead end with logical atomism, a group of philosophers in Vienna were inspired by Russell's work to develop what they called "logical positivism." Their intent was to create a perfect philosophy based on a method of rigorous logical analysis. They came to be known as the "Vienna Circle." Rudolf Carnap, Otto Neurath, Herbert Feigl, and Friedrich Waismann were the most active members of the Vienna Circle, and they evangelized their new method across Europe, successfully igniting a philosophical movement.

Foremost in the minds of the logical positivists was a fierce distaste for metaphysics—the philosophy of the nature of reality, which they interpreted as speculation beyond what is observable. Like Russell, they sought to build a logically perfect language. Their method was the "verifiability principle": They insisted that only propositions that could be verified by logical or scientific observation should be permitted. With that core principle as a battle-ax, they removed most of the history of philosophy before them.

The verifiability principle stated that a factual statement is meaningful only if it can be verified in experience. A statement, "There is a tree next to the driveway," is meaningful because it can be verified as being either true or false by going to the driveway and observing. The meaning of any factual statement is the method of its verification. The meaning of the statement just given can be expressed by the explanatory statement, "If I go to the driveway, I will see a tree." In science, a theory is meaningful only if the theory can be tested and verified. In the opinion of the logical positivists, statements such Hegel's "Freedom is the idea of *Geist*...," discussed in Chapter 15, are meaningless because they cannot be verified. But also eliminated by the verifiability principle was Kant's synthetic *a priori* judgments because they cannot be verified by observation; they can only be inferred. All theological statements are rejected. Both the theists' "God exists" and the atheists' "no God exists" are unverifiable and meaningless. Similarly, the logical positivists rejected all moral theory. Its English convert, A.J. Ayer (1910–1989), went so far as to dismiss all moral statements as mere emotional reactions. He claimed that saying an act was morally wrong was simply saying "boo!" and saying an act was morally good was simply rooting "hooray!"

The logical positivists' ideal principles ran into real-life issues similar to Russell's. The verifiability principle immediately ran into a feasibility problem. "There is a mountain on the far side of the moon" was not verifiable in the 1930s. That objection was easily remedied by adjusting the principle to state verifiable in experience *in principle*. Sure enough, technology advanced to where we could observe the far side of the moon. Scientists objected that many important scientific statements, including the laws of physics, were not conclusively *verifiable* through observation but could only be *supported* by observation. This corresponded to Hume's observation that science can only infer probable truths because the next experiment could always yield a different result (see Chapter 12). The logical positivists had to concede that point, and Carnap replaced "verification" with "confirmation" in the principle.

Then developments in subatomic physics and quantum mechanics forced them to modify their principle again to accept that statements about unobservable subatomic particles are meaningful because other observations suggest their existence is probable. Logical positivism completely melted down in the face of Heisenberg's uncertainty principle and Schrödinger's cat being both alive and dead (see your friendly, neighborhood physics professor). The final blow to logical positivism was the critique that its central principle of verifiability was itself unverifiable by either logic or observation. Hume would be laughing out loud at this point because the verifiability principle is neither a relation of ideas nor a matter of fact; it is simply an assertion. The logical positivists had to admit that their verifiability principle was only a recommendation. The demand of the logical positivists that all human knowledge conform to a specific structure ultimately was an empty demand.

PROCESS: CONTINENTAL PHILOSOPHY

At the same time that Russell was developing positivist analytical philosophy, French philosopher Henri Bergson (1856–1941) was developing a very different philosophy. For several decades, he was probably the most famous philosopher in the world. He is now tragically largely forgotten because his work is incorrectly dismissed as mere speculation because it is not reducible to the methods of analytical philosophy. Bergson, similar to Hegel, thought of knowledge as an ongoing process of development, but he rejected the mechanistic causality of Hegel's historicism (see Chapter 14). Bergson developed a highly original approach to philosophy that took into account elements of Kant, Hegel, and pragmatism.

BERGSON EXPLAINS THE ANALYTICAL/ CONTINENTAL DIVIDE

Bergson proposes that in the quest for understanding the world, there are two methods of gaining knowledge of an object. There is analysis, which seeks to know an object absolutely, and there is intuition, which seeks to understand an object relatively.

The method of analysis is how science and analytical philosophy think empirical knowledge of the world is obtained, and it is the habitual way that Western people have learned to think. Since Aristotle, philosophy had seen everything in the universe as discrete substances that maintain their identity even while undergoing change. When you look back at all of the philosophers we've covered so far, you can see how much of their work was dealing with the problems created by that assumption that everything is a substance: how objects are, how they are similar yet different, how they change, and how we can have knowledge about them. Analysis is the method that comes from this assumption. It is the detached and disinterested method of separating the object from its surroundings, conceptually breaking down an object into parts, interpreting the divided parts, and reconstituting a view of the object after analysis. But, Bergson says, analysis depends on symbols that represent parts of the objects and then uses symbols to reconstruct a picture of the object. This is similar to Locke's epistemology (see Chapter 8) in which simple ideas combine into complex ideas, but this is the approach that Bergson wants us to stop using. Symbols, words, and language are, he said, barriers between us and reality. Bergson's philosophy is not an epistemology in the usual sense.

Bergson says that the true empiricism is intuition. Bergson uses "intuition" differently from what we've seen previously. Philosophers like Descartes used "intuition" to describe an immediate knowing. Bergson used "intuition" as a sympathetic entering into what is observed, rather than going around it from the outside. By "sympathetic," Bergson does not mean an emotion but operating through affinity and interdependence, as in a sympathetic vibration of two strings. Intuition is entering into experience to be a part of what is observed. Intuition is an integral experience, a series of acts within what Bergson calls "duration," (explained soon) and thus a method of experience.

One of the examples Bergson gives of the difference between the method of analysis and the method of intuition is experiencing a city. Looking at photographs of a city, even a collection taken from every viewpoint and perspective, you can't reconstruct what it is to be in the city. Only by entering the city and walking through it can you grasp what it is to be there. His other example is reading a commentary on a poem by Homer. No matter how many commentaries you read, you can never grasp the value of experiencing the poem in its original language. Analysis can give us photographs and commentary, but it can't give us the experience of the things themselves. Analysis has its own value and provides us with some understanding, but knowing the things themselves requires the sympathetic entering into of intuition. Bergson says that by intuition we can seize reality from within.

Duration—Bergson's Philosophy of Time

Intuition begins with entering into the "duration," another original concept from Bergson. Duration is Bergson's conception of time and consciousness that he proposed to help correct the problems with the method of analysis. Bergson realized that reality is a continuous flow of activity, not static substances. Everything is constantly changing, and fundamental to the flow of reality is time. We experience time, he realized, but not with our senses or by reason, but through an inner sense. Bergson's philosophy of time is an ingenious and highly original exploration of a topic that few philosophers take on.

Bergson identifies two ways that we can think about time. One he calls "scientific time" or "clock time." This is time as conceived by the method of analysis, discussed earlier. The other is "duration" or "real time." This is time as we live it. Science attempts to measure time with precision, but science's concept of time is actually an abstraction based on the concept of space.

Bergson's first book on duration was *Time and Free Will: An Essay on the Immediate Data of Consciousness* (1889). As the subtitle indicates, Bergson is studying the contents of consciousness, similar to Husserl's project of phenomenology (see Chapter 21). Bergson accepted the reality of free will and said that other philosophers only saw free will as a philosophical problem because of their detached and disinterested method of analysis. Kant had to locate free will outside of time and space because he confused all time with immobile space that is subject to causality. Bergson differentiated time and space, removing time from mechanistic spatial causality and placed it within duration. Free will is also located within duration.

So what is duration? Our language isn't fully adequate to define it, but Bergson gives some analogies. Bergson visualizes duration as being like two spools. The first spool is constantly unrolling as time flows forward, and the second spool is rolling up, continually collecting memories left by the other spool. The second spool is consciousness, symbolizing how we take up duration and gather experiences in it. Each moment in consciousness is different from all previous moments because the present is added onto the memories of the past.

His next analogy is how we experience time like we experience the color orange, which also illustrates how duration is connected with intuition. If we sympathize with, enter into, orange, we would sense ourselves between red and yellow. Making the effort to perceive orange, we perceive a variety of shades of orange between red and yellow. Further effort opens us up to perceiving lighter and darker shades of each color and the whole spectrum of colors and saturation. Similarly, we can be introspective and sympathize with and enter into our own duration. When we do, we can sense ourselves among many other durations. Making an effort, we can expand our intuition to come into contact with a community of durations of different shades and saturations. We can follow durations upwardly toward spirit and downwardly toward inert matter—indeed, in a manner similar to that of Plotinus (see Chapter 4).

Reality is more like a fluid than a sequence of discrete units, so, for Bergson, duration is not a perception of images as an empiricist would understand it but the entering into a flow. We can, to use a contemporary analogy, "dial up or down" our experience of time. We do this unconsciously, as indicated in the old saying, "Time flies when you're having fun." Also, you know how time can drag when you have to wait for an unpleasant experience to finish, like listening to a dull professor lecture. Not a philosophy lecture of course, philosophy is riveting! (Just seeing if you are still paying attention.) Time is a flowing indivisible continuum. Clock time is an artificial abstraction created by humans. We can and do divide time into distinct, measurable entities: hours, minutes, seconds. These divisions are useful, but an hour does not in itself exist. Bergson says units of time become harmful to us when we mistake them for reality.

Experiencing Process

When we don't treat objects as substances and don't treat time as a sequence of discrete units, we open ourselves to see how reality truly is. When we understand that process, spontaneity, and creativity are fundamental to reality, we can understand order and stability in objects as patterns within the flux of the dynamic flow.

This reality is mobility. Not things made, but things in the making, not self-maintaining states but only changing states, exist. Rest is never more than apparent, or, rather, relative. The consciousness we have of our own self in its continual flux introduces us to the interior of a reality, on the model of which we must represent other realities. All reality, therefore, is tendency. (*An Introduction to Metaphysics*, 65)

This idea that reality is mobility and tendency, a process, is incredibly influential in continental philosophy and all of the sciences and humanities that take inspiration from it. Bergson's process philosophy finds resonance in quantum physics and chaos theory, among other branches of the hard sciences.

Through intuition and duration, we see that we aren't dealing with substances. The question, "What will the weather be tomorrow?" is not inquiring about a substance. A friendship, a vacation, a university, an ecosystem, and public opinion are all concepts we can think about and use meaningfully in sentences, but they aren't things or substances. Such concepts are expressions of collections of more primary activities and events. Rain is not a quality of a substance called weather; rain happens in the course of weather as a result of the interplay of various forces and objects. Weather is a dynamic process, ever changing as one set of events gives way to a new set of events. There are recurring patterns (it rains more in the autumn than in the summer, perhaps), but not permanent qualities.

The core of Bergson's philosophy is that we will better understand objects when we consider them as dynamic processes, like weather, rather than as substances. Objects find their identity within a set of relations and events. A friendship does not have a static character, no matter how strong it is; it has its ups and downs, its ebbs and flows. Public opinion is ever changing within shifting demographics. An ecosystem is a community of living organisms interacting and flowing as a system with no exact boundaries. You might think that a university has a static geographical location, but is a university a set of GPS coordinates? Would it cease to be if it moved location? Or if it changed its name? What universities are, and most of what we experience and think about, are entities not reducible to substances.

With reality being a dynamic process of change, we do well to make the effort to put aside the habitual method of analysis and enter into the process of reality, allowing our mind's categories to be shaped by reality. Entering into the duration, we can expand our awareness to experience that each duration that comes into existence must be related to others.

Self, Life, and Élan Vital

Bergson applied his concepts of intuition and duration to the consideration of who we are and the living world around us. We've seen that Hume dismissed the idea of a self (see Chapter 12) and that Kant accepted Hume's idea that we don't experience a self in itself but argued that we can rationally assume that there's a noumenal self underneath our experiences (see Chapter 13). Bergson believes we do have a self that can be observed and known, and we do so the same way we observe and understand other things.

We can encounter our real self by the method of intuition, which, remember, is a sympathetic entering into what is observed. Bergson criticized the then growing fields of psychology and psychiatry as seeing the human self as nothing but a sequence of separate psychological states—what Bergson called the method of analysis. This led practitioners of psychology and psychiatry to believe that each distinct psychological state was caused by the previous state and, therefore, that human behavior is determined. Belief in determinism follows from a false assumption about the human self. The self is not a sequence of separate psychological states. We experience our self as a seamless totality. Our actions flow from our whole self as free actions. Bergson is overstating his case here, because we are aware that we can be "of two minds" and that we occasionally act from compulsions, but his argument that determinism is a belief that comes from a faulty psychology is valid. Bergson's sympathetic intuition reveals that we have free will. We saw William James (see Chapter 18) make a not too dissimilar argument for free will. Late in his life, James read the younger Bergson's books and hailed Bergson as a genius.

Somewhat like the existentialist philosophers (see Chapter 21), Bergson said that people can choose to live on a superficial level, passively reacting to the world, or they can choose to live authentically. It's easy to see how Bergson's theory that there are two methods of approaching the world—analysis and intuition—apply to living life. Bergson is consistent throughout his philosophy in claiming that reality *is* a seamless continuous flow of activity and that intuition is the way to experience reality clearly. In terms of who we are, he says that we discover our freedom in our own experience. Psychology, using the method of analysis, views *other people* as objects whose behavior is determined. However, and this is Bergson's crucial observation, no one can view his or her *own* self as determined because we all experience ourselves as a creative, spontaneous agent capable of responding with free will to the external world. Sure, you can *choose* to become like an object by denying your own deep, authentic self, but that is denying the reality of who and what you are.

Interestingly, Bergson does not reserve the idea of a creative, spontaneous agent to human beings. He saw this power as existing to an extent in all life. He called it "*élan vital*," literally "vital force" in French, and saw it as the creative principle immanent in all living organisms. We can see the *élan vital* in our continuous experience of duration: our ability and desire to experience, express, and grow. "Our personality shoots, grows, and ripens without ceasing. Each of its moments is something new added to what was before" (*Creative Evolution*, 8). This vital life force is present in all of nature. Its surging, expressing, growing force will strain against inert matter to overcome or get around resistance. We can see this in how plant roots and stems will find any cracks in rocks or walls to break through and grow. In this way, life is ceaselessly changing into something new and adding to what was before.

Bergson extends this idea to the whole biosphere, seeing *élan vital* as the engine of evolution. Bergson accepted biological evolution, which had been discovered independently by Herbert Spencer (1820–1903) and Charles Darwin (1809–1882) in the mid-1800s. Bergson rejected Spencer's positivist "survival of the fittest" model of evolution. He also disagreed with Darwin's theory that evolution was driven by random variations, some working, some not, in helping an organism survive. Bergson responded that if mere survival was the force in evolution, it would have stopped at single-cell organisms. The appearance of complex "higher" organisms must have had some other force at work. That force, Bergson said, was the élan vital. It is a force that comes from life itself, not from an outside realm—Bergson also rejected Hegel's idea that *Geist* drives development (see Chapter 14). Evolution isn't driven by power, randomness, or reason but rather grows organically from the free will of life. Evolution is an unceasing gushing out of life, continually rising, falling, and rising again into new forms. In the vital activity of evolution, we see "a reality which is making itself in a reality which is unmaking itself" (*Creative Evolution*, 248).

Bergson's Legacy

Few remember Henri Bergson's name today, but the influence of his philosophy has rippled throughout society. In a number of ways, he was ahead of his time, and we can see many of his themes echoed in current continental philosophy and popular culture. Those who practice the method of analysis—many scientists and, of course, analytical philosophers—have dismissed Bergson as an irrational antiscience mystic. But Bergson was not antiscience. He cautioned against the reductionist method of doing science that reduced reality to static discrete entities. He pointed out that infinitesimal calculus, now central to physics, is based on the realization of continuity and change over the earlier static conception of the world. A number of theories in physics, increasingly being accepted now, consider the universe to be dynamic in the way Bergson described. It remains to be seen, but a revival of interest in Bergson may soon happen, just as some other past philosophers have found renewed fame and discussion long after they formed their ideas.

ALFRED NORTH WHITEHEAD'S NATURAL THEOLOGY

Yes, you saw Whitehead's (1861–1947) name earlier as the coauthor with Bertrand Russell of *Principia Mathematica*. That was in Whitehead's first life as a professor of mathematics. His second life, as a professor of philosophy, was, he said, inspired by his wife's vivid appreciation of beauty and capacity for love. From her vital force, he realized that there was more to appreciate beyond the confines of logic and science. Whitehead's dramatic transformation from mathematician to philosopher, from a professor teaching mathematics and logic to a professor sharply critical of logical and scientific reductionism, is unparalleled in academia. The themes and direction of Whitehead's philosophy are similar to those of Bergson, but there's no evidence of any interactions between the two.

The Quest to Understand the Ultimate Categories

Immanuel Kant's Copernican revolution had reset the foundation of philosophical inquiry (see Chapter 13). That the mind is active in structuring experience was now accepted by all except for some within analytical philosophy. Whitehead accepted the basic idea of Kant's Categories, but he did not like that Kant had left open the possibility that the human mind's structures might not mirror the structure of reality. Whitehead thought that the successes of science in discovering truths about the world must indicate that the structures imposed by the human mind on experience must emulate structures found in reality. Evolutionary theory backed up Whitehead's idea: Wouldn't the human species develop mental abilities in concord with how reality is? This gave Whitehead the hope that it was possible to attain an understanding of the structure of reality itself.

Whitehead's method was to start with an understanding of a particular region of experience and then take the concepts discovered in that region and use reason and "free imagination" to see if those concepts could be generalized to describe other regions of experience. Whitehead described the method by using the analogy of an airplane flight (a new technology at that time). The flight starts from the ground of experience, elevates into the air of imaginative generalization, and lands again for new observations now enhanced by rational interpretation. It's important to realize that Whitehead is not talking about flights of fancy beyond reason. His point is that good explorers of reality need to be imaginative in their thinking.

The region of experience from which Whitehead preferred to start was biology. Similar to Bergson, he saw life and its dynamic, vital processes as a key to understanding all of reality. Whitehead referred to his method as the "philosophy of organism." Being organisms, we human beings can use our own flow of dynamic experiences as a great place to begin our flight of discovery. To the positivists who dismissed metaphysics (the philosophy of the nature of reality), Whitehead countered that everyone has metaphysical beliefs; such beliefs are unavoidable. Every scientific man (sic), Whitehead said, feels he has to say he dislikes metaphysics to preserve his reputation, but that what he means is he dislikes having *his* metaphysics criticized. Indeed, the positivists, analyticals, and scientists all operate based on a system of metaphysical beliefs that guide their thinking. The fashion to deny that truth, rampant in Whitehead's time and still present today, is sheer conceit. Whitehead said that as long as metaphysics is grounded in logical principles of coherence and consistency, rather than undisciplined speculation, it was healthy and necessary.

Against the Metaphysical Assumption of Reductionist Materialism

Whitehead pointed out that it is a common metaphysical belief that reality can be reduced to a collection of fundamental units of matter independent of one another. Whitehead rejected that positivist assumption in favor of a process view of reality that looked at events as primary, all events being interrelated and interdependent. He proposed his event-based or process metaphysics as a replacement for the reductionist, materialist metaphysics of classical Newtonian physics. He identified four metaphysical assumptions in reductionist materialism: that particles of matter retain their essential identity through time, that each particle's essential identity is self-contained and independent of relations with other particles, that each particle has a definite location in time and space, and that the state of each particle in a specific time is completely determined by prior causes.

Anyone familiar with advances in physics in the last century will recognize that most in the field now agree with Whitehead's idea that these metaphysical assumptions are false. Whitehead was aware when he was writing in the 1920s that quantum physics was beginning to question these assumptions. He was still ahead of the curve and, in one way, still is. Being consistent with his idea that concepts discovered in one region of experience can be applied to other regions, Whitehead was keenly interested in applying the concepts in nonclassical physics to other areas of reality. He saw a correspondence between the reductionist tendency in physics to consider particles in isolation from each other and people's growing sense of alienation from the natural world.

Whitehead traced people's alienation back to the rise of the modern mechanistic view of the world in 1600s philosophy. That tendency, from Hobbes and Descartes on down, led to what Whitehead called "the bifurcation of nature": separating the world of experience from the world of objects. Whitehead is in agreement with the German idealists (see Chapter 14) on the need to reconnect with nature. He called the reductionist, mechanistic view strained and paradoxical. He questioned if the standardized concepts of science were too limiting and narrow for science itself. They certainly were too limiting and narrow for our lives. Process philosophy overcomes this false separation, denying neither the world of experience nor the world of objects.

> *For us the red glow of the sunset should be as much part of nature as are the molecules and electric waves by which men (sic) of science would explain the phenomenon. It is for natural philosophy to analyze how these various elements of nature are connected.* (*The Concept of Nature*, 29)

Process and Reality

Reality is always in process, always changing in an indivisible flow of time. The fundamental units of reality are not material particles but events or momentary actions. Whitehead calls events the "actual entities" of reality. Actual entities range from the single vibration of an electron to a single thought within your stream of consciousness and everything in between and beyond. The temporal extension of an event is as much a part of any entity's identity as is its spatial extension, though science had only considered spatial extension. The only actual entity that could be atemporal, or without extension in time, would be God. Everything else would be temporal occasions of experience. When we perceive an object in the world, what Whitehead's event-based philosophy tells us we are perceiving is a composite of many occasions of experience that have occurred over time. What an object is, then, is how it became what it is. For each actual entity, its being is constituted by its becoming.

Seeing reality as temporal process allows us to see how actual entities are interrelated, not separate things. Every entity in the universe has its particular character that comes from its relationship with everything else. Other philosophers discuss the importance of understanding objects within their context, but Whitehead takes the idea to the level of existence itself. Actual entities *are* all affected by each other.

Again ahead of the curve, Whitehead wrote in 1925 that, in a sense, every entity is everywhere at all times and every location involves an aspect of itself in every other location. Therefore, every spatiotemporal standpoint mirrors the world, and reality is a web of interconnected events. Whitehead's conception was met with astonishment at the time, yet at the same time, theoretical physics was beginning to confirm his conception, and it is now widely accepted within physics that it is at least a possibility (for example, the theories of quantum entanglement and the wave function).

Whitehead's interest wasn't in physics per se but in a mix of biology and philosophy. For him, the interconnectedness of actual entities manifested in subjective feeling. This is where Whitehead's philosophy loses some people because he states that every entity in reality has subjective experience and can be said to have some level of awareness and feeling. Not only humans but also all organisms, even single-celled organisms, have feelings. One way to understand what Whitehead is saying is to avoid overly anthropomorphizing it as conscious self-awareness but instead see it as every organism responding to its environment and seeking out conditions more conducive to its health and survival. This fits with Whitehead's statements that electrons are not passive entities but are active entities that react to their environment. Here, too, multiple theories in physics describe electrons and other subatomic particles in ways that Whitehead would find familiar.

Ultimately, for Whitehead, the web of interconnected events and the actual entities in it are all characterized by creativity. Similar to Bergson, Whitehead saw everything as lively and continually evolving. Entities come into existence, their becoming a process of self-creation reacting to their immediate past in synthesis with their environment. The universe is dynamic, constantly creating and changing. Entities are aware and interconnected. Nothing can be considered in isolation because particular entities form societies of larger entities. This last idea by Whitehead is the same as the current scientific idea of ecosystems: communities of organisms interacting as a system.

TWO DIFFERENT QUESTS FOR UNDERSTANDING?

The analytical/continental divide in philosophy is often the split between two different approaches. One could look at the difference as the analytical approach studies the parts and the continental approach studies the whole. Both approaches are valid if they then use the one to move to the other: using the whole to explain the parts or the parts to explain the whole. Philosophers on both sides aren't always successful at this move. Interestingly, both sides claim science is on their side, but continental philosophy is based more on social and life sciences and analytical more on physics, logic, and mathematics. Philosophy of language, on the analytical side, has given us some important insights into social behavior, but it also tends to reduce social issues to problems of language and reduce language to logic. Despite all protests to the contrary, we cannot prove that mathematics and logic exist outside the mind (hello, William). So how do we think of logic when we try to apply it to the world? Continental philosophy doesn't deny the value of logic but instead looks at the world as a system more akin to an organism than a set of mathematical equations. The continentals tend to base their work on Hegel and Marx and tend to reduce social issues to problems of socioeconomic systems like Marx did. But, of course, you can take what I write in this paragraph to four different philosophers and get seven different opinions on how wrong what I just wrote is. Such is the nature of our profession.

REFERENCES

Henri Bergson, *Creative Evolution*, tr. Arthur Mitchell, New York, Henry Holt and Company, not in copyright. Internet Archive. https://archive.org/details/creativeevoluti01mitcgoog. (accessed April 24, 2021)

Henri Bergson, *An Introduction to Metaphysics*, tr. T.E. Hulme, G. P. Putnam's Sons, 1912, not in copyright. Internet Archive. https://archive.org/details/anintroductiont02berggoog. (accessed April 23, 2021)

Alfred North Whitehead, *The Concept of Nature,* Project Gutenberg. https://www.gutenberg.org/files/18835/18835-h/18835-h.htm. (accessed April 25, 2021)

Proof 54-43 in Principia Mathematica, Volume I, 1st edition, p. 379. Public domain source: http://quod.lib.umich.edu/cgi/t/text/pageviewer-idx?c=umhistmath&cc=umhistmath&idno=aat3201.0001.001&. (accessed April 22, 2021)

CHAPTER 20

LUDWIG WITTGENSTEIN

Straddling both sides of the analytical/continental divide is the Austrian-born Ludwig Wittgenstein (1889–1951) who did most of his philosophical work in England. He was a student of Bertrand Russell (see Chapter 19), trying to understand the foundations of logic, and his early work galvanized analytical philosophy and remains an influence. He then stepped away from philosophy for a decade; when he returned, he rejected his own early work and adopted a kind of pragmatism, centered on a new view of how we use language, the meaning of which philosophers still debate. How best to consider Wittgenstein's philosophy career is a matter of debate, but I'll opt for the view that we can see Wittgenstein as having three stages: the early period of the *Tractatus*, a middle period in the 1930s, and a later period during and after World War II.

THE EARLY WITTGENSTEIN: THE TRACTATUS

Ludwig Wittgenstein was originally an engineering student when he learned about Russell's work on the foundations of mathematics. Ever the strong-willed and impetuous person, Wittgenstein traveled to the University of Cambridge where Russell taught and requested to be his student. Russell quickly saw Wittgenstein's potential and took him on, mentoring him in philosophy and his theories on mathematics.

Wittgenstein was inspired by Russell and Gottlob Frege to write a book that combined Russell's logical atomism with the philosophy of logic. He wrote much of the book, *Tractatus Logico-Philosophicus* (1921), while serving in the Austrian army in World War I. It is a bizarre book, and Wittgenstein knew it. In the preface to the book, Wittgenstein wrote the odd comments that its value consists of two things: that thoughts are expressed in it and that it shows how little is achieved when these problems are solved. The problems he refers to are the problems of philosophy defined by the work of Frege and Russell. The second comment is the first hint that Wittgenstein thought the *Tractatus* was a failure.

The short book consists of numbered propositions in seven sets. That format is similar to Russell's *Principia Mathematica*, which was a list of numbered mathematical proofs. In the *Tractatus*, there are seven main propositions, with sets of numerous sub- and sub-sub-propositions. Proposition 1.2 belongs to the first set and is a comment on proposition 1. Proposition 1.21 is about proposition 1.2, and so on. I'll start with some important and representative propositions from the first part of the book, and this is leaving out many propositions:

1 *The world is everything that is the case.*
1.1 *The world is the totality of facts, not of things.*
2 *What is the case, the fact, is the existence of atomic facts.*
2.1 *We make to ourselves pictures of facts.*
3 *The logical picture of the facts is the thought.*
3.4 *The proposition determines a place in logical space.*
4.001 *The totality of propositions is the language.*
4.01 *The proposition is a picture of reality. The proposition is a model of the reality as we think it is.*
4.0311 *One name stands for one thing, and another for another thing, and they are connected together. And so the whole, like a living picture, presents the atomic fact.*
4.04 *In the proposition there must be exactly as many things distinguishable as there are in the state of affairs, which it represents.*
4.121 *...Propositions show the logical form of reality. They exhibit it.*
4.2 *The sense of a proposition is its agreement and disagreement with the possibilities of the existence and non-existence of the atomic facts.* (*Tractatus*)

I'll pause there for now. Make sense? No? Well, philosophers still argue about what it all means, and I just gave you some of the easier bits. Let's look at what Wittgenstein was trying to accomplish in the early part of *Tractatus*. In its first part, the book is a description of logical atomism and the basic elements of a logically perfect language. That was Wittgenstein's goal. He was essentially laying out the idea that the world is a logical world (the totality of facts) and that what we do is represent the facts in the world with our own logical pictures, with each picture, each word, corresponding to a fact. That is what Wittgenstein is claiming that thinking is. When we learn the proper methods of constructing and using logical propositions, we cannot fail. There can never be surprises in logic, he said (*Tractatus*, 6.1251). Except...well, we'll get to that in a second.

Philosophers are guilty of taking from the *Tractatus* what they like and leaving the rest. The logical positivists loved the complex rules for constructing logical propositions that Wittgenstein gave in the middle of the book and just ignored the statements Wittgenstein made about the limits of logic in the last part of the book. Here are some of those important and representative propositions from that part of the book, again leaving out many of the more complicated propositions:

5.43 *...all propositions of logic say the same thing. That is, nothing.*
5.6 *The limits of my language mean the limits of my world.*
5.621 *The world and life are one.*
5.63 *I am my world.*
5.641 *There is therefore really a sense in which in philosophy we can talk of a non-psychological I. The I occurs in philosophy through the fact that the "world is my world." The philosophical I is not the [hu]man, not the human body or the human soul of which psychology treats, but the metaphysical subject, the limit—not a part of the world.*
6.1 *The propositions of logic are tautologies.*
6.11 *The propositions of logic therefore say nothing. (They are the analytical propositions.)*
6.41 *The sense of the world must lie outside the world.*
6.42 *Hence also there can be no ethical propositions. Propositions cannot express anything higher.*
6.432 *How the world is, is completely indifferent for what is higher. God does not reveal himself in the world*
6.522 *There is indeed the inexpressible. This shows itself; it is the mystical.*
6.54 *My propositions are elucidatory in this way: he (sic) who understands me finally recognizes them as senseless, when he has climbed out through them, on them, over them. (He must so to speak throw away the ladder,*

after he has climbed up on it.) He must surmount these propositions; then he sees the world rightly.

7 *Whereof one cannot speak, thereof one must be silent.* (*Tractatus*)

The logical positivists, and many analytical philosophers to this day, avoid these passages. Wittgenstein is admitting the very things they are most against accepting: Logic tells us nothing about the world, perception is subjective, there is a real nonpsychological "I," and there is a mystical realm beyond logic and philosophy that cannot be reduced to words. Not that Wittgenstein gave us any help in understanding what he was getting at with these concepts or what to do with them. Are we to accept what he says, climb this "ladder" over them (to what? the mystical?), and then be silent?

And Wittgenstein seemed to adopt silence after finishing his book in 1919 (though it was only published 2 years later). He went back to Austria, apparently walking away from philosophy.

THE MIDDLE WITTGENSTEIN: THE BLUE AND BROWN BOOK LECTURES

About 8 years later, Wittgenstein came to one of the meetings of the Vienna Circle (see Chapter 19), invited to talk with them about the *Tractatus*. They greeted him like a hero because in their mind, Wittgenstein's book (except for that last icky bit) could form the basis of a logical language. Rudolf Carnap, a member of the Vienna Circle, later wrote that it soon became apparent that they weren't thinking the same as Wittgenstein anymore, if they ever had. Wittgenstein told them he no longer agreed with much of the *Tractatus*. His later work showed that he agreed only with the statements toward the end of that book, the last few that I listed. His later thought focused on the meaning of language and the word outside of logical atomism and pure propositional logic.

Wittgenstein was persuaded by contacts at the University of Cambridge to return. He was now famous, and not only in philosophy circles, because of the *Tractatus*. He returned in 1929. Cambridge University wanted to hire him as a professor, but he did not have a PhD. At Russell's urging, Wittgenstein submitted the *Tractatus* for his PhD in philosophy at Cambridge. Bertrand Russell was one of the examiners. Russell loved parts of the book but confessed he didn't understand all of it. The story is told that in the middle of the viva (where a candidate defends his or her thesis to be confirmed for the PhD), in response to Russell again expressing confusion over a passage in the book, Wittgenstein stood up, said "It's okay, you'll never understand it," and walked out. He was awarded a PhD and offered a teaching position.

For the next 12 years, Wittgenstein was a lecturer at Cambridge. He published nothing, but his lectures began to show a bold new style of philosophy. His students reported that his lectures were highly unconventional. He did not have a set topic but instead talked about whatever was on his mind, with long pauses as he thought deeply about a philosophical problem. What was usually on his mind were the philosophical problems of language. He had come to realize that he had not solved all the philosophical problems of language in the *Tractatus*. In two academic years, several of his students took lecture notes and made copies of them with a mimeograph machine, bound them in cloth, and shared them with other students and faculty. The lecture notes are known by the color of their cloth covers: the 1933–1934 lectures were in the blue book and the 1934–1935 lectures were in the brown book.

What was in these books were the roots of a new philosophy. Wittgenstein had abandoned logical atomism and had developed a different view of language's relation with the world. He now realized that we didn't learn language through strict rules, and we don't use language according to strict rules. Yes, most of us were taught the rules of grammar, but how we use language are ways that we learned through a plethora of life experiences. We learn how to use language by using language. We learn by doing, applying ways of doing things with language to our activities.

Wittgenstein's insightful analogy is to call what we do with language a "language-game" (*Sprachspiel* in German). In any game—from checkers to baseball—we learn the basic rules, but it is only through practice that we *really* learn how to play. We learn by doing. Language is the same. There are rules, but the rules are not all-encompassing, and we can know the rules but still not know how to speak the language. It is by playing the language-game that we learn the language. That's because words do not have the logical one-to-one correspondence with objects that Wittgenstein had learned from Russell and had written in the *Tractatus*. Words are inexact. An example he gives of how this works is learning the word "pencil." One could try to teach the word by pointing at a pencil and saying "pencil." But the listener could associate the word with a number of things: the pencil as a whole, the wood it is made of, the shape of it, and so on. Only through context and use of the object do we come to understand the words for it. Then, when we use language, we are playing a language-game. In this middle period, he was still working out the implications of this new theory of language.

THE LATER WITTGENSTEIN: THE PHILOSOPHICAL INVESTIGATIONS

Wittgenstein continued to develop his new philosophy through the 1930s. He largely stopped during World War II, volunteering instead for the British war effort for several years. By 1946, he had written a new book, part one of what would be a two-part book. It was accepted for publication, but Wittgenstein, being a perfectionist, withdrew it before publication, worried that it wasn't finished. Only after his death did several of his former students gather his first part and, along with some of his other notes that would have been components of the second part, publish the book as *Philosophical Investigations* in 1953.

Philosophical Investigations expands on the themes of his lectures in the 1930s. It's less bizarre than the *Tractatus* but similarly is a collection of thoughts rather than a systematic narrative. What becomes obvious from the contents is that Wittgenstein is doing philosophy as an activity of open imagination and thinking. Often, he is telling stories of real-life situations that demonstrate how language works. His style is like using Whitehead's method of imagination taking flight to go from one region of certainty to a new one.

Wittgenstein's stories demonstrate his new theory of language and what it means for philosophy. He begins by, at length, indirectly criticizing his theory of language in the *Tractatus*. Words do not get their meaning from a logical one-to-one correspondence with objects but from their use. That shift in definition leads to a further shift from the *Tractatus*. Instead of seeing philosophical problems as problems of logic, he now sees them as the lack of a clear view of the use of our words. To get a clear view of the meaning of words, we need to examine their use in the language. Three of Wittgenstein's important concepts are revealed when we start to examine words in this way: that word meanings rely on family resemblances, that words make sense only in the context of language-games, and that language-games make sense only in the context of forms of life—particular sets of interlaced practices and understandings of our culture.

To discuss the first two concepts, he uses the example of the word "game." What is a game? How would we define it? We can't, as he says, just point to various games and define the word by examples. A short clarification: Wittgenstein wrote in German, and the German word he uses for "game" is "*Spiel.*" The German word has a broader sense than the English word "game." *Spiel* extends in its use to the act of "play" and "playing," so this German sense of the word is more suggestive of an action or activity, which helps us understand Wittgenstein's meaning in his discussion of games.

Wittgenstein discusses several possible meanings for "game"—competition, enjoyment, having a set of rules, and so on—but shows how each is inadequate to describe games. What we see when we think about the meaning of the word "game" is that all of the many objects and activities that we call "games" share family resemblance. When you look at a biological family, they don't all look exactly the same, but they share enough common features of appearance that you recognize them as members of the same family. They may all have "the same nose," but they don't need to all share one particular feature to resemble each other. They have enough similar features that we see the family resemblance. The same is true for the word "game," Wittgenstein says. Solitaire, checkers, water polo, slot machines, and mind games all share enough similar features that we can see the family resemblance that they are all games. What he takes from this exercise is that an exact definition is neither possible nor required for the word to have meaning. If someone says, "Let's play a game," we understand what is meant despite the lack of specificity.

Words get their meaning from their use, and Wittgenstein talks about their use in terms of language-games. Similar to the pragmatists, Wittgenstein said that we use words as tools to do things in the world. Language is part of our activities in the world, and our uses of language are as varied as our activities are. Wittgenstein describes the many activities in which we use words as various language-games. He mentions giving orders, describing an object's appearance, speculating about what may happen, making a joke, translating from one language to another, requesting something, thanking someone, cursing, praying. Each activity is a language-game. Within each type of activity, the various ways of expressing ideas and actions have internal family resemblances that show they are related and can be called "language-games," despite how much they vary.

Our many ways of speaking do not all conform to a single model, but their commonalities include that they are all activities, all have purposes and goals, and they all are used by people who have a shared understanding about the rules of the language-game. This last resemblance is crucial. Words and sentences do not have meanings in themselves; they have the meanings that we give them, and those meanings are how we use the words. If I say "table," I have not communicated anything to you unless we are both playing the same language-game. If you are asking me where to set something, you'd know I mean to put it on the table. If I'm teaching you English, you know to point to the table. If I am quizzing you on German, you could respond with "Tisch." As Wittgenstein says, we don't simply speak; we do things by speaking.

Language-games, then, are human activities in which words help us accomplish our goals. Words are tools, and just like we would use a hammer to pound nails, but not to cut a board in two—we'd use a saw for that—we use different words for different purposes in different situations. Plus, we often will use the same word in multiple different situations or different language-games. Take the word "lose." We can lose our keys, lose sleep, lose a game, lose our train of thought, lose confidence in someone. If we are playing the language-game of talking about going for a drive, if you say you lost your keys, I can help you find them. But "can I help you find it" is without sense if we are talking about how you are very worried about something and losing sleep over it.

Wittgenstein illustrates his concept by imagining a language-game of two people building a stone wall. Because language helps us accomplish our goals, the workers could accomplish their task with a language of very few words. Builder A could communicate to his helper B by calling out "brick," "cube," and "slab" to request a stone of a certain size to build the wall. Builder B would understand and respond to the request. Within the context of that language-game, "brick" is all A needs to say to ask B to bring a brick. But outside that particular language-game, if A says "brick," no one would know for sure what A means. All words have meaning within a particular context of actions.

The point to all of this, according to Wittgenstein, is that the demand of the logical positivists that we have one set of logical language rules to which all language must conform is wrong. There are as many sets of rules as there are language-games; though again, the sets of rules have family resemblances. Wittgenstein now realized that the mistake he made in the *Tractatus* was to try to force language to conform to the crystalline purity of logic. But language isn't calculus. Language is living.

Wittgenstein now saw that philosophical problems arise when "language goes on holiday." That's a Britishism there—"holiday" in the British language-game is like the American "vacation." So, in this language-game, when the proper use of language has gone away and is no longer "on the job," philosophical problems arise. The logical positivists were mixing language-games by trying to force the rules of logic onto other language-games. Speculative philosophy, such as Leibniz's (see Chapter 13), can make the same mistake by trying to impose the language-game of talking about worldly things onto higher, deeper ideas. This is one area where Wittgenstein still agreed with his *Tractatus*—there is indeed the inexpressible, the mystical that is beyond words. The role of philosophy is not to try to impose structure on language or life but to learn from them. He states that when philosophers use a word like "knowledge," and try to grasp the essence of it, they need to ask how the word is used in the language-game that is its original home. The philosopher needs to bring the word back to its everyday use. Wittgenstein uses "everyday" similar to the way Heidegger does (see Chapter 21): how we act in normal life without introspection. Wittgenstein seems to suggest that philosophy needs to stop trying to find perfect forms and perfect knowledge and step aside to let everyday normal life show us what is the case. He says at various points in the *Philosophical Investigations* what he sees as the proper role of philosophy. Philosophy simply puts things before us open to view and need not explain things. Philosophy should not question or interfere with how language is used but can only describe it.

As said previously, people use language within language-games, and language-games are played within an activity. Wittgenstein further describes our activities as occurring within a "form of life." Our actions, and thus our language, are interlaced with our practices, interests, goals, and understandings, which are shaped by our culture and our place within it. On a social level, the interlaced practices and understandings of a culture are its form of life. The point is that it is the cultural forms of life that provide people with the meanings of words, and it is this social backdrop of meanings that renders language intelligible. This is a similar idea to Peirce's interpretant—that which gives signs their meaning (see Chapter 18). Human culture is organic—it grew and continues to evolve on its own; it did not and does not ask philosophers to justify what it does. For that reason, forms of life are the justification for definitions of words and the rules of language. No further justification is needed, and there is no further logic to it. Language simply works. It enables us to communicate and do things. It lives and grows with us.

REFERENCE

Ludwig Wittgenstein, *Tractatus Logico-Philosophicus*, https://www.gutenberg.org/ebooks/5740. (accessed April 26, 2021)

CHAPTER 21

PHENOMENOLOGY AND EXISTENTIALISM

Phenomenology is exactly what it sounds like: the study of phenomena. We've seen philosophers discussing mental phenomena before. What the philosophical movement of phenomenology does differently is establish a method of analyzing mental phenomena and making those observations the foundation of philosophy. It's a process similar to what Descartes was doing, and both supporters and critics of phenomenology have compared it with Descartes' *Meditations*. There are multiple flavors of phenomenology, as we shall see, depending on what a phenomenologist is seeking. What they all have in common is the phenomenological method. Instead of trying to understand the essence of an object like the medieval philosophers did or look only at the facts about an object like the philosophers who are of a scientific bent did, we observe what is present in consciousness during experience.

Existentialism is, almost exactly as it sounds, about the issue of our existence. The name comes from the French writer, Jean-Paul Sartre (1905–1980), to describe his idiosyncratic take on philosophy. "Existence precedes essence," he declared as the fundamental issue facing not only philosophy but also every person. Because there are similarities between Sartre's approach and those of Kierkegaard and Nietzsche, those two earlier philosophers (see Chapter 17) have also been called "existentialists," though they would not have recognized the term.

There are also some similarities between phenomenology and existentialism. You will see why as we go through this chapter.

EDMUND HUSSERL

Few philosophers can be said to have founded a new branch of philosophy. The Moravian philosopher Edmund Husserl (1859–1938) is one. His training was in mathematics, and his early writings were on the philosophy of mathematics. Franz Brentano's (1838–1917) teachings changed Husserl's thinking.

Brentano said that we should look more carefully at our mental processes. Philosophy and psychology were presuming too much about how consciousness operates and were, therefore, not learning what actually transpires in human consciousness. Brentano proposed that we try to eliminate all assumptions about causes and consequences of consciousness, to bracket them out. By "bracketing out," he means placing the content of our inquiry in the center and temporarily ignoring everything outside of it (like this).

Bracketing Perception

Bracketing at first sounds simple enough, but how best to do it so that it yields us useful information took up the rest of Husserl's life. In a long and prolific career of writings and lectures (1894–1936), Husserl developed and redeveloped his methodology of phenomenology. Husserl was blazing a new trail, and he acted as the pragmatists said we should, building knowledge step-by-step by testing hypotheses and altering our beliefs on the basis of the evidence. Husserl was a perfectionist to a fault, constantly tinkering with his methodology and trying to identify the best method and understanding of consciousness. Trying to condense Husserl's highly complex and technical phenomenology into something easily digestible and understandable is difficult, but I'll try to give you the most important elements.

Husserl's initial priority was to understand how to bracket our perceptions off from preconceptions so that we can directly observe the workings of our consciousness. In simplest terms, bracketing is our "suspension of judgment," for which Husserl adopted the Greek word for that idea: "*epoché*." It's an idea similar to Descartes' rule of avoiding precipitancy (see Chapter 7), and Husserl, following Brentano idea of bracketing, called for the *epoché* to be the first act of our analysis. We suspend all of our judgments. We do not assume that what we are experiencing is caused by external objects, much less an accurate representation of them. We do not assume that any external objects exist. Here, too, this is similar to what Descartes was doing, and both Descartes and Husserl were seeking certainty of knowledge. The difference between their approaches is that Descartes' method focused on the world of objects, whereas Husserl's method focused on what mental phenomena reveal about the structures of consciousness.

The first purpose of the *epoché* was to free us from what Husserl called the "natural standpoint." This is the assumption that we all make that there is a world that exists independently of us and that our consciousness is caused by objects in that world. Husserl is not suggesting that the natural standpoint is an illusion or foolish to hold. It is a natural assumption that we accept without question, and it serves us well when we are immersed in everyday concerns. The problem with the natural standpoint is that when we stand in it, we cannot see our own experience. Bracketing it off is necessary to get to pure experience.

Immersion in Experience

The object of Husserl's study is the pure experiences in the phenomenal world of consciousness. Kant had identified the noumena, that which is outside of our experience and thus unknowable by us. The German idealists had rejected the idea of the noumena, but Husserl cautioned that philosophy had gone astray in debating the noumenal world and was neglecting the important study of consciousness. Many philosophers had tried to understand consciousness—for example, Locke (see Chapter 8) and Hume (see Chapter 12). Husserl's study was both more intensive and without as many presuppositions.

Husserl wanted to focus on the first-person experience. What is it that **I** experience? What is experience, and what does it mean to have experience? Husserl is using "experience" in its broadest sense of anything that is mental awareness or consciousness. Applying the *epoché*, he, and we, can focus on the contents of consciousness and identify what is intrinsic to all of our mental processes. We can then understand what features of consciousness transcend any particular phenomenon and are present in all experience. We accept only what is directly evident in consciousness, and what is left is the essence of the experience. The essence is in the experience itself, not in the external object.

Applying the *epoché*, Husserl identifies that what immediately comes to our awareness is our consciousness itself. In the natural standpoint, we are unaware of our own consciousness and how our consciousness contributes to our experiences. When we bracket off the world, we can discover our consciousness at work. Husserl does not see consciousness as a thing; it does not have qualities like an object or a substance. On the one hand, Descartes was mistaken in thinking of the "I" as a substance. On the other hand, Hume was mistaken in thinking there is nothing to consciousness but a collection of different perceptions. We can see in our consciousness a structure that is independent of the contents of consciousness.

A key feature of the structure of consciousness is what Husserl calls "intentionality." All consciousness, every thought and feeling that we have, is aimed at something—it has an intention. If you are consciously perceiving or thinking of a tree, the perception of the tree is the "noema" of your consciousness—"noema" being the word Husserl developed (from the Greek "*noesis*," meaning "thought") to describe that object of our conscious intention. Husserl said that consciousness is a relation of knower and known. The intention of our consciousness, what our thought is directed at, need not actually exist. When we are imagining something, we are still intending our consciousness toward a mental object. Even a hallucination is an act with a conscious intention—our consciousness is directed at the hallucination. The basic structure of consciousness is the intentional act of experience and the object that is experienced.

Having established that most basic structure of experience, Husserl then applies a process of phenomenological reduction to uncover the essential features of the phenomena of the objects we experience. One important feature is our "time-consciousness." If we are looking at the tree, the noema is the visual phenomenon of the tree. When we close our eyes, the noema is the memory of the tree. These are two different perceptions, but we understand that they are both of the same tree separated by duration in time. That separation is in our consciousness, not in the object. That last point is important because consciousness is continually processing the contents of consciousness. Hegel (see Chapter 14) had delineated the differences between sense certainty and perception, the latter being the mind's active interpretation of sense experience. Husserl similarly saw sense impressions as nonintentional, the raw materials presented to consciousness on which consciousness acts. What we are capable of doing, Husserl says, is taking the noemata (plural of "noema") in our consciousness of the object and using our imaginative capabilities to consider the object behind the noemata. We can consider the various phenomena we sense, separated by time. We can hold in our thoughts our past experiences and can imaginatively experiment with the noemata: "What if the object was this other color, what would it look like upside down," and so on. Through comparisons and imagination, we develop an objective understanding of the object. Crucially, Husserl points out, this objectivity belongs to the experience, not to the external object. The object is unaffected by our contemplation of it.

Layers of Consciousness

It's not wholly wrong to say we experience objects in the world, but it is far more correct to say that we experience objects in consciousness. Objects exist for us, Husserl said, as objects of actual and possible consciousness. There's a hint of Berkeley (see Chapter 11) in this, and another sign that Berkeley wasn't so daft. A rock on a planet light-years away from you is not an object that you can actually or even possibly perceive. Weirdly, however, it kind of is because now you are thinking about such a possible object. That proves Husserl's point. Nothing is meaningful for us unless our consciousness makes it so by our consciousness intending toward the object.

This connection between meaning and consciousness creates a problem. If objective understanding is within our consciousness and it is our intentional consciousness that makes things meaningful, then how can we have certain knowledge of objects independent of our mind? Are we left with nothing but completely subjective judgments about objects? Husserl's intriguing and insightful answer is to embrace the subjectivity and include that in our consideration of the world.

There are two levels of this subjectivity, both of which affect our consciousness. The first level is within you, the individual. The *epoché* shows that the phenomena are constituted by our consciousness, as Kant and the German idealists (see Chapters 13 and 14) all agreed. What Husserl adds to this is that our past experiences contribute to how our consciousness constitutes phenomena. Every act of consciousness, both sense experiences and thinking, affects our consciousness, and that affects our future experiences. Husserl calls it the "sedimentation of meanings" that builds up, layer by layer, within our consciousness. Our experiences, our reactions to those experiences, our thoughts and feelings about those experiences and reactions, all create sediments in our consciousness. They literally change how we perceive and think about things. Consider experiencing a person. You meet the individual, you develop a first impression, and that first impression, as we all know, affects how you experience that individual. As you interact more with that person, you learn more about the individual and you develop a fuller conception of who that person is. Let's say that over time you become friends with this person, and of course that friendship affects your perception of the person; the more time you share with this person, the more those experiences and feelings about the person shape your perception of your friend. But now suppose this friend betrays you in a serious way that hurts you badly. Can you ever look at this person the same way again? That's sedimentation. Using your time-consciousness, you can look back through your memories and think about past good times and warm feelings you had, but now things are different.

The second level of consciousness is beyond you as an individual but is particular to your individual life. Husserl introduces an idea that becomes very important in continental philosophy: the "*Lebenswelt*" in German or "lifeworld." The lifeworld is the world in which we live; it is the world that we experience. Just as we don't experience objects apart from our own sedimentations in consciousness, we can't experience objects apart from the context of a world. For example, you don't experience a computer; you experience it as being on a desk, in a room, in a building, in a society. We never experience anything isolated from its surroundings. Moreover, we never experience anything apart from the collection of meanings that social life places on them. You experience objects in a social context that imbues those objects with meaning, and those meanings affect your experiences of objects. The lifeworld is another set of layers of consciousness.

Taking these layers of consciousness into account, Husserl calls scientists "self-forgetful theorizers." The central assumption in science is that it can reveal the true reality to us. This was the optimistic hope since science's beginning in the late 1500s (see Bacon in Chapter 8), and it continued up to Husserl's time. The truth, Husserl stresses, is that we do not experience pure objects; we experience objects through the filters of our own sedimented consciousness and the lifeworld in which we live. Scientists are not exempt from that truth. Science gives us an idealized and naively objectivized nature, Husserl said. Scientists forget that they are doing science as people within a lifeworld. Science is a social activity within a social context that instills activities with social meanings. Scientists also forget that they are individual people who experience everything, including their experiments, through their personal sedimented consciousness.

Husserl is not saying science is too biased to be of use, but he is saying that we need to be aware of the layers of meaning and consciousness within which and through which science is conducted. Science is an attitude that sees the world through its particular understanding of it. Because our knowledge structures how we perceive the world, the scientific approach structures perceptions to see the world in a certain way. Forgetting the effects of our biases makes us blind to them.

Husserl's critique that people are self-forgetful is not limited to scientists. We all suffer that implicit bias of seeing the world through our own sedimented consciousness and limited lifeworld. Husserl in 1930 bemoaned the lack of dialogue among philosophers. He thought that philosophers with differing views needed to discuss their conflicting theories seriously to find a basis for common ground and together grow their knowledge. This is similar to what the pragmatists were suggesting (see Chapter 18). Instead, Husserl said, philosophers remain in their own subjective views and narrow fields of study and don't consider other views.

This criticism can apply not only to philosophy but also to all academic fields and subfields. Academics are only human, of course, and the criticism that people remain within their subjective biases and don't listen to others applies universally. The antidote to this is found in the philosophy of Husserl and other phenomenologists and existentialists. We need to acknowledge that every one of us experiences the objectively real world as individuals and that that understanding is a process that includes listening to each other.

MAX SCHELER

German philosopher Max Scheler (1874–1928) is tragically still virtually unknown in English-speaking countries, but his influence on philosophers in Europe is immense. Scheler studied Husserl's published writings and developed his own version of phenomenology. Scheler stated that phenomenology is not a methodology for studying static objects but an engagement with phenomena, an attitude of seeing what otherwise remains hidden. Husserl could legitimately answer that his method did not assume static objects and was focused on mental phenomena, but his method was one based on logic. Scheler emphasized phenomenology's focus on original experiences, which we have before we apply logic and other interpretive criteria to them. Our sense experiences of objects are given to us only in the experiencing act itself. By extension, the phenomenologist needs to engage with the phenomenological facts of experience without first applying a logical or scientific method.

What motivated Scheler was to steer philosophy away from the reductionism of positivism and toward the question of the meaning of human life. He saw people as more than rational beings or practical tool makers (as he saw pragmatism depicting humanity). We are those things, he said, but we are also beings who can seek and understand the world in its essences and being. In other words, we are capable of more than dealing with practical concerns; we are also capable of wondering about the deeper meaning of life. Scheler called philosophy a loving act of participation in the essence of all things. This appearance of the concept of love in philosophy may seem surprising, and it is something we haven't seen since Augustine (see Chapter 4). But Scheler brought back to philosophy something significant and influential: a sense of wonder about the world and a willingness to engage with it and have feelings about it rather than hold the world at arm's length.

Partially influenced by Husserl, Scheler recognized the importance of the philosopher's attitude. He did not discount the importance of emotions as most philosophers have. Love, for Scheler is not sentiment or yearning but an attitude of wonder and openness. Love, Scheler said, is a movement of opening oneself up to the world of values—that which we find valuable. In contrast, hatred is closing oneself off from the world of values. Love involves acts that extend into the world, and hatred involves acts that narrow one's reach into the world. Phenomenology is an attitude of openness. It does not negate the practical or scientific attitude, but it suspends judgment on them. Scheler saw phenomenology as a trusting attitude toward the world instead of the skeptical attitude of the modern era.

Scheler also applied the attitude of love to moral and political philosophy. He adopted Kant's idea that morality must be based on duty without regard to consequences (see Chapter 16). But he rejected Kant's insistence that the Categorical Imperative must be universal and instead said that our duty is the specific duty that one has to another person. Scheler corrects the cold rationality of Kant's Categorical Imperative by realizing that all of our perceptions are also experiences of values. A tree has green leaves and is tall, but it is also beautiful and gives cooling shade, and often these values of beauty and pleasure are what are important to us. All objects of experience carry values. Their values do not exist in the object but in the act of perception. Scheler said that when we perceive a painting, we "see" its beauty like we "see" its shapes and colors. Our awareness of value is our most primordial relation to the world. Objects have value for us before we perceive or know them.

Following Franz Brentano, Scheler conceived of our relations to things as having positive and negative values. Values are objectively real, Scheler said, though we experience and act on them subjectively. Positive values are those that we find desirable and as those that we feel ought to be. Conversely, negative values are those that we find undesirable and those that we feel ought not to be. Differing from Kant, and most philosophers going back to Aristotle, Scheler said that what ought to be is not derived through logic. We intuitively feel what ought to be and what ought not to be, and we intuitively feel that some values are higher than others. The specific type of being who can experience values is a person, Scheler said, and other people are values in and of themselves. This is similar to Kant's Imperative that other people should be treated as ends in themselves. The person is a moral actor, present in every act; however, the person is not reducible to any particular act but is the unity of all acts the person performs. That means every person is unique because each person is a unique center of acts, and every person has his or her own unique style of acting, loving, and assigning meaning. Therefore, the person cannot be objectified—or subsumed under stereotypes or categories. A person's meaning is determined by the unique way in which that person brings meaning to the world.

Because every person is a unique center of acts with unique meaning, Scheler said we ought to value every person. This idea forms the foundation of Scheler's political philosophy, or truer to his wording, a philosophy of community. Community is about shared values and love. We understand each other through valuing others, and through valuing others we form community. In turn, the sharing of values and responsibilities within a community is the context (or "lifeworld" to use Husserl's term) in which people form and realize themselves. Permeating all of Scheler's lengthy and detailed discussion about building a community of love and solidarity is the "attitude of valuing." An attitude of valuing someone or something is an act of giving or creating meaning and is, therefore, an intentional act, not of intellect but of love. Sharing, empathy, and respect are some of the ways that we value other people. We will see a very similar idea, recognition, in Chapter 24.

EDITH STEIN

Husserl, as a philosophy professor at the University of Freiberg, had two particularly notable students. One was Edith Stein (1891–1942). Born into a practicing Jewish family, she converted to Catholicism and eventually became a nun. Her conversion was after, but not incompatible with, her philosophical career, in which she studied the philosophy of emotions, especially empathy. She also studied under Max Scheler, and her PhD thesis advisor was Edmund Husserl, for whom she later worked as his teaching assistant. Despite fulfilling all of the qualifications, Stein was refused habilitation (a postdoctoral certification required to be a professor in the German system) by the University of Göttingen because she was a woman. After reading the autobiography of Theresa of Avila, Stein converted to Catholicism in 1921 and became a Carmelite nun. Her order encouraged her to teach instead of joining a convent, which she did at several Catholic institutions until 1933, when the Nazis banned people of Jewish heritage from teaching positions.

Stein applied Husserl's phenomenological method to understand consciousness and human empathy. Her application of the *epoché* led her to discover "life-feelings" (German: *Lebensgefühle*), which are experiential states in a person's consciousness. Life-feelings affect what a person perceives, thinks, feels, and wills and determine how the person experiences conscious states and bodily awareness. Stein's examples of life-feelings include weariness, freshness, vigor, and irritability, which affect one's feeling toward the world and influence the whole course of one's experiences. In her example of weariness, she points out what we have all experienced, that when we feel weary, it affects all of our sensations, deadening colors, sounds, and so on. She said that life-feelings are experiential causality, and she compares them to mechanical causality. It is as inconceivable that weariness would enliven our stream of consciousness as it is that throwing a ball downward would cause it to rise upward. Mechanical causality has external effects on us, but experiential causality has internal effects not wholly determined by the external world. Stein defends human free will and personal agency by observing that we can control life-feelings, at least to a degree. By engaging with and controlling our life-feelings, we effect our self and our experiences of the world. When we feel weariness, we can choose how much attention we pay to it and, to a degree, how much we let it affect us.

Scheler had said that we intuitively feel that some values are higher than others, and Stein builds on this idea. Stein identifies five levels of feelings. The first four are sensory, common (bodily life-feelings that affect us), moods (spiritual life-feelings that affect us but objectively connect with the external world), and emotions that are intentional states (feelings directed at an object). For example, I can be looking at a tree in the sunshine, have the sensory feelings of the light reflecting off shimmering leaves, and a cheerful mood starts to take hold of me, but my (common) feeling of bodily weariness deadens my cheerful mood, and about that I feel disappointed. We can't make moral judgments about the first four types of feelings, but we can and should make rational judgments about emotions. This is because emotions are intentional states anchored in the "I." We can consider whether someone is keeping his or her emotions within an appropriate hierarchy of values. Stein's idea is similar to Mill's idea (see Chapter 16) that some pleasures are higher than others because they have greater long-term benefit for someone. Stein's fifth type of feeling is sentiments, the attitudes we direct toward other people. In sentiments, she includes love and hatred (like Scheler) and other feelings like gratitude and vindictiveness. Sentiments are emotions that have conscious intention toward another person and always are correlated to personal values. Sentiments are subject to moral judgments in the same way emotions are.

After the Nazis banned her from teaching, Stein joined a Carmelite convent. Because Stein was born Jewish, the Nazi regime arrested her at her convent in 1942 and shipped her to the Auschwitz concentration camp, where they murdered her. Pope John Paul II beatified Stein in 1987 and canonized her in 1998. Years earlier, in 1954, Pope John Paul II, then known as Karol Wojtyła, earned a PhD with his thesis on the moral philosophy of Max Scheler.

MARTIN HEIDEGGER

Understanding Martin Heidegger (1889–1976) is no easy task. That statement is not only about his philosophy but about him as a person. He was Husserl's other most notable student, working as Husserl's assistant after Edith Stein had moved on. When Husserl retired in 1929, he recommended Heidegger be his successor to the chair of philosophy in Freiburg, Germany, a recommendation the university accepted. When the Nazis came to power and seized control of all universities, Heidegger joined the Nazi Party. He was then appointed rector of the University of Freiburg, but he resigned a few months later for reasons he never made clear. Scholars have ever since debated how much Heidegger agreed with Nazi ideology. The position that he did is buttressed by statements in his written papers and the fact that even though he lived and lectured for more than 30 years after the war, he never formally condemned the Nazis. We will talk about Heidegger's ideas, just as, for example, we talked about Aristotle's ideas even though Aristotle supported the abhorrent idea of slavery. Being involved in the quest for understanding means being able to consider ideas and take what is valuable and leave behind what is not.

A Phenomenology of Being

Heidegger is described as either a phenomenologist or an existentialist. Each description is true, to an extent, but it is more accurate to say Heidegger presents a unique hybrid of the two. His philosophy captures the spirit of Husserl's study of phenomena by focusing on the phenomena in experience, but his *epoché* led him to focus on the science of Being. That's "Being" with a capital "B." All objects are beings (small "b"), and all objects have Being (capital "B"). Particular beings pass in and out of existence, but Being remains. One can try to study Being in and of itself. Some Roman era and medieval philosophers did, some associating Being with God. Heidegger rejects this idea, pointing out that God is simply the highest being among all others.

When Heidegger brackets off the world and all assumptions about it, what he finds left is Being—the fundamental phenomenon in which all experience is grounded and from which all experiences derive meaning. Every object that we encounter in the world is a manifestation of Being. Heidegger finds one particular manifestation: our existence.

We exist. But that is a qualitatively different statement for us than "that tree exists." To describe the distinctive character of our existence, Heidegger used the concept that we are *Dasein*. The term "*Dasein*" could be literally translated as "being there," but typical of Heidegger's thought, it means "being there" and other concepts implied by it. That we are *Dasein*, in essence, means that we are beings *in* the world, not separate from it, and we are beings for whom our Being is a central concern for us. The biggest misunderstanding that one can have about this concept of being concerned about our existence is that it is simply a concern about whether we are alive. That is only a small part of it. We are also concerned about the quality and meaning of our life. For Heidegger, it is not enough for us merely to live—we also want to live meaningfully. But that's getting ahead of ourselves.

Dasein is not one object among the many objects in the world. Heidegger describes *Dasein* as a clearing in the midst of a dense forest of Being. It is a clearing in the sense that *Dasein* is a region where Being is fully revealed to us. It is from the vantage point of this clearing that we can analyze the meaning of Being. Looking at *Dasein*, we are aware, first and foremost, of our existence and that we exist within a world. Our essence as beings is that Being is an issue for us. What happens to us matters more than what happens to other things, and all that we experience we relate to ourselves in one way or another. From that perspective, from our clearing, we can relate to the world. It is not an objective understanding, but such an understanding is not possible. We work with what we have and what we are.

So far, so good. Quickly after that, Heidegger's study of *Dasein* and Being becomes very complex. He invents multiple terms to describe deep and sophisticated concepts that philosophers have spent thousands of pages trying to define and explain what they mean. We don't have that much space, so let's try to break it down as simply as possible.

Being-in-the-World

"*Dasein*" means "being there," and the "there" is the world. One of Heidegger's most significant ideas is that we are not detached from the world. We are not a consciousness trying to understand a world that is separate from us. Instead, Heidegger said we are Being-in-the-World (German: *In-der-Welt-sein*). The hyphenation in this word expresses that our Being and the world cannot be separated. The best way to think about Being-in-the-World is that you are a consciousness *embedded* in the world. "Embedded" means that we are inextricably in the world. Heidegger says we *dwell* in the world; we fully exist within it, are absorbed in it, and are taken up with it. All of our thinking and acting is not *about* the world, or *at* the world, but an inextricable part of the world in which we are embedded. I use "we" in these sentences, but with reason; Heidegger uses only "*Dasein*." That's because he is trying to capture in *Dasein* the uniqueness of the type of beings we are beyond the fact that we are embedded in the world.

Heidegger's most famous book is *Being and Time* (1927). He used that title because *Dasein* has two unique characteristics that make it distinct from all other beings (animals, plants, rocks, and so on): awareness of its own existence and awareness of time. *Dasein* exists, and it is aware that it exists—and Heidegger refers to *Dasein* as an "it." *Dasein* can question why it exists in ways that all other worldly objects cannot. *Dasein* can also question why it is situated in the world the way that it is and what its possibilities are in the world. We are beings who can ask—not so much in an intellectual way as in a practical, worldly way—what we can do in the world. Considering possibilities entails an awareness of time. *Dasein* is oriented not only to the present; *Dasein* can also remember its past and project itself into the future. Heidegger saw this as a crucial element of *Dasein*. It is always living-ahead; its here and now is always oriented toward future possibilities. That *Dasein* is aware of time means it is Being-ahead-of-itself, which affects *Dasein's* everyday actions and its anxiety. First, we need to discuss the everyday.

Regions, Involvements, and the Everyday

Ultimately, *Dasein's* situatedness is not the world itself but its set of relations to the world. Because *Dasein* is Being-in-the-world, it necessarily has an understanding of its place and possibilities in the world, even if that understanding is without reflective intellectual content. Most individuals think of themselves in terms of their social acceptance or their material comforts while they are immersed in the everydayness of life. We can take a detached view from life, considering the world and ourselves as a philosopher or scientist might, but that is not how we live. We live in our everyday Being-in-the-world.

The "everyday" is an often neglected key aspect of Heidegger's philosophy. To understand it, we also need to understand two other important concepts in Heidegger: regions and involvements. We are embedded in the world, but, more accurately, we are embedded in very small regions of that world. Where you live, where you work, who you interact with, what information you take in—these are small regions of the wider world. You, as *Dasein*, are embedded in a number of regions: home, work, school, friends, and so on. What makes regions important is that they are modes of *Dasein's* existence where *Dasein* works out its involvements. All of our actions and relations are tempered by and structured by our involvements. Husserl said that every one of our experiences is structured by our past experiences. Heidegger accepts that and adds the idea of involvements—which is a concept similar to goals, but because they are related to *Dasein* and Being-in-the-world, involvements have meaning for us beyond simple goals. Objects in the world are matters of concern for us. We care about what happens, and we are concerned that our actions work for us. Each of us has our own projects that we care about—for example, passing a course. We want equipment to work for us, like our computers, cars, and phones. We act on projects and use equipment to fulfill our involvements.

An important insight for Heidegger that is revealed in the phenomenological analysis of *Dasein* is that, contrary to almost all previous philosophy, we do not experience a world of objects. Instead, we engage with *equipment* that we use to fulfill our involvements. When all is going well—the equipment works and people behave as we expect them to—all is fine, and these objects become invisible to us; they recede into the everyday. For example, we never think about what our computer mouse does until it doesn't work. It's transparent to us. You don't think, "I am moving the mouse and the mouse is helping me do my work." No, you think about the tasks you are performing. The intentionality of your consciousness is on the work that you are doing. The mouse is invisible equipment. This is the case as long as everything is going according to plan and your intentions and your concerns are lined up and you're getting the results that you want. As soon as something interrupts that flow, that's when you start to think of equipment in a different way. Only then do you consider the mouse as an object of inspection. Your intention then shifts to how to get the object to work to fulfill your involvements. You are constantly thinking or not thinking about things, but you're always involved in the world in which you are embedded through your concerns. You are Being-in-the-world, and you are involved in the world and the regions in which you are embedded.

Heidegger's concept of involvement has deeper meaning than having goals; it also includes the question of who we are. *Dasein's* identity exists as *Dasein's* own first-person evaluation of its place in the world that reflects its involvements. As *Dasein*, we cannot disentangle our sense of who we are from our relations with what is around us. Who we are is a matter of concern to us. Heidegger said that it is not enough for us simply to survive; we wish to have a series of relations with our regions and the people and things in our regions, and even in relation with our life itself. It is not enough simply to live; one must live meaningfully. If this reminds you of Kierkegaard, good! You are paying attention, because that is where Heidegger got it from. But while Kierkegaard was very emotional about the meaning of our life, Heidegger is eerily dispassionate about the meaning of a person's life. There is nothing warm and personal about Heidegger (*Dasein* is an "it," remember), even though his philosophy is perhaps the most personal of all.

Thrownness, Authenticity, and Anxiety

The cold aspect of Heidegger's thought is found most vividly in what he calls the "thrownness" of our existence. We are beings who are thrown into the world. We're born. We didn't choose where; we didn't choose when; we didn't choose our parents; we didn't choose our siblings. We were thrown into a region of the world, and because we are thrown into these choiceless realities of our life, our life is a matter of constant tension. Now this is where Heidegger probably goes a little off the deep end because when he tries to talk about authentic versus inauthentic existence he gets into difficulties. What being authentic means for Heidegger he never quite makes clear, but his discussion centers on being aware. We need to be aware that we are *Dasein*, that we are embedded in a world as Being-in-the-world, and that we are continually in time as *Dasein* Being-ahead-of-itself. Above and beyond our everyday involvements, we constantly have to think about our place in the world and who we are now, have been in the past, and could be in the future. If you're not thinking of these things, that seems to be what Heidegger means by an inauthentic existence. If we are lost in the everydayness of life, we are fallen. When we don't deal with the fact that we are thrown into a world that we did not choose, we have nothing but anxiety. Not that we never do not have anxiety. Influenced by Nietzsche, Heidegger thought that part of our thrownness is that we realize that our system of social meanings has no ultimate ground; those meanings are simply what has developed over time. Influenced by Kierkegaard, Heidegger accepts that we are beings who must choose and act; therefore, Being-in-the-world means being forced to act despite having no absolute values or directions on which to base our actions. To be *Dasein* is to be finite and full of anxiety. We simply exist in the world into which we've been thrown.

What any of this has to do with Nazism no one can explain. It is true that, when Hitler came to power, Heidegger was slightly friendly to the Nazis, but then he mysteriously resigned the university position the Nazis gave him and never spoke of it again. Maybe Heidegger saw himself as being thrown into that world and convinced himself that he didn't choose to be a German in the 1930s and shouldn't concern himself with the everydayness of politics. Plus, after all, he thought that there is no ultimate ground for moral values. That would certainly be a grotesque denial of moral responsibility, especially since Heidegger writes about the importance of a moral conscience, but it's a possible explanation because, again, there's no sense in Heidegger of a warm and personal relationship with the world or people. His discussion of "care" is not related to love, family, or community but is about resolving one's own anxiety. He says some things about obedience to your society and the law as part of being authentic, but his discussion of conscience is about *Dasein* being called to make itself aware of its potential. That's the big, big paradox and irony of Heidegger. His philosophy deals with that fundamental questions of who are we and what we want from life, but the closest he comes to an answer is letting-be: being open to *Dasein* returning to its potentiality-for-Being-its-Self.

KARL JASPERS

German Karl Jaspers (1883–1969) applied the phenomenological method to clinical psychiatry. His 1913 book, *General Psychopathology*, described diagnosing mental illnesses by the form of a patient's symptoms and personal history, rather than by preconceived notions about psychological delusions. The role of the psychopathologist, he said, is to learn how to observe, ask questions, and analyze phenomena. Jaspers is better known for his later work in existentialism. He was, in the 1930s, the first to identify the common theme of personal freedom in Kierkegaard and Nietzsche. Jaspers's blend of psychology and existentialist philosophy uses expert empirical knowledge but goes beyond it.

Like the other existentialists, Jaspers saw that our existence and our freedom are challenges, but he was more optimistic than the others about facing those challenges. He acknowledged that most people retreat from the challenge. Most people, when they encounter the frighteningly limitless possibilities of human existence, retreat into false certainties. People construct psychological worldviews that interpret the world in inflexible subject–object terms. Using the Karl Jaspers antinomy inherent in a worldview, a person incorporates strategies of defensiveness, suppression, and deception against the world, forming an objectivized cage of false certainty. We can see how these inflexible worldviews work in attitudes of prejudices that limit a person's ability to take in information. Jaspers saw the role of psychology as helping people past the restricted antinomies of worldviews.

Jaspers's philosophical project was to retain Kierkegaard's decisive and passionate commitment to authenticity, while overcoming what he saw as the limitation of Kierkegaard's interiority and sense of inability to speak to the world that prevented authenticity (see Chapter 17). Jaspers stated that an individual's authenticity can come only from shared dialogue with others. To accomplish an existentialist view of communicative dialogue, Jaspers combined elements of Kant's doctrine of transcendental ideas (see Chapter 13) with Hegel's idea that consciousness forms through our actively cocreating our understanding—we learn through experience and by applying reason to our perceptions (see Chapter 14). Jaspers says we must be in continual dialogue with those around us because, although our knowledge frames our orientation toward the world, our existence is formed by our active self-reflection.

Jaspers argued that when we question reality, we encounter borders that cannot be crossed with the empirical approach of science. The problem isn't rationalism, per se, but the approach to the world of narrowly functional rationality. Most rational approaches block genuine knowledge, he said, because they are forms of ideology that conveniently serve subjective and objective functions. Jaspers is taking an existentialist approach to the central idea of positivism (see Chapter 19) that by focusing on rationality we find truth. We can find truth, Jaspers said, not by rationality alone but by applying reason to vital experiences, confronting oneself through decisive acts, and taking a leap of faith over borders and limits into existential communicative transcendence. Open consciousness is when one abandons the limits of oneself and communicates intersubjectively with the world. In transcendence, we do not attain positive knowledge in an analytical sense or in a Kantian sense of transcendental ideas of pure reason. Transcendence is what Jaspers calls an "existence" (German: *Existenz*)—an awareness that our authentic existence is not as an isolated rational consciousness but as a beingness of shared humanity found in the resources of social life and cultural tradition. In other words, we become authentic through communication with other people.

JEAN-PAUL SARTRE

Then there is the Frenchman Sartre (pronounced, SART, 1905–1980). If Heidegger is cold, Sartre is frozen solid. Some people find some things to like in Sartre, but others hate his philosophy of nihilistic existentialism. "Life's a bitch and then you die" is a flippant but not entirely inaccurate summary of Sartre's philosophy. He was also influenced by Kierkegaard but with even more fear and trembling.

Heidegger's principle book was *Being and Time*, but Sartre's principle book was *Being and Nothingness* (1943, written after he read Heidegger's book), and this gives a hint as to what separates their philosophies. Sartre agreed with Heidegger that we are finite beings thrown into the world without absolute values or directions on which to base our actions. But whereas Heidegger writes about our involvements and our concerns, Sartre wrote that we simply exist and are full of anxiety. Sartre does not agree with Heidegger's notion of *Dasein*, or that we are Being-in-the world. Sartre thought that knowledge of facts has no meaning in an objective sense but also oddly decides that subjective consciousness has no meaning in a subjective sense. Consciousness is nothingness, Sartre claimed. The root of this concept comes from Husserl's realization that consciousness is not a thing like a tree is a thing. Sartre takes that concept to the extreme conclusion that consciousness is separate from the world of things. At first that may sound like Descartes, but Sartre means something very different. Sartre labels objects "in-itself," signifying that they are self-contained entities that are static entities. He labels human consciousness "for-itself," signifying that it is a self-aware and self-projecting entity. Objects in-itself have static identities determined by external sources. Consciousness, as for-itself, is spontaneously free and lives in terms of possibilities.

After deciding that we are conscious beings separate from the world, Sartre embraces a stark conclusion. We are not so much thrown into a world of objects as we are thrown into freedom. That we have complete and total freedom is a logical consequence of Sartre's belief that there are no values, no structure, and no meaning to life. We can do whatever we want. Sartre also said that because there are no objective values, structure, or God, our existence precedes our essence, meaning that we are not defined by the essence of "humanness" as so many previous philosophers had believed. We are, Sartre wrote, nothing but what we make of ourselves. Similar to the pragmatists, Sartre believed that bare facts have no meaning until we assign a meaning to them.

We might ask, well, that's all good, yes? Sartre said, no, freedom is a horrible thing. It's a horrible feeling of discomfort to know that you are free and that the type of entity you are is incompatible with the type of entities that are the objects all around you. You exist, and Sartre says that you have nothing behind you or before you. You have no objective values, no means to justify or excuse your actions. We are left alone, he says, with the overwhelming burden of freedom. Humans are condemned to be free, and our existence is absurd and meaningless.

Even worse (yes, even worse) according to Sartre, he knows that other people are free, totally free to think about him whatever they want. His most famous play, "No Exit" (1944) ends with the often quoted line "hell is other people," an appropriate conclusion to a play that explores how helpless we are in the company of others. His semi-autobiographical novel, *Nausea* (1938), details the rest of his ideas about the absurdity of existence. He describes objects in the world as grotesque, bloated existence. Other people he describes as empty beings practicing "bad faith" in that they live in the everyday, denying their freedom. However, when the central character of *Nausea* acknowledges his freedom, all it does is make him nauseated, hence the title. The realization of freedom and taking responsibility for one's actions are the only authentic acts of which we are capable, but if our very existence is absurd, and there are no values, what good is freedom?

Perhaps Sartre was so pessimistic because he lived through the Great Depression, Nazi occupation of France during World War II (he was imprisoned by the Nazis), and the end of France's empire. Other French intellectuals of that period were also gloomy about life and the future, but few, if any, as much as Sartre.

SIMONE DE BEAUVOIR

Simone de Beauvoir (pronounced, da-bo-VWAR, 1908–1986) was a longtime confidant and companion of Sartre's. They are philosophy's most famous couple. Because they lived together for many years, it is not surprising that they shared themes and ideas. It is fair to say, though, that de Beauvoir's philosophy surpassed Sartre's in depth, clarity, and optimism.

de Beauvoir realized that Sartre's philosophy left no possibility for meaningful moral philosophy. She resolved to fix this shortcoming in her book, *The Ethics of Ambiguity* (1947). Her first step is to ground the concept of freedom in human actions. Freedom requires the realization of the goals of particular projects, de Beauvoir said, in an idea closer to Heidegger's than to Sartre's. There are no absolute moral values, but we create them from our choices and actions. She agrees with Sartre that freedom is discomfiting and that most people avoid their own freedom, but not to the extremes that he thought. In a Kierkegaardian manner, she saw people moving from less adequate to more adequate moral responses to freedom. Our freedom includes the freedom to try to avoid our freedom. People, especially children, avoid their freedom by adopting society's values. At a slightly higher level, others recognize their freedom but misuse it by denying all values (nihilism), by adventurously taking on projects without regard to goals or consequences, or by passionately focusing on their own goals with contempt for others. The highest moral level is genuine freedom, when one's passion for one's own freedom extends to others. To will oneself free also means to will that others be free, she said. Freedom and moral choices are never without ambiguity. We have freedom, but that freedom is not absolute. Our freedom is always constrained by our situation. Maintaining our own freedom while at the same time allowing other people their freedom is a constant challenge.

de Beauvoir is most famous for her book, *The Second Sex* (1949), which became one of the foundational texts for feminist philosophy. Her title evokes the central issue of feminism: that human society has always treated women as an "other" secondary to men. The first volume of the two-volume *The Second Sex* is a brilliant, detailed history of the subordination of women in all aspects of society. de Beauvoir sets forth the theory that women's second-class status can be explained largely by motherhood. Being pregnant, giving birth, and nursing the baby left a woman "riveted to her body" and made it possible for men, who are free from "reproductive slavery," to dominate her. Social institutions, science, and writers—from philosophers to poets—have contributed to myths about women being an "everlasting disappointment." de Beauvoir gives numerous examples of how revered men in history have perpetuated the great collective myths about women as unclean, inferior, and insignificant beings.

Like Wollstonecraft (see Chapter 10), de Beauvoir said that in those few circumstances when women are not denied opportunity, they prove that the historical insignificance that men have forced on women is the reason for their inferiority, not any inferiority in women, that has led to their insignificance. One is not born a woman, de Beauvoir declared, but is made a woman by society. (We will see an identical claim made about society making one black in Chapter 26.)

de Beauvoir is the first to make the distinction between sex, which is biological, and gender, which is a social construction. She observes that society oppresses women from birth, through childhood, adolescence, and into adulthood, forcing the social construction of gender onto them. She especially decries marriage as an absurd and perverted social institution that oppresses both men and women. She says that women obviously get the worse end of marriage, imposing on women a servitude that almost always destroys them, denying them their sexual and life desires, and turning them into passive instruments. She also has a negative view of traditional motherhood that forces a woman to give up her identity and self in sadomasochistic living through her children without end. She suggests instead communal child-rearing. In like manner, de Beauvoir analyzes many aspects of women's lives, from how society expects women to dress to how society expects women to behave. The common denominator is that society continually places women in a situation in which they can be nothing more than useful servants to men and children. She says only a very few women in history have achieved any real independence, but these have had little significant effect on challenging the human condition. She concludes by calling for women to be left to take their own chances in life, and she is hopeful for a future when women and men are equals. As we will see in Chapter 25, feminist philosophy picked up many of de Beauvoir's themes.

MAURICE MERLEAU-PONTY

Frenchman Maurice Merleau-Ponty (pronounced mar-lo-PON-tee, 1909–1961) was influenced by Husserl and Heidegger, but created a radical phenomenological approach to analyzing human perception. He proposed that the material body, not consciousness, is the source of human knowledge. All perception, he argued, was of the body, so philosophy should center on the body-subject not the Cartesian self. Therefore, Merleau-Ponty's phenomenology focused on the body's sensorimotor functions, and his version of the *epoché* was to bracket off all propositions about the world beyond the body's involvement with the world.

What Merleau-Ponty arrives at through his *epoché* is that perception is primary to thought. Merleau-Ponty claimed that there are bodily perceptions that do not fit Husserl's idea that consciousness is always intentional, that it always takes an object. Examples include phenomena of the body that Merleau-Ponty considered to be immediately known, not separable between knower and known. Merleau-Ponty adopts Heidegger's concept of Being-in-the-world as bodily perception, not mental perception, and that the body's involvements in the world is the condition of experience. We understand ourselves as a body in space, and all that we perceive comes from bodily perception. Merleau-Ponty's reconception of phenomenology inspired an exploration in epistemology known as "bodily cognition."

CHAPTER 22

ANALYTICAL PHILOSOPHY

Despite its inherent difficulties and weaknesses, analytical philosophy has been the dominant approach to philosophy in the United States for decades. Its appeal lies in the ease with which it can connect with logic and mathematics and to a lesser degree with the "hard" sciences. Logic and mathematics have always held out the promise of certain knowledge, and there is a strong allure to a method that can break down problems into small discrete chunks and solve them.

Analytical philosophy was founded by Bertrand Russell (see Chapter 19). He described his philosophy as "logical atomism," which had both a metaphysical meaning and a methodology for doing philosophy. Russell's metaphysical view was that the universe consists of many independently existing things exhibiting qualities and standing in relations with each other. Although few subscribe to a strict logical atomism today, analytical philosophy has the basic metaphysical assumption that logic can tell us about the world. In its essence, analytical philosophy is the faith in logical analysis to solve all problems. It focuses on logical problems and says that anything that is worth discussing is worth discussing in terms of getting at the underlying logic of the problem.

PHILOSOPHY OF LANGUAGE

Perhaps analytical philosophy's greatest contribution has been in establishing the importance of the consideration of language. It is surprising how little attention was paid to language in philosophy prior to the 1900s. We saw in Chapters 19 and 20 that philosophers started to note the importance of language in how we frame and solve philosophical problems.

Charles Sanders Peirce, Gottlob Frege, and Ferdinand de Saussure (1857–1913) independently and around the same time put forward theories about the connections between words and their objects. They shared the same idea that a word (a "signifier") has a meaning (the "signified"), though Frege used the terms "sense" and "reference," respectively. The study of signs—semiology or semiotics—looks at how language shapes society and human behavior. Saussure said that signs are arbitrary. For example, the signifier "dog" has no actual connection to the particular animal that it signifies in the English language. In other words, the word that is used is a matter of social convention. Take the signifier "gift." It means a present in English but a poison in German. Differences are crucial.

Structuralism

The study of semiotics gave rise to the philosophical field of structuralism, which was led by French anthropologist Claude Lévi-Strauss (1908–2009). He applied the semiology of Saussure to anthropology and language and believed that human culture is a system of symbolic communication. From that he reasoned that the structure of language is the prototype of familial and social relations. All human cultures, he claimed, share the same structure, which is a set of rules that are communicated by mythology. The linguistic structures of the myths express the basic unconscious structures of the mind, which are universal to all human beings. Lévi-Strauss claimed that structure is dominant. The structures of the mind determine how people live and make sense of the world—that is, language. Culture is a signifying system. It *is* language. For Lévi-Strauss and other structuralists, this means two things. One is that in trying to understand anything about humanity, we need to analyze the system of signs that structure society. The other is that humans do not create language. Instead, language structures humans at social and individual levels. We do not use language to describe and create reality. Instead, language constitutes reality for us. The structure fixes the system of culture, all human culture being fundamentally the same, and the structure positions all individuals within the system of culture. Consequently, structuralism denies free will.

Some analytical philosophers reject structuralism because it assumes its metaphysical basis of the structure, which cannot be verified. Others have adopted the basic idea that human thought and society are governed by essential structures. French literary theorist Roland Barthes (1915–1980) agreed with Lévi-Strauss on the importance of understanding how myth structures human society, but he emphasized myth as a narrative. He was much more open than was Lévi-Strauss about different cultures interpreting the narrative of myth in different ways. He also was willing to use structural analysis to critique the myths of bourgeois society. French psychiatrist Jacques Lacan (1901–1981) applied structuralism to the field of psychoanalysis that had been invented by Sigmund Freud (1856–1939). Lacan argued that the structure of language also determined the structure of the human unconscious. Lacan's structuralist psychoanalysis interpreted Freud's concepts in terms of the all-encompassing hegemony (dominance) of language. He developed an elaborate and hopelessly complex symbology mapping how the unconscious and conscious parts of the mind are structured.

Ordinary Language Philosophy

Wittgenstein's philosophy has spawned its admirers; detractors; and, more than all else, people struggling to understand what it all means. His ideas are deceptively straightforward; we get what he seems to mean, but then when we consider the deeper implications of his ideas, we see we are only just beginning a journey of understanding. One important offshoot of Wittgenstein's later philosophy is "ordinary language philosophy."

Ordinary language philosophy is so called because it operates from the idea that philosophy should look at how language is used in everyday life. It shares concepts with Wittgenstein's language-games and forms of life, but it has its roots in the philosophy of Englishman Gilbert Ryle (1900–1976), who, in 1949, independent of Wittgenstein, published *The Concept of Mind*, which had many ideas similar to Wittgenstein's in *Philosophical Investigations*. Ryle laid out a map of human thinking as consisting of categories to which concepts belong. Within a category, there are concepts and associated words that logically fit together, and it is the language category that gives them meaning. His example is a visitor being shown around a university campus. After the full tour, the person says, "I have seen all the classroom buildings, research centers, and dormitories, but when are you going to show me the university?" This, Ryle called a "category mistake." The visitor has placed the concept "university" in the wrong category, thinking it is an entity separate from the buildings, faculty, and activities. The university is the way in which all of its parts come together to form an organized whole.

Ryle uses his concept of a category mistake to attack Descartes' division of the human into two substances, mind and body. Descartes assumed that the mental and the physical were different substances, but Ryle counters that they belong to different categories. Ryle argues that when we encounter a noun, we assume that the word refers to a distinct thing. Descartes assumed the noun "mind" referred to a substance. Ryle's provocative idea is that "mind" is a misleading concept, similar to the university example. Mind is not separate from the acts of learning, remembering, imagining, knowing, or willing. "Mind" is a term we use to describe the abilities and dispositions that explain a person's public actions. Thus, he argues, Descartes was wrong to assume there are mental acts separate from physical acts. Ryle, in *The Concept of Mind*, derides that idea as "the dogma of the ghost in the machine." It is a category mistake, according to Ryle, to talk about mental acts causing physical acts, such as, "I will to raise my arm, and I raise my arm." For Ryle, they are correctly seen as one in the same act. All issues of intelligence, he claimed, are not clues to the inner workings of minds; they *are* those workings. He is not claiming that there aren't mental processes, only that there are no hidden chambers from which these processes are directed. Ryle's work is categorized as ordinary language philosophy because of his efforts to get us to clarify our use of words to describe the world. However, his philosophy is more influential in the field of philosophy of mind.

John L. Austin (1911–1960) was another English major proponent of ordinary language philosophy. In his most important book, *How to Do Things With Words* (1962), he takes the position that philosophy can contribute to an understanding of our language and concepts. Austin proposed that we classify uses of language similar to the way in which science classifies species of organisms. Instead of Wittgenstein's claim that philosophy can only clarify language, Austin's position is that the analysis of ordinary language is the first step in improving our knowledge.

Similar to the pragmatists and Wittgenstein, Austin views words as tools. That being the case, he says, we should use clean tools, and we should know what we mean and what we do not mean when we use them. Austin also sides with Wittgenstein's position that the meanings of words lie in their use. As Austin frames it, we have a common stock of words that embodies meanings and distinctions that people have found worth making and have found to be successful. Because our words have stood the test of time, he says we should be analyzing those words rather than trying to create a better language ourselves. This is a rejection of the agenda of the logical positivists (see Chapter 19), which Wittgenstein had also rejected. Instead, Austin says an analysis of ordinary language will give us an understanding of human experience.

Austin develops the idea of "speech acts," his version of Wittgenstein's language-games. Remember that Wittgenstein's German word *Spiel* includes the idea of action, and that is the sense that Austin wants to express in his term, "speech acts." He identifies three components in speech acts. When a person says something, there is the locutionary act, which is the act of saying or writing words; the illocutionary act, which is what the person is doing by speaking or writing (informing, ordering, warning, and so on); and the perlocutionary act, which is the response of the listener or reader that the speaker/writer hopes to elicit. For example, in this speech act of writing this sentence to you, my locutionary act is these actual words, my illocutionary act is to inform you, and my perlocutionary act is for you to learn something. Another way to think of it is to ask what is said, why the speaker is saying it, and what the speaker hopes will happen as a result. We can, Austin says, learn a great deal about human behavior by examining speech acts in this way. As you can quickly imagine, there are many, many possibilities for what lies behind any speech act. Is the speaker reporting a fact, expressing an opinion, trying to inform me, distract me? Analysis of speech acts quickly becomes very complicated and subject to interpretation and debate. Still, interest in what Austin proposes is high in analytical philosophy.

PHILOSOPHY OF MIND

Philosophizing about the nature and workings of the human mind has been around since Augustine (see Chapter 4), but the development of computer technology, particularly artificial intelligence research, has raised new questions and suggested new methods and directions within the philosophy of mind. A relatively new field has emerged called "cognitive science," which reduces the human mind to a biological computer and uses artificial intelligence, analytical philosophy, psychology, neuroscience, and linguistics to build a deterministic model of human mental functioning. The "computational model of the mind" is the basis for cognitive science; but, although computers are new, cognitive science's assumption of a deterministic mind equivalent to a programmed computer picks up the deterministic visions of Hobbes (see Chapter 8); Leibniz (see Chapter 13); and, in particular, Julien Offray de La Mettrie (1709–1751) in his 1747 work, *L'homme machine (Machine Man)*. Many cognitive scientists work in the field of artificial intelligence in the attempt to make computers duplicate the deterministic model of human intelligence.

Analytical philosophers of mind such as Patricia and Paul Churchland adopt the computational model and believe that an adequate scientific understanding of the material brain will expose terms such as "mind," "self," "beliefs," "desires," and "intentions" as "folk psychology." They believe that all future talk about human cognition will be in terms of brain states. Their neurological approach is a strong movement within philosophy of mind, leading to either a denial of human consciousness or a reduction of consciousness to the firing of neurons in the brain. The problem with cognitive neuroscience and related analytical philosophy of mind is their methodology of assuming the conclusion of biological determinism. As Husserl had pointed out (see Chapter 21), science, as a social activity, gives us an idealized and naively objectivized nature. The lifeworld of cognitive neuroscience assumes biological determinism and the computational model, assumptions that structure the experiments they design, and this bias of assumption leads to confirmational bias in the results. The assumption that a blip on a monitor has captured a brain state and thus explains conscious activity may be no more than the logical fallacy of conflating cause and effect.

One of the leading critics of the computational model of the mind and the possibility of artificial intelligence duplicating the human mind is John Searle (1932–). His now famous 1980 "Chinese room" thought experiment goes like this: Imagine that you are in a room with a large rule book giving you directions in English on how to respond to Chinese phrases with appropriate Chinese replies. You have no knowledge of the Chinese language, but the manual contains formal rules for syntactically analyzing one set of Chinese symbols and constructing another set of Chinese symbols that a native Chinese speaker would recognize as an appropriate response. However, the manual does not explain what any of the symbols mean. While you are in the room, Chinese speakers slip messages written in Chinese under the door. These slips of paper contain various marks made up of straight and curved lines, none of which you understand. You find the symbols in the rule book, and, following the instructions, you write out appropriate sets of symbols on new slips of paper and pass these messages back under the door. The Chinese speakers outside read the slips you gave them, and they read them as articulate Chinese responses.

You have fooled the people outside into believing that you are fluent in Chinese. However, you still don't understand any Chinese. Searle argues that something different clearly is going on when you copy the Chinese symbols from the rule book than would be the case if you were receiving and responding to messages in a language that you do understand. Searle claims that this formal manipulation of symbols is comparable to what goes on in a computer's artificial intelligence program. His point is that no matter how effective a computer program may be in simulating human conversation, it will never produce actual understanding of language. A computer program can only simulate intelligence; it can't duplicate it. Searle claims that a computer program is nothing like a human mind and that artificial intelligence does not duplicate human cognitive states.

Another critic of the attempt to explain our mental life in terms of brain states is David Chalmers (1966–). In his highly influential book, *The Conscious Mind* (1996), he divides the neuroscience approach to human consciousness into the easy problems and the hard problem. Easy problems are problems on which neuroscience has made some progress, including the mind's ability to discriminate, categorize, and react to environmental stimuli; the integration of information; the ability of a cognitive system to access its own internal states; and so on. However, Chalmers says that even if all of these sorts of problems have been solved by the neuroscientist, there still remains the hard problem of consciousness.

The hard problem for neuroscience is to explain the subjective experiences of awareness that characterize human consciousness. To be conscious means that one is a self who has an inner life. Consciousness is the subjective quality of experience. When you view a tree, your eyes and brain are physically affected by the light reflecting off the tree. Obviously, though, there is more going on in your mind than what happens when a photoelectric cell is affected by the light reflecting off the tree. You have a subjective experience of the qualities of the tree, experiences the machine does not and cannot have. From this, Chalmers argues that all of the progress claimed by the brain sciences has been on the easy problems. They have not and, Chalmers claims, will not be able to solve the hard problem of explaining consciousness.

Chalmers is open to alternative theories, but his suspicion is that consciousness is a fundamental and irreducible feature in reality that operates according to its own set of laws. He points to how scientists in the 1800s had to introduce the new entity of the electromagnetic charge because the existing physics of the day could not explain certain observed phenomena. Similarly, Chalmers thinks that there is an explanatory gap in existing scientific models of our mental life. Eventually, we will need to introduce a new, nonreductive theory of consciousness. Or, perhaps, accept one of the nonreductive theories that have long existed.

ANALYTICAL POLITICAL PHILOSOPHY

A nonstructuralist but still analytical approach to human society can be found in two diametrically opposed traditions—liberalism and analytical Marxism. In the context of analytical philosophy, "liberalism" does not mean liberal politics as most people think of it now and certainly does not mean what continental philosophers think of as liberal. Continental political philosophers focus on the ideas of greater distribution of civil liberties, fair application of the rule of law, and freedom from oppression. Liberal analytical political philosophers focus on the ideas of laissez-faire government, meaning minimal regulatory intervention and oversight of business and low or even no taxation. The different approaches include different definitions of what liberty and equality mean. We'll look at continental social and political philosophy in Chapter 24.

Liberalism

Again, "liberalism" is not liberal or progressive politics but political theory based on the rational ideal of liberty or freedom and may or may not include the idea of human rights. John Rawls (1921–2002) is a highly influential analytical political philosopher is. In his classic book, *A Theory of Justice* (1971), Rawls tries to answer the question of what justice is (a question as old as Plato, see Chapter 2). Rawls's answer is that justice is fairness. He believed that the common view that freedom and equality are in conflict is an illusion. His answer was that freedom and equality can be integrated into a unity when we see that justice is a matter of fairness. He demonstrated his answer through a thought experiment similar to Locke's thought experiment about the state of nature (see Chapter 9).

Rawls's thought experiment is to imagine all of us in what he called the "original position." Like Locke, Rawls asks us to imagine a world without social institutions and ranking of social status. Unlike Locke, Rawls offers a hypothetical scenario that is grounded in logic, not the natural world. He says to imagine that we are deliberating on how we want society to be structured politically and economically. Society doesn't exist in this scenario, so anything is possible. What kind of society would we agree to want to live in? The catch is that we are in the original position, before reality. We are behind what Rawls called the "veil of ignorance"; we do not know, once society is created, what gender, race, age, intelligence, wealth, skills, education, religion, and so on that we will have in this society. All we would know, Rawls says, is a sense of justice and that we would be able to pursue our conception of the good life. So now what kind of society would we agree to want to live in?

The idea behind this thought experiment is that if we are not guaranteed any kind of social status in this to-be-created society, we logically would not choose any political and economic structure that would deny justice and the pursuit of the good life to anyone. Rawls says it would be irrational for us to propose a society in which certain people are denied justice because, behind the veil of ignorance, we would not know if we would end up being one of those people denied justice. In other words, it would be illogical for anyone to agree to a society that discriminates against women or Black people if there was a chance you would be a woman or Black person in that society. We would instead choose a society that guarantees equal justice for everyone. That is the only logical choice for us, Rawls says.

Rawls's purpose in giving us this thought experiment is to clarify our thinking and get us to the correct standpoint in thinking about justice. The original position removes all presuppositions and focuses our attention on what is truly just. He thinks that we would agree to general principles of equal freedoms for all, including freedoms of conscience, association, expression, and democratic rights, and that we can establish a just society. We would agree that society would have adequate structures to ensure basic rights and freedoms for all. We would never agree that one gender, race, age, or any other property that a person could possess would entitle someone to more rights than those without that property would possess. A just society, for Rawls, would be one that is based solely on a rational implementation of the good without regard to hierarchical divisions.

Rawls's theory has been much discussed, and he has both defenders and critics. Not surprisingly, much of the division is along the lines of the analytical/continental divide. Rawls called his thought experiment an engagement in "ideal theory," meaning that it reasons from idealized assumptions about rational norms to discover the best possible social structure. Ideal theory, by design, does not attempt to address real-world problems but seeks instead to establish rational general principles, an approach similar to Plato's and Hobbes's. Rawls and his theory are for this reason best categorized as analytical philosophy. But philosophers such as the Indian-British Amartya Sen (1933–) and the Jamaican-American Charles W. Mills (ca. 1950–) have criticized ideal theory as too idealized. Sen published a book directly addressing Rawls, *The Idea of Justice* (2009), arguing that a thought experiment about justice should not be like Rawls's transcendental and institutional approach but instead should be a comparative approach that is focused on people's capabilities concerning what they are and can realize in society. Mills similarly argues that ideal theory is overly idealized and is, in fact, an ideological denial of the real-world realities of racism and sexism, among other forms of oppression (see Chapter 26). Sen and Mills both agree with Rawls that equality and justice are important norms. Mills does think that Rawls provides us with some good ways to think about these norms, but he thinks Rawls's theory is utterly unfit to deal with racial justice.

An analytical response to Rawls, and a highly political one, came from American Robert Nozick (1938–2002). In his book, *Anarchy, State, and Utopia* (1974), Nozick applies his own version of ideal theory but has sharp disagreements with Rawls. He agrees with the norm of justice but not with equality. Nozick objected to Rawls's idea that justice should consider the well-being of those who are worse off—Rawls having argued that lifting up those who are worse off benefits everyone in society. Nozick counters that those who are well-off have no obligation to assist others for the sake of bettering society. Nozick bases his argument on the idea of inviolable natural rights for individuals. From this he states that an individual can do whatever he or she wants as long as he or she respects the rights of others. But what "respect" means for Nozick is the respect for the right to "positive freedom"—to do what they want. He makes the extraordinary claim that any behavior is allowed as long as compensation is paid for any damage caused to others. Critics have pointed out that such a view favors those with greater financial resources.

Nozick offers a modified version of Locke's social contract (see Chapter 9) in which people agree to the convenience of a state, but the only role for the state in Nozick's vision of utopia is to defend the rights of individuals. Nozick also adopts a strict version of Locke's labor theory of property; Nozick claims that acquisition of property creates an inviolable right of the individual to do whatever he or she wants with the property. He offers no means to correct abuses of property acquisition, only a suggestion that such abuses are wrong but wouldn't happen in an ideal society. Nozick ends up with a tamer version of Hobbes's state of nature (see Chapter 9), but Nozick's is made less nasty and brutish by a minarchist state—a government with only the minimal powers to enforce the law. A state is preferable to anarchy in that it can protect individuals' rights, mainly property and financial rights. Throughout his philosophy, Nozick favors the assumption that those who are well-off acquired their property justly and are thus justified in their wealth. Nozick thus rejects all ideas of social welfare, equates taxation with theft, and even frowns on nongovernmental efforts to promote greater social equality.

Nozick's book has been cemented into the foundation of the political ideology of libertarianism: an extremist view that there should be no government at all. Libertarianism has a social component and an economic component. In social theory, libertarianism states that individuals should have complete freedom to do whatever they want as long as they are not aggressive or coercive toward others. This is similar to the views of John Stuart Mill (see Chapter 16). Most libertarians reject the idea of positive human rights ("I have a right to…."), believing instead in negative rights ("No one has the right to coerce me.") In economic theory, libertarianism rejects governmental regulation of business. One branch of this theory, anarcho-capitalism, states that corporations should be allowed to create their own private enforcement agencies to defend their property rights. Nozick had said that the minarchist state was preferrable to anarchy, but libertarianism generally prefers anarchy to the state.

Many analytical political philosophers, including libertarians, accept the view of economic liberalism that economic activity is governed by laws similar to the way in which the motion of bodies is governed by physical laws of motion. That view, which has its roots in Adam Smith (1723–1790), a friend of David Hume and the "father of capitalism." Recent economic liberalism includes the idea that human society, especially government, should not interfere with the natural processes of financial transactions. A milder form of libertarianism is known as "neoliberalism" or "corporatism," which sees the role of government as existing to protect the interests of business corporations, with minimal oversight and regulation, though not to the complete absence thereof.

Analytical Marxism

Similar to liberalism in its analytical approach but leading to diametrically opposed conclusions is analytical Marxism. Karl Marx (see Chapter 15) could be considered an analytical philosopher if you look at his theory of economic determinism as an exercise of logical analysis. Certainly that was the view of French Marxist Louis Althusser (1918–1990). He divided Marx's philosophy into two time periods—the earlier humanist Marx who wrote about human alienation and the later scientific Marx who wrote about structures of capital. Althusser dismissed Marx's early writings as consisting of bourgeois delusions and instead insisted on a structuralist interpretation of Marx. He saw capitalist society in terms of a totality, with the structure of the social totality dominating all social life. He rejected being associated with the structuralists because he didn't agree that signs determine the structure. He thought that the complex social totality structures all social practice, including a person's characteristics, desires, intentions, and choices. Althusser thought Marx's economic determinism was just one level of the totality; Althusser places more importance on the role of ideology as forming people into concrete subjects filling concrete roles within the totality. He saw the structure of ideology as unchanging throughout history, or, as he said, ideology has no history, and history is a process without a subject. In Althusser, there is no individual to feel alienated from life; there is only the totalizing theory of the ideological structure.

Another enthusiastic analytical Marxist, but highly critical of Althusser's structuralist reductionism, was Canadian philosopher G. A. Cohen (1941–2009). In his book, *Karl Marx's Theory of History: A Defence* (1978), Cohen updated Marx's theory to include technological advancements but otherwise gave a version of economic determinism faithful to Marx's original theory. A key addition by Cohen is the idea of "rational choice theory"—an analytical theory in economics that states that people make rational cost–benefit calculations to determine what option is best for them. Cohen's application of this theory to Marx is to explain the changes in economic epochs, with new modes of production being adopted when it is rational for people to do so. Human history is thus explained as a series of rational steps to increase productivity.

American economist John Roemer (1945–) applies analytical rational choice theory to Marx's observation that workers are in competition with each other for jobs (the fourth alienation). He also argues that economic exploitation is generated not in production itself but in the market exchange of commodities, which in turn reflects wider exploitation in society on the basis of property relations.

In reaction to Rawls's ideal theory, a number of analytical Marxists have taken on the challenge of what justice is. The challenge is to develop a concept of justice liberated from bourgeois ideology. Cohen argued that a theory of justice must be built from the idea that all people are fundamentally equal in worth and moral status, a position not far off from Rawls's. Cohen restates the Marxist idea of the unjust exploitation of workers. Instead of Marx's contention that the capitalist steals the workers' labor, Cohen says it is the system that denies workers autonomy. This exploitation would be overcome when there is a society in which no class controls the means of production and workers not only own the product of their labor but also have sovereignty over their own selves. Cohen stresses that his concept of self-ownership is egalitarian, distinguishing it from Nozick's notion that an individual's right to himself or herself extends to a right to acquire external resources.

ANALYTICAL EPISTEMOLOGY

The most opaque area of analytical philosophy (save formal logic itself, which we will leave to courses devoted to advanced logic) is epistemology. We have seen, so far, a great deal of epistemology based on sense perception. Analytical epistemology is based on logical analysis of propositions. The analytical take on epistemology largely rests on the short three-page paper, "Is Justified True Belief Knowledge?" (1963), by American Edmund Gettier (1927–2021). Perhaps no paper in the history of philosophy has caused more discussion and uproar than Gettier's simple little paper. It has spawned a cottage industry in creating examples that prove Gettier's point. They have come to be known as "Gettier problems." Gettier takes on the ancient idea, going back to Plato, that we can say that justified true belief is the definition of knowledge. In short, if you believe something and have a good justification for holding that belief, and that belief is in fact true, then you can be said to have knowledge of that truth. The point is that it's not knowledge if your belief just happens to be true; you need to have a good, justified reason for believing it. This idea was so well accepted as common sense that few philosophers ever discussed the topic, which is why we haven't addressed it in this book up to now. What Gettier pointed out is that one can believe something, that one can have very, very good justification for that belief, and that the belief is true but that one being correct in all this could be a matter of luck, so it cannot count as knowledge.

A simpler version (many dozen have been offered over the years) of Gettier's convoluted original examples was given by Alvin Goldman (1938–). Henry is driving through Barn County and sees numerous structures that look like barns. Unknown to Henry is that Barn County is littered with barn facades, structures that aren't barns but from the road look exactly like barns. Henry therefore has a justified belief that he is seeing barns, but it is a false belief. When he next looks at one particular structure, he is looking at the one real barn in Barn County. In this instance, Goldman says, Henry's belief is justified and true, but it is a result of luck, so it cannot count as knowledge. Other examples of Gettier problems include a farmer who believes there's a sheep in the field because he sees what looks like a sheep, but he does not know that it is a dog disguised as a sheep; the actual sheep is hidden behind the dog. So the farmer's belief that there's a sheep in the field is correct but cannot count as knowledge.

Analytical philosophers have offered many solutions to the quandary Gettier created. Some add additional conditions to the argument; others substitute "adequate evidence" for "justified"; and some others add causal conditions, defeasibility (canceling) conditions, and so on. You may have noticed that some subterfuge is involved in the barn and sheep examples. Henry and the farmer believe for incorrect reasons because they were deceived. This is true for Gettier's original examples in which the believer holds a belief because of deliberate deception or ignorance caused by bad luck. This has led some to propose the "no false premises" solution, which, exactly as the name suggests, says that a belief can count as knowledge if its justification does not rely on false premises. This does clear up Gettier's original examples, the barns and sheep examples, and most if not all other Gettier problems. However, the no false premises solution requires the believer to check for the possibilities of deception and even self-deception. This is the simple solution offered by the pragmatists (see Chapter 18) long before Gettier—in particular Peirce, who said that what is true is determined by the opinion that is ultimately agreed to by all who investigate. As you've probably thought, Henry can get out of the car and look more closely at the barn facades; the farmer needs simply to walk into the field to see the dog is disguised as a sheep. William James would say that all of this arguing about the Gettier problems is an exercise in pedantry. There is no absolute truth or knowledge, so what is true, and by extension what is justified knowledge, is tangible experience that works for us.

The no-false-premises solution requires us to accept that we have fewer justified beliefs than we think we have. Pragmatism says that's what we have to live with so we do our best to be sensible and verify our beliefs and carry on. These conclusions are not acceptable to most analytical epistemologists. They carry on with ever more detailed and elaborate logical analysis of propositions. Ignoring Wittgenstein, they have returned to the logical positivist dream of a logically perfect language. This effort was led by Polish logician Alfred Tarski (1901–1983) who proposed the "correspondence theory of truth," which says that "p" is true if and only if p, where p is the proposition expressed by "p." A real-world analogy being as follows: "Snow is white" is true if and only if snow is white. But Tarski stresses that any ordinary language examples are not illustrations of the theory of truth that works only in logical language. In many ways, Tarski's program is a revival of Russell's program of reducing everything to logic (see Chapter 19). If you took a course in advanced epistemology at a U.S. university today, you would probably spend most of the course discussing Gettier and Tarski.

The analytical epistemology course *may* mention analytical philosopher Willard Van Orman Quine (1908–2000), who in his paper, "Two Dogmas of Empiricism" (1953), demonstrated that all analytical statements are actually synthetic statements that appeal to the way in which people normally define terms in social discourse, people including analytical logicians. The classic example of an analytical statement, "All unmarried men are bachelors," is defined by the meaning of the terms as people use them (hello, Wittgenstein). Logical notation of "if p then q" doesn't escape this problem because the meanings of those terms—"p" and "q"—are as people use them, even if logicians are the only ones using them. Quine also conclusively showed that the entire analytical project was based on reductionism, the belief that particular statements can be verified or falsified in isolation from other statements. This dogma is false, Quine says, because no statement, even ones of formal logic, can be verified outside of a broader belief system and all of its assumptions about the world. Quine says that all of our knowledge, from observations to laws of logic, is part of a human-made fabric of beliefs that impinges on experience only along the edges. He adopts the approach of pragmatism that the efficacy of a belief, not logic, is what makes the belief true. He also adopts the continental approach that terms are defined by the broader social environment. Quine essentially guts the entire analytical project. And yet it continues because some people choose to believe in it for their own reasons.

CHAPTER 23

TEARING DOWN PHILOSOPHY: POSTMODERNISM

In philosophy, around 1600 is considered the beginning of the "modern era." Philosophers from Descartes to Kant are often referred to as "early modern philosophers," and the post-Kant era as "modern philosophy." The concept of "modernity" is loosely defined as the Enlightenment worldview that there is one true picture of reality that humans can know through reason and science. Modernity has a firm faith that it has a superior and enlightened form of universal, objective knowledge. Analytical philosophy is an example of modernism. Enlightenment modernity in philosophy is associated with the Cartesian concept of the autonomous, knowing subject as the source of all ideas and that collectively, rational autonomous subjects have discovered theories that increasingly better describe reality. From these assumptions, modernity has an optimistic view of human progress.

"Postmodernist" is the name given to a loose-knit group of thinkers united in their opposition to modernity and its assumptions. There is an almost bewildering array of postmodernist thinkers, and we will have to restrict our discussion to a few significant ones. Their postmodern tradition—though they'd reject being called a tradition—is based on the observations and arguments of philosophers like Nietzsche, Scheler, Heidegger, and the later

Wittgenstein. Those philosophers themselves were inspired by the long tradition of unmasking the pretensions of rationalism and the illusions of dogmatic speculation.

Postmodernists emphatically believe that the modernist dream of discovering the central theme or set of rational categories for understanding reality is dead. Reminiscent of Nietzsche's metaphor that "God is dead," the death of modernity means we must now face our stark and uncharted lives with no essences to which we can appeal or certitudes on which we can base our lives. We are the products of history, but history is just a purposeless interplay of shifting material and social forces. All we can do is critically analyze or "deconstruct" the modernist dream of reason to reveal how its illusions arose and why it seemed so real. Continuing with the false paradigm of the Enlightenment, we remain stuck. Postmodernists call for philosophy, as it has traditionally been understood, to be torn down, including the modern conceptions of epistemology, metaphysics, logic, and science. Postmodernism obviously rejects analytical philosophy. Postmodernism could be categorized as continental philosophy, with which it has significant cross-pollination, but it is probably more honest to consider postmodernism as detached from, if not opposed to, much of continental philosophy.

THE HAZY BEGINNINGS OF POSTMODERNISM

One cannot reduce the breadth and complexities of postmodernism to a single source, but it's helpful to consider a significant spark: Claude Monet's (1840–1926) painting of boats in the morning haze, "Impression, soleil levant" (1872). Not that it occurred in isolation, of course. Nothing does. Here is some context. In the 1860s, the French art scene was dominated by the Académie des Beaux-Arts. They controlled what art was exhibited at the Salon de Paris, the largest and most influential juried art exhibition in France. The Académie insisted that paintings displayed the staid, traditional style, including that the brushstrokes were blended to invisibility so as to portray realistic historical, religious, or mythological scenes and portraiture. Four painters, Claude Monet, Pierre-Auguste Renoir, Alfred Sisley, and Frédéric Bazille, partly inspired by Romanticism (see Chapter 14), broke from the staid tradition of the Académie to gather to paint in the open air rather than in a closed studio. Their purpose was to capture the sunlight and the feel of nature better. Importantly, they wanted to capture the *feeling* of what they saw in nature and social life. They didn't try for lifelike realism, and they didn't hide their brushstrokes. The artists had inserted their personal feelings and style into the paintings, and they weren't afraid to use bold colors and new techniques. The Académie rejected their submissions to the Salon de Paris as too radical.

Essentially censored by the Académie, in 1873 Monet, Renoir, and Sisley, along with fellow painters Camille Pissarro, Paul Cézanne, Berthe Morisot, and Edgar Degas, founded the "Cooperative and Anonymous Association of Painters, Sculptors, and Engravers" and exhibited their creations independently of the Académie. Their rogue exhibitions, held eight times over the next 12 years, were ridiculed by the establishment, the artists even harassed by authorities. One art critic derided Monet's painting as being only an impression and not a finished work of art. Owning the mockery, the embryonic movement embraced "impressionism" as the label for their movement, a movement that changed art forever. Artists ever since have tried to capture that air of the rebel artist defying convention and snobbery. But that unique era, the same decade in which Nietzsche exploded into prominence, can't be replicated. The impressionist art movement had little immediate effect on philosophy, but it served as a backdrop for a general skepticism about cultural conventions, a skepticism that fully blossomed in the 1960s.

JACQUES DERRIDA

Derrida (1930–2004) was born of Jewish ancestry in French-occupied Algeria. He originally studied phenomenology, and he came to prominence in 1959 by using Husserl to critique structuralism (see Chapter 22). Derrida emphasized the thread of Husserl's thought that sought to understand phenomena by identifying the processes and events that led to them. Derrida's simple question was this: If there is an all-encompassing structure as structuralists supposed, what led to it? Any structure has to have a genesis that itself had to have its own structure in order to be the genesis of something else. Change had to come from a complex structure, what Derrida called an "original complexity" capable of generating change. He used this idea of original complexity in multiple applications. One was to expose the central flaw of structuralism as its assumption of a transcendental constant signifying system. In other words, within the structuralist approach, the answer to all questions is "the structure." Structuralists didn't see this as a problem, but Derrida did.

Derrida's conclusion was that despite its positive contributions to understanding cultural myths, Structuralism suffered from a pretension of reason that had plagued the whole history of philosophy. Derrida called this the "myth of presence." His concept is best understood as pointing to the false idea that there is a central presence that is given or fixed and that anchors the rest of the structure. The center was whatever the philosopher or school of thought assumed was the foundation of certainty on which the rest of the philosophical inquiry or system was built. Examples include Plato's Forms, Aristotle's substance, Descartes' thinking self, Newton's material particles, and so on. The center serves the useful function of orienting, balancing, and organizing the structure, but, Derrida claims, it mostly serves to anchor thought and language in the center, limiting what he calls the "play" of the structure. Derrida uses "play" to describe openness to unexplored possibilities and new approaches. Another effect of fixing the center is that it sets up binary oppositions defined in terms of good/bad, right/wrong. These oppositions are used to repress and marginalize that which differs from the center or foundation that is considered good and right. People, especially women, people of color, the poor, and so on, are deemed bad and wrong. Derrida thus favors an abandonment of the reassuring foundation of the center and an affirmation of play or openness. This decentering he calls "deconstruction," a deliberate play on the pretensions of structuralism.

For Derrida, deconstruction means rejecting the myth of the center or foundation and exposing and dismantling any philosophical constructs that depend on foundationalism or binary oppositions. This deconstruction of philosophy, he hoped, would reveal that which has been repressed and marginalized. In turn, that means accepting that there is no certainty and no possibility of finding any. Derrida took this line of thought to a set of radical conclusions about texts. There are no meanings to the language we invent, and everything is interpretation, he declared. He means this in terms of understanding texts, not morality or scientific truths, asserting that there is nothing that is out of context. A text must be understood within its context, but because there are no transcendental meanings of language, language cannot refer to anything beyond itself. All words receive their meaning from distinctions within the language. This is not as weird as it may at first sound because if you look up the meaning of a word in a dictionary, you find that the word is defined by other words.

This being the case, Derrida says that there are no limits to the play of meanings and interpretations that a reader can bring to a text, which implies that the author is less important, an implication that Derrida accepts, even in his own books. He endorsed the thesis of Frenchman Roland Barthes' (pronounced BART) book *The Death of the Author* (1967), which rejected the traditional idea of incorporating the author's intentions when interpreting a text. That would assign a single interpretation to the text: the author's. The text's meaning lies with the reader. The creator and the creation must be considered separate, Barthes said, and Derrida agreed.

The problem for Derrida and all deconstructionists is that believing the assertions that there are no author, no rational subject, and no fixed meaning to anything leaves the believer with no basis or justification for a critique of philosophy and society at large. If one wants to stand up for subaltern people who are repressed and marginalized by the "myth of presence," one must be able to appeal to some source of validity for the claims that repression is wrong and rectification of justice is good. Deconstruction offers the tools to tear down pretensions but not the tools to build up the good.

MICHEL FOUCAULT

French philosopher and historian Michel Foucault (pronounced FOO-koh, 1926–1984) is a central figure in postmodernism. His most influential books, all published in the 1960s, are *Madness and Civilization*, *The Birth of the Clinic: An Archaeology of Medical Perception*, *The Order of Things: An Archaeology of the Human Sciences*, and *The Archaeology of Knowledge*. He saw his postmodernist task as being an archaeologist digging beneath the surface of our social-intellectual traditions to expose the strata—which he called "*épistémès*," the Greek word for "knowledges"—of historical eras that led to our current "knowledge." Each *épistémè* is the dominant conceptual framework of a given historical era, that era's definition of "truth"—"a system of ordered procedures for the production, regulation, distribution, circulation and operation of statements." Throughout history, each era's truth is the product of that particular historical era. Foucault insists that the modernist notion of one, universal truth belongs to the *épistémè* of an earlier era and is no longer viable for our postmodern era.

Foucault considered an *épistémè* to consist of structured linguistic or discursive patterns. The particular patterns that Foucault is interested in are those that society had awarded the status of truth and were used to control that society. His archaeological approach looks at the normative discourses of medicine, psychiatry, law, and morality to expose the dominant discursive practices of an era. These discursive patterns define what is permissible and impermissible for people to say, what questions are meaningful, and how human behaviors are to be described. These patterns define social reality and indicate how the world should be divided into categories such as true/false, moral/immoral, rational/irrational, madness/sanity, and normal/perverse.

Foucault applies this idea of discursive patterns to the meanings of words themselves. The meaning of a word is not the object to which it refers because words don't really refer to objects as much as they constitute them. Similar to Wittgenstein in his later philosophy, Foucault said that words receive their meaning from their role within the network of social discourse and practices. To understand the meaning of a word, you can't point to a certain object or action. Instead, you have to understand the complex network of words and practices of the *épistémè* in which the word occurs. True to the emerging postmodernist tradition, Foucault says there is no universal, objective meaning of words. Their meaning is part of the world of social institutions and ideals within a historical era. Words don't literally create a tree, but we know a tree as the sort of thing that it is in terms of a network of social meanings.

Reversing the modernist assumption that philosophers' ideas create society, Foucault claimed that the system of social structures (*épistémè*) determines our ideas. The Enlightenment *épistémè* created the Enlightenment intellectuals; the intellectuals did not create their age. Foucault says that the discursive practices of a society are governed by "rules of production." These rules aren't consciously invented and are never explicitly expounded but are part of an unconscious play of forces within each historical era. We can understand these rules, Foucault said, by "decoding" their patterns. Through this decoding, we can expose as an illusion the notion that human institutions and history exhibit rationality and continuity. Instead, he claimed, we see that history is an aimless sequence of ruptures, displacements, transformations, and gaps as socially created institutions and *épistémès* rise and fall without order or reason.

After the violent May 1968 French general strike against capitalist imperialism, Foucault turned his attention to the role of power structures in society. His thinking shifted from placing discourse as primary in the constitution of social reality to seeing discourse as merely one product of the ever-expanding institutionalized social power structures. His focus also shifts from "archaeology" to "genealogy." Nietzsche used the word "genealogy" to describe how the will to power expressed itself in covert ways, and Foucault had a similar idea. Foucault invents the term "power-knowledge" to indicate that power and knowledge directly imply one another. He claimed that there is no power relation without the correlative constitution of a field of knowledge, nor is there any knowledge that does not presuppose and constitute power relations. From this, Foucault concludes, similar to the way Marx does, that intellectual history is nothing more than a demonstration of the ways in which the conception of truth has been used by power structures to mask the will to power that always operates just beneath the surface. Each society, Foucault said, has its own régime of truth, its 'general politics' of discourse which it accepts and makes function as truth.

Foucault's increasingly political philosophy has inspired a number of later philosophers. His emphasis on power structures seems to duplicate much of the structuralist program, but Foucault is correctly seen as a fierce critic of those structures, one who is unearthing how those structures are used to oppress people. He goes beyond descriptions of structure to an analysis of the power inherent in the structure. His analysis weighs very heavily on how social institutions and the prevailing *épistémè* use power to control and discipline people's minds and bodies. Similar to, if not inspired by, analytical Marxism's theory of power relations (see Chapter 22), Foucault's theory saw power as an all-encompassing set of social relations used by the ruling class to maintain inequality.

In his 1975 study, *Discipline and Punish: The Birth of the Prison*, he used the evolution of the architecture, policies, and practices of prisons in the 1800s to illustrate how the mechanisms of power and control evolved. Foucault referenced historical documents to show how the same "technologies of control" employed in prison systems were mirrored in the organization of armies, schools, hospitals, and factories. All of these institutions exercised new mechanisms of power and control under the disguise of scientific, enlightened, humanitarian social reforms. Through its régimes of truth, society's power structures impose their historically relative truths on people, inventing labels such as "criminals," "students," "patients," and "workers" to divide them into categories such as moral/immoral, sane/mad, and normal/perverse. One of Foucault's examples of how power relations use these labels is from his own life as a homosexual person—all his life he was told he was immoral, mad, and perverse for being who he was.

JEAN-FRANÇOIS LYOTARD

French philosopher and sociologist, Lyotard (1924–1998) was a fierce critic of universalizing theories and "metanarratives" (narratives about narratives). He portrayed postmodernism as essentially antagonistic against modernism and as the savior of humanity against modernism. In his book, *The Postmodern Condition: A Report on Knowledge* (1979), he proclaimed that we have outgrown our need for metanarratives or grand narratives. Metanarratives are—grand totalizing theories and explanations about why everything is the way it is. Hegel, Marx, and structuralists (and perhaps even Foucault) all offered metanarratives. They are also found more subtlety in widespread assumptions like the idea that science will provide us with all knowledge. Lyotard claimed that people have lost faith in these grand narratives and are forced to find new, smaller narratives to address social issues. His idea is similar to Nietzsche's idea that "God is dead" (see Chapter 17). The old stories are no longer believed, and society is now fractured as people search for knowledge and meaning.

For Lyotard, the fracturing of metanarratives is what postmodernism is. He took the *post* in postmodern very seriously. We are moving out of modernism. What we are moving into, Lyotard said, is the postmodern awareness that we are not all the same and that the grand narratives don't describe most of us. We have become aware of our differences and are beginning to accept the reality of human diversity. The shift from modernity to postmodernity is a shift from metanarratives to micronarratives. To explain micronarratives, Lyotard uses Wittgenstein's concept of language-games (see Chapter 20), though Lyotard prefers the term "phrase regimens", which he uses to map society's diversity. Human society is not the monoculture that is portrayed by the grand narratives. Society is a multiplicity of communities, and each community has its own language-game of the meanings and rules it has developed. The grand narrative of human progress and human emancipation favors the wealthy and powerful but does not offer progress and emancipation to all communities. Those communities have to develop their own understandings about the meanings of morality.

Lyotard's postmodern theory of justice takes on how the loss of faith in grand narratives affects the narrative that morality is universal. Kant had encapsulated the view that for moral laws to be meaningful, they had to apply universally—the Categorical Imperative (see Chapter 16). Lyotard acknowledges this long-held view of moral laws and that the loss of grand narratives would seem to call morality itself into question. Issues of justice and injustice are concepts within language-games, and if language-games are diverse, reflecting social diversity, then the concepts of justice and injustice must also be diverse. Concepts of justice and injustice remain in postmodernity, but we now can see (should see) that injustice includes imposing the rules of one language-game onto another. Morality requires being aware of this threat of injustice.

Lyotard explains this threat of injustice through his term "differend," coined in his 1983 book, *The Differend: Phrases in Dispute*. Differend is when the language-game of the dominant power structure denies other communities the language to express the injustices they experience. Lyotard's prime example was Holocaust denier Robert Faurisson, who took the logically contradictory position that the only person who can legitimately testify to the existence of gas chambers is somebody who actually died in one. Faurisson was using this fallacious reasoning to negate discussion of the injustice of the Holocaust. Another example Lyotard gave was a court case in which the judge does not allow one party to state its case. The concept of the differend extends into more general social circumstances of language use within popular culture when victims of injustice lack the language to express their victimization. Here, Lyotard lays some groundwork for the later concept of "epistemic injustice"—the silencing and exclusion of people to the extent that their own understandings are distorted. We'll see a fuller explanation of epistemic injustice in Chapter 25.

Lyotard explains how the differend deprives victims of language by rejecting the common notion that the meaning of a word or phrase is determined by that to which it refers. This notion is the pairing of signifier and signified we've seen in both pragmatism and analytical philosophy. Lyotard counters that the meaning of a phrase cannot be fixed by the reality of the signified. This is because reality does not conform to modernity's narrative that reality is fixed and objective. Similar to Wittgenstein in his idea that the meanings of language come from its use, Lyotard says the meanings of phrases come from a set of complex interactions. Every phrase exists in a context, has a number of possible significations, a speaker/writer, and those to whom the phrase is addressed. There is a certain degree of play (in Derrida's sense of "play") for interpreting any phrase, so its meaning is ambiguous. Our various phrase regimens—knowing, describing, recounting, questioning, showing, ordering, and so on—have meanings and rules for linking phrases within the phrase regimens that cannot be wholly translated to other phrase regimens of discourse.

There is also a political dimension to the meaning of a word or phrase. A community in power can use the phrase regimen of a grand narrative to colonize and silence other communities. Colonialism is the perfect example, as are the many ways that the rich dictate meaning to the poor. In so doing, the community in power can silence discourse by using the ambiguity of meaning, thereby forcing its interpretation on others, denying diversity, and causing injustice. It is possible for people in different communities and phrase regimens to find links between their diverse rules and meanings, but this requires the willingness of all sides to do so.

JEAN BAUDRILLARD

Yet another French postmodern philosopher (France was the hotbed of postmodernism from the 1960s through the 1980s) was Jean Baudrillard (1929–2007). Baudrillard (bo-dree-AR) could be classified more as a social critic than as a philosopher. His philosophy was based on the life of signs and how technology affects people and society. In three books, *The System of Objects* (1968), *The Consumer Society* (1970), and *For a Critique of the Political Economy of the Sign* (1972), Baudrillard combined the philosophy of semiology with French sociologist Henri Lefebvre's (1901–1991) critique of everyday life. Lefebvre (le-FEV), a Marxist, argued that capitalism had colonized everyday life and had turned it into a zone of consumption, pushing people to believe that they needed to relieve the boredom of everydayness through purchasing products or experiences. Lefebvre had also shown how space is a complex social construction based on social values, and he considered capitalism to be the dominant social value that produces social space.

Baudrillard thought that Lefebvre's Marxist critique of the everyday life had some merit but was insufficient and needed to be enhanced by a theory of signs. Baudrillard accepted that signs are an integral part of society because they articulate meanings and are organized into systems of meaning. He saw that commodities should be characterized not strictly through their use and exchange value, as Marx had said, but by their "sign-value." For example, the value of a luxury watch lies more in its sign-value as an expression of prestige, wealth, and style than in its "use-value" as a timekeeping device or its monetary exchange value. In everyday life, people purchase and display their commodities as much for their sign-value as for their use-value. This insight from Baudrillard is even more true now, decades later, as consumerism is increasingly dominated by the sign-values of brand loyalty and the need to be "on trend."

Presaging developments in the early 2000s is Baudrillard's notion of the "simulacra" and the "real." He sees as fundamental to the rupture between modernity and postmodernity that modern societies are organized around commodities but that postmodern societies are organized around simulation and play. He laid out in his 1981 book, *Simulation and Simulacra*, that we are ruled by simulation. Identities and meanings are constructed by the appropriation of cultural signs—images, codes, and models—that determine how we view ourselves; how others view us; and, therefore, how we relate to each other. Baudrillard broke with the Marxist grand narrative that social class differentiated boundaries between people. That was true in modernity, but in the postmodern world, differentiation by class, gender, politics, economics, culture, and sexuality are imploding under the force of simulation. Baudrillard said that people have so much access to signs, which are exchanged so freely, that differences between groups collapse amid the dissolving social boundaries and structures on which society is built and on which social theory is focused.

Electronic media and digital technologies propel this transformation. They deliver a constant stream of signs and references to viewers without any consequences to them. For example, the top-grossing film in 1980, the year Baudrillard was developing his theory, was *The Empire Strikes Back*. Millions watched the film, but none of it was real. The death and destruction on-screen had no consequences for the viewers, yet the images and signs of the film excited people into a state of what Baudrillard called "hyperreality," in which entertainment provides experiences more intense and involving than the realities of everyday life. We see how common it is for people to identify themselves by their fandoms of television shows or music artists. From amusement parks, to shopping malls, to television shows, to video games, to social media, the images, codes, and models of hyperreality are more real to people than real life is. Real life is a desert compared with the fantasylands offered by simulation.

The postmodern person is awash in simulacra. Baudrillard defines the simulacrum as the truth that conceals that there is no truth; the simulacrum is true. Human society has always had signs that mediated reality for us—that's what words are (hello, William). Now in the postmodern world, society has replaced reality with signs, and our human experience is a simulation composed of simulacra. Postmodern life is a procession of simulacra—all of culture's images, codes, and models that construct our perceived reality—and our society is so saturated with simulacra that meaning is infinitely mutable to the point that meaning is now meaningless. Now, wait one moment and understand something important here. As I write this in 2021, people debate the effects of virtual reality, computer simulations, and deepfake videos. These are *not* what Baudrillard was talking about 40 years ago. He's talking about the broader cultural forces of which these new simulation technologies are simply expressions.

Virtual reality is an extension of television and films, which immerse viewers in simulacra. Television at best shows us copies of reality. Watching television, we don't see the U.S. president giving a speech; we see an image of that person. That's not in itself problematic, but when the copy on screen is unfaithful to the underlying reality, it obscures what's real. The image before us is what's real for us. If the image is fictional, maybe a TV drama about a real U.S. president that has an actor pretending to be that person, it is a copy divergent from an original, even though it pretends to be a faithful copy. Then there's the pure simulacrum—perhaps a TV show about an entirely fictional president. In these images, signs reflect other signs without any claim to reality. The simulacra of the president are what is real and become more familiar and real to viewers than the actual president. Sounds far-fetched? Well, a 2015 opinion poll found that the fictional president of the TV show, "The West Wing," had a higher favorability rating than the actual U.S. president, Barack Obama.

Baudrillard's notion of the simulacra isn't just limited to the realm of entertainment. Their more pernicious appearances are in advertising and political propaganda. We are besieged by advertising, and Baudrillard is dead on in describing it as simulacra that at best pretend to be real but more often present a completely manufactured set of signs that is connected only to other signs. Advertising sells a fake world, a hyperreality in which things are better than everyday life; all you have to do is purchase what the simulacra are selling. Political propaganda similarly provides signs that are conjured up to seem to be connected with reality but are engineered to deceive. Today, some people talk about us living in a "post-truth" society. Baudrillard observed in the 1980s that simulacra have always existed. What differs now is that there is only the simulation, only copies of copies, and originality is a meaningless concept in our society.

On the one hand, it is almost eerie how Baudrillard's ideas seem much more true now than when he proposed them. Baudrillard mentions the "ecstasy of communication," a state in which a person has close instantaneous access to a plethora of information and images. In this state of ecstasy, a person becomes a pure screen. The person is pure absorption, a surface on which is shown an overexposed, transparent world of simulacra. Baudrillard expressed these thoughts before the Internet, before smartphones, before advanced video games.

On the other hand, it is easy to criticize Baudrillard's claim that postmodernity would result in differentiation imploding as partly naive. He was correct that electronic media and digital technologies have brought about much easier sharing of cultural and intellectual ideas. Concepts of cultural identity and gender are more fluid than ever, but differentiation of categories of class and race are still sharply drawn.

RICHARD RORTY

American Richard Rorty (1931–2007) became disillusioned with analytical philosophy's pursuit of finding universal foundations of knowledge, and he adopted pragmatism. Rorty is the epitome of the open-minded philosopher willing to listen to and take wisdom from other philosophers. John Dewey (see Chapter 18) is his main influence, but he also takes seriously Wittgenstein's later philosophy (see Chapter 20) and Heidegger's (see Chapter 21). Rorty said that the main problem of modern and analytical epistemology was the assumption that the mind is trying to mirror external reality faithfully. A second, related problem is the attempt to find a foundation of all knowledge—beliefs that are not justified by other beliefs but are self-justifying. Rorty rejects both of these ideas, saying that we will understand knowledge when we understand the social justification of belief. When we do that, we will have no need to judge perception on the accuracy of mental depictions. Accepting the social justification of our beliefs allows us to see knowledge as a product of conversational social practice rather than as attempts to mirror nature. He calls this idea "epistemological behaviorism," claiming it is the view adopted by Dewey and the later Wittgenstein.

Rorty applied his epistemological behaviorism in ways that puzzled other philosophers. He dismissed science as being the business of controlling and predicting objects thereby making science largely useless for philosophy. He said that philosophers have made a mistake in trying to imitate scientific methods. Science's success in describing objects does not translate to philosophy. He also claimed that there is no worthwhile theory of truth aside from a narrow formal logic unconnected to epistemology. Rorty instead developed a vision of human community bound together not by abstract foundational ideas like the justice of a common humanity but by a shared opposition to cruelty. He does not offer the belief that cruelty is horrible as a foundational belief but as a behavior justified by our social experience. We cannot give a clear reason why cruelty is wrong, but we don't need one. It is what we feel—shades of Hume's moral sentiments (see Chapter 12).

Rorty's idea of the proper political mindset is what he calls "ironism." He says the ironist fully understand she has been socialized into certain understandings, but society may have given her the wrong understandings and the wrong language to discuss them. Nevertheless, the ironist combines the contingency of her beliefs with a commitment to reduce cruelty and suffering. The ironist mindset is consistent with epistemological behaviorism in that it rejects the rationalist, foundationalist mindsets of conservatism (including totalitarianism) and radicalism (including Marxism). Rorty advocates incremental reforms, not the extreme conflict and sweeping changes demanded by radicalism. At the core of Rorty's political ironism is the acceptance that one's own perspective has no universality; therefore one must persuade others not by arguments but by conversations that expand the vocabularies of all participants.

CHAPTER 24

CONTINENTAL SOCIAL PHILOSOPHY

We saw several analytical approaches to political philosophy in Chapter 22. In this chapter, we will look at some continental approaches. A common argument against analytical philosophy is that it does not challenge prevailing power structures. All of the philosophers in this chapter thought it necessary to describe oppressive power structures and provide alternatives to them, so they adopted the approach of process rather than positivism (see Chapter 19) in social and political philosophy. We earlier saw the rise of modern political philosophy in the 1600s and 1700s (see Chapter 9), but by the early 1900s, human society had changed significantly, as had ways to think about it.

Multiple factors influenced social and political philosophy in the 1900s. One influence was the second industrial revolution of the late 1800s, sparked by technical advances in steel, chemicals, petroleum products, and electricity. Society was transformed to an even greater degree than it had been during the first industrial revolution of the late 1700s. The transformation was most keenly felt in capitalism, which expanded and strengthened, instead of collapsing as Marx had predicted.

The political philosophy of Karl Marx was also a major influence, as was the Bolshevik Revolution in Russia, eventually creating the Soviet Union, which described its ideology as Marxism–Leninism but which became a totalitarian state more akin to fascist dictatorship than a workers' revolution. Some philosophers criticized the Soviets for not following Marxism, as we shall see. By the 1920s, the fact that capitalism was now stronger than ever forced those who agreed with Marx's critique of capitalism to figure out why it had not collapsed as Marx had said it would.

Philosophers also had to deal with the rise of fascism in the 1920s and 1930s. For various reasons, Europeans had been optimistic that science, technology, and increased communication and social freedoms would lead society into more reasonable and peaceful forms. Instead, an unimaginable darkness descended over Europe. The Nazis and their regime of terror directly affected several of the philosophers in this chapter. Everyone had to deal with fascism in one way or another.

Phenomenology and existentialism (see Chapter 21) had brought to the fore the importance of how individuals perceive and live their lives. This awareness ushered in a shift from political philosophy—macrostructures of governments and nations—to social philosophy—the structures of life as lived by groups and individuals.

MARTIN BUBER—I AND YOU

Martin Buber (1878–1965) was an Austrian Jewish existentialist and interpreter of Jewish spiritual traditions. Buber was greatly influenced by Kierkegaard and Nietzsche (see Chapter 17), but he belongs in this chapter because he gave existentialism a decidedly social dimension very different from the negative views of Heidegger or Sartre.

Buber's masterpiece was his German-language book *Ich und Du* (1923), the title of which is also Buber's central philosophical concept. The book's title and concept have always been translated into English as "I and Thou," which is technically correct, but truly to understand Buber's meaning, we need a short German lesson. German, like many other European languages, has a formal "you" and an informal "you." "*Du*" is the informal "you" and is used to address people you know well, signifying equality or a closer relationship. "*Sie*" is the formal "you," which acknowledges a more distant or formal relationship. Buber's use of *du* is significant. The English "thou" seems formal, largely because of its use in antiquated biblical translations, but is actually a very old form of the informal "you" from when English made that distinction. "You" might be an easier modern translation of *du*, especially as Buber uses it, but because you will see it written everywhere else as "I and Thou," I will keep with that convention.

Buber said that there are two ways in which we as the "I" can address existence. We can address something as an "It," signifying it is an object separate from us. We can also address something as a "Thou" (*Du*), signifying we are in relationship with another rather than separate from an "It." For these two attitudes, Buber uses the shorthand of "I-It" and "I-Thou." We have an I-It attitude when we deal with particular objects. They are an It to us, an object we perceive and experience. We have an I-Thou attitude when we have a living relationship with something or someone. The I-Thou relationship is sustained as long as the mind of the "I" is predominantly feeling or thinking of the other with that attitude. That means that we can have an I-Thou attitude toward an inanimate object. Buber gives the example of experiencing a tree not merely as a discrete object drawn from a set of objects but experiencing the tree as being in relationship with the tree. Your attitude toward the tree is one of open participation, a melting of the separation between the "I" and the tree, the tree becoming another "I." That may sound a little odd, but think of it as how we can relate to things, especially beautiful things like a tree, with a positive attitude of openness to it—not thinking of it as a distant object but rather feeling it intimately. We all relate to objects in this way sometimes.

There is a readily apparent morality to these two attitudes when it comes to dealing with other people. If we treat another person as a mere object, the I-It attitude, then we are not giving that person his or her due. When we think dismissively about someone else, we objectify the person, turning the person into an It. This impersonal attitude produces possibilities for using and abusing other people. When instead we open up to a relationship and dialogue with another person, that is the I-Thou attitude, and we are seeing and listening the person as the person is. Buber saw the I-Thou relationship as a symmetrical co-presence. The other person becomes another "I" same as we are. There need not be actual intimacy in this relation; we may not even talk to the other person. The positive attitude, even if it is just to people in general, is enough to form the I-Thou relationship. Every thought and action we have attaches our "I" to the other. The question is whether we remain separate from the person on the I-It attitude or enter into an I-Thou relationship with the person. In the I-Thou attitude, we are communicating instead of ignoring, valuing instead of dismissing. It is easy to see which attitude promotes justice.

NEO-MARXISM

A large number of philosophers can be called neo-Marxists. What they had in common was the desire to separate Marxism from the distorted version practiced by the Soviet Union. Beyond that common ground, there has been a bewildering array of different theories, emphasizing different aspects or outgrowths of Marx's ideas. Neo-Marxist philosophies include historicist, scientific, analytical, and sociological Marxism, all competing for the label of the "real" Marxist theory and often with antagonism for each other. All but lost in the ideological jostling were a few democratic socialists, like Rosa Luxemburg (1871–1919). She placed the honor and voice of the workers in the center of neo-Marxist thought, calling for a revolutionary socialist democracy in which workers had a direct voice in government, instead of the Leninist one-party totalitarianism under the guise of revolution. Luxemburg was killed by a paramilitary unit amidst a failed workers' uprising in Germany in 1919.

In the historicist camp was Hungarian György Lukács (1885–1971). He wanted to return Marxism to its totalizing vision of historical determinism. He agreed with most of Marx's economic analysis but said that, ultimately, it is not economic motives that drive history and class consciousness but the all-pervasive supremacy of the totality over all its parts. He saw capitalism as an objective totality of social relations in which the bourgeoisie is not conscious of the transitory character of capitalism. Only the proletariat, who receive no benefit from capitalism and no interest in its continuance, can see the reality that capitalism is doomed for what it is. Lukács was involved in the failed Hungarian Soviet Republic of 1919, but he survived and continued to be involved in revolutionary activity and then involved in government when the Soviets took over Hungary in the late 1940s. Marx's early writings on alienation were uncovered and translated by Lukács, who in 1932 published them as "Economic and Philosophic Manuscripts of 1844."

A sociological Marxist was Italian Antonio Gramsci (1891–1937) who introduced perhaps the most important concept in neo-Marxism: cultural hegemony. Marx and most Marxist theorists had seen the bourgeoisie as maintaining control through political and economic coercion. Gramsci extended this idea of coercion to all of culture. Capitalism was maintained by the hegemony of bourgeois ideology in cultural institutions. Marx had mentioned this, but Gramsci moved it to the forefront of social critique. The bourgeoisie propagate their values through their control of the press, the education system, and the arts. Their values become "common sense," and the proletariat learns to associate their good with the good of the bourgeoisie. Bourgeois culture and values have hegemony throughout society.

Gramsci and others could now explain why the proletariat had not revolted: More than economic factors were at work. This concept allowed Gramsci to develop a view of emancipation from capitalism not dependent on the fatalism of economic determinism. Influenced by Henri Bergson (see Chapter 19), Gramsci accepted that there were forces beyond the material. This informed his idea of cultural hegemony and his division of society into the political (police, military, legislative, and judicial systems) and the civil (family, trade unions, and other forms of social activism). He proposed that the working class develop a counter-hegemony, a working-class culture that would develop alternative values to bourgeois ideology. Working-class people were not stupid, he stressed; they can organically grow their own intellectuals. Organic intellectuals will not be separate from the people, as the intelligentsia too often are, and won't reduce society to scientific rules, but will, in dialogue with the working class, help them develop ways to articulate their feelings. Gramsci saw it as a duty of intellectuals to speak for those who are excluded from the cultural hegemony. He introduced the term "subaltern" to describe the segment of society that is denied agency and a voice in society. Gramsci died in prison, a victim of Benito Mussolini's brutal fascist suppression of intellectual freedom.

THE FRANKFURT SCHOOL

Gramsci wasn't exactly an optimist, but he seems one compared with the pessimism of the Frankfurt School. The most prominent members of the Frankfurt School were Germans Max Horkheimer (1895–1973), Theodor Adorno (1903–1969), and Herbert Marcuse (1898–1979). They were consternated about why capitalism had not collapsed and why the workers' revolutions of 1919 had failed. Like other neo-Marxists, they opposed Soviet totalitarianism and sought a new theoretical basis for emancipating the working class from capitalism. They called their approach "critical theory" because they saw their project as a theoretical critique of society as a whole. Their use of the term "critical theory," a term still used in philosophy, should not be confused with the use of the term in other disciplines, such as literary theory and literary analysis. In the late 1920s, the Frankfurt School developed a system of critique founded on the social sciences. The plan was to use sociology's empirical research methods developed by Max Weber (1864–1920) and Georg Simmel (1858–1918). This interpretative method was deliberately anti-positivist (see Chapter 19) in not reducing social science to logical, deterministic categories but instead trying to understand cultural groups on their own terms and from their own points of view. They did, however, bring to their social science the assumptions of Hegel's historicism (see Chapter 14), Marx's economic theory (see Chapter 15), and the psychoanalytical theory of Sigmund Freud.

The Frankfurt School's program was deeply affected by the rise of the Nazis. Horkheimer, Adorno, and Marcuse were all Jewish, and they were fortunate enough to be able to flee Germany shortly after the Nazis came to power. Horkheimer and Adorno found academic refuge at Columbia University in New York City. While there, they wrote *Dialectic of Enlightenment* (1944), a deeply Hegelian take on Marxism. In their view, historical determinism had led not to the collapse of capitalism but rather to its strengthening in new forms of domination—fascism and state capitalism—that amounted to a one-party police state. Like Gramsci, Horkheimer and Adorno saw society as being dominated by bourgeois culture, but unlike Gramsci, they were fatalistic about the prospects of overcoming the cultural hegemony. Horkheimer and Adorno condemned fascism, but they said that its state capitalism had abolished the competitive tensions in market capitalism. Marx had said that those tensions among capitalist producers and the demands that capitalist production places on labor and raw materials were contradictions that would bring down capitalism. This prediction had obviously failed, and from Horkheimer's and Adorno's perspective as German Jews, who had lived through the failed workers' revolutions of 1919, fascism had "won." Their task then was to explain why.

Dialectic of Enlightenment was their attempt to answer the "why?" question, an attempt more scattershot than precise. They prudently rejected totalizing theories, such as those in positivism and the yet-to-come structuralism, and instead drew on a variety of sources, but primarily they combined Marx's historicism and Freud's theory of repression of human drives. What they came up with was that historical determinism had produced the modern culture industry, the method authoritarianism used to manipulate and dominate the masses, repressing their independence and agency. They pointed to the rise of technological methods of culture dissemination, most notably radio, that assimilated people into a mass consciousness dominated by the bourgeoisie. Again, this is similar to Gramsci's idea of cultural hegemony, but Horkheimer and Adorno saw no way out, alluding only to a vague notion of gradual cultural awareness.

Adorno doubled down on this pessimism in his solo book, *Minima Moralia* (1951). Adorno saw historical determinism as an overwhelming objectivity that has ended the subject (his word for "person"). The subject still thinks of itself as autonomous but has been historically condemned and nullified by the concentration camp. Adorno saw the Nazi concentration camps as emblematic of the despair of the time. There is no poetry after Auschwitz, he declared, and the possibility of progress is now in doubt. Adorno turned his back on the promise of the working class's redemption within Marxism, declaring that the reality or unreality of redemption or human emancipation hardly matters. All was despair for Adorno, even music, which he declared in *The Philosophy of Modern Music* (1949) was a tool of the culture industry that saw absolute oblivion as its goal. His only answer was what he called a "negative dialectic," a negation of existing cultural forms among small groups of men (his gender-exclusive language). He also saw these small groups as determined by history, which fates certain individuals and certain arts to hold out the possibility of future truth.

Adorno's cynical condemnation of nearly everything, and his notion that only a select few chosen by history can fully discern what's happening, has appealed to some, but Adorno has been widely criticized. Lyotard rejected Adorno's negative dialectic, saying Adorno was seeking a therapeutic resolution in the framework of a religion of history. Lukács accused Adorno of inhabiting the Grand Hotel Abyss, equipped with comfort, perched on the edge of the abyss of absurdity, and contemplating that abyss. Axel Honneth (see later in this chapter) said Adorno's historical-philosophical negativism was a failure of critical theory. Honneth and Emmanuel Habermas (see later in this chapter) are considered a second generation of critical theory related to but separate from the Horkheimer and Adorno generation.

HANNAH ARENDT—AGAINST TOTALITARIANISM

Arendt (1906–1975) is most famous for her book, *Eichmann in Jerusalem: A Report on the Banality of Evil* (1963), her report of the trial of Nazi war criminal Adolf Eichmann. Her philosophical views expressed in that book, however, were formed much earlier. At the University of Marburg, Germany, when only 17, Arendt began a long romantic relationship with Martin Heidegger, 18 years her senior. They kept their relationship completely secret, and it wasn't discovered until 1982 when Arendt's biographer discovered their hidden correspondence. Heidegger's philosophy was a major influence on hers, as was the philosophy of Karl Jaspers (see Chapter 21), who was the advisor on Arendt's doctoral dissertation, entitled "On the Concept of Love in the Thought of Saint Augustine," and with whom she remained friends for the rest of his life. She was also influenced by the movement of Romanticism, though more by its literary side than its philosophical side.

Being a German Jew, Arendt had believed in Jewish assimilation into mainstream culture, but the rise of the Nazis forced her to radical action. She used her home as a way station to help those persecuted by the Nazis (socialists, Jews, Marxists, and others) to escape the country—like the American Underground Railroad that helped people escape enslavement in the 1800s. She wrote essays opposing the Nazis and became involved in Jewish political resistance until she was arrested at a state library in 1933 for conducting "illegal" research—namely, the extent of Nazi anti-Semitism. She was released to await trial, but realizing she had little hope for a future in Germany, she and her mother fled using the underground escape route she had helped others to use. She later only narrowly escaped the Nazi occupation of France and was one of the fortunate few helped to emigrate to the United States.

The Nazi tyranny deeply affected her personally and philosophically. Her book, *The Origins of Totalitarianism* (1951), took aim at what she called this "novel form of government." She argued that totalitarianism differs from despotism, tyranny, and dictatorship in its use of terror to subjugate mass populations instead of subjugating only political adversaries. Totalitarianism also seeks to control all aspects of society as a prelude to world domination, whereas autocratic regimes seek only regional political power. This led her to the claim that the operative factor of Nazi terror was not the Jewish populations—they were merely a convenient excuse for the general Nazi practice of subjugation. Arendt's highly controversial claim is supported by the fact that the Nazi concentration camps were initially built not for Jewish people but for leftist political activists. That fact, however, calls into question Arendt's theoretical division between totalitarianism and other forms of autocracy. There is no denying that the Nazis hated and murdered both their political adversaries and the Jewish people. Arendt in no way diminishes the anti-Semitism of the Nazis but places it into the wider historical context of the marginalization of minority populations, including colonialism. It is true that Jewish people had long suffered persecution in Europe, and it would be wrong to say that Naziism was a specifically anti-Jewish movement. Still, it is a dubious claim made by Arendt that, because Judaism was associated with the nation-state, the Nazis exploited general hatred of the Jewish people as a proxy for their real target, the nation-state.

On firmer ground is Arendt's claim that totalitarianism seeks to eliminate the intellectual, spiritual, and artistic initiative of the individual. She considered the persecution of intellectuals, religious leaders, and artists by both Nazi Germany and Stalinist Russia as springing from their resentment of everything they could not understand. Total domination of society cannot allow people to have free creative initiative because creative energies are not predictable. Totalitarianism, preferring predictable mediocrity, persecutes all who show talent and initiative and replaces them with crackpots and fools because those with a lack of intelligence and ingenuity are the most likely to stay loyal to the regime.

No doubt, it was Arendt's conception of the uncreative, unintelligent functionary within the totalitarian state apparatus that led her to see Adolf Eichmann in that way. In *Eichmann in Jerusalem*, she wrote that he was an unthinking dutiful functionary who was "terribly and terrifyingly normal." She concluded that evil isn't always radical; it can also be simply a function of thoughtlessness. Totalitarianism exploits the tendency of ordinary people to conform willingly to mass opinion and obey orders. Such behavior is easier for people than critically evaluating the consequences of their actions. This allows evil to become banal—something normalized as acceptable behavior. She described Eichmann as a human example of the banality of evil—a bureaucrat who facilitated horrific crimes because he found meaning and importance within the Nazi movement.

In her book, *The Human Condition* (1958), Arendt argued that people develop within the social realm more than within the political realm. Showing Jasper's influence, she outlines a view of the human condition as one of existential and aesthetic action. Central to her discussion is her concept of "natality," which she first used in her doctoral dissertation on Augustine that Jaspers oversaw. Natality is in sharp contrast to the pessimism of the obsession with mortality found in later existentialist philosophers like Heidegger and Sartre (see Chapter 21). She says that people are not born in order to die but in order to begin. Natality is the root of the human "faculty of action," by which people can continually find new beginnings. It is a more existential version of Bergson's *élan vital* (see Chapter 19) that generates not only life but also choices in how to live. Arendt identifies two essential human actions: forgiving past wrongs that unfix the fixed past and promising future benefits that fixed the unfixed future.

Furthermore, Arendt distinguishes among labor, work, and action. "Labor" is action directed at biological survival—procuring food and shelter—and is therefore a repetitive, cyclical process with an air of futility. "Work" is different from labor in that it has clearly defined beginnings and endings because work produces durable objects. The concept of work fits both making instrumental tools (like hammers) and creating works of art. "Action" is the ways in which people disclose themselves to each other. Our actions distinguish us as unique people. What we do and what we say establish and communicate our individuality. Unlike labor and work, which are directed at material objects, action is always directed at other people. Action generates human relationships. Action, because it is an expression of an individual, leads to human plurality: individual expression. Arendt notes that philosophers since Plato have disliked and dismissed human plurality, but she considers it a basic human condition that has the twofold character of equality and distinction. Acknowledging the diversity of people allows us to see what is possible in action and to see how action generates a kind of objectivity in the understanding of the ways in which action can be witnessed from different perspectives. Human plurality creates tensions, to be sure, but Arendt's answers to those problems are the two essential actions of forgiveness of the past and promises for the future.

EMMANUEL LEVINAS—THE ETHICS OF THE OTHER

Born in Russian-occupied Lithuania, Emmanuel Levinas (1906–1995) was educated in Germany, where he studied under Husserl. He became a French citizen in 1939. He was Jewish, but because he served in the French army and was captured as a prisoner of war, he avoided the concentration camps. Still, he was imprisoned in a German prisoner of war camp for the duration of the war. His experiences in the camp were formative for his philosophy, though he didn't publish philosophy stemming from those experiences until much later, his first book on it being *Totality and Infinity* in 1961.

Levinas referred to philosophy as "the wisdom of love" rather than "the love of wisdom." Central to Levinas's wisdom of love is the ethics of our encounter with the face of the Other. By "face," he refers both to the literal visible face of another person and the phenomenon of this existential encounter. Husserl (see Chapter 21) had introduced the concept of the Other to describe our encounter with other people. Levinas saw this encounter, and the ethical obligations it places on us, as the starting point for philosophy.

Unlike Buber's symmetrical I-and-Thou relation, Levinas saw the face-to-face encounter as asymmetrical in that the appearance of the face places a demand on us. According to Levinas, the face declares "you shall not kill me," prior to any reaction we may have to the person or that person's request for moral consideration. The face of the Other is "where God passes," according to Levinas, where "God" is not understood in the sense of either the religious lawgiver or the philosophical source of Being or Intellect. Levinas's God is the trace of the divine in every person. To that face, that trace, I owe the Other everything, but the Other owes me nothing. The presence of the face is a divine commandment, but without divine authority. Our ethical relation to it is beyond Being, and we cannot reduce the Other to a thing.

The face of the other person in its defenseless nudity is a passive resistance to my own freedom. It stops me from doing whatever I want to the other person. If this sounds odd, realize that Levinas is identifying a common phenomenon. To deny the ethical obligation that we have to Others, we must first deny their faces. Executioners place a bag or blindfold on the condemned so as not to look on the face. If we think someone is lying to us, we say, "Look me in the eye and say that." When we see someone suffering, we may be tempted to turn away, to not see the face in its suffering. We should see the suffering of Others as a demand on us because ethical responsibility for the Other is embedded in our subjective constitution. In other words, part of what we are as human beings, is to feel sympathy for others.

Levinas separates ethics from morality, terms that usually are synonymous. He took ethics of the Other as that obligation beyond Being, the primary face-to-face encounter. He considered morality to be the set of rules that emerge within social life that address situations among people beyond the face-to-face encounter. Morality can construct rules that deceive us into denying the ethics of the Other, and it is that type of morality against which philosophy must guard us.

JÜRGEN HABERMAS

Habermas (1929-) is a German sociologist and philosopher who originally associated with the Frankfurt School but branched out into other areas of social philosophy. He was influenced by fellow German Hans-Georg Gadamer (1900–2002) who had argued similarly to Heidegger (see Chapter 21) that people are embedded in a particular culture and from that culture have a historically effected consciousness. Gadamer saw the role of philosophy as the interpretation of culture to understand what happens to us over and above what we want and do. Habermas took on that project by seeking to understand communication in culture and how everyday communication affects consciousness.

Habermas's two key concepts are the "public sphere" and "intersubjective communication." In *The Structural Transformation of the Public Sphere* (1962), he departed from a strict Marxist interpretation of history by considering the rise of the public sphere. Habermas saw it as a bourgeois sphere, but not one completely controlled by the ruling powers. Historically, the public sphere grew from the noncapitalist merchant class in the late 1600s (Locke's time, see Chapter 9) as society shifted away from feudalism into a liberal constitutional order. Before then, Habermas said, European culture was dominated by the ruling powers who imposed their views and values on people. The growth in the 1600s and 1700s of printed materials like newspapers and broadsheets and the rise of coffeehouses created the public sphere. This gave the emerging middle class opportunities to learn about and discuss each other's ideas. This social sphere was still dominated by men of some economic means and was, therefore, not an ideal form, but it was a significant historical development. Habermas credits the public sphere for innovations in political philosophy like those of Locke and Rousseau and for the development of liberal constitutional governments. He argued that the public sphere began to decline with the rise of commercial mass media, consumer capitalism, and the post-World War II social welfare state. Habermas said the latter development had good intentions but ended up collapsing the bourgeois public sphere. The historical triumph of consumer culture and mass media serving capitalist interests has stifled rational and critical dialogue. This leads to Habermas's second key concept.

His book, *Theory of Communicative Action* (1981), is an analysis of how our everyday lives are affected by formal social systems and how we can revive the public sphere. Habermas had become pessimistic about the state of society, and this book was his ambitious program to set things right. The book is more a work of sociology than philosophy, but it makes several important philosophical observations. The first is his rejection of the assumption of the primacy of purposive rationality in people's actions. This common positivist, objectivist assumption in philosophy and the social sciences obscures the subjective intentions of human actions. Habermas pushed for a practical, pluralist approach to understanding human behavior that examines intersubjective communication shared among people.

His second observation is the division of social life between the systems of modern capitalist society and the lifeworld of personal everyday life. His two-level concept of society is perhaps his most important concept. As we've seen discussed by a number of philosophers, society is composed of systems that shape human life. Habermas agrees with the general Marxist conception that social systems are dominated by the capitalists and that the political, legal, and media systems serve the capitalists' interests. Habermas adds the lifeworld, using the concept in a manner similar to Husserl's (see Chapter 21), but with greater emphasis on community. He sees the lifeworld as formed by "communicative action"—the cooperative acts taken by individuals within a continual process of deliberation. Communicative actions transmit cultural knowledge, mold new mutual cultural understandings, coordinate individuals in moving toward social integration and solidarity, and continually enable individuals to form their identities. Communicative action forms the lifeworld in which people live and coordinate their behaviors on the basis of consensual norms.

That's Habermas's descriptive definition of communicative action, but he also adds a prescriptive definition in distinguishing communicative action from "strategic action." In strategic action, individual actors are primarily interested in achieving their individual goals rather than in cooperation and mutual benefit. This potentially leads to manipulation and coercion instead of cooperation. The systems of capitalism encourage strategic action. Habermas advocates for communicative action, in which people discuss and coordinate their desires and goals, seeking a shared understanding that their goals are inherently reasonable or worthy. Habermas gives a lengthy discourse on appropriate speech acts that lead toward successful communicative action. The bottom line is that Habermas stresses the importance of the rationality of discourse, in which individuals provide reasons for their speech acts and claims that are open for discussion—both criticism and justification. In this view, communication is judged not by claims of empirical facts—as found in positivism and analytical philosophy—but by where the speech act falls on the spectrum of "validity claims," which are claims that include appeals to moral rightness, authenticity, sincerity, and so on. The person making a speech act still must provide justification for his or her claims, but the validity is not an appeal to logic or science. Instead, it is an appeal to validity within a social context. Habermas is being prescriptive in calling for an intersubjective dialogue that is both consensual and reasonable—a process that leads to justified cooperation. When the intersubjective dialogue is practiced and communicative action is strong, the lifeworld is healthy, and individuals can better resist the coercive forces of the systems that attempt to colonize the lifeworld and stifle communication and cooperation.

Communicative action can therefore be seen as a means toward advancing democratic public life and the revival of the public sphere. Habermas's goal is for the current social systems to be replaced by political organisms of deliberative democracy in which people are actively involved in dialogue about issues and decision-making.

AXEL HONNETH—RECOGNITION THEORY

German philosopher Axel Honneth (1949-) is, with Habermas, considered the second generation of the critical theory trajectory established by the Frankfurt School. Honneth takes on critical theory's mission of critiquing society to bring about human emancipation from injustice. His distinctive approach to critical theory is to replace Marxism as the center of the critical project with Hegel's theory of recognition (see Chapter 14). This enables Honneth to talk about how social institutions affect people positively and negatively and what causes people to demand justice.

Honneth's hypothesis is that all social integration depends on reliable forms of mutual recognition. There are two keys to Honneth's conception of recognition. The first is that individuals are socialized into a lifeworld of recognition norms that prescribe how we should respond to people's behaviors. Social norms inform us about what behaviors are worthy of praise or censure in ourselves and in others. They tell us what is expected of us, from moral behavior to social niceties, creating shared communal bonds. The second is that receiving recognition on the basis of these norms enables an individual to develop a positive "relation-to-self"; his or her sense of place in society; and, most importantly, his or her autonomy to be able to determine and realize his or her own desires and intentions freely. Thus, individuals desire and need to both receive and give recognition to achieve their goals in society. When we receive recognition and enter into relations of mutual recognition with others, we develop an identity.

Honneth sees himself as continuing the critical theory project but rejects the historicism and pessimism of Horkheimer and Adorno. Honneth extends Habermas's idea of communicative action into everyday intersubjective relations in which people can form rational responses to their suffering of moral injustices. Honneth expands the usual definitions of injustice as violations of laws or rights to the idea that people experience moral injuries when recognition is lacking or an individual is actively misrecognized. In his book, *Disrespect* (2007), he says that misrecognition is an active withholding of recognition such as denying rights or refusing social inclusion. Exclusion, insult, and degradation violate and damage one's self-confidence, self-respect, and self-esteem. These injuries to one's integrity, honor, or dignity, Honneth argues, are the core of the experience of injustice. People learn what justice is through processes of socialization. They come to expect that society will recognize them in accordance with social recognition norms of just treatment. When instead they receive misrecognition, people experience the resulting disappointment as violence to their sense of identity. Honneth's view of justice extends beyond capitalist exploitation, oppressive laws, or unequal distribution of resources to receiving exclusion, insult, or degradation.

Struggles for Recognition

In *The Struggle for Recognition: The Moral Grammar of Social Conflicts* (2003), Honneth states that most social movements for justice are in fact struggles for recognition. Even social conflicts over resources or political power are at their heart struggles based on the concern that moral values are not being reflected in actual recognition relations. Groups denied rights or integrity seek to reestablish relations of mutual recognition. We can see a recent example of Honneth's idea in the Black Lives Matter movement. Yes, this group is struggling for legal rights, but at the heart of their movement is the struggle for recognition—that they are human beings who deserve to be treated according to the moral values that society claims it believes in but is not fully extending to Black people. That denial of recognition of Black people is what Honneth calls a "pathology of reason." It should be obvious that Blacks are people with the same rights as other people. However, capitalism has distorted people's ability to reason about moral relations and norms, leading to a failure to identify misrecognition.

When individuals experience misrecognition, Honneth says, their suffering motivates them to take action. Their damaged self-esteem and relation-to-self can be repaired only by recognition. They therefore join an existing political movement that is struggling for recognition. Honneth also sees large-scale political movements as necessary to motivate an individual to take on a struggle for recognition.

This position leaves him unable to explain how such movements get started. His theory also can't explain how a person damaged by misrecognition could manage to resolve to struggle for recognition or why many people who suffer from misrecognition don't enter into a struggle for recognition. Also, Honneth's reliance on a Hegelian view of society as institutional spheres of family, civil society, and state leaves him unable to recognize the myriad ways that individuals respond to experiences of misrecognition outside of institutional paths. Despite the shortcomings of Honneth's version of recognition theory, he has established recognition as a social reality that political philosophers need to address.

Freedom and Socialism

More recently, Honneth has turned his attention to the ideal of social freedom. In *Freedom's Right: The Social Foundations of Democratic Life* (2014), he moves the discussion of justice away from abstract principles and toward normative claims anchored in real-world situations and institutionally established practices. Influenced by his own theory of recognition, and Habermas's view of the public sphere, Honneth establishes the paradigm of the "democratic ethical life." He argues that a grounded theory and practice of justice requires concrete social spheres that generate the standards of what is just. Ideally, particular social spheres define a particular aspect of individual freedom and bring about its realization. Here, too, however, Honneth focuses on social institutions, neglecting possibilities for individual social actions.

In *The Idea of Socialism* (2015), Honneth seeks to reclaim the idea of socialism from the damage caused by many decades of capitalist defamation of socialism. Socialism, he says, is the realization of personal freedom in social solidarity. He reclaims socialism by renewing its basic tenets that were originally formed in the industrial era of the 1800s. To respond to the realities of our postindustrial society, Honneth replaces archaic Marxist assumptions with Dewey's instrumentalism (see Chapter 18) to expand social freedom through mutual dependence, cooperation, and shared social experimentation with new forms of mutual recognition and participatory democracy. It is in keeping with Honneth's career-long avoidance of totalizing theories.

CHAPTER 25

RETHINKING PHILOSOPHY: FEMINIST PHILOSOPHY

Feminist philosophy could be said to be part of postmodernism (see Chapter 23) in that it also seeks to tear down the modernist view that there is one superior form of universal, objective knowledge. What feminism adds to, when it does not diverge from, postmodernism is a focus on the role of beliefs about gender in shaping the historical patterns of thought and society. It is very wrong to consider feminism a hatred of men. Feminism is an acknowledgment of the ways in which our male-dominated social traditions have excluded women and feminism, and it is an attempt to decode and change those traditions. Feminist philosophy calls for women to be given full intellectual and political participation in society. Advocates seek to open up social institutions, correct traditional distortions about gender roles, and modify intellectual disciplines to bring about the emancipation of women from patriarchy—the system of male domination.

There are multiple ways to describe feminism because it is not a monolithic entity; it is as diverse as society itself. Feminism is essentially a philosophical movement because it is a quest to understand the nature of society, the nature of people, and how traditional assumptions about men and women have affected society. Because society has historically silenced women's voices, the history of philosophy is dominated by male voices. Too many philosophy textbooks either entirely leave out women philosophers or they tack on a brief mention almost as an afterthought. In this book, I've included several important women philosophers, Mary Wollstonecraft (see Chapter 10), Madame de Staël (see Chapter 14), Edith Stein (see Chapter 21), Simone de Beauvoir (see Chapter 21), and Hannah Arendt (see Chapter 24). Because this book is ordered chronologically, it is appropriate to bring up feminist philosophy at this point, not as an afterthought, but because society had taken this long before philosophy began to take seriously the issue of the rights of women and society's systemic sexism.

THE FIRST WAVE—HUMAN RIGHTS

Mary Wollstonecraft was an early feminist who decried the exclusion of women from full freedom and social equality in her book, *A Vindication of the Rights of Woman* (1792). John Stuart Mill, in *The Subjection of Women* (1869), made arguments similar to Wollstonecraft's that women of sufficient intellect and abilities should be given equal place with men in education, opportunities, and intellectual and political leadership. Both of these philosophers are part of what's been called "equity" or "first-wave" feminism.

First-wave feminism is exemplified by American Margaret Fuller (1810–1850), a member of the Transcendental Club (see Chapter 17). Her book, *Woman in the Nineteenth Century* (1845), directed the philosophy of transcendentalism to the question of the place of women in society. People were burdened with selfish desires, Fuller said, but are now on the verge of an awakening when men and women will be equals. She argued that people in the United States were not achieving equality because they had inherited the depravity of Europe, as evidenced by its horrific treatment of Native Americans and Blacks, who were then still enslaved. Fuller criticized the hypocrisy of people who claimed to believe in divine love but did not practice it. She finds this hypocrisy in slavery and in marriage, though she doesn't equate marriage with slavery. She does condemn the legal reality of her time that women were considered equal to children but not to men. Similar to Wollstonecraft, Fuller calls for women to receive the same intellectual and religious freedom as men. The highest marriage, she said, is a union of equals on a pilgrimage toward a common shrine. Fuller suggests that an "old maid" (the colloquial term in her time for an unmarried woman) would have the best opportunity for close communion with the divine. Fuller also discussed the subject of gender, saying that the souls of men and women are the same but that individuals vary in their levels of masculine and feminine energies. There is no wholly masculine man and no purely feminine woman, she said.

Fuller touched on some of the primary issues for which first-wave feminists fought: the right to vote (women's suffrage), the right to employment, the right to inherit, and the right to divorce. In the last part of the 1800s and early 1900s, many brave women in many countries struggled for recognition of their human rights. This era of activism, by both philosophers and nonphilosophers, won a number of key reforms. Women could vote in most countries by the 1920s, but they still were denied equal opportunities in many areas of society and still were seen as second-class citizens.

THE SECOND WAVE—LIBERATION

In the 1960s, the "second wave" of feminists claimed that the fundamental structures, assumptions, and discourse of human society reflect male domination. The second wave was clearly fundamentally different from the first wave in its motivations and scope. It was also separated by four decades and existed in quite different social realities. It's arguable whether the second wave continues or that it ended in the 1980s as some claim, replaced by a third wave; indeed, feminists still argue over that question. Another way to look at feminism since the 1960s is the difference between "mainstream feminism" and "radical feminism," which have, as the names denote, a difference in philosophical positions. In some respects, the second wave can be seen as more mainstream and the third wave as more radical, though some feminist philosophers would not fit into that characterization. I'll stick with a chronological order of second- and third-wave feminism.

The second wave was informed by two important books. The first was Simone de Beauvoir's *The Second Sex* (1949), which we discussed in Chapter 21. The second was American Betty Friedan's *The Feminine Mystique* (1963). Friedan (1921–2006) continued the critique made by Wollstonecraft and de Beauvoir that women were treated as second-class humans and denied opportunities and rights allowed to men. Friedan updated the critique to the post–World War II period and took a more psychological perspective on how women were personally faring in that society. Women are being denied their basic human need to grow, Friedan said, and the "feminine mystique" is to blame. That mystique is the twofold assumption that truly feminine women had no desire for an advanced education, a career, or a political voice because women are predisposed to find personal fulfillment in marriage, child-rearing, and keeping house. Friedan argued that the mystique had strengthened after World War II, when men returned from war and women, who had capably filled many traditionally male occupations, were expected to return home and return to being more "feminine." This expectation was strengthened by the cultural propaganda of the Cold War that portrayed the idealized American nuclear family as a bulwark against the Soviets. American media and popular culture fortified the feminine mystique, but when Friedan interviewed women, she found that women felt pressured to live up to the mystique, which was leaving them unhappy, unfulfilled, and even neurotic, all of which was affecting families and the broader society. Friedan called the symptoms these women were suffering the "problem that has no name."

Friedan didn't engage with political remedies for the feminine mystique, opting instead to encourage women to believe they can have a successful career along with a family. That encouragement spoke to many women who wanted more for their lives than what society dictated as a woman's place. In the United States, women who had been active in the Civil Rights Movement and the anti-war movement saw that a struggle for recognition was also needed for women. The political successes of the Civil Rights Movement encouraged second-wave feminists to push for political action on women's issues. In 1966, the National Organization for Women was established, with Friedan as its first president. Feminist activism won several legislative victories for women's equality in the 1970s, including equal education funding in schools (Title IX), equal access to credit and financial services (such as being able to have their own bank accounts and credit cards), and the outlawing of marital rape. However, their efforts to pass the Equal Rights Amendment failed, leaving the unfathomable reality that in the United States, the equal rights of women are not constitutionally guaranteed. The 1973 *Roe v. Wade* Supreme Court ruling striking down laws against abortion was not a result of legislative action but fit in with the growing awareness of women's equality and rights.

Second-wave feminism also enacted changes in the broader society. In 1970, San Diego State University was the first to offer women's studies courses, which remain an important part of higher education to this day. *Ms.* magazine, devoted to women's liberation, was founded in 1972 and was an immediate success. Institutions that had traditionally excluded women, from golf clubs and business associations to the U.S. military, now integrated women into their membership. Women were increasingly visible in mass media, in television in particular. In 1966, *That Girl*, played by Marlo Thomas, was the first TV show centered on a woman who was not married or living with her parents. It wasn't until 1976 that the first woman was named a TV news anchor, but Barbara Walters had to share the role with a man.

Women philosophers became more common in the 1970s as barriers to women earning advanced degrees eroded and women's interest in philosophy increased. Kate Millet's *Sexual Politics* (1970) analyzed how sexual relations are infused with politics and dominated by patriarchy. She looked at fiction and nonfiction writing and showed how they propagate patriarchal myths that subjugate women. Deconstruction of the underlying patriarchy in texts became, and still is, a major thread in feminist philosophy. A feminist critique of science began with a 1978 journal article, "Women, Science, and Society," by Catherine Stimpson and Joan Burstyn. They critiqued the gender bias in science that had for centuries prevented women from being leading scientists; they has been allowed to work only as assistants to men who did the "real" science. In the second wave of feminism, the focus in science was on the lack of equal opportunity for women within it. As we shall see later, the feminist critique of science developed into a critique of the way science was conducted.

Some feminists used Marxism or neo-Marxism to explain the subordination of women. Italian-born Silvia Federici (1942–) provides a good example of Marxist feminism. She argues that because capitalism needs a constant supply of expropriated capital to perpetuate itself, it extends this need to the expropriation of women's unpaid labor. She sees the labor women perform in child-rearing and keeping house as a condition for a capitalist economy that also depends on the exploitation of wage labor. Feminists have frequently debated how to think about housework, tasks overwhelmingly still performed by women. Feminists have widespread agreement that women should not be restricted to a life of housework with no other options, but they have not arrived at a consensus on how exploitative of women housework is.

One thread in second-wave feminism was to employ the then-current faith in technology to solve all human problems. Emblematic of this was Canadian Shulamith Firestone's (1945–2012) *The Dialectic of Sex: The Case for Feminist Revolution* (1970). Firestone claimed that gender equality could not be achieved until women's identity is separated from their biological traits. Firestone drew on Marx to develop the idea that biological sex was a class in itself, and Firestone argued that the distinctions between the male class sex and the female class sex were caused by the traditional division of labor and roles in childbirth and child-rearing. The biological division of labor in reproduction is the root cause not only of male–female inequality but also of economic class exploitation, racism, imperialism, and even men's reckless exploitation of the environment. She acknowledged there were real biological differences between men and women, but she said these should not be a basis for discrimination of one class of sex over the other. Firestone said the goal of feminist revolution must be not just the elimination of male privilege but, through technological advances, the elimination of the sex distinction itself. The centerpiece of Firestone's vision of a future utopian society was replacing what she called the barbarity of pregnancy and natural childbirth with artificial means of gestation and birth.

American Mary Daly (1928–2010) offered a more radical version of feminism in the 1970s. She said that feminism's issue shouldn't be the push for equality with men but the abolition of patriarchy. Almost all societies in history have been male dominated. Men hold political and economic power and therefore enjoy social privilege and first access to natural and social resources. Patriarchal society subordinates women under men. Daly's mission was to overcome patriarchal oppression through an analysis of language and ethics. Daly's method was *not* like the analytical philosophy of language methods we saw in Chapters 19 and 22. She looked at how words are used, especially how words are used to assert patriarchal power and disempower women. Her first two books dealt with the use of patriarchal language in religion: *The Church and the Second Sex* (1968) and *Beyond God the Father: Toward a Philosophy of Women's Liberation* (1973). Daly applied the approach of existential theologian Paul Tillich (1886–1965) who had been influenced by Kierkegaard and Heidegger. Tillich had written about replacing theology's abstract and impersonal language with the language of the personal encounter with the divine. Tillich's personalism allows us to move away from the language of God as the invincible tyrant that characterizes both the "theological theism" of traditional religion and the atheist revolt against it and reclaim religious language and signs for ourselves. Daly expanded Tillich's personalism to replace theology's patriarchal language, observing that the impersonal language of traditional religion expressed the impersonal hierarchy of male domination. She set out a way to rehabilitate "God-talk" in religion and spirituality for the women's liberation movement, creating a woman-centered theological anthropology. Her approach has inspired others, women and men, pro-religion and anti-religion, to take on a deconstruction of patriarchal language in religion and make it more gender-neutral or woman-centric.

Daly then turned to the wider society in her book, *Gyn/Ecology: The Metaethics of Radical Feminism* (1978). Her central premise is that men have always sought to oppress and use women. Patriarchal language and behavior are far larger than religion, and all of society can and should be rehabilitated. Religion didn't create patriarchy; patriarchy is itself a religion. Daly was not anti-religion—she maintained an affinity for Christianity—she was only anti-organized religion because, like all social institutions, it was structured on the basis of patriarchal interests. In her highly influential *Gyn/Ecology*, Daly showed how women had historically been portrayed as emotional creatures subversive to rationality, objectivity, and morality. Women's contributions were thus dismissed and women oppressed as unhelpful, if not dangerous and evil. Daly called for women to embrace the traits that patriarchy ascribed to them—emotionality, nurturing, and so on—and reclaim them as good moral traits rather than as harmful and wicked traits. She called for women to embrace their femininity, not as men defined it, but as women find in their own female energy—an energy that includes the ability to create and nurture life. This female energy lay dormant, suppressed by patriarchy, and needs to be revived. She associated male energy with death-dealing and even evil and female energy with birth and goodness.

Daly's philosophy captured two crucial questions that have since become major topics within feminist philosophy. One is the question of whether men and women have essentially different natures, which we'll discuss in the next section. The other is whether we should try to reform the current system and win equality for women or acknowledge that the system is too corrupt so that the answer is to smash the system of patriarchy. Daly was one who felt that reforming patriarchy was impossible and that women needed to separate wholly from men in order to express themselves freely and bond with each other. Only clear of oppressive male energy can female energy thrive. Contributing to the revolutionary camp was Australian Germain Greer's *The Female Eunuch* (1970), in which she analyzed how patriarchy has shaped women's views of themselves. As her title suggests, Greer (1939–) argues that women's sexuality has been lost, a result of the limitations imposed on them by society. Women need to come to know and accept their own bodies and liberate themselves. Men hate women, Greer contended, and women need to realize this. Change can come only through revolution.

THE THIRD WAVE—INTERSECTIONAL FEMINISM

Some have characterized the third wave of feminism that began in the early 1990s as a more radical version than the second wave. There is some validity to that, but radical versions of feminism have been around for a long time. The birth of third-wave feminism was openly declared in a *Ms.* magazine article, "Becoming the Third Wave," (1992) by Rebecca Walker, daughter of novelist Alice Walker. Only 22 years old, Rebecca Walker was responding to the confirmation to the Supreme Court of Clarence Thomas, despite the testimony of Professor Anita Hill, who gave credible testimony that Thomas had sexually harassed her. Walker pointed to Hill's testimony being disregarded as an example of the oppression of the female voice. Her call for a new wave of feminism was a call to integrate equality and female empowerment into the very fiber of life. Women needed to search for personal clarity and join together in sisterhood to understand power structures with the intention of challenging them. This, Walker defined as the third wave.

Third-wave feminists address multiple issues, but we can focus on three: the issue of complacency over past feminist gains, intersectionality—the idea that feminists also need to include considerations of race and class, and the need to expand feminism to confront more issues. We'll look at each in turn.

Complacency and Backlash

By the late 1990s, anyone under the age of 30 had lived his or her whole life in the presence of feminism. It had retreated into the background as just part of the landscape. Women were in Congress, women were TV and movie stars, women were topping the pop music charts. Many felt that gender equality had been achieved. Young women, who benefited from the gains won by the second-wave feminists but had no awareness of the prior reality, couldn't relate to that older generation of feminists. The emergence in the mid-1990s of a strongly reactionary strain of right-wing politics in the United States stoked a backlash against feminism, both politically and culturally. Radio personality Rush Limbaugh, mouthpiece of the political movement, invented the myth of the "feminazi," dismissing all feminists as un-American man haters who wanted female supremacy. As had happened so often in history, women who spoke out were being vilified. Women, too, were starting to waver about feminism. Friedan's idea that women can have a career outside of the home was now being accused of pressuring women into believing they *needed* to "have it all": career, marriage, and motherhood. Helped along by the propaganda that feminism had gone too far, some women were turning against the word and concept of feminism.

Aware of the problem, some third-wave feminists turned to personal narratives as a form of feminist theory. The first and second waves had focused on specific legal issues: the right to vote and the end of workplace, educational, and financial discrimination. Those legal rights were under threat from the right wing, but in an age dominated by mass media consumer culture, third-wave feminists needed new ways to raise the consciousness of younger women. That meant shifting feminism from a focus on mass political agendas to a focus on the experiences of individual women and from universal definitions of "woman" to personalist definitions of what it means to be a woman. In *Manifesta: Young Women, Feminism and the Future* (2000), Jennifer Baumgardner and Amy Richards wrote about not doing feminism in the same way that the second wave had done but instead women finding their own way genuine to their own generation. That sentiment fit nicely with the growing awareness of intersectionalism.

Intersectionality

Intersectionality was born out of the feminist struggle for recognition and the realization that it wasn't the only struggle to overcome injustice. The term "intersectionality" was introduced by Kimberlé Williams Crenshaw in her paper "Demarginalizing the Intersection of Race and Sex: A Black Feminist Critique of Antidiscrimination Doctrine, Feminist Theory and Antiracist Politics" (1989), though Crenshaw says the idea of intersectionality is as old as Black feminist experience. One way to look at intersectionality is to see that society marginalizes and excludes groups of people, and though those groups have tangible differences, they all share the common experiences of being marginalized. Uniting around common ground and common cause to emancipate all marginalized groups, while not forcing those groups to minimize their differences, is the basic idea of intersectionality.

Perhaps no one epitomizes intersectionality better than American Audre Lorde (1934–1992). She described herself as "Black, lesbian, mother, warrior, poet." She is best known for her poetry, but she also wrote several interesting works of philosophy. Her book, *Sister Outsider: Essays and Speeches* (1984), lays out Lorde's intersectional strategy. Different groups of people need to come together over a common cause, emphasizing their shared lived experiences. She focuses most on the need for white women and Black women to find common ground. They need to face their differences directly and use those differences as a source of strength rather than as an excuse for alienation. The patriarchal divide and conquer, she wrote, must become define and empower.

Lorde's overarching philosophy of intersectionalism is best expressed in her essay, "Age, Race, Class, and Sex: Women Redefining Difference," within *Sister Outsider*. There, she speaks from the perspective of being a Black lesbian from a poor family experiencing social structures of dominance. Lorde's ability to think of herself beyond single components—Black, lesbian, woman—and as a whole person empowered her to see the qualities of each aspect of herself. She then turned this self-awareness to people in general and society at large to see how people are conditioned to respond to difference with fear and loathing. They are further conditioned to ignore difference, reassert dominance, or destroy what they are told is subordinate. From this, Lorde concluded that people need to recognize all forms of oppression, not just one. The structure of all forms of oppression is composed of similar beliefs in the inherent superiority of one group over another and the right and privilege of dominance of one over the other. Racism, sexism, ageism, heterosexism, elitism, classism—these forms of dominance all share the same belief structure of dominance and oppression. Women in the feminist movement, Lorde wrote, felt pressure from patriarchy to conform to their oneness as women and thus didn't recognize their "manyness"—the different aspects of their identities. That behavior explains the feminist movement's inability to form the alliances needed to create a better world.

She underscored the need for people to educate themselves about oppression. It is not up to the marginalized groups to educate the oppressors, as though the marginalized are still servants of the oppressors. When people do educate themselves, they will see that a major tool used by the masters is to keep the oppressed busy dealing with the master's interests. That pattern must be broken, Lorde said, because real change will never come from working with the racist, patriarchal system, because any changes brought about within the system will be diverted and not last.

Lorde stresses the importance of speaking. "Your silence will not protect you," she wrote. People understandably are afraid to speak the truth because of potential retaliation, but silence will never protect the marginalized from being oppressed. Silence will choke us anyway, she wrote. Lorde calls for the transformation of silence into language and for all marginalized people to speak up and take action despite the danger of others' reactions.

Another important intersectional feminist is Gloria Jean Watkins (1952–), who chooses to write under the name "bell hooks" after her maternal great-grandmother. As a Black woman, she experienced the effects of both racism and sexism, which she wrote about in her book, *Ain't I a Woman? Black Women and Feminism* (1981). The book is a historical view arguing that Black women have suffered the lowest status and living conditions of any group. She claims that white female abolitionists and suffragettes were more comfortable with Black male abolitionists than they were with Black women. Hooks says that white reformers were concerned with white morality and ignored the effects on Black people. She also says that Black nationalism, led by men, was a patriarchal movement. Even feminism itself is a mostly white middle-class movement that does not speak up for the needs of nonwhite women or poor people.

Hooks advocates for a broad social movement that challenges sexism, racism, and classism, overcoming them all to create loving communities. Her version of feminism is more inclusive but still is radical in its fight against oppression. In her book, *Feminist Theory: From Margin to Center* (1984), she points out that women's equality with men is not enough because it doesn't address economic inequality. She calls for women to acknowledge their differences as they build a sisterhood. Feminism should not be led by only bourgeois white women. The feminist movement should also include men, she says, because for real restructuring of the power structure to occur, men must do their part. In all relations, she calls for camaraderie rather than separation so that there is no need for hierarchy or oppression. This restructured feminist movement shifts the focus from victimization to mutual understanding and appreciation among all who wish to control their own destinies uncontrolled by patriarchal, capitalist tyrants. That movement requires what she calls "transgressive education," meaning that educators teach students to transgress the racial, sexual, and class boundaries that oppress people. Teachers need to stop using control and power, confining students to an assembly-line approach to learning. Instead, educators should offer students the space to be inventive and make spontaneous shifts. Through acts of transgression, people can achieve freedom.

Expanding Feminist Issues

Beyond opening up to a new generation and non–middle-class whites, third-wave feminism also opened up to new issues, many of which reflected more personal issues for women. Anita Hill's testimony had brought into the public eye the concept of sexual harassment to the United States. Women began to share their experiences of being harassed and molested by men. Years of concerted activism by women brought the problem to public consciousness, and now nearly everyone in business and education is trained in the prevention of sexual harassment. However, that the #MeToo movement began in 2019 shows that it is still a large problem.

A related issue is the problem of rape. Everyone would agree in the abstract that rape is wrong, but the question is what constitutes rape and what the wrongness of it is. Feminist philosophers began to confront this issue in the late 1990s. They faced two main challenges. The first was overcoming the perception that rape was rare. This required debunking the stereotype that rape was committed by a stranger choosing a random victim. Feminist researchers showed that rape was most commonly committed by men who knew their victims. The second challenge was the recognition of rape as a crime against the victim herself. Patriarchal culture had always seen women as the property of men—of the father until she was married and then of the husband. In patriarchal societies, the wrongness of rape was construed as a property crime against the woman's father or husband. A raped woman was less valuable, so if the rapist was caught, he was forced to pay compensation to the man who "owned" his victim. Worse, one punishment was that the rapist and his victim were forced to marry; the rapist was forced to take ownership of the property he had damaged. Shifting awareness to the reality that the woman was the true victim of rape was helped along by philosopher of law Keith Burgess-Jackson's history, *Rape: A Philosophical Investigation* (1996).

Another feminist view of rape was that it must be recognized as a pillar of patriarchy. In Allan Johnson's (yes, men can be feminists, too) book, *The Gender Knot: Unraveling our Patriarchal Legacy* (2005), he takes the view that rape is a consequence of patriarchal gender constructions and of sexuality as expressions of male power. He argues that rape also harms women as a group. Third-wave feminists remind us that rape is not about sex; it is about power. In recent years, feminists increasingly have talked about the proliferation of "rape culture"—namely, that women are seen as objects to be used by men. Feminists also observe that society may no longer see rape as a crime against a woman's male owner but still assume that the woman "did something" to bring on the rape. This is another expression of patriarchy in the implicit assumption that women are wicked and tempt men to do wrong.

Violence against women is a clear aspect of patriarchy. The pervasive ideology of male dominance that says that women are the property of men condones violence against women. Rape is an act of violence. Domestic violence is, of course, acts of violence. Iris Marion Young (1949–2006) said violence was one of the "five faces of oppression" (the others being exploitation, marginalization, powerlessness, and cultural domination), which she said were methods of social dominance of groups. Women as a group were dominated by men using these five faces of oppression. Some feminists have extended the concept of violence from the physical to the psychological. One does not need to hit someone to dominate that person but could use mental and emotional violence. The word "violence" is related to "violation," and any act that violates a person's integrity or autonomy is an act of violence. Young gives examples of this in her early book, *Throwing Like a Girl: A Phenomenology of Feminine Body Comportment Motility and Spatiality* (1980). She argues that young girls are socialized to restrict their bodily movements and are conditioned to think of their bodies as fragile. They will "throw like a girl" not because their bodies are different from boys' bodies but because they are conditioned to think they have less physical capability. Many feminists would argue that restriction of free bodily movement is a violation of a person.

Some talk of a fourth-wave of feminism on the basis of the use of social media and an increased focus on violence against women, though the claim that this is a "wave" distinct from the third wave is not yet widely accepted.

GENDER AND THE FEMINIST CRITIQUE OF SCIENCE

Central to feminist philosophy is the critique of the notion of "gender." Feminism makes a distinction between the biological category of sex and the social category of gender. Gender includes social definitions of masculine and feminine and the many accompanying assumptions about social roles, sexuality, and psychological and mental differences between men and women. Some feminists are "essentialists" who claim that there is an essential female nature distinct from a male nature. (Ironically, some male misogynists agree with this idea.) Essentialists include biological determinists who see female nature as rooted in women's unique biology and social determinists who see the female nature as created through the unique and common features of female social experience. Both kinds of essentialists assume that the female gender is composed of stable properties that cannot be changed without great effort, if at all. Other feminists are nonessentialists who reject the idea that gender characteristics are fixed, viewing gender as socially constructed concepts that are open to change and redefinition. Simone de Beauvoir had a view between the extremes saying in her book, *The Second Sex* (1949), that "one is not born, but rather becomes, a woman." She argued that gender characteristics are not biologically or culturally determined but can be either socially imposed or subjectively chosen.

Regardless of how feminists view the genealogy of gender, they tend to agree that women and men experience the world from different standpoints. Because experience and knowledge are situated within a person's social environment, individuals who are socially situated differently will have different experiences; therefore, they will have different views of what is true. This notion, called "standpoint theory," applies to gender, race, economic class, sexuality, and any other socially situated circumstance. There are major movements in philosophy that attempt to address the social situatedness of marginalized groups by critically analyzing gender, race, and sexuality.

Feminism rejects modernist epistemology such as that of analytical philosophers. These feminist philosophers critique traditional theories of knowledge as having been based on the assumption that there is one universal human nature and therefore the gender, race, class, and other social–historical circumstances particular to the knower are irrelevant to how that person perceives and understands anything. Feminists reject the traditional assumption that it is possible to obtain purely objective, value-free, and politically neutral knowledge.

Third-wave feminists claim that perception is always relative to the standpoint of a particular knower; therefore, claims to knowledge reflect the dominant values and political structures of a society. Feminists claim that the philosophical picture of a generic universal human nature has actually enshrined men's experiences and interests as the paradigm for all knowledge. The majority position in the Western philosophical tradition has defined rationality as male and emotionality as female and has devalued the emotions. Points of view, particularly those of women, that deviate from the standard picture of universal rationality have been marginalized and excluded as being too subjective and unconventional. Traditional epistemologists seek the universal standard of rationality, but feminists ask, "standard and rational for whom?" Most feminist philosophers contend that women's experiences and ways of thinking differ from those that have been the basis of traditional (male) epistemologies. Philosophy must make room for other nontraditional ways of experiencing the world and gaining knowledge.

The feminist theory about standpoint has been significant in the feminist critique of science's assumption of objectivity. Some suggest that what is called "objectivity" is actually the subjective male viewpoint that is an expression of patriarchy. That doesn't mean science is worthless, but whether male scientists see phenomena and data differently from female scientists is an open question. Men and women may frame questions differently, leading to different experimental approaches, leading to different data being collected, leading to different conclusions. An issue raised by feminists interested in science is that women may be more likely to ask questions and notice phenomena that men deem irrelevant. Empirical research has partially verified that more medical research studies are conducted on diseases that affect men than on diseases that affect women. Judith Stacey and Barrie Thorne in "The Missing Feminist Revolution in Sociology" (1985) observe that in the social sciences, male-dominated scientific paradigms systematically ignore and erase women's experiences. This means that science is not value free and objective as is assumed. It instead reflects the values of patriarchy. Some feminists believe that the notion of objectivity is false and should be dispensed with. Others believe that objectivity is possible and desirable but that to achieve a sufficient level of objective perspective requires deconstructing patriarchal bias.

One major area of contention about patriarchal bias is in biology, which has long characterized male organisms as active and female organisms as passive. Evelyn Fox Keller in, "Making a Difference: Feminist Movement and Feminist Critique of Science" (2001), argued that this assumption is so fundamental that it extends to the portrayal of the sperm as masculine and the ovum as feminine. This may seem self-evident at first, but Keller points out that it is a projection of gender onto cells resulting in false assumptions. We were all taught in high school biology that the male sperm actively competes to get to the passive female ovum and win the race to fertilize the ovum. This well-worn story hides the reality that the ovum is in fact just as active in the process. As Keller observes, this illustrates the ways that language shapes the thinking and acting of working scientists. The patriarchal paradigm frames the scientists' attention and shapes their perception. It also structures and limits the fields of inquiry that scientists are willing to explore. Biology similarly also sees the males of species as active and females as passive, projecting onto animals the patriarchal conception of the strongest male winning the right to pass on his genes.

Feminists also see strong gender bias in psychology. Sigmund Freud was a common target of feminists criticizing how patriarchy dominated psychology and psychiatry. Early psychiatry was indeed rife with patriarchal gender bias. For example, the term "hysteria," used to describe a psychological disorder, came from the Greek word *hystera*, meaning "womb." (Some male physicians thought the womb wandered around the woman's body and made the woman crazy.) The idea that women were unable to control their emotions and thus were easily excitable and out of control was common in psychology. American feminist psychologist Carol Gilligan (1936–) saw the Freudian tradition and the psychology of child development as fields dominated by men who deemed women deficient in development. In her book, *In a Different Voice* (1982), Gilligan observed that psychologists had always assumed that men were the measure of humanity. Their gender bias assumed that the "masculine" qualities of autonomy and rationality were the signs of maturity. Gilligan found in her own experiences working in psychology that it was a culture that counted on women not speaking for themselves. When she worked in child psychology, she found that the established gauges of child development were predisposed to measure boys as being more mature than girls. This led her to develop her own moral theory (as we shall see a bit further on).

Another aspect of standpoint theory is seen predominantly in the social sciences regarding the question of people's lived experiences. The male objectivist paradigm ignores individual experiences in favor of reductionist paradigms that see particular people as examples of general types. Social science, therefore, has been a matter of collective quantitative data because it is considered more objective. Feminist scientists have pushed back on this assumption, saying that if the purpose of social science is to understand people, then social scientists need to listen to *people* and collect qualitative data about individuals' lived experiences. Sociologist Joey Sprague, in *Feminist Methodologies for Critical Researchers* (2005), called for awareness that gender, race, and class are key organizers of social life and that social science therefore needs to engage in qualitative ethnographic research through conducting interviews and direct participant observations. Sprague also argues that for feminist researchers, understanding how things work is not enough; they need to take action to make the world more equitable.

FEMINIST MORALITY

Most feminists agree that morality as traditionally construed and discussed within philosophy has been male dominated. This view is consistent with seeing society as historically dominated by patriarchy. Traditional moral theories reflect the male viewpoint, feminists claim, and do not include female perspectives or women's voices.

Carol Gilligan developed her own moral philosophy in her book, *In a Different Voice*, on the basis of her work in psychology. She argued that humans are exposed to two different moral voices. The masculine voice is individualistic and logical. Its emphasis in the making of moral decisions is based on the defense of rights and the dispensing of justice. The feminine voice emphasizes interpersonal relationships and taking care of people as individuals. She calls the feminine voice the "care perspective." The dominant theories of psychology and child development accentuate the masculine voice, and that both reflects and buttresses cultural beliefs. Gilligan said that this bias made it difficult to evaluate a woman's moral development. She argued for an androgynous approach that integrated the masculine and feminine moral voices as the way for each individual to reach his or her potential. At times, Gilligan seems to adopt an essentialist notion of gender—that women and men inherently perceive morality differently—but she says her theory of moral voices is characterized by theme not by gender. The different voices come from cultural traditions not inherent biology.

Gilligan's most significant contribution is her advancing of the "theory of care." Her theory is that women's moral viewpoints focus on a person's own moral responsibilities and relationships, whereas men's moral viewpoints focus on a rational understanding of rules and rights. Men tend to define moral situations in formal and abstract terms, whereas women define them in terms of context and narrative. At the heart of the feminine moral voice and viewpoint is care for other people. Gilligan says the voice of care is a different voice within patriarchal culture that joins reason with emotion, self with relationships, and men with women in resisting the divisions that maintain the patriarchal order. Within a democratic framework, care is human morality. Since Gilligan's description of "care ethics," as it has come to be known, a number of feminist philosophers have embraced the concept. Nel Noddings and Joan Tronto, for example, have developed theories of care ethics. Tronto says that because moral philosophy is engaged with human goodness, then care needs to assume a significant role. She states there are five qualities of care: attentiveness, responsibility, competence, responsiveness, and solidarity or caring with.

A recent innovation in moral philosophy is the concept of "epistemic injustice," developed by British philosopher Miranda Fricker (1966–). These injustices are epistemic in that the problem is one of knowledge or understanding. Fricker identifies two forms of epistemic injustices: testimonial injustices and hermeneutical injustices. A testimonial injustice occurs when social prejudice causes people to give a speaker less credibility, the lack of knowledge occurring in the listener. An example Fricker gives is a woman in a business meeting whose presentation is not given much credibility by others because of the prejudice that women are less competent. The woman who is being considered less believable is being wronged specifically in her capacity as a knower and tangentially in that she may be passed up for promotion or other opportunities. A hermeneutical injustice occurs when social prejudice blocks a speaker's access to conceptual resources, hindering that person's ability to interpret, understand, and speak about his or her experiences. An example of this is the times before the language of sexual harassment was widely known. Women who suffered sexual harassment lacked the conceptual resources to interpret, understand, or claim a hearing for their experiences of being morally wronged. The earlier cited example of Anita Hill, a target of sexual harassment whose congressional testimony was disregarded, can be seen as a victim of epistemic injustice.

CHAPTER 26

PHILOSOPHY OF RACE

Feminist philosophy deals with the problem of sexism, and philosophy of race deals with the problem of racism. Feminist philosophy critiques patriarchy, and philosophy of race critiques white supremacy. I discuss philosophy of race late in this book not as an afterthought but because, as with feminism, society has taken that long before philosophy began to take the issue of racism seriously. It's a statement of historical fact, not of politics, that Europeans did not see many non-Europeans as their equals, in particular the indigenous peoples of the Americas and Africa. The enslavement of Black people was legally abolished in France in 1794 (though not until 1848 in its colonies), in Spain in 1811 (though also later in some of its colonies), in the Netherlands in 1814, in Portugal in 1819 (though not until 1858 in its colonies), in the United Kingdom in 1833, and finally in the United States in 1865. However, the end of enslavement did not mean equal rights for Blacks in any of these countries. It wasn't until the early 1900s that the idea emerged of a philosophy dealing with issues of race. Unsurprisingly, the philosophy of race was begun by people of color.

It is important to realize that into the late 1800s, many supposedly educated and intelligent people held the belief that Europeans and Negroes were two different species. Among those who saw that all humans are of a single species, most thought that humans could be divided into anywhere from three to seven separate races, roughly parallel with the continents. Because it was Europeans and Americans of European ancestry doing the classification, however many races they classified the European race was seen as superior to all other races. The legacy of dividing people into biological races persists to this day, but we will wisely avoid biological debates and consider only cultural ideas about race.

Philosophy considers race in terms of its social construction, and it analyzes the cultural and moral effects of attitudes toward race. The "philosophy of race" deals with how ideas and attitudes about race developed and with understanding race relations in the context of social and moral philosophy. The *critical* philosophy of race analyzes and critiques racism and its effects on ideas, beliefs, values, practices, and social institutions. Similar to feminist philosophy, critical philosophy of race is a focus on the role of racism in shaping the historical patterns of thought and society. Critical philosophers of race acknowledge the ways in which European-dominated social traditions have excluded non-Europeans, and critical philosophy of race is an attempt to decode often hidden words and ideas and change those traditions. It is also critical in its calling for an end to the denial of society's past and ongoing racism, including an end to racial segregation, exploitation, and genocide. Being philosophers, critical philosophers of race are especially critical of their own field's denial of its racial past.

W.E.B. DU BOIS—DOUBLE CONSCIOUSNESS

William Edward Burghardt Du Bois (last name pronounced du-BOYCE, 1868–1963) was an American sociologist and activist for the civil rights of people of African ancestry in the United States. He was the first Black person to earn a PhD from a U.S. university; he earned a doctorate in sociology from Harvard. Du Bois's early work in the sociology of Black communities led him to the position that Negroes (as Blacks were widely referred to at that time) should not assimilate into white society but should accept their African heritage as members of a vast historic race. His was not an anti-white or Black nationalist sentiment but a rejection of the idea that Negroes would overcome discrimination by acting white.

Du Bois's philosophy was American pragmatism, influenced by William James (see Chapter 18) whose courses Du Bois had taken while at Harvard. His primary philosophical work consisted of several essays in his book, *The Souls of Black Folk* (1903). He stated that the problem of that time was the problem of the "color line," indicating the segregation of whites and Blacks. From this social fact, he developed the concept of "double consciousness," a phenomenon he felt was unique to Black people. Du Bois said that Black Americans developed the sense of always looking at themselves through the eyes of white Americans, of measuring one's soul by the tape of a world that looks on in amused contempt and pity. These experiences of discrimination that denied their identities inflicted moral injuries on Black people, yet as Du Bois wrote, Blacks possessed a dogged strength to resist the strife of prejudice and to attain self-consciousness. This was because they developed a double consciousness—the consciousness of oneself but also the consciousness of seeing oneself through the misrecognizing eyes of the whites. Despite the realities of white domination, a Black person retains a sense of the dichotomy between the discrimination expressed by the oppressors and a love for oneself that is not defined by white domination. The Black person, Du Bois says, simply wishes to make it possible for a man (sic) to be both Black and an American without being cursed and spit on by his fellows, and without having the doors of opportunity closed roughly in his face. Du Bois's portrayal of the double consciousness of oppressed people has been broadly influential in critical philosophy of race and postcolonial theory.

FRANTZ FANON—BLACK SKIN

Fanon (1925–1961) was born in the French Caribbean colony of Martinique. He left the island in 1943 to fight with the Free French Forces. After that, he studied in France to become a psychiatrist. His experiences in the colony of Martinique and in France influenced his important book on racism, *Black Skin, White Masks* (1952). Fanon's central idea is that Black people are condemned by their skin to be a lesser creature in the white world in which they live. Fanon observed that racism reduces Black people to nothing more than skin, a skin to which they are chained and determined. The prejudiced views of the dominant culture are imposed on the oppressed who are represented as mere animal bodies less able to think, reason, or speak properly. The inferiority of Black people is determined by the Other, by the "white gaze" that sees only the skin. Within white supremacy, Black people experience the image of their own body as alien to them, an image of a third person.

Black people have to learn how to navigate the world in two dimensions. They are one person with their fellow Black people, but have to behave differently with white people. Black people are at home in their own bodies only when the white gaze is absent. In the presence of white people, Black people have to move differently, act and speak differently, according to the norms of the white world. This self-division is the direct result of colonial oppression. In the white world, the Black person has to be Black in relation to the white, while still being Black. It is similar to Du Bois's description of double consciousness, though there is no indication Fanon knew Du Bois's work. Fanon criticized philosophy (mostly Sartre, see Chapter 21) for not permitting us to understand the Black person's Beingness because it ignores the lived experience of being Black. Blackness was created in the white world and continues to exist in negation to whiteness. But rational categories can't be used to understand the lived experience of Black people. Sartre talked a lot about suffering, but Fanon said that white philosophers like Sartre forget that Black people suffer quite differently from white people, again, because of colonialism.

JAMES BALDWIN

Baldwin (1924–1987) was a novelist and playwright, but his writings had a definite philosophical tone and dealt with topics significant to the philosophy of race. Born in New York, he emigrated to Paris to escape American racism and to develop his voice as a writer outside of being a Black man in America. His one major work of nonfiction, *The Fire Next Time* (1963), was influential in the U.S. Civil Rights Movement of the 1960s and as a testament to Black experience within racist society. Baldwin set out to reach a white readership to help white people understand the Black experience and their motivations to struggle for civil rights. He was telling whites his story, educating them, an approach that influenced a number of later philosophers and activists.

Baldwin's book contains two essays. The first, "My Dungeon Shook," is styled as a letter to his 14-year-old nephew in which he cautions the young man about racism and how he should react to racial oppression. America has the ability to destroy Black men, Baldwin wrote, but he challenged his nephew to convert his anger over his mistreatment into having a passionate view for other Black people's experience. His second essay, "Down at the Cross," describes his journey away from organized Christianity, which he felt had repressed his full experience of humanity. His feelings of being repressed came from a combination of his experience as a Black man but perhaps more from his experience as a homosexual. Baldwin also describes the attempt by Nation of Islam founder Elijah Muhammad to convert him. Baldwin wrote that the Black Muslim movement had replaced Christianity's "white God" with a "Black God." In response to both sides, Baldwin asserted that such binary orientations of white versus Black and an insatiable quest for power underpinned American society's predicament. The attempts to make God one color or another were attempts to legitimize discrimination on the pretext of safeguarding the truth. He rejected hatred and affirmed the dignity of all people regardless of color. The upheaval of that time in America, Baldwin wrote, was not caused by a Black revolution. The social strife in the 1960s reflected white America losing its sense of exclusive power to define Black identity. America was seeing the rewriting of history, not only for the liberation of Black people, but for white people who did not really know their own history.

The American Civil Rights Movement was a long and complicated struggle for recognition. It peaked in intensity in Baldwin's lifetime but had roots going back a further century. I cannot hope to cover it adequately in this book, and I hope your other courses will give it the thorough treatment that it deserves. Similar to the first and second waves of feminism (see Chapter 25), the American Civil Rights Movement was originally focused on achieving human rights related to employment, housing, education, and so on. Like feminist philosophers, philosophers of race have views across a spectrum of more moderate to more radical. We also saw in Chapter 25 how Black women developed intersectionalism as a method of being open to people's diverse experiences of gender, race, class, and sexuality. Many of the same themes about cultural hegemony and oppression discussed in Chapters 24 and 25 definitely also apply to the topic of race. In the rest of this chapter, we look at philosophers of race who wrote after the 1960s, who considered what had and had not been accomplished by the American Civil Rights Movement, and what still needs to be accomplished for the full emancipation of Black people.

CORNELL WEST

West (1953–) is arguably the U.S.'s most widely known philosopher at the time of this writing and is certainly the only philosopher ever named MTV's Artist of the Week (2016). West's first book was *Prophesy Deliverance! An Afro-American Revolutionary Christianity* (1982) that expressed a radical Christianity that worked for the emancipation of all people. He chose "Afro-American" rather than the common "African-American" to denote the Black experience as being not that of immigrants but that of descendants of people who were enslaved and were still experiencing the legacy of slavery. Like Fanon, West focuses on the lived experiences of Black people, but unlike Fanon, who was hostile toward religion, West highlights the revolutionary experience of Black American churches. West adopts the interpretation of Jesus as a liberator of the poor and downtrodden, a common theme in Black American church communities. West urges Afro-Americans to understand their dual status as being oppressed by both white supremacy and capitalism. He accepts Marx's critique of capitalism (see Chapter 15) and his contribution to the growth of self-consciousness in the proletariat, but he rejects Marx's materialism, moral relativism, and strangulating totalitarianism. His version of a revolutionary Christianity is one that replaces the class structure and class antagonisms of bourgeois society with a new association in which the free development of each person is the condition for the free development of all. West embraces a Christian spirituality in which loving concern for others is central. Justice, he says, is what love looks like in public.

West has been compared with Du Bois, on whom West has written a large amount, mostly in solidarity. Published 90 years after Du Bois's *The Souls of Black Folk*, West's *Race Matters* (1993) assesses the position of Black people in the United States and finds that Black people still suffer greatly from white supremacy. West says that the U.S.'s history of white supremacist beliefs and images have permeated society and culture and have inflicted on Black people emotional scars and existential angst. The lived experience of Black people is to feel unsafe, unprotected, subject to random violence, and hatred for who they are. West stresses that experiencing this trauma doesn't excuse immoral acts by Black people, but it does mean that we must be cognizant of the circumstances into which people are born and under which they live. The circumstances for Black people are a combination of historical white supremacy built into social structures, the continued resistance on the part of white people to accept the humanity of Black people fully, and neoliberal economic structures (see Chapter 22). West opposes what he calls the "free-market fundamentalism" of neoliberalism. This ideology that puts corporate interests first trivializes concern for the common good and puts fear and insecurity into the hearts of workers. West says this ideology is also at the heart of American imperialism and militarism abroad. Despite his opposition to capitalism, West says he is a non-Marxist socialist and a democratic socialist because he is suspicious of authority and believes in people having a voice in government.

LEWIS GORDON

American Lewis Gordon (1962–) has applied phenomenology and existentialism (see Chapter 21) to the lived experiences of Black people, developing a distinctly "Africana existentialism." His perspective is that while existentialism is a historically European movement preoccupied with freedom, anguish, responsibility, embodied agency, sociality, and liberation, an Africana existentialism examines the question of what it means for Black people to exist and live as a problem to the white world and to understand Black people's suffering. His existential and phenomenological study of racism was *Bad Faith and Antiblack Racism* (1995).

For Gordon, the issue is the status of Blackness because, historically, the question of race has been directed at "the Blacks." Gordon's concept of "bad faith" includes a variety of phenomena that in one way or another are a choice against choice and an effort to avoid freedom and responsibility. Antiblack racism includes white people's bad faith efforts of a flight from and war against social reality. This reflects a common theme in philosophy of race that critiques white people's denial of the humanity of Black people and the history of antiblack racism. But Gordon also labels as "bad faith" a spirit of sincerity, calling instead for "critical good faith" that respects evidence and accountability, building a world of intersubjective relations.

Gordon emphasizes antiblack racism rather than white supremacy because the former can exist without the latter—people can reject white supremacy and still think that Blacks are inferior. In his phenomenology of racism, Gordon observes that racism requires the rejection of other people's humanity, which is a denial of reality. Because communication is possible between the racist and the people at whom racist hatred is directed, the social reality that those people are indeed human will appear. In antiblack racism, the existence of the Black person is a problem. The racist must therefore avoid and deny the social reality of the Black person's existence. In particular, the racist must avoid the embodied reality of the people whom the racist hates—to make invisible the bodies that are visible. This avoidance, he says, tries to make embodied realities be without points of view and/or make points of view as being without bodies. In other words, racists dismiss Black people as having a point of view, or dismiss their point of view as having no tangible embodied reality. Gordon, agreeing with an argument made by Fanon, says that racists aren't irrational; they are expressing a hyper-rationality of justification for their bad faith of racist thinking. That racist hyper-rationality is what causes the highly emotional passions of racists. Feeding that hyper-rationalization is the notion that moral obligations are founded on similarity and therefore do not extend to people who are different. White people within white supremacy only recognize people who are similar to them and do not feel the need to extend moral consideration to Black people. This is an antiblack misrecognition that lies at the core of racism.

In *Existence in Black* (1997) and *Existentia Africana: Understanding Africana Existential Thought* (2000), Gordon frames Black existentialism as a discipline that studies the problematics of Black existence, such as Black social invisibility. Therefore, contributions to Black existentialism can be made by anyone; one does not have to be Black. For this reason, Gordon applies an intersectionality to his philosophy, looking at and welcoming the contributions of people of all genders, races, and religions. Gordon further elaborates on the observations of Du Bois and

West that Black people are treated as problems instead of as people, saying that Black people suffer from demands to justify their existence. From those demands of antiblack racism, Black people suffer dread, a sense of absurdity, and loss of freedom—common themes in European existentialism. Unlike European existentialism, Black existentialism has to argue that not all Black people are the same; they are not all reducible to antiblack stereotypes. Gordon combines existentialism with religious thought because, in his opinion, similar to West's, religion offers unique paths to be taken in struggles for recognition and liberation.

DERRICK BELL—CRITICAL RACE THEORY

American Derrick Bell (1930–2011) was a professor of law and legal theory who, along with Richard Delgado and Jean Stefancic, developed critical race theory. Unlike other approaches to critical philosophy of race, critical race theory looks at racism within legal theory and scholarship. It has its roots within critical legal theory, which had critiqued the assumption within legal scholarship of judicial neutrality and objective truth. Bell's research in legal aspects of civil rights convinced him that racism is an ordinary presence at the center of society and, thus, that traditions of racial subordination are stronger than legal standards, which affects legal proceedings. He says that race is a social construction and that the domination of whites over people of color served important psychological and material purposes for whites. Racism is not a binary white-Black relation but is a pattern of dominance that has shifted to different minority groups at different times, usually in response to economic considerations. Bell therefore adopted intersectionality—that each race has its own ever-evolving history. From that, he said that people of color need to communicate their histories and experiences to white people, who are unlikely to know the circumstances faced by racialized minorities. The history of race relations in the United States shows that, from the framing of the Constitution, whites have chosen property over justice and that whites will promote civil rights advances only when they also serve white self-interest.

CHARLES W. MILLS

Jamaican-born Mills (ca. 1950–) is a political philosopher of race. He is a critic and commentator on John Rawls (see Chapter 22). Mills accepts the Rawlsian goal of the flourishing of the individual and justice as fairness but rejects the notion of ideal theory as ignoring the reality of structural racism. He therefore prefers "nonideal theory" as responding to the reality of racism, thus providing a way to explain and expose it. Nonideal theory begins from the standpoint that structural inequalities exist and moves from that to the question of how to reverse those inequalities. Mills's starting point is the idea that white supremacy is a political system in which white political philosophers are so embedded that in their ideal theories of justice and morality they never consider actual practice. Mills therefore employs "contract theory," which seeks to rectify racial injustices, rather than Rawls's ideal theory, which considers justice in the abstract.

Mills sees liberalism, as was defined in Chapter 22, as a political ideology steeped in racism. In his book, *The Racial Contract* (1997), Mills deconstructs the history of liberalism through an analysis of "social contract theory," another form of ideal theory. Mills argues that the social contract is not, as assumed, neutral with respect to racial and ethnic differences. Instead, it was intended as a contract only among white people and thus establishes obligations and regulates interactions only among white people. Racism is at the core of the social contract, Mills says. Racism is not an unintended side effect; racism has really been the rule—an agreement among the tribes of Europe to spread and maintain white supremacy against all nonwhite tribes the world over. When white people say, "Justice," they mean, "Just us." Therefore, Mills contends that it is more reflective of the nonideal reality to think of the racial contract as the real character of the world in which we live. The "racial contract" of white supremacy is the actual social contract. Mills's conception of a racial contract fits well with postcolonial theory (see Chapter 27).

It is not only analytical political theory that Mills says is steeped in white supremacy. He also targets Marxism (see Chapter 15) as not taking racism into account. In *From Class to Race: Essays in White Marxism and Black Radicalism* (2003), Mills, consistent with his views in *The Racial Contract*, says that racism was not an unintended side effect of capitalism but that white supremacy was central to the creation of the capitalist modern world. He calls on "white Marxism" to learn from the radical critique by Black philosophy and activism. He gives the example of his own journey from a self-described orthodox Marxist to a radical Black theorist. He outlines how the Marxist critique of class strongly parallels a critique of structural racism, with white supremacy essentially acting in the same role in which Marx saw the bourgeoisie acting. Mills defines the central foundational categories of oppression in both internal structural racism and white settler colonialism, and he refers to white supremacy as a worldwide "domination contract." He also claims that race, not gender, is the primal contradiction, with race being the stable reference point for identifying "them" and "us." This contention raises the ire of radical feminists. Mills in recent years has written on the need for whites who see themselves as progressive "liberals"—those wanting to expand recognition, rights, and opportunities—to learn from and unite with Black radicalism to generate a new social contract that will rectify injustices.

OTHER NOTABLE PHILOSOPHERS OF RACE

Philosophy of race is a vibrant and growing field and, regrettably, this chapter can be only a brief introduction. Even a few years from now, this chapter will need to be expanded substantially, and that is a good thing. The Black Lives Matter movement will surely inspire more people to explore the causes of and remedies for structural racism, not only in the United States but also throughout the world. In the meantime, several more philosophers of race active within the past decade require our attention.

American Tommie Shelby (1967–) constructs a new pragmatic theory of Black political theory in *We Who Are Dark: The Philosophical Foundations of Black Solidarity* (2005). Shelby is more friendly to liberalism (see Chapter 22) than is Mills and brings in some of its values of individual liberty and social equality to help form what he calls a "pragmatic Black nationalism." He sees the principles of equality and justice as being important to form an organic Black identity that can generate Black solidarity across cultural or class lines. This empowers Black people to ground their solidarity not on a sense of shared identity but on a principled response to the oppression they all face. Also unlike Mills, Shelby is open to connecting his theory of Black solidarity with Rawls's ideal theory of justice. Shelby argues that a concept of justice that seeks to rectify racial injustices presupposes an ideal theory of justice that can be the standard by which we make judgments about when injustices have occurred and when they have been rectified.

American George Yancy (1961–) followed in Franz Fanon's line of thinking with his book, *Black Bodies, White Gazes: The Continuing Significance of Race* (2008). Yancy continues the approach of telling stories from the lived experience of being Black in a white world. He tells the powerful story of being a Black body entering an elevator that has a white person in it. Because of antiblack racism training that a Black man is essentially dangerous, the white person, especially if she is a white woman, is immediately put on guard. As a Black person with a Black body, he is immediately dehumanized by the white gaze. Of course, the white gaze has power far beyond such interpersonal encounters. Yancy says that the white gaze in its active form is the site of white power, hegemony, and privilege. Using Husserl's (see Chapter 21) concept of sedimentation, Yancy says that the white gaze, sedimented with experiences of white power and privilege, sees the Black body with disgust and perpetuates violence against it. Writing amidst the spate of police killings of Black people, Yancy establishes the difficult concepts of suturing and unsuturing—difficult to understand and even more difficult to accept. He says that white people "suture" over the festering reality of lies about their violence against Black people. Sutured, they believe themselves closed off to the reality of Black people as people and closed off to Black people as suffering. White people, he says, must strive to be unsutured—the powerful step of openness to the ways in which their whiteness is a problem. Being unsutured is an openness to the loss and great discomfort of challenging their own identities. Yancy links this to Baldwin's call for a dialogue between Black and white people, a dialogue that necessarily involves an accusation that will require white courageous listening.

We also need to mention feminist philosophies of race. We met two intersectional feminists in Chapter 25, Audre Lorde and bell hooks, and they also wrote about philosophy of race. American Kimberlé Williams Crenshaw (1959–), who introduced the term "intersectionality," has argued within legal theory that the law looks at gender and race discrimination separately but that Black women suffer not simply from a sum of those two discriminations but also from an intersection of them that overlaps the two forms of discrimination. Arguably the first book on intersectionality was Angela Davis's (1944–) *Women, Race, and Class* (1981), an orthodox Marxist analysis of the three topics in the title. Davis covered the problems of second-wave feminism being run by and for white middle-class women, and she discussed the economic role of enslaved Black women. Davis's answer to the problems of race and gender was Marxist revolution.

In a different vein, American Kathryn Sophia Belle (1978-), formerly known as Kathryn T. Gines, has written critiques of Simone de Beauvoir, Jean-Paul Sartre, W.E.B. Du Bois, Charles W. Mills, and in general analytical philosophy and continental philosophy, pointing out the absence of the perspective of Black women in those philosophies. Belle wrote a book, *Hannah Arendt and the Negro Question* (2014), in which she argued that Arendt's discussion of the "Negro problem" failed to recognize that it was actually a "white problem." Belle holds up Arendt as an example of how a rigid distinction between the social and the political stops philosophers from recognizing that racism is both a political and a social problem.

Finally, there is the idea of getting rid of the concept of race altogether. This is the view of American Lawrence Blum (1943-) and British-Ghanian Kwame Anthony Appiah (1954-) who argue that we should dispense with the concept of race. Their basic argument is that because race is a social construction with no biological basis, we should talk about "racialized groups" or "racial identities." Making this shift in language, they believe, will make it easier for us to eliminate discrimination based on racialization.

CHAPTER 27

CRISES OF THE NEW CENTURY

I write this book at the beginning of the third decade, the 2020s, of the 21st century. It says something that the first thirteen chapters covered all of philosophy's history prior to 1800, the next five chapters covered the 1800s, and the next eight chapters covered the 1900s. Philosophy is accelerating and diversifying. I could easily have written much more about the philosophy of the late 1900s and early 2000s. As you have probably gathered, the field of philosophy has become increasingly fragmented, no longer the fairly linear development of the first eighteen or so chapters. That is because philosophy is becoming increasingly dynamic and involved in the world, despite those people who want to dismiss philosophy because it challenges their assumptions. The quest for understanding is alive, bigger than ever, and never more needed than now. Too many introduction to philosophy courses treat philosophy as a collection of "dead white guys," but the reality is that the quest for understanding is ongoing. This book is about to end, but philosophy will not. I could write a great deal about the challenges facing us in the future and how philosophy can respond to them. For this last chapter, I want to talk about a few of the topics that are much discussed in this decade of the 2020s but not covered in Chapters 24, 25, and 26. Those three chapters and several of the topics in this chapter address social crises.

PHILOSOPHY OF SCIENCE

We are a civilization increasingly dominated by science and technology. What effects that has on us goes far beyond simply having new tools that make our lives easier. We've seen a number of philosophers who were critical of science, and that critique continues. Some speak of a crisis of science in that science's pervasive reach into our lives is largely unquestioned, despite the real possibility that our science can harm if not destroy us. We can't afford to pretend that science is value neutral—science will reflect our values. The question then becomes what values do we want science to reflect?

Simply put, philosophy of science is the philosophical exploration of the roots and methods of scientific inquiry. Every discipline of science has its own corresponding "philosophy of ___" that examines the underlying foundations of that scientific discipline and the implications of the questions and results generated by that discipline. Like most philosophy, though, a serious exploration of science is not simple. Like all good philosophy, philosophy of science tries to improve our understanding and quality of life, and like all good philosophy, it does not simply accept the dominant paradigm. The dominant paradigms of science have been positivism and coherentism. Positivism we saw before in Chapter 19; it basically is the assumption that scientific statements are verified through observation and reason. "Coherentism" is the idea that scientific statements are justified by being part of a coherent system of theory and observations. Unlike positivism, coherentism understands that no scientific theory or observation exists in isolation, nor can they be validated on their own. All theories, predictions, and observations are cognitive acts that rely on a broad set of beliefs. Therefore, it is impossible to test a theory in isolation; we can only justify the overall system, but even then only in an ad hoc way. Both positivism and coherentism assume that science is a gradual, methodical process of discovery of facts about the world. Some still hold to one of these views, despite the work of Thomas Kuhn.

Thomas Kuhn's (1922–1996) book, *The Structure of Scientific Revolutions* (1962), radically changed our understanding of science. Kuhn's ideas on epistemology were influenced by philosophers such as Wittgenstein (see Chapter 20) and his own studies of the history of science. He rejected the traditional view that science advances through the gradual accumulation of new discoveries. He argued that science is "a series of peaceful interludes punctuated by intellectually violent revolutions" in which "one conceptual world view is replaced by another."

Kuhn said that scientific work in these longer-lasting, more tranquil periods of "normal science" is guided by a dominant paradigm. By "paradigm," Kuhn means an attitude similar to what Peirce had defined as truth—a consensus within the community of scientists. Science is an approach to reality and questions about it that operates from a set of assumptions and preconceptions. Formally or habitually, scientists establish the paradigm of how the universe should be conceptualized, including what fundamental laws and theoretical assumptions we must accept, what problems need to be solved, and what phenomena are relevant to their solution. In normal science, the task is attempting to answer questions raised by the paradigm and fitting all new data into the paradigm. Eventually, however, phenomena will emerge that don't conform to the paradigm. Kuhn describes the process science goes through: initially dismissing such maverick data as "anomalies" or minor difficulties that science will eventually solve and fit into the paradigm. Science resists the idea that the prevailing theory and paradigm are false, and it resists alternative theories to explain the anomalies. As anomalous data increase, normal science enters a crisis; eventually, a new paradigm will gain a following and will overthrow the established theory, and a scientific revolution has come about. Kuhn points to the scientific revolutions of Galileo's rules of motion replacing Aristotelian science and Einstein's theory of relativity replacing Newtonian mechanics.

Kuhn claims, as Husserl had (see Chapter 21), that all scientific observation is "theory laden." This means that we don't see objects simply as they are; we see objects in terms of our theoretical, interpretive framework. Because we operate within our paradigm, our belief system, we observe objects according to what our "knowledge" tells us we see, and we consider this to be "normal" and our interpretations "true." Despite our best intentions, we make the phenomena we observe fit the preconceptions of our paradigm. An Aristotelian scientist had the paradigm that rest was the "natural" condition for an object. Therefore, motion was abnormal and needed to be explained. Galileo, and later Newton, operated under a different paradigm, which said an object in motion "naturally" stayed in motion. Therefore, motion didn't need to be explained, but any change in its motion did. An Aristotelian, seeing a weight swinging on a string, would seek to answer what was preventing the weight from coming to rest. A post-Galilean, seeing the same swinging weight would seek to answer what was preventing the weight from continuing to move in a straight line. This difference may seem subtle on the surface, but because the two paradigms organize and view phenomena according to different assumptions, they ask different questions and look at different data—and come to different conclusions.

If all observations are theory laden, Kuhn argues, then there are no theory-neutral observations. That means there is no privileged viewpoint that can decide which of the competing scientific theories is the winner. Numerous philosophers had been making this point for centuries, but science still saw itself as being above this. Nevertheless, no pure observation could decide between Aristotle's or Galileo's physics of motion. What's more, scientists operating under their own theory will interpret the empirical data to make them consistent with their preferred theory's claims. What counts as scientific inquiry, acceptable standards of scientific evidence, and even rationality itself will be defined in terms of the particular preferred paradigm. Accordingly, Kuhn concludes that we have no purely objective, rational path from an old paradigm to a new one, and, therefore, a scientific revolution (like a political one) is more the result of sociological factors than objective, impartial evidence.

Critics charge that Kuhn has denied the objectivity of science and its goal of producing a true account of reality. But isn't that Kuhn's point? And isn't Kuhn following a trajectory of philosophical thought that goes back to Kant if not William or even Socrates? Philosophers have long debated how much our so-called knowledge is based on a "true" encounter with objective reality and how much is our own mental construction. In current philosophy of science, the debate is between the various versions of scientific realism and anti-realism. Scientific realism is the standard scientific view that the objects that scientists talk about exist independent of human theories and that, therefore, science can give us objective knowledge about the world. Scientific anti-realism is the contrary claim that scientific theories are products of humans and do not give us a purely objective account of the world.

Scientific theories are tools that provide us with fruitful models, "useful fictions" as Nietzsche would say (see Chapter 17), and ways to systematize and make sense of our experiences. The realists correctly point out that it is undeniable that scientific theories can be useful guides to explain the phenomena we observe. The anti-realists reply that past theories continually made successful predictions—for example, Ptolemy's cosmology—before they were abandoned because of a paradigm shift. Truth is not essential for a theory to be accepted and successful. Furthermore, inspired by pragmatism (see Chapter 18), anti-realists argue that theoretical models are helpful because they are abstractions, not because they are real. The "average American family" is a useful fiction for economists and social planners, but the average American family does not exist as an entity in the world. Similarly, entities like subatomic particles, genes, and DNA molecules are theoretical constructs that serve a scientific purpose whether or not they are real. Is light a particle or a wave? Both paradigms are useful, and no amount of experimentation can prove one theory or the other the winner. The pragmatic usefulness of a scientific model does not prove that it is providing us with the one and only true depiction of the world. Realists offer a number of responses, mostly centered on the argument that the realist account best fits the success of science.

Taking a more radical position than Kuhn was Austrian philosopher Paul Feyerabend (1924–1994) who said that science had lost its original purpose and needed to be saved from itself. Feyerabend contends that science began as a movement to liberate human thinking and inquiry but had devolved instead into an increasingly dogmatic and rigidly oppressive ideology. He warned against the authoritarian dominance of science. Scientific "facts" are now taught in much the same way that religious "facts" are taught, and science is obsessed with its own mythology, making claims far beyond its ability to justify. He objected to the dogma of a single scientific method as limiting the activities of scientists. Similar to Kuhn, Feyerabend saw how many significant scientific advances came not from methodical processes but from serendipitous discoveries. The only "method" of science that made sense, he said, was "anything goes."

ENVIRONMENTAL ETHICS

The field of environmental ethics concerns human beings' ethical relationship with the natural environment. Advances in science and technology have for centuries increased human destruction of the environment, and humans need to accept their culpability in this destruction, which may endanger our own lives. Environmental ethics developed into a specific philosophical discipline in the 1970s. Philosophy's interest coincided with increased awareness in the 1960s and 1970s of the effects that industrialization, economic expansion, and population growth were having on the environment. Rachel Carson's 1962 exposé, *Silent Spring*, warned that the widespread use of chemical pesticides was causing the destruction of wildlife and posed a serious threat to public health. Paul Ehrlich's 1968 book, *The Population Bomb*, raised the alarm about the effects that the exploding human population would have on Earth's resources. (In 1968, the world population was about 3.5 billion. In 2021 it is about 7.7 billion.)

Pollution, depletion of natural resources, dwindling plant and animal biodiversity, the loss of natural habitat, and global warming are all environmental concerns that have become part of the public consciousness. Human concern over the looming climate crisis is slowly seeping into debates over public policy. The task for environmental ethicists is to outline our moral obligations in the face of the climate crisis and other environmental concerns. The fundamental questions that environmental ethics must address are what moral and practical duties humans have with respect to the environment and why. To understand what our obligations are, it is necessary to consider first why we have them. Philosophers ask whether we have duties to protect the environment for the sake of human beings living in the world today, for humans living in the future; or for the sake of nonhuman forms of life in the environment itself, irrespective of benefits to humans. Different philosophers answer these questions differently, leading to the emergence of different environmental ethics.

What obligations do we have to our natural environment? If our concern for the environment extends only to our own desires and self-preservation, then that ethic is by definition "anthropocentric," literally "human centered." In a real sense, our ethics have to be anthropocentric. For one thing, there is nothing wrong with caring about yourself and your interests. In a broader sense, it seems that only human beings are capable of reflecting on ethical questions and reasoning to ethical decisions, thus giving all moral debate a definite human centeredness. However, in the field of environmental ethics, the charge of anthropocentrism is directed at any ethical framework that grants moral weight only to human beings and thus implicitly or explicitly holds that we have no moral duty to other forms of life.

Much of human history is dominated by this kind of anthropocentrism, but its assumptions have been challenged by many environmental ethicists. These philosophers have insisted that ethical consideration must extend beyond human beings to the nonhuman natural world. Some say this consideration should extend to animals, others to all living organisms, and still others to natural entities like rivers and ecosystems. They agree that we have obligations to the environment because we actually owe moral recognition to other living things and to the environment itself. How wide and to what extent our moral obligations extend to the nonhuman environment are matters of debate among environmental ethicists. All of these philosophers are united in the conviction that our moral framework needs to change if our planet is to survive.

POSTCOLONIAL PHILOSOPHY

The age of colonialism that began in 1492 (see Chapter 6) supposedly ended sometime in the 1960s by which time most former colonies had become independent nations. Postcolonial philosophers look at the ongoing legacy of colonialism, in particular the ideological justifications for colonial imperialism and oppression of non-European peoples. In short, colonialism justified itself as the enlightened Europeans bringing civilization to the rest of the world, whether the rest of the world wanted it or not.

Franz Fanon inaugurated the philosophy of colonialism with his book, *The Wretched of the Earth* (1961). The book was certainly informed by Fanon's thinking in *Black Skin, White Masks* (see Chapter 26), but it broadens those ideas about the experiences of Black people to the experiences of all oppressed people. Fanon had become deeply involved in the Algerian liberation movement, Algeria then being a colony of France, which kept control through harsh suppression of the Algerian people. Fanon was also interested in the Pan-African movement, the vision of uniting all of Africa in opposition to European colonialism. In a foreshadowing of intersectionalism (see Chapter 25), Fanon looked at oppressions based on class, race, or national culture and considered them as having similar effects. All forms of prejudice rip away a person's ability to feel human, depriving him or her of the possibility of being a person. Fanon said that the tensions caused by settler colonialism grow over time because the relationship of the settler and the native is one between binary opposites. Those tensions eventually become the catalyst for native violence against the settler, the colonizer who occupies native land. In this way, Fanon defended colonized people's use of violence to gain independence. He also stated that because the colonizers did not consider the natives as human beings, the colonizers should not expect the natives to be bound by moral principles that apply to human beings. Also, because the colonizer maintains occupation of the land and control over the native population through violence, violent resistance by the natives is justified because it is the only language that the colonizer speaks. Despite his condoning of violence, Fanon stressed the best solution to colonialism was to build up the humanity of the native. The native people needed to learn their own true history, reestablish their own culture, develop their own consciousness of self. *The Wretched of the Earth* quickly became inspirational to anticolonial movements, including violent ones, across the world.

Palestinian cultural critic Edward Said (1935–2003) originated postcolonial theory with his book *Orientalism* (1978). In the book, he described how Western Europe had intellectually divided the world into a binary social relation, inventing the concepts of Occident and Orient. The "West" created the concept of the "East," despite the reality that those living in the "East" did not see themselves as such. So much discourse still today refers to "Western" and "Eastern" cultures as somehow qualitatively different. Said argued that the social construction of Orientalism depicted the Middle East and Asia as a homogeneous cultural entity, unified in its inferiority to the European "West." Said thus reveals how white supremacy extends beyond the issue of blackness. The reality of the enslavement of black Africans created a distinct dynamic for antiblack racism, but Orientalism is also a white supremacist dominance and dehumanization of the people of the Middle East and Asia.

Like blackness, the Orient was created in the white world and continues to exist in negation to whiteness. The attitude of Orientalism has its roots in the Crusades of the 1000s, which saw the Islamic states of the Middle East as an evil scourge that needed to be eliminated. (Granted, the Islamic states had similar feelings about the Europeans, especially after the Crusades.) Said focuses less on the political and economic exploitation of people in the "East" and mainly on the academic fields of Orientalism popular in Western Europe in the 1700s and 1800s. French and British scholars developed a structured set of assumptions and discursive practices that described and interpreted the people of the Orient. European paternalism exercised authority over the cultural product of Oriental societies, explaining their history, practices, and especially their literature. The Europeans pretended to know more about these people than they did about themselves, often getting things very wrong. Said stated that this paternalistic characterization allowed Europeans to create a binary relation that could make them feel better about themselves. They were rational, ordered, and sensible people, whereas the people of the "East" were irrational, chaotic people who had strange and primitive beliefs. In this way, Europeans were able to justify their expressions of power and superiority under the guise of their supposed knowledge about the "East." Said exposes the pretense of European scholarship being value free. It expressed the values of the "West."

Indian philosopher Gayatri Spivak (1942–) applied Said's concept of Orientalism to her native land. She says that Western scholars dismiss all non-Western forms of knowledge and discourse as mere myth and folklore. Using Gramsci's concept of the subaltern (see Chapter 24), Spivak explores the experiences of women who are socially and politically excluded from the hierarchy of power. She criticizes the ongoing cultural appropriations of Westerners who do not seek to listen to or understand subaltern peoples.

Brazilian philosopher of education Paulo Freire (1921–1997) sought to tackle the problem of illiteracy in his country. He grew to realize that the problems of illiteracy and poverty were related to authoritarian attitudes that were deeply ingrained in all aspects of society, even in how parents related to their children. Influenced by John Dewey (see Chapter 18), Freire saw that education is more than learning skills; education is about people discovering themselves as creative agents and becoming more human. The value of education, for Freire, was not simply being better able to make a living in a profession but rather empowerment and transformation for an individual and community. Education, well done, leads to social justice. His philosophy of education was a response to the legacy of colonialism. Freire believed that political and legal reforms on their own were insufficient to change oppressive dynamics because people in all classes had internalized the historically pervasive authoritarian oppression. All people, both colonizers and the colonized, have been conditioned to maintain the dynamic of authoritarian oppression. The oppressed have internalized oppressive structures and are conditioned to keep their place in the social hierarchy. Worse, Freire realized, the oppressed, instead of striving for liberation, tend themselves to become oppressors when possible. People embedded in oppressive dynamics become opportunistic oppressors: bosses of their workers, parents of their children, and others in situations in which there is an imbalance of power. Education needs to empower people by raising their consciousness of their own internalized oppression. Education changes people, and people change the world, Freire said.

GLOBALIZATION AND TECHNOLOGY

We are becoming one world, though some nationalists still resist the long trend of increasing interconnectedness among the people of the world. Technology has enabled communication, trade, and travel to become quicker and easier. Anyone can converse with anyone anywhere in real time. The Internet has empowered people to access incredible amounts of information, learn almost everything about anything. People instead just watch videos of celebrities and post stupid memes. Too cynical? Well, like Nietzsche (see Chapter 17), some philosophers who have high hopes for humanity look at our global age of technology and are rather disappointed by people's behaviors.

Globalization has implications for political philosophy. Plato, Aristotle, and the modern political philosophers all held the view that states were relatively isolated and homogeneous. Not that states in prior centuries didn't have trade and immigration, but the idea of distinct societies with distinct cultural, if not geographical, borders was considered the norm. Globalization has forced people to give up the notion of cultural isolation. Some have welcomed it; some have resisted it. Powered by technology, the wave of globalization will continue, shrinking our world and our distance from each other.

We need to differentiate the globalization of the 2000s from the type of globalization that occurred during the age of colonization. Colonialism was an expression of economic exploitation and military power that inflicted European culture on other cultures. Today's globalization must be assessed in terms of the legacy of colonialism, but there is more openness from the "West" toward other cultures, and there is less, though still too much, denial and suppression of other cultures. Still, the ethics of cultural appropriation must be considered. What right do

Western people and companies have to use and profit from the cultural creations of non-Western people? Economic exploitation of workers in "third world" countries is still a significant problem. Marx's critique of 1800s European capitalism (see Chapter 15) seems more true than ever when we consider the plight of workers in East Asian and Latin American countries.

Some philosophers predicted problems associated with the pace of change and globalization. As early as 1927, John Dewey warned that it is difficult to organize the public sphere when it does not stay in place and that this would have negative effects on democracy. Heidegger in 1950 expressed concerns that technology was dehumanizing us, successfully predicting that television would soon come to dominate all communication. Canadian cultural critic Marshall McLuhan (1911–1980) wrote about the coming "global village" in which humanity is connected by technology. However, McLuhan predicted bad consequences, saying that the technological medium by which a message is transmitted would become more important than the content of the message. Anyone who didn't think of social media when they read that sentence is not paying attention. Indeed, the moral issues of social media and social networking are the subjects of a very new but very important field in philosophy. Phenomenologist and existentialist Hubert Dreyfus (1929–2017) in his paper "Nihilism on the Information Highway: Anonymity Versus Commitment in the Present Age" (written in 2004, before Facebook, Twitter, and Instagram), observed that the anonymity and distance allowed by electronic media meant that online interactions intrinsically lacked exposure to risk. Dreyfus says that we are not fully bodily present on electronic media, so we are shielded from the social risks of our behavior being disapproved of by others. Without risk, he said, there can be no true meaning or commitment in the social media realm. The Internet is, he says, like Kierkegaard's aesthetic sphere (see Chapter 17)—promising us new and exciting experiences, and to be whoever we want to be, but without a chance of gaining a history and authentic self that is founded on firmness, balance, and steadiness.

It is not all negative. British-Ghanaian philosopher Kwame Anthony Appiah (1954–), who has written primarily on moral philosophy, has addressed globalization with his theory of "cosmopolitanism." In his book, *Cosmopolitanism: Ethics in a World of Strangers* (2006), Appiah defines cosmopolitanism as "universality plus difference," meaning that we don't ignore cultural diversity but that our universal humanity always takes precedence. Cultures matter, but people also matter. Cultural differences are to be respected, but only insofar as they do not harm our universal concern for people. We should first and foremost understand ourselves as citizens of the world. He goes on to say that our obligations to others go beyond sharing citizenship. We have a responsibility to learn about the practices and beliefs of others and their identities. Appiah is critical of all ethnocentrism, both the Eurocentrism of white supremacy and the Afrocentrism of some radical black philosophers of race.

NONHETERONORMATIVE PHILOSOPHY

Definitely not least, but last in chronology, is the new and growing field of philosophy about people outside the traditional binary designations of norms about gender and sexuality. Nonheteronormative sexuality has long been dismissed or repressed by European and American societies. In one respect, the suppression and oppression of nonheteronormative people is similar to that suffered by women and people of color. However, heteronormative supremacy has a distinct character. The fear and loathing of nonheteronormative people cuts across gender, racial, and class distinctions. What should be obvious is that nonheteronormative people are people and, therefore, are entitled to recognition as people with basic moral consideration. We've seen some philosophers in this book whose nonheteronormative sexuality, and the oppression they suffered from society for it, formed part of their philosophy—for example, James Baldwin and Audre Lorde. In the 1970s, serious academic study of homosexuality as a nonaberrant identity began. The gay rights movement also began, which has since expanded into rights for other nonheteronormative identities.

One philosopher who has written about nonheteronormative philosophy is Judith Butler (1956–). She has written a series of books that have shown gender to be a social construction and that gender is therefore a set of concepts and stylized repetitive acts that reflect the dominant power structure. Gender, she argues, is performative; one *acts* male or female within the frameworks that determine for people what their possibilities are for gender, sex, and sexuality. The supposed binary nature of biological sex has led to assumptions that gender and sexuality should also be binary. Butler calls instead for an open critique of sex and gender. For her, that includes how feminism has used the concept of "women" as an objective, discrete, ahistorical group. Butler sees this as a mistake that has reinforced the binary view of sex and gender. Instead of trying to define "women," Butler says that feminism should focus on providing an account of how power functions and shapes our understandings of womanhood. Butler also takes aim at the concepts of homosexual and heterosexual, seeing them as limiting, binary identities. Her idea that sexuality is performative applies here also. One repetitively *acts* as homosexual or heterosexual, imitating how the categorized identity is defined.

This is the case even though acting as a homosexual may include exclusions and concealments.

Butler says that many of the performative acts of sex, gender, and sexuality are performed without conscious awareness. The social constructions of gender identities are social norms to which we conform because we are taught to do so. Such is the case for all social norms—that's why they are *norms*—these are the definitions of how we are to act (see Honneth in Chapter 24). Butler calls for breaking the socially defined linkage of sex with gender, allowing for people to develop their gender and desires freely and flexibly. One's gender and sexuality would still be performative, but an individual's acts would stem from who that person is, not from a social construction. Individuals would not have an identity limited to the expression of any binary structure.

Butler's work has been instrumental in the development of ideas of nonbinary gender identities and has helped establish the field of queer theory. Butler opened a door onto possibilities for dispensing with the traditional narratives that heterosexuality is the only acceptable norm and for people not needing to take on compulsory identities as "man," "woman," "heterosexual," or "homosexual." We've seen in this book how when someone opens a door, people will go through it. This has indeed happened with this door to a society accepting of nonheteronormative identities. When we've looked at previous times when these philosophical doors have opened, we've had the advantage of being able to analyze what happened from the perspective of many years later. Butler and others have opened this philosophical door less than 30 years ago. It should not surprise us that the field of nonheteronormative philosophy is still very much in flux. Currently, there is much debate over approach, terminology, and goals. One problem the field must resolve is that if "queer" is defined in opposition to "normal," than no matter how broad the concept of "queer" is, it remains a binary definition that can quickly become yet another us-and-them binary opposition and excuse for division and oppression.

That all nonheteronormative people should be recognized as having full human rights should be obvious. Actually, that all people should be so recognized is obvious. As we've heard a number of philosophers of feminism and race say, we need to respect differences and listen to individuals' lived experiences. We are all on a quest for understanding. The best approach to our personal quest for understanding is to be open to understanding people for who they are and listening to what they have to tell us.

CHRONOLOGY

ANCIENT ERA

BCE

509	Roman Republic established
449–431	"Golden Age" of Athens
431–404	Peloponnesian War ending in defeat of Athens
399	Death of Socrates
398–347	Plato active
347–322	Aristotle active
311–270	Epicurus active
ca. 290	Zeno of Citium founds Stoic school
31	Octavian establishes Roman Empire

CE

ca. 30–50	Philo active
93–138	Epictetus active
245–270	Plotinus active
313	"Edict of Milan" proclaims religions toleration
325	Council of Nicaea
384–430	Augustine active
410	Visigoths sack Rome
410–895	Age of "barbarian" invasions
455	Vandals sack Rome
476	Last Roman Emperor deposed

MEDIEVAL ERA

ca. 830–873	Al-Kindi active
ca. 930–950	Al-Farabi active
ca. 1010–1037	Ibn Sina active
1168–1204	Maimonides active
1169–1198	Ibn Rushd active
1204	Sack of Constantinople
1209–1229	Albigensian Crusade against Gnostic Christians in Languedoc
1212	Battle of Las Navas de Tolsa; beginning of end of Muslim rule in Spain
1240	Translations of Aristotle and Islamic commentaries on Aristotle widely available in Catholic Europe
1265–1274	Thomas Aquinas writes *Summa Theologica*
1277	Papal condemnation of 219 theses from Aristotle and Islamic philosophy, but not Thomas's reinterpretations of those philosophers

RENAISSANCE ERA

1290–1307	John Duns Scotus active.
1298	Publication of Marco Polo's journeys in Asia
1317–1349	William active.
1347–1351	Black Death kills one-third of population throughout Europe
1380s	John Wyclif translates Bible into vernacular, inspires the Lollardy movements
1381	Venice wins war with Genoa, gains upper hand in Mediterranean trade.
1397	Medici banking house founded in Florence
1398	Jan Hus begins lecturing at Charles University in Prague; develops Hussite church reform movement influenced by Wyclif
1415	Jan Hus burned for heresy
1419–1434	Hussite rebellions in Bohemia
1425	Tommaso Masaccio paints using perspective, birth of Renaissance art
1447	Invention of the printing press
1453	Constantinople falls to Ottomans, Greek scholars and manuscripts flee to Latin west transmitting the rest of Plato to the west

1480–1519	Leonardo DaVinci active
1492	Ferdinand and Isabella expel all Jews in Spain
1492	Christopher Columbus's first voyage to the new world
1494	Spain and Portugal agree to Treaty of Tordesillas which divides the world between them, ushering in the age of colonialism
1500	First Portuguese trading posts in India
1502	First slaves taken from Africa to the new world
1513	Niccolo Machiavelli writes *The Prince* though it is not published until 1532
1514	Mikołaj Kopernik begins development of heliocentric theory though he does not publish until on his deathbed in 1543
1517	Martin Luther produces his *95 Theses* intended to stimulate debate about church corruption and abuses
1521	Pope Leo X excommunicates Luther
1521	Spain conquers the Aztec Empire
1524	First rebellions and defections from Catholic rule commence over a century of wars in central Europe
1532–1533	Spain conquers the Incan Empire
1534	Henry VIII breaks with Rome and declares himself head of Church of England
1572	A bright nova (new star) appears in the sky, undermining the concept of celestial unchangeability
1577	The Great Comet appears, also questioning the concept of celestial unchangeability
1588	English navy defeats Spanish Armada; beginning of English military ascendency.

MODERN ERA

1589–1613	William Shakespeare active
1597–1627	Francis Bacon publishes works on methods of philosophy and science
1600	Giordano Bruno burned at the stake for heresy
1604	"Kepler's Nova" lends further credence to notions of change in the heavens
1609	Kepler publishes his theory of planetary motion showing planetary orbits are not circular but elliptical
1610	Galileo publishes his discoveries in astronomy, the *Sidereus Nuncius*
1632	Galileo publishes *Dialogue Concerning the Two Chief World*

	Systems explaining the heliocentric theory; a year later the Inquisition forced him to recant
1618–1648	Thirty Years War
1624–1643	Political theory of Absolutism develops in France under reign of Louis XIII
1626–1649	Rene Descartes active; publishes *Discourse* in 1637, *Meditations* in 1641
1628	William Harvey publishes his theory of circulation of blood
1633	Galileo forced by The Inquisition to denounce his teachings on a sun-centered universe
1638	Galileo publishes *Two New Sciences* advancing theories on motion of objects
1637–1656	Thomas Hobbes active; publishes *Leviathan* in 1651
1642–1660	English Civil War, Oliver Cromwell's rule (1649-1658), Restoration in 1660
1643–1715	Reign of French King Louis XIV
1660	The Royal Society of London for Improving Natural Knowledge founded two months after the Restoration
1661	Robert Boyle in *The Sceptical Chymist* rejects the Aristotelian four elements and adopts a corpuscular view of matter
1663–1677	Spinoza active; *Ethics* published after his death
1665	Robert Hooke publishes *Micrographia* detailing his microscopic observations
1665–1666	Great Plague of London, ended by the Great Fire of London
1666–1714	Leibniz active, invents calculus in 1675
1670–1675	Isaac Newton lectures and writes on theories of optics and light
1678	Peace of Westphalia ends the Thirty Years' War
1685	Louis XIV revokes legal protections for protestants; brutal persecutions begin
1687	Isaac Newton publishes *Principia Mathematica*
1689	William and Mary are named co-rulers of the United Kingdom
1689	British "Bill of Rights" lays out basic rights for all male citizens
1689–1695	John Locke's published writings on epistemology and political philosophy
1707	The "Acts of Union" unifies Scotland and England
1709–1713	George Berkeley's published writings
1726	Jonathan Swift publishes *Gulliver's Travels* satirizing scientists, especially the Royal Society
1739–1762	Hume active
1754–1799	Kant active

1755	Lisbon earthquake devastates Portugal
1762	Rousseau writes *The Social Contract*
1772–1775	Carl Scheele, Joseph Priestley, and Antoine Lavoisier independently discover oxygen
1774	Johann Wolfgang von Goethe publishes the novel, *The Sorrows of Young Werther*
1776	Adam Smith publishes *Wealth of Nations*
1776	James Watt sells the first copy of his vastly improved steam engine
1776	Declaration of Independence and Articles of Confederation written establishing the ideas of natural rights and the social contract in the new United States of America
1781	Kant's first edition of *Critique of Pure Reason*
1782	The Montgolfier brothers launch the first hot air balloon
1787	United States Constitution written
1789	Jeremy Bentham publishes his moral theory of utilitarianism
1789	Antoine Lavoisier publishes the first modern list of chemical elements
1789	French Revolution; "Reign of Terror" 1793–1794, chaos and war until 1799
1792	Mary Wollstonecraft publishes *A Vindication of the Rights of Woman*

POST-KANTIAN ERA

1794–1814	Fichte active
1794–1833	Schelling active
1798–1802	The Jena Romantic circle meets
1799	Napoleon grabs power in France
1803–1815	Napoleonic Wars
1807	Hegel publishes *Phenomenology of Mind* and *Phenomenology of Spirit*
1808	Beethoven's Fifth Symphony
1813	Madame de Staël publishes *De l'Allemagne*, introducing German idealism to the rest of Europe
1830–1842	Auguste Comte develops positivism, which leads to analytical philosophy
1836	Transcendental Club founded in Cambridge, Massachusetts
1841–1855	Søren Kierkegaard active
1842–1883	Karl Marx active

1843–1869	John Stuart Mill active.
1845	Margaret Fuller publishes *Woman in the Nineteenth Century*
1848	"The Year of Revolutions"—peasant and worker rebellions across Europe
1848	Marx and Engels' *Manifesto of the Communist Party*
1857	Herbert Spencer publishes the first theory of evolution
1859	Charles Darwin publishes *Origin of Species*
1863	John Stuart Mill publishes *Utilitarianism*
1864–1909	Charles Sanders Pierce active
1896	John Stuart Mill publishes *The Subjection of Women*
1872	Claude Monet's painting, *Impression, soleil levant*, sparks the Impressionist art movement
1872–1888	Nietzsche active, publishes *Beyond Good and Evil* in 1886
1874	Franz Brentano publishes *Psychology from an Empirical Standpoint*
1881–1949	John Dewey active
1889–1932	Henri Bergson active, publishing *Time and Free Will* in 1889 and *Creative Evolution* in 1907
1890–1910	William James active, beginning with *The Principles of Psychology*
1891–1936	Edmund Husserl active, publishes *Ideas* in 1913, the founding text of phenomenology
1895–1969	Bertrand Russell active, with Alfred North Whitehead publishes *Principia Mathematica* in 1910-1913
1897–1919	Rosa Luxemburg active
1897–1963	W.E.B. Du Bois active, publishes *The Souls of Black Folk* in 1903
1904–1969	György Lukács active, publishes *History and Class Consciousness* in 1923
1913–1928	Max Scheler active
1916–1933	Edith Stein active
1917–1918	Ludwig Wittgenstein writes the *Tractatus Logico-Philosophicus* while a soldier and then prisoner of war in World War I
1918–1939	The Frankfurt School is active
1920–1938	Alfred North Whitehead develops his natural theology, publishes *The Concept of Nature* in 1920 and *Process and Reality* in 1929
1923	Martin Buber publishes *Ich und Du*
1926–1937	Antonio Gramsci writes his philosophical works while a political prisoner under the Italian fascists
1927	Martin Heidegger publishes *Being and Time*

1929–1941	Ludwig Wittgenstein develops his later philosophy which goes against the *Tractatus*
1929–1975	Hannah Arendt active
1932–1969	Karl Jaspers active, publishes *Reason and Existenz* in 1935
1933–1945	The Nazis suppress many philosophers' ideas
1939–1945	World War II

POST-WORLD WAR II ERA

1936–1976	Jean-Paul Sartre active
1946	Max Horkheimer and Theodor Adorno publish *Dialectic of Enlightenment*
1946–1997	Paulo Freire active
1947–1986	Simone de Beauvoir active, publishes *The Second Sex* in 1949
1949	Gilbert Ryle publishes *The Concept of Mind*
1951	Hannah Arendt publishes *The Origins of Totalitarianism*
1952	Franz Fanon publishes *Black Skin, White Masks*
1953	W.V.O. Quine writes "Two Dogmas of Empiricism"
1955–1968	Martin Luther King, Jr. active in Civil Rights Movement, wins Nobel Peace Prize in 1964
1955–1994	Claude Lévi-Strauss active
1959–2003	Jacques Derrida active
1960–1978	Louis Althusser active
1961	Emmanuel Levinas publishes *Totality and Infinity*
1961	Franz Fanon publishes *The Wretched of the Earth*
1961–1984	Michel Foucault active
1962	Thomas Kuhn publishes *The Structure of Scientific Revolutions*
1962	John L. Austin publishes *How to Do Things With Words*
1962	Rachel Carson's environmental exposé, *Silent Spring*
1962–	Jürgen Habermas active, publishes *Theory of Communicative Action* in 1981
1963	Betty Friedan publishes *The Feminine Mystique*
1963	Edmund Gettier publishes "Is Justified True Belief Knowledge?"
1963	Hannah Arendt publishes *Eichmann in Jerusalem: A Report on the Banality of Evil*
1963	James Baldwin publishes *The Fire Next Time*
1963	President John F. Kennedy is assassinated
1967–2016	Hilary Putnam active
1968	Summer of student and worker protests in France, events influential on postmodernist and political theory

1968–2004	Jean Baudrillard active, publishes *The Consumer Society* in 1970
1968–2010	Mary Daly active, publishes *Gyn/Ecology: The Metaethics of Radical Feminism* in 1978
1969	The Stonewall uprising in New York City, sparking the gay liberation movement
1969–	John Searle active
1970	Shulamith Firestone publishes *The Dialectic of Sex: The Case for Feminist Revolution*
1970	Germain Greer publishes *The Female Eunuch*
1971	John Rawls publishes *A Theory of Justice*
1973	*Roe v. Wade* U.S. Supreme Court decision protects a woman's right to terminate her pregnancy
1974	Robert Nozick publishes *Anarchy, State, and Utopia*
1978	Edward Said publishes *Orientalism*
1979–1998	Jean-François Lyotard active
1979–2005	Richard Rorty active
1980–2006	Iris Marion Young active
1981–	bell hooks active
1982	Carol Gilligan publishes *In a Different Voice*
1982–	Cornel West active, publishes *Race Matters* in 1993
1984	Audre Lorde publishes *Sister Outsider: Essays and Speeches*
1988–	Judith Butler active
1989	Kimberlé Williams Crenshaw introduces the concept of intersectionality in "Demarginalizing the Intersection of Race and Sex"
1991–	Axel Honneth active, publishes *The Struggle for Recognition: The Moral Grammar of Social Conflicts* in 2003
1994	The World Wide Web comes into general public use
1995–	Lewis Gordon active
1996	David Chalmers publishes *The Conscious Mind*
1997	Charles W. Mills publishes *The Racial Contract*
2001	September 11 terrorist attacks
2007	Miranda Fricker publishes *Epistemic Injustice*
2008	George Yancy publishes *Black Bodies, White Gazes: The Continuing Significance of Race*

CPSIA information can be obtained
at www.ICGtesting.com
Printed in the USA
LVHW081234040821
694272LV00002B/2

9 781792 457609